# WISDOM WELL SAID

Anecdotes, fables, legends, myths, humor, and wise sayings that capture the human condition.

collected by

## Charles Francis

**Editorial assistance**
Jay Levine

**Cover and interior page design**
Beth Levine

# www.wisdomwellsaid.com

LEVINE MESA PRESS

levinemesapress.com
El Prado, New Mexico

Published by:
Levine Mesa Press
PO Box 2218
El Prado, NM  87529

LEVINE MESA
PRESS

levinemesapress.com

ISBN: 978-0-9823887-0-9

Library of Congress Control Number:  2009924171

This book is printed on acid-free paper.

Printed in the United States of America

# INTRODUCTION

As a writer and professional corporate communicator, I spent many years collecting anecdotes, myths, fables and short interesting stories to help articles and speeches come alive for the reader or audience. This book contains a lifetime's collection of the items I found most useful.

Most of the collection are anecdotes, a language form that causes many people to ask the question, "What is an anecdote anyway?" The actual form goes back to the ancient Greeks. The word comes from the French, who use it to describe "any interesting circumstance." *Webster's Dictionary* defines an anecdote as an "usually short narrative of an interesting, amusing, or biographical incident." However, my favorite definition is by the late Sam J. Ervin, Jr. (1896-1985), a United States Senator from North Carolina who, at the age of 76, headed the Senate Select Committee investigating the Watergate scandal. Senator Ervin was talking about humor, but his remarks apply equally well to anecdotes, a great many of which contain humor along with wise insights into the human condition.

> "Humor," he said, "endows us with the capacity to clarify the obscure, to simplify the complex, to deflate the pompous, to chastise the arrogant, to point a moral, and to adorn a tale."

Anecdotes are simply very short stories, the best of which have a lesson to teach us. Jesus used anecdotes (then called parables) to teach his followers. Abraham Lincoln used them to slice through complicated subjects and to teach listeners a lesson thereby. Most of his anecdotes had humorous content. Once criticized by a cabinet member for telling "jokes" in the midst of the horrors of the Civil War, Lincoln replied, "If I could not tell jokes, I think I would die." Mark Twain, who earned much of his living on the lecture platform, was equally adept at coining and using humorous anecdotes. Will Rogers, a famous actor and humorist, was also skillful at saying humorous things on every subject imaginable.

For ease of use, I have organized the items in this collection in alphabetical order. Underneath each category are listed relevant items (Examples, "Accounting," "Action," "Actors," etc.) each with a subhead printed in bold-face type. By going to each category listed in the index, you can easily locate an item on almost any subject you desire.

In selecting individual items, I have not felt bound to follow the strict construction of an anecdote. As mentioned above, the collection includes not only anecdotes but ancient myths, fables and other folk tales, each of which has a point to make. In a few cases, I have included some quotations.

Every attempt has been made to make sure that the items included in this collection are accurate. However, because some of the items are born out of folklore and verbal transmission over many years, this is not always possible. Mark Twain once observed that Adam was the only person able to say something and be certain that he was the first person to say it.

Using short stories such as anecdotes can transform your personal communications in a way that is absolutely magical. I hope the contents of this book will help you do exactly that.

Charles Francis

# TABLE OF CONTENTS

ACCOUNTING . . . . . . . . . . . . . . . . . . . . . . . . . . . . . . . . . . . .1

ACTION . . . . . . . . . . . . . . . . . . . . . . . . . . . . . . . . . . . . . . . .3

ACTORS . . . . . . . . . . . . . . . . . . . . . . . . . . . . . . . . . . . . . . . .5

ADAPTABILITY . . . . . . . . . . . . . . . . . . . . . . . . . . . . . . . . . .7

ADVERSITY . . . . . . . . . . . . . . . . . . . . . . . . . . . . . . . . . . . . .8

ADVERTISING . . . . . . . . . . . . . . . . . . . . . . . . . . . . . . . . . .10

AGRICULTURE . . . . . . . . . . . . . . . . . . . . . . . . . . . . . . . . .16

ALCOHOL . . . . . . . . . . . . . . . . . . . . . . . . . . . . . . . . . . . . .19

AMBITION . . . . . . . . . . . . . . . . . . . . . . . . . . . . . . . . . . . . .23

AMERICANA . . . . . . . . . . . . . . . . . . . . . . . . . . . . . . . . . . .24

ANGER . . . . . . . . . . . . . . . . . . . . . . . . . . . . . . . . . . . . . . .32

ANIMALS, LESSONS FROM . . . . . . . . . . . . . . . . . . . . . . .34

ATTITUDE . . . . . . . . . . . . . . . . . . . . . . . . . . . . . . . . . . . . .46

BOOKS . . . . . . . . . . . . . . . . . . . . . . . . . . . . . . . . . . . . . . .47

BUREAUCRACY . . . . . . . . . . . . . . . . . . . . . . . . . . . . . . . .49

BUSINESS, SERVICE . . . . . . . . . . . . . . . . . . . . . . . . . . . .55

CAREER . . . . . . . . . . . . . . . . . . . . . . . . . . . . . . . . . . . . . .72

CHANGE . . . . . . . . . . . . . . . . . . . . . . . . . . . . . . . . . . . . . .74

CHARACTER . . . . . . . . . . . . . . . . . . . . . . . . . . . . . . . . . .77

CHILDREN . . . . . . . . . . . . . . . . . . . . . . . . . . . . . . . . . . . .83

CITIES . . . . . . . . . . . . . . . . . . . . . . . . . . . . . . . . . . . . . . .85

CLOTHING . . . . . . . . . . . . . . . . . . . . . . . . . . . . . . . . . . . .88

COMMITMENT . . . . . . . . . . . . . . . . . . . . . . . . . . . . . . . . .91

COMMUNICATIONS . . . . . . . . . . . . . . . . . . . . . . . . . . . . .92

COMMUNITY SERVICE . . . . . . . . . . . . . . . . . . . . . . . . . .99

COMPROMISE . . . . . . . . . . . . . . . . . . . . . . . . . . . . . . . .102

CONFORMITY . . . . . . . . . . . . . . . . . . . . . . . . . . . . . . . .104

COURAGE . . . . . . . . . . . . . . . . . . . . . . . . . . . . . . . . . . .106

CREATIVITY . . . . . . . . . . . . . . . . . . . . . . . . . . .109

CRITICISM . . . . . . . . . . . . . . . . . . . . . . . . . . . .111

CULTURAL DECLINE . . . . . . . . . . . . . . . . . .114

CURIOSITY . . . . . . . . . . . . . . . . . . . . . . . . . . .115

DEATH . . . . . . . . . . . . . . . . . . . . . . . . . . . . . .117

DECISION MAKING . . . . . . . . . . . . . . . . . . . .118

DENIAL . . . . . . . . . . . . . . . . . . . . . . . . . . . . . .120

DIPLOMACY . . . . . . . . . . . . . . . . . . . . . . . . . .121

DISCOURAGEMENT . . . . . . . . . . . . . . . . . . .125

DIVERSITY . . . . . . . . . . . . . . . . . . . . . . . . . . .126

ECOLOGY . . . . . . . . . . . . . . . . . . . . . . . . . . . .127

ECONOMICS . . . . . . . . . . . . . . . . . . . . . . . . . .128

EDUCATION . . . . . . . . . . . . . . . . . . . . . . . . . .130

EGO . . . . . . . . . . . . . . . . . . . . . . . . . . . . . . . . .138

ENGINEERING . . . . . . . . . . . . . . . . . . . . . . . .139

ETHICS . . . . . . . . . . . . . . . . . . . . . . . . . . . . . .142

ETIQUETTE, MANNERS . . . . . . . . . . . . . . . . .143

EXCELLENCE . . . . . . . . . . . . . . . . . . . . . . . . .147

EXPLORATION . . . . . . . . . . . . . . . . . . . . . . . .150

FAILURE . . . . . . . . . . . . . . . . . . . . . . . . . . . . .154

FAME . . . . . . . . . . . . . . . . . . . . . . . . . . . . . . . .158

FATE . . . . . . . . . . . . . . . . . . . . . . . . . . . . . . . .160

FEAR . . . . . . . . . . . . . . . . . . . . . . . . . . . . . . . .161

FOOD AND UTENSILS . . . . . . . . . . . . . . . . . .164

FREEDOM . . . . . . . . . . . . . . . . . . . . . . . . . . . .171

FRIENDSHIP . . . . . . . . . . . . . . . . . . . . . . . . . .173

FUTURE . . . . . . . . . . . . . . . . . . . . . . . . . . . . . .176

GENIUS . . . . . . . . . . . . . . . . . . . . . . . . . . . . . .178

GLOBAL . . . . . . . . . . . . . . . . . . . . . . . . . . . . .182

GOOD LUCK . . . . . . . . . . . . . . . . . . . . . . . . . .187

GREED . . . . . . . . . . . . . . . . . . . . . . . . . . . . . . . .188

GRIEF, LOSS . . . . . . . . . . . . . . . . . . . . . . . . . . . .195

HELPING OTHERS . . . . . . . . . . . . . . . . . . . . . . . .196

HOLIDAYS . . . . . . . . . . . . . . . . . . . . . . . . . . . . . .201

HOLIDAYS – JANUARY . . . . . . . . . . . . . . . . . . . .201

HOLIDAYS – FEBRUARY . . . . . . . . . . . . . . . . . . .204

HOLIDAYS – MARCH . . . . . . . . . . . . . . . . . . . . . .205

HOLIDAYS – APRIL . . . . . . . . . . . . . . . . . . . . . . .208

HOLIDAYS – MAY . . . . . . . . . . . . . . . . . . . . . . . .209

HOLIDAYS – JUNE . . . . . . . . . . . . . . . . . . . . . . .211

HOLIDAYS – JULY . . . . . . . . . . . . . . . . . . . . . . . .213

HOLIDAYS – OCTOBER . . . . . . . . . . . . . . . . . . . .216

HOLIDAYS – NOVEMBER . . . . . . . . . . . . . . . . . . .219

HOLIDAYS – DECEMBER . . . . . . . . . . . . . . . . . . .223

HOLLYWOOD . . . . . . . . . . . . . . . . . . . . . . . . . . .233

HUMILITY . . . . . . . . . . . . . . . . . . . . . . . . . . . . . .236

INCOMPETENCE . . . . . . . . . . . . . . . . . . . . . . . . .238

INFERIORITY COMPLEX . . . . . . . . . . . . . . . . . . .240

INVENTION, TECHNOLOGY . . . . . . . . . . . . . . . . .242

IRISH . . . . . . . . . . . . . . . . . . . . . . . . . . . . . . . . .263

KINDNESS . . . . . . . . . . . . . . . . . . . . . . . . . . . . .264

LANGUAGE . . . . . . . . . . . . . . . . . . . . . . . . . . . . .267

LAUGHTER . . . . . . . . . . . . . . . . . . . . . . . . . . . . .271

LAW ENFORCEMENT . . . . . . . . . . . . . . . . . . . . .273

LEADERSHIP . . . . . . . . . . . . . . . . . . . . . . . . . . . .274

LEGAL . . . . . . . . . . . . . . . . . . . . . . . . . . . . . . . .280

LISTENING . . . . . . . . . . . . . . . . . . . . . . . . . . . . .285

LOVE, MARRIAGE . . . . . . . . . . . . . . . . . . . . . . . .287

MATHEMATICS . . . . . . . . . . . . . . . . . . . . . . . . . .304

MEDIA . . . . . . . . . . . . . . . . . . . . . . . . . . . . . . . .307

MEDICINE . . . . . . . . . . . . . . . . . . . . . . . . . . . . .309

MISTAKES . . . . . . . . . . . . . . . . . . . . . . . . . . . . . .318

MONEY . . . . . . . . . . . . . . . . . . . . . . . . . . . . . . . .321

MUSIC . . . . . . . . . . . . . . . . . . . . . . . . . . . . . . . .325

NEGATIVE THINKING . . . . . . . . . . . . . . . . . . . . .336

NEGOTIATION . . . . . . . . . . . . . . . . . . . . . . . . . .342

NOBEL PRIZE . . . . . . . . . . . . . . . . . . . . . . . . . .344

OLD AGE . . . . . . . . . . . . . . . . . . . . . . . . . . . . . .345

OPPORTUNITY . . . . . . . . . . . . . . . . . . . . . . . . . .354

PARENTING . . . . . . . . . . . . . . . . . . . . . . . . . . . .356

PATRIOTISM . . . . . . . . . . . . . . . . . . . . . . . . . . .360

PERSISTENCE, PERSEVERANCE . . . . . . . . . . . . .372

PERSONAL GROWTH . . . . . . . . . . . . . . . . . . . . .380

PERSONAL HEALTH . . . . . . . . . . . . . . . . . . . . . .384

PERSPECTIVE . . . . . . . . . . . . . . . . . . . . . . . . . .385

PERSUASION . . . . . . . . . . . . . . . . . . . . . . . . . . .387

PHILANTHROPY . . . . . . . . . . . . . . . . . . . . . . . . .391

POLITICS . . . . . . . . . . . . . . . . . . . . . . . . . . . . . .393

POSITIVE THINKING . . . . . . . . . . . . . . . . . . . . . .407

PROBLEM SOLVING . . . . . . . . . . . . . . . . . . . . . .416

PRODUCTIVITY . . . . . . . . . . . . . . . . . . . . . . . . .427

PROFANITY . . . . . . . . . . . . . . . . . . . . . . . . . . . .429

PRUDENCE . . . . . . . . . . . . . . . . . . . . . . . . . . . .431

QUALITY . . . . . . . . . . . . . . . . . . . . . . . . . . . . . .433

READING . . . . . . . . . . . . . . . . . . . . . . . . . . . . . .437

REFORM . . . . . . . . . . . . . . . . . . . . . . . . . . . . . .439

RELIGION . . . . . . . . . . . . . . . . . . . . . . . . . . . . .439

RENEWAL . . . . . . . . . . . . . . . . . . . . . . . . . . . . .447

RESPECT . . . . . . . . . . . . . . . . . . . . . . . . . . . . . .448

RESPONSIBILITY . . . . . . . . . . . . . . . . . . . . . . . .450

RETIREMENT . . . . . . . . . . . . . . . . . . . . . . . . . . . . . . . . . .452

SCAM . . . . . . . . . . . . . . . . . . . . . . . . . . . . . . . . . . . . . . .454

SCIENCE . . . . . . . . . . . . . . . . . . . . . . . . . . . . . . . . . . . . .455

SELF-CONFIDENCE . . . . . . . . . . . . . . . . . . . . . . . . . . . . .460

SELFISHNESS . . . . . . . . . . . . . . . . . . . . . . . . . . . . . . . . . .462

SEX . . . . . . . . . . . . . . . . . . . . . . . . . . . . . . . . . . . . . . . . .464

SLEEP . . . . . . . . . . . . . . . . . . . . . . . . . . . . . . . . . . . . . . .467

SMALL TOWNS . . . . . . . . . . . . . . . . . . . . . . . . . . . . . . . .468

SPEAKING . . . . . . . . . . . . . . . . . . . . . . . . . . . . . . . . . . . .469

SPORTS, BASEBALL . . . . . . . . . . . . . . . . . . . . . . . . . . . . .484

SPORTS, BASKETBALL . . . . . . . . . . . . . . . . . . . . . . . . . . .495

SPORTS, BOXING . . . . . . . . . . . . . . . . . . . . . . . . . . . . . . .500

SPORTS, FOOTBALL . . . . . . . . . . . . . . . . . . . . . . . . . . . . .501

SPORTS, GENERAL . . . . . . . . . . . . . . . . . . . . . . . . . . . . . .514

SPORTS, GOLF . . . . . . . . . . . . . . . . . . . . . . . . . . . . . . . . .506

SPORTS, HOCKEY . . . . . . . . . . . . . . . . . . . . . . . . . . . . . .508

SPORTS, OARSMEN . . . . . . . . . . . . . . . . . . . . . . . . . . . . .500

SPORTS, SOCCER . . . . . . . . . . . . . . . . . . . . . . . . . . . . . .513

SPORTS, THE OLYMPICS . . . . . . . . . . . . . . . . . . . . . . . . .509

STATISTICS . . . . . . . . . . . . . . . . . . . . . . . . . . . . . . . . . . .516

SUBSTANCE ABUSE . . . . . . . . . . . . . . . . . . . . . . . . . . . . .518

SUPERSTITIONS . . . . . . . . . . . . . . . . . . . . . . . . . . . . . . .521

TACT . . . . . . . . . . . . . . . . . . . . . . . . . . . . . . . . . . . . . . . .523

TAXES . . . . . . . . . . . . . . . . . . . . . . . . . . . . . . . . . . . . . . .525

TEAMWORK . . . . . . . . . . . . . . . . . . . . . . . . . . . . . . . . . .527

TESTIMONY . . . . . . . . . . . . . . . . . . . . . . . . . . . . . . . . . . .531

THRIFT . . . . . . . . . . . . . . . . . . . . . . . . . . . . . . . . . . . . . .532

TIME . . . . . . . . . . . . . . . . . . . . . . . . . . . . . . . . . . . . . . . .577

TRAVEL, TRANSPORTATION . . . . . . . . . . . . . . . . . . . . . .536

TRUST . . . . . . . . . . . . . . . . . . . . . . . . . . . . . . . . . . . . . . .538

TRUTH . . . . . . . . . . . . . . . . . . . . . . . . . . . . . . . . . . . . . . .540

UNEXPECTED CONSEQUENCES . . . . . . . . . . . . . . . . . . . . . .542

VANITY . . . . . . . . . . . . . . . . . . . . . . . . . . . . . . . . . . . . . . .543

WAR . . . . . . . . . . . . . . . . . . . . . . . . . . . . . . . . . . . . . . . . . .546

WATER . . . . . . . . . . . . . . . . . . . . . . . . . . . . . . . . . . . . . . .561

WINNING . . . . . . . . . . . . . . . . . . . . . . . . . . . . . . . . . . . . .563

WOMEN'S RIGHTS . . . . . . . . . . . . . . . . . . . . . . . . . . . . .564

WORK . . . . . . . . . . . . . . . . . . . . . . . . . . . . . . . . . . . . . . . .566

WRITING . . . . . . . . . . . . . . . . . . . . . . . . . . . . . . . . . . . . .568

YOUTH . . . . . . . . . . . . . . . . . . . . . . . . . . . . . . . . . . . . . . .574

# ACCOUNTING

## 1. Once They Used Notched Sticks

Charles Dickens (1812-1870) writes in *David Copperfield* that, until the reign of George III (1738-1820), accounts in the Court of Exchequer in England were kept on notched sticks. The sticks were splints of elm wood called "tallies." It was 1826 before these cumbersome sticks were finally abolished.

## 2. Inventor of Double-Entry Book-Keeping

Few people have heard of Fra Luca Pacioli (1446/7-1517), the inventor of double-entry bookkeeping. The German philosopher Goethe (1749-1832) called Pacioli's invention (around 1494) "one of the finest discoveries of the human intellect" and said that Pacioli should without hesitation be ranked with his contemporaries Columbus and Copernicus.

## 3. Duties of Auditors

It has been said that auditors are the troops who watch a battle from the safety of a hillside and, when the battle is over, come down to count the dead and bayonet the wounded.

## 4. A Nation's Budget

U.S. Senator J. William Fulbright (1905-1995) used to say that priorities are reflected in the things we spend money on. Far from being a dry account of bookkeepers, a nation's budget is full of moral implications; it tells what a society cares about and what it does not care about; it tells what its values are.

## 5. The Need for CPAs

The legendary entertainer Elvis Presley (1935-1977) used to say, "I have no use for bodyguards, but I have very special use for two highly trained certified public accountants."

## 6. The Balance Sheet

*The Accounting Review* in 1971 published the following item:

"We have audited the balance sheet and here is our report;
The cash is overstated, the cashier being short;
The customers' receivables are very much past due,
If there are any good ones, they are very, very few;
The inventories are out of date and practically junk,
And the method of their pricing is very largely bunk;
According to our figures the enterprise is wrecked...
But subject to these comments, the balance sheet's correct."

## 7. President Hoover on Budgets

Herbert C. Hoover (1874-1964), the 31st President of the United States, once said, "My sympathy often goes out for the humble decimal point. He has a pathetic and hectic life wandering around among regimented ciphers, trying to find some of the old places he used to know when budgets were balanced."

## 8. Accounting as a Profession

In 1993, *Time* said "accounting is a profession whose idea of excitement is sharpening a bundle of No. 2 pencils."

## 9. Accounting As a Bikini

A textbook on accounting published some years ago said that creative accounting practices have given rise to the following quip: "A balance sheet is very much like a bikini bathing suit. What it reveals is interesting, what it conceals is vital."

## 10. An Ex-Accountant Looks Back

The famous comedian Bob Newhart (1929- ) once said, "I was a lousy accountant. I always figured that, if you came within eight bucks of what you needed, you were doing okay. I made up the difference out of my own pocket."

# ACTION

## 11. No Time to Lose

The great French Marshall Lyautey (1854-1934) once asked his gardener to plant a tree. The gardener objected that the tree was slow growing and would not reach maturity for 100 years.

The Marshall replied: "In that case, there is no time to lose; plant it this afternoon."

## 12. Committee on Snakes

Ross Perot (1930- ) is an American business executive famous for his hatred of bureaucracy. The following is typical of his views made during his candidacy for president of the United States: "I come from an environment where, if you see a snake, you kill it. At General Motors [where he was a director], if you see a snake, the first thing you do is go hire a consultant on snakes. Then you get a committee on snakes and then you discuss it for a couple of years. The most likely course of action is — nothing. You figure, the snake hasn't bitten anybody yet, so you just let him crawl around the factory floor. We need to build an environment where the first guy who sees the snake kills it."

## 13. Immediacy

Leo Tolstoy (1825-1910), famed Russian novelist, wrote about this important aspect of time, "There is only one time that is important — NOW! It is the most important time because it is the only time that we have any power."

## 14. Making Decisions

T. Boone Pickens (1925- ), successful entrepreneur and corporate raider, said in commencement remarks at George Washington University, "Be willing to make decisions. That's the most important quality in a good leader. Don't fall victim to what I call the 'ready-aim-aim-aim-aim syndrome.' You must be willing to fire."

## 15. Risk Taking

In a memorable speech given at the Sorbonne in Paris, France, in 1910, President Theodore Roosevelt (1858-1919) spoke about the credit that should go to someone willing to take controversial positions in public life. Richard M. Nixon (1913-1994) quoted Roosevelt verbatim and from memory during his farewell remarks in the East Room of the White House on the morning of his resignation from the presidency in 1976.

There are versions of the speech that vary slightly from each other but here is one that is most widely accepted.

Roosevelt said, "It is not the critic that counts, not the man who points out how the strong man stumbles, or where the doer of deeds could have done better. The credit belongs to the man who is actually in the arena, whose face is marred by dust and sweat and blood; who strives valiantly; who errs and comes short again and again; because there is no effort without error and shortcoming, but who does actually strive to do the deeds; who knows the great enthusiasms, the great devotions; who spends himself in a worthy cause; who at the best, knows in the end the triumph of high achievement; and who, at the worst, if he fails, at least fails while daring greatly, so that his place shall never be with those cold and timid souls who know neither victory nor defeat."

## 16. Difficult Decisions

Admiral Arthur William Radford (1896-1973), while chairman of the U.S. Joint Chiefs of Staff, once said about making difficult decisions, "A decision is the action an executive must take when he has information so incomplete that the answer does not suggest itself."

## 17. Good Intentions

An anonymous verse maker once made this insightful observation:

MR. MEANT-TO

Mr. Meant-to has a comrade,
And his name is Didn't-do.

Have you ever chanced to meet him?
Did he ever call on you?
These two fellows live together
In the house of Never-win,
And I'm told that it is haunted
by the ghost of Might-have-been.

# ACTORS

## 18. Don't Forget to Leave a Tip

When Billy Crystal (1948- ), the famous comedian and actor, moved to Los Angeles in an attempt to break into the big-time, he felt that he had mastered every trick and nuance of his business. To evaluate his performance, he arranged for Jack Rollins, a well-known manager of comedians, to catch his first appearance in L.A.

Crystal did a 25-minute routine including imitations of several famous characters. When he ended, the audience applause was deafening. Exuberant with success, Crystal went next door with Rollins for a talk and some evaluation.

Expecting praise from the agent, Crystal asked Rollins, "How did I do?"

"You were effective," said the agent, "but I don't think good."

Remembering the audience's thunderous applause, Crystal was hurt and totally thrown by the unexpected criticism.

"You made the audience laugh all right," said Rollins, "and they certainly loved everything you did. Your entire performance was fresh and inventive. But never once did you give them your point of view."

Crystal remained puzzled and crestfallen. His ego had taken a beating.

"Listen," Rollins continued, "the problem is there was not enough of your own personality in that performance. You didn't leave a tip."

"I didn't what!" Crystal exclaimed.

"You didn't leave a tip." said Rollins. "You didn't leave a little something on the table for the audience to remember you by."

Crystal still did not understand.

Rollins continued in a kindly but serious tone. "Look, these people tonight, they saw professional razzle-dazzle. They saw talent. But when they left, I assure you they couldn't remember your name or anything else about you. Why? Because you didn't do anything personal or unexpected. There was no risk taking. A comedian's job is to take risks, and you're playing it too safe. Don't be afraid to fail. And don't ever forget, 'Leave that tip.'"

Crystal says he has remembered the agent's sage advice all during the amazing career. No matter how or where he performs, and no matter who is the audience, he always remembers to "leave a tip" for them to remember him by.

## 19. Roosevelt and Orson Welles

President Franklin Roosevelt (1882-1945) once told the famous actor Orson Welles (1915-1985), "There are only two great actors in America – you are the other one."

## 20. Managing Actors

The English film director Alfred Hitchcock (1899-1980) denied ever saying that actors are cattle. According to Hitchcock, "What I said was that actors should be treated like cattle."

## 21. Sound and the Movies

In 1927, before movies had sound tracks, Harry Warner (1881-1958), co-founder of Warner Brothers Pictures, told a reporter, "Who in blazes wants to hear actors talk?"

## 22. Actors and Egos

Michael Wilding (1912-1979), a British movie actor, told a friend, "You can pick out actors by the glazed look that comes into their eyes when the conversation wanders away from themselves."

# ADAPTABILITY

## 23. Better to Bend Than to Break

This is an Aesop fable about a proud oak that grew upon the bank of a stream. For a full hundred years it had withstood the buffeting of the winds, but one day there came a violent storm. The great oak fell with a mighty crash into the swollen river and was carried down toward the sea.

Later the oak tree came to rest on the shore where some reeds were growing. The tree was amazed to see the reeds standing upright.

"How ever did you manage to weather that terrible storm?" he asked. "I have stood up against many a storm, but this one was too strong for me."

"That's just it," replied a reed. "All these years you have stubbornly pitted your great strength against the wind. You were too proud to yield a little. I, on the other hand, knowing my weakness, just bend and let the wind blow over me without trying to resist it. The harder the wind blows the more I humble myself, so here I am!"

Moral: It is better to bend than to break.

## 24. Adaptability in Sport

Sir Roger Bannister (1929- ) was the first man in history to run the mile race in less than four minutes (3:59.4) on May 6, 1954, at Oxford's Iffley Road Track. He later became a doctor and was knighted for his running successes. Here is what he said about the need for adaptability in sports:

"Sport is not about being wrapped up in cotton wool. Sport is about adapting to the unexpected and being able to modify plans at the last minute."

## 25. Darwin on Adaptability

Charles Darwin (1809-1882), the famous English naturalist who first formulated the concept of evolution, wrote in his history-making *Origin of the Species*: "In the struggle for survival, the fittest win out at the expense of their rivals because they succeed in adapting themselves best to their environment."

## 26. Shaw on Adaptation

George Bernard Shaw (1856-1950), the Irish-born British playwright and critic, said of adaptability in his classic *Man and Superman*: "The reasonable man adapts himself to the world. The unreasonable man persists in trying to adapt the world to himself. Therefore all progress depends on the unreasonable man."

# ADVERSITY

## 27. Triumphs over Adversity

Adversity is the grindstone of life. Intended to polish you up, adversity also has the ability to grind you down. The impact and ultimate result depend on what you do with the difficulties that come your way. Consider the phenomenal achievements of these people who experienced extreme cases of adversity:

- Beethoven (1770-1827) composed his greatest works after becoming deaf.

- Sir Walter Raleigh (1552-1618) wrote *History of the World* during a thirteen-year imprisonment.

- If Christopher Columbus (1451-1506) had turned back, no one could have blamed him, considering the constant adversity he endured. Of course, no one would have remembered him either.

- Abraham Lincoln (1809-1865) achieved greatness by his display of wisdom and character during the devastation of the Civil War.

- Martin Luther (1483-1546) translated the Bible while enduring confinement in the Castle of Wartburg.

- Under a sentence of death and during twenty years in exile, Dante Alighieri (1265-1321) wrote the *Divine Comedy*.

- John Bunyan (1628-1688) wrote *Pilgrim's Progress* while in an English jail.

- Handicapped at birth, Helen Keller (1880-1968) was not able to speak, hear or see during her long life. Yet she became a famous author and worldwide celebrity for her charm and wisdom.

## 28. How to Conquer Fear

A famous trapeze performer was instructing his students how to perform on the trapeze bar. After full explanations and instruction in this complicated skill, he asked them to demonstrate.

However, one of the students, looking up at the insecure perch upon which he must perform, was suddenly paralyzed with fear. He had a terrifying vision of falling to the ground and being seriously injured. Frozen with fear, he was unable to move a muscle.

"I can't do it! I can't do it!" he cried.

The instructor put his arm around the boy's shoulder and said quietly, "Son, you can do it, and I will tell you how."

Speaking slowly and with conviction, he said, "Throw your heart over the bar and your body will follow."

That is what the boy did and he turned in a performance on the bar high above the ground that surprised even him. He was never afraid again.

## 29. Inspiring His Troops

When Julius Caesar (100 BC-44 BC) sailed over the English Channel from Gaul and landed with his Legions in what is now England, he knew he had no other choice but to succeed.

To ensure his success, he made an irreversible move. He halted his soldiers on the chalk cliffs of Dover; and looking down over the waves two hundred feet below, his troops saw fire consuming every ship on which they had crossed the channel.

In the enemy's country, with the last link with the continent gone, the last means of retreat burned, there was but one thing left for his army to do — to advance, to conquer! That is precisely what they did. They had no other choice.

### 30. Advice from St. Francis

The renowned founder of the Franciscan order, St. Francis of Assisi (1182-1226), advised, "Start by doing what's necessary, then do what's possible, and suddenly you are doing the impossible."

### 31. Trees and Adversity

Botanists say trees need the powerful March winds to flex their trunks and main branches, so that the sap is drawn up to nourish the budding leaves.

Perhaps people need to meet the stresses of life in the same way, though we dislike enduring them. A stormy period in our life can be prelude to a new spring of life and health, success and happiness. That is, if we keep our self-confidence and faith in the future.

# ADVERTISING

### 32. Advertising Frequency

A businessman once complained to the famous showman P.T. Barnum (1810-1891) that he had tried advertising and that it didn't do any good.

"How often did you advertise?" asked Barnum.

"I put an ad in a weekly newspaper three times," said the businessman, "and got very poor results."

"Sir," said Barnum, who had spent a lifetime successfully promoting things, "advertising is like learning — a little is a dangerous thing."

## 33. Samuel Johnson on Advertising

Note: The following are generous excerpts from an article about advertising that appeared in the English publication, *The Idler* (Number 40) on January 20, 1759. The author was Samuel Johnson (1709-1784), an English man of letters who compiled the first real dictionary. Many of his remarks are as timely as if they appeared yesterday. His article begins:

"The practice of appending to the narratives of publick transactions more minute and domestick intelligence, and filling the newspapers with advertisements, has grown up by slow degrees to its present state.

"Genius is shown only by invention. The man who first took advantage of the general curiosity that was excited by a siege or battle, to betray the readers of news into the knowledge of the shop where the best puffs and powder were to be sold, was undoubtedly a man of great sagacity and profound skill in the nature of man. But when he had once shown the way, it was easy to follow him; and every man now knows a ready method of informing the publick of all that he desires to buy or sell, whether his wares be material or intellectual; whether he makes clothes, or teaches the mathematicks; whether he be a tutor that wants a pupil, or a pupil that wants a tutor.

"Whatever is common, is despised. Advertisements are now so numerous, that they are very negligently perused, and it is therefore become necessary to gain attention by magnificence of promises, and by eloquence sometimes sublime and sometimes pathetick.

"Promise, large promise, is the soul of an advertisement...there are some, however, that know the prejudice of mankind in favour of modest sincerity. The vendor of the 'beautifying fluid' sells a lotion that repels pimples, washes away freckles, smoothes the skin, and plumps the flesh; and yet, with a generous abhorrence of ostentation, confesses that it will not 'restore the bloom of fifteen to a lady of fifty.'

"The trade of advertising is now so near to perfection, that it is not easy to propose any improvement. But as every art ought to be exercised in due subordination to the publick good, I cannot but propose it as a moral question to these masters of the publick ear, whether they do not sometimes play too wantonly with our passions..."

## 34. Violin Advertising

In the late 1600s, the finest instruments originated from three rural families whose workshops were side by side in the Italian village of Cremona. First were the Amatis, and outside their shop hung a sign: "The best violins in all Italy." Not to be outdone, their next door neighbors, the family Guarnerius, hung a bolder sign proclaiming: "The Best Violins In All the World!" At the end of the street was the workshop of Anton Stradivarius, and on its front door was a simple notice that read: "The best violins on the block."

## 35. Does Advertising Pay?

An acquaintance seated next to Philip K. Wrigley (1894-1977) on a flight to Chicago asked the multimillionaire why he continued to advertise his chewing gum when it was far and away the most successful product in its field.

Wrigley replied, "For the same reason the pilot keeps this plane's engines running even though we're already 30,000 feet in the air."

## 36. Broken Pencils

The creative director of a large advertising agency assembled a group of copy supervisors for a training session.

First, he handed out to each of them a new pencil.

Then he told them, "Hold the pencil over your head."

As they held the pencil over their heads, he said, "Now break it in two."

With a puzzled look, each member of the class did as they were told, breaking the pencil they held in two.

"Now that your pencil is broken," said the creative director, "you are ready to supervise and critique copy handed into you without trying to rewrite it yourself. Remember that lesson now that you are a member of management. Your pencil is broken."

## 37. Hiring Advertising People

David Ogilvy (1911-1999) built one of world's greatest advertising agencies during his lifetime. In addition to being a wonderfully creative person, he was also a great administrator and business builder.

In his book *Ogilvy on Advertising*, Ogilvy tells how, when someone was appointed to head one of Ogilvy and Mather's growing number of offices, he would send as a gift a Russian nesting doll. Inside the smallest doll, he placed this note:

"If each of us hires people who are smaller than we are, we shall become a company of dwarfs. But if each of us hires people who are bigger than we are, we shall become a company of giants."

A good philosophy for any company that wants to grow and succeed.

## 38. How to Kill a Business in 10 Easy Steps

1. Don't Advertise. Just pretend everybody knows what you have to offer.

2. Don't advertise. Tell yourself you just don't have the time to spend thinking about promoting your business.

3. Don't Advertise. Convince yourself that you've been in business so long customers will automatically come to you.

4. Don't Advertise. Forget that there are new potential customers who would do business with you if they were urged to do so.

5. Don't Advertise. Forget that you have competition trying to attract your customers away from you.

6. Don't Advertise. Tell yourself it costs too much to advertise and that you don't get enough out of it.

7. Don't Advertise. Overlook the fact that advertising is an investment in selling — not an expense.

8. Don't Advertise. Be sure not to provide an adequate advertising budget for your business.

9. Don't Advertise. Forget that you have to keep reminding your established customers that you appreciate their business.

## 39. Editing Copy

A man opened a fish market and made a sign for it. The sign read:
FRESH FISH FOR SALE HERE.

The first passerby said: "Why did you put the word 'fresh?' You wouldn't sell them if they weren't fresh, would you?" So the merchant crossed out the word FRESH.

The second passerby said: "Why do you say 'here?' You're not selling them anywhere else, are you?" So he crossed out the word HERE.

The third passerby said: "Why use the phrase 'for sale?' Obviously, you are in business to sell fish; you're not going to give them away." So he crossed out the words FOR SALE.

That left just the word "fish" and the owner thought: "No one can find fault with the sign now."

However, the next passerby said: "Why do you have that sign saying 'fish' up there? Anybody can tell there are fish here; you can smell them from a block away."

So he crossed out the word FISH.

And shortly afterward, because he had no sign describing his business or the product he was selling, the fish market owner went bankrupt.

## 40. It Pays to Advertise

Early in his career, the famous humorist and author Mark Twain (1835-1910) was editor of a small-town newspaper in Missouri. In this capacity, he got a letter from a subscriber who reported he had discovered a spider when he unfolded his newspaper.

"Is this good luck or bad?" asked the subscriber.

Twain replied: "Finding a spider in your paper is neither good luck nor bad. The spider is merely looking over our paper to see which merchants were not advertising so that he can go to one of their stores, spin his web across the door, and lead a life of undisturbed peace ever afterward."

## 41. Salesmanship in Print

In a book about Albert Lasker (1880-1952), the famous advertising pioneer, John Gunther tells the story of how a complete stranger put him on to one of the most powerful advertising ideas of all time.

As Gunther tells it, Lasker was in his office in 1904 when he received the following note from a John E. Kennedy, a former clothing salesman and a former member of the Royal Canadian Mounted Police. The note read:

"I am in the saloon downstairs, and I can tell you what advertising is. I know what you don't know. It will mean much to me to have you know what it is and it will mean much to you. If you wish to know what advertising is, send the word 'Yes' down by messenger."

Lasker asked Kennedy to come to his office and, after an hour, the two men returned to the downstairs saloon and talked until midnight.

Kennedy asked Lasker for his definition of advertising and Lasker replied, "News."

"No," said Kennedy. "News is a technique of presentation, but advertising is a very different thing. I can give it to you in three words. It is 'Salesmanship in Print.'"

Lasker was so impressed he hired Kennedy at a salary of $28,000 a year and raised it two years later to $75,000. Kennedy went on to establish the "reason why" concept of advertising persuasion and, along with Lasker, developed the concept of modern copywriting.

## 42. Product Appeal

The following advertising copy was run for E.R. Squibb and Sons in 1921. It says some very profound things about what it takes to make a product successful.

"In the city of Baghdad lived Hakeem the Wise One, and many people went to him for counsel, which he gave freely to all, asking nothing in return.

"There came to him a young man who said, 'Tell me, Wise One, what shall I do to receive the most for that which I spend?'

"Hakeem answered, 'A thing that is bought or sold has no value unless it contains that which cannot be bought or sold. Look for the Priceless Ingredient.'

"'But what is this Priceless Ingredient?' asked the young man.

"Spoke then the wise one: 'My son, the Priceless Ingredient of every product is the Honor and Integrity of its maker. Consider this name before you buy.'"

# AGRICULTURE

## 43. The Peanut

No one's life has been more inspiring than that of George Washington Carver (1864-1943), son of a slave who single-handedly saved agriculture in the American South by discovering uses for the lowly peanut.

On September 8, 1890, Carver walked 30 miles on a dirt road to Simpson College at Indianola, Iowa, a white college with white students and white teachers in a white state. He had been refused elsewhere. To its everlasting credit, Simpson accepted him for $12 in tuition.

Later at Iowa State, Carver was forced to eat at first with the kitchen help rather than in the dining hall. To earn his keep, Carver worked as a janitor, waiter, and as caretaker of the greenhouse and laboratory. He studied mycology (fungus growth) and he had some 20,000 specimens.

Graduating in 1896 with a Master's Degree in Science, Carver was hired by Booker T. Washington for the Agriculture Chair at the Normal and Industrial Institute at Tuskegee, Alabama. He lived there until his death in 1943, unmarried, devoted to the science of living plants, and residing in a small furnished room.

During his career, Carver created more than 300 products from peanuts and more than 100 products from sweet potatoes. By persuading southern farmers to plant peanuts as a cash crop, he saved southern farmers during the depression years from being devastated by the boll weevil invasion that nearly destroyed farmers existing solely on cotton crops.

About the peanut, Carver used to tell this story:

"When I was young, I said to God, 'God, tell me the mystery of the universe.'

"But God answered, 'That knowledge is reserved for Me alone.'

"So I said, 'Then God, tell me the mystery of the peanut.'

"And God said, 'George, that's more nearly your size.'

"And so he told me."

## 44. Farm Subsidies

The number of farmers in the nation may be dropping dramatically, but the number of employees in the Department of Agriculture stays steady. Some old Washington hands like to tell the story of the tour group that was visiting the Department of Agriculture.

Seeing one of the department's employees seated at an empty desk and crying, the visitors asked why.

The answer was: "His farmer died."

## 45. Importance of Agriculture

George Washington (1732-1799), the first President of the United States, described in a letter to John Sinclair in 1794 the importance of agriculture to any nation. He wrote, "I know of no pursuit in which more real and important services can be rendered to any country than by improving its agriculture, the breed of useful animals, and other branches of a husbandman's cares."

## 46. A Farmer's Creed

The following description of the importance of farming was captured long ago by an unknown farmer who loved everything about it:

"I believe a man's greatest possession is his dignity and that no calling bestows this more abundantly than farming.

"I believe hard work and honest sweat are the building blocks of a person's character.

"I believe that farming, despite its hardships and disappointments, is the most honest and honorable way a man can spend his days on this earth.

"I believe farming nurtures the close family ties that make life rich in ways money can't buy.

"I believe farming provides education for life and that no other occupation teaches so much about birth, growth and maturity in such a variety of ways.

"I believe many of the best things in life are indeed free: the splendor of a sunrise, the rapture of wide open spaces, the exhilarating sight of your land greening each spring.

"I believe true happiness comes from watching your crops ripen in the field, your children grown tall in the sun, your whole family feels the pride that springs from their shared experience.

"I believe that by my toil I am giving more to the world than I am taking from it, an honor that does not come to all men.

"I believe my life will be measured ultimately by what I have done for my fellow man, and by this standard I fear no judgment.

"I believe when a man grows old and sums up his days, he should be able to stand tall and feel pride in the life he's lived.

"I believe in farming because it makes all this possible."

## 47. National Wealth

In a paper describing how nations can build wealth, Benjamin Franklin (1706-1790) in 1769 wrote the following, "There seems to be but three ways for a nation to acquire wealth. The first is by war, as the Romans did, in plundering their conquered neighbors. This is robbery. The second is by commerce, which is generally cheating. The third is by agriculture, the only honest way, wherein man receives a real increase of the seed thrown into the ground, in a kind of continual miracle, wrought by the hand of God in his favor, as a reward for his innocent life and his virtuous industry."

# ALCOHOL

## 48. Foiled Character Assassination

During the famous debates between Abraham Lincoln and the noted Senator orator Stephen Douglas (1813-1861), Douglas let it be known that Lincoln used to run a store where you could buy whiskey.

Lincoln replied: "It is true what Mr. Douglas said, that I did run a grocery store and I did sell goods including whiskey. But I remember that in those days that Mr. Douglas was one of my best customers. Many a time have I stood on one side of the counter and sold whiskey to Mr. Douglas on the other side. But the difference is that I have left my side of the counter but Mr. Douglas still sticks tenaciously to his."

## 49. How to Talk When Drunk

At a speech on his 67th birthday at the Metropolitan Club in New York, humorist Mark Twain (1835-1910) talked about the difficulty of expressing one's self clearly when overcome with emotion or some other impediment.

He said it reminded him of a man who came home drunk one night and tried to explain why it happened to his wife, who said:

"John, when you have drunk all the whiskey you want, you ought to ask for sarsaparilla [a soft drink]."

The husband replied, "Yes, but when I have drunk all the whiskey I want, I can't say sarsaparilla."

## 50. Mark Twain and Strong Drink

Those who have sworn off strong drink will appreciate this story told by Mark Twain (1835-1910) to a New Zealand audience in November of 1895. The story goes like this:

"In our country several years ago," said Twain, "there was a man came into a prohibition town and they said to him, 'You can't get a drink anywhere except at the apothecary.'"

So he went to the apothecary (we would say druggist today) and asked for a drink of alcoholic spirits.

"You can't get a drink here," said the apothecary, "without a prescription from a physician."

"But," protested the man, "I'm perishing. I haven't time to get a prescription."

The apothecary shook his head and said, "Well, I haven't the power to give you a drink except for snake bite." And the apothecary gave him the address of a snake.

Soon after, the man was back again, saying, "For goodness sake, give me a drink. That snake is engaged for months ahead."

## 51. Biblical Moderation

In Marc Connelly's (1890-1980) famous play, *Green Pastures*, God instructs Noah to build an ark to save himself and his family from a flood to be caused by 40 days and 40 nights of rain.

He also instructs Noah to take two of every kind of animal and bird on the ark so that they will be preserved from the deluge to come.

Noah asks God if he wants snakes to be included and God replies, "Certainly."

In that case, says Noah, he would like to provision the ark with a keg of liquor in case of snakebite. Agreeing, God replies, "You can have one keg."

Noah argues that he really needs two kegs of liquor, one for each side of the ship to balance it during the downpour.

"One keg," says God firmly. "You can balance the ship by placing the keg in the middle."

## 52. W.C. Fields Preparing for War

On the day the Japanese attacked Pearl Harbor, the famous actor John Barrymore was visiting the comedian-actor W.C. Fields (1880-1946) at his home in Hollywood. Fields is known even today for his legendary alcoholic capacity. John Barrymore (1882-1942) was no slouch either when it came to imbibing alcoholic spirits.

When news of the Japanese attack came on the radio, Fields picked up the phone and ordered forty cases of gin from his liquor dealer.

"Are you sure that is going to be enough?" asked Barrymore.

"Yes," replied Fields, "I think it's going to be a short war."

## 53. Don't Sell That Cow

The humorist Mark Twain (1835-1910) liked to tell this story about an itinerant preacher during frontier days who held his audiences spellbound talking about the evils of alcohol.

Before one of his sermons in a farming community, the preacher asked the church elder serving as his host to provide him with a glass of milk to refresh himself during his long sermon. He placed it in an inconspicuous place on the pulpit's lectern. Without the preacher knowing it, the elder had put some home-made whiskey in the milk.

When the minister reached an impassioned point in his sermon, he took a big swallow from the glass of milk on the lectern. Then he paused a moment, took an appreciative look at the glass, and drank all that was remaining.

Putting the glass down slowly, the minister exclaimed to the congregation, "O Lord, what a cow!"

## 54. Churchill's Thirsty Goals

Winston Churchill (1874-1965) once, believe it or not, came to America after World War II to receive an award for temperance. For people who know something about Winston Churchill, that is an improbable award.

Before presenting Churchill with the award, the Chairperson turned to him and said, "You know, Sir Winston, we've actually done some research and found that you imbibe a little bit. In fact, we found out that you have wine with lunch, you go to the pub in the afternoon, you have cocktails before dinner, wine with dinner, and a nightcap of brandy before you go to bed. We calculated that if one took all the liquor you have drunk during your lifetime it would fill up a room to this level." And she pointed to a line drawn halfway up the huge auditorium wall.

Sir Winston pushed his chair back and he looked up at the line drawn halfway up the wall. He looked at the Chairperson, then looked up at the ceiling, and said quietly, "So far to go, so little time."

# AMBITION

## 55. Lincoln's Ambition

The early years of Abraham Lincoln's (1809-1865) career passed without much distinction and left him with more than his share of self-doubt.

From his teenage years onward, Lincoln had been keen to advance, pursuing a rigorous program of reading, study, and self-improvement. Observing this, Lincoln's law partner, William Herndon, would say later that Lincoln's ambition was "a little engine that knew no rest."

In 1841, the melancholy Lincoln, doubting whether his life would amount to anything, confessed to a friend, "I would be more than willing to die, except that I have done nothing to make any human remember that I have lived."

## 56. How Coolidge Saw Ambition

President Calvin Coolidge (1872-1933) was very skillful at turning away any question he didn't like.

In 1928, after Coolidge issued his famous "I do not choose to run" statement, a persistent reporter in search for more details followed Coolidge to the door of his library.

"Exactly why don't you want to be president again," the reporter asked.

Coolidge looked the reporter squarely in the eye and replied, "Because there is no chance for advancement."

## 57. Ambition Has Not Always Been Admired

In the past, ambition was condemned as unnatural, even immoral. The Latin word "ambitio" referred to those who would scurry about soliciting popular favor, drumming up votes, rather than allowing people to recognize true worth and character.

In the age of William Shakespeare (1564-1616) and John Milton (1608-1674), ambition was often equated with the sin of Lucifer, or of Adam and Eve, the unlawful desire to be of higher estate than God had intended. Many of Shakespeare's protagonists such as Richard III, Henry IV, and Macbeth seek to reinvent the identities bequeathed to them and find themselves cut-off from their true selves, their lives given over to shipwreck.

"I charge thee, fling away Ambition," Shakespeare wrote in *Henry VIII*. "By that sin fell the angels." Ambition seemed like rebellion in a society that defined one's identity largely by birth and inherited status.

In the modern world, and particularly in America, by contrast, we have come to idealize self-made figures like Abraham Lincoln, the rail splitter who went to the White House; Frederick Douglass (1817-1895), the ex-slave who became a learned and articulate advocate for his people; Andrew Carnegie (1835-1919) and John D. Rockefeller (1839-1937), who without education or status, transformed the scale of business corporations. In the modern world, there is a widespread conviction that you are what you make of yourself.

# AMERICANA

## 58. Seeing the Elephant

To the adventurers drawn by it, no expression characterized the California gold rush more than the words "seeing the elephant."

Those planning to go west in search of gold announced to their friends that they were "going to see the elephant." Those who turned back discouraged claimed they had seen "the elephant's tracks" or the "elephant's tail," and admitted that view was sufficient.

People painted colorful names on their wagons like "Prairie Bird," and one teamster scribbled on his words, "Have You Saw the Elephant?" Another forty-niner observed, "As matters turned out, this last legend, despite its bad grammar, was the most appropriate and prophetic of all."

There remains considerable confusion as to just what this expression means in American slang usage.

The *Oxford Dictionary* has this entry: "to see the elephant (U.S. slang); to see life, the world, or the sights (as of a large city); to get experience of life, to gain knowledge by experience."

## 59. How Mt. Rushmore Got Its Name

Millions of tourists from all over the world have journeyed to South Dakota's Black Hills to view a national monument called "Mt. Rushmore." The faces of the four American presidents carved on the mountain are familiar to almost every American, but probably none of them could tell you how the mountain got its name.

The granite and limestone mountain was first sculpted by nature. Harsh Dakota winds and water produced a distinctive peak which went without a name until 1885.

In that year, Charles E. Rushmore (1883-1931), a New York attorney, was traveling through the Black Hills on horseback accompanied by a guide. Rushmore asked the guide what was the name of the impressive peak, and the guide, with tongue in cheek, replied, "Actually, it doesn't have a name. But from now on we'll call the damn thing Rushmore." And, for some reason, the name stuck.

Later, Charles Rushmore became one of the earliest contributors ($5,000) to the Presidential memorial carved there by sculptor Gutzon Borglum (1867-1941). It was completed October 31, 1941.

## 60. Pilgrims Liked Their Beer

Some historians believe that beer was the reason the Pilgrims landed at Plymouth Rock. It's clear from the Mayflower's log that the crew didn't want to waste beer looking for a better site. The log goes on to state that the passengers "were hasted ashore and made to drink water that the seamen might have the more beer."

## 61. An Amazing Pioneer Tale

In early frontier days, pioneers often burned down their houses when they planned to move. Why? They wanted to save their nails. The value of the nails was greater than the value of the entire structure and the labor that had gone into building it.

## 62. Movable Plymouth Rock

Tourists interested in the Pilgrims who go to see Plymouth Rock near the shoreline at Plymouth, Massachusetts, aren't looking at its original location, wherever that was.

The rock was ignored for 150 years until, during the Revolutionary War, the "Liberty Boys" decided it was a historic landmark. By this time the rock was partially buried in the middle of a roadway leading to a wharf and had to be dug out and hauled to the town square.

In the course of several additional moves, the rock fell from a wagon and had to be cemented back together. By 1920, tourists were disconcerted when they found the rock was not at the water's edge. So for the 300th anniversary celebration of the arrival of the Mayflower, Plymouth Rock was moved to the shoreline and a Greek-style temple was erected over it.

It is estimated that Plymouth Rock was probably once 80 percent larger than it is today. Prior to it being housed in the Greek-style temple and protected by an iron grill, many people had chiseled off parts of the rock as souvenirs.

## 63. What Does the Term "Jim Crow" Mean?

The term Jim Crow originated in a song performed by Daddy Rice, a white minstrel show entertainer in the 1830's. Rice covered his face with charcoal to resemble a black man, and then sang and danced a routine in caricature of a silly black person.

By the 1850s, this Jim Crow character, one of several stereotypical images of black inferiority in the nation's popular culture, was a standard act in the minstrel shows of the day. How it became a term synonymous with the brutal segregation and disfranchisement of African-Americans in the late nineteenth century is unclear.

What is clear is that by 1900, the term was generally identified with those racist laws and actions that deprived African-Americans of their civil rights by defining blacks as inferior to whites, as members of a caste of subordinate people.

## 64. Some Texas Expressions

From the Austin (Tex.) American-Statesman

- "He's all hat and no cattle." (All talk and no action.)
- "Big as all hell and half of Texas." (Perpetuating the everything's bigger-in-Texas myth.)
- "He's riding a gravy train with biscuit wheels." (Lucky.)
- Hot as a stolen tamale." (The Texas heat.)
- "She could talk a coon out of a tree." (Either persuasive or simply talks too much.)
- "He's grinning like a mule eating cockleburs." (Nervous.)
- "He's in tall cotton." (A rich dude.)
- "She's two tacos short of a No. 2 dinner." (Crazy.)
- "There are two things in the middle of a road – a yellow line and dead armadillos."

## 65. First Visitors to America

Christopher Columbus (1451-1506) was not the first European to meet Native American people. A much earlier meeting happened when Viking explorers landed in the extreme northeast of North America, around the year 1000.

The landing was part of a great exploratory wave, when the Vikings sailed all around the north Atlantic visiting Iceland, Greenland, and northern North America. They found these lands almost entirely uninhabited.

There are two stories from the 13th and 14th centuries, written records of much older transmitted tales, that tell the story of their encounters with Native Americans. They are *The Saga of Erik the Red*, and *The Saga of the Greenlanders*, both about the explorer Erik the Red and his son, Leif Eriksson.

## 66. A Famous Quotation Wrongly Attributed

Next to a few lines from the Declaration of Independence and Lincoln's Gettysburg Address, the most famous remark in American history may well be the quotation, "Go west, young man, go west."

The quotation is almost never recalled without mentioning the name of Horace Greeley, a famous journalist in the 1800s. The only problem is: Horace Greeley never said it.

The author of the quotation was actually John L. Soule, a little-known Indiana journalist, who published it in the *Terre Haute Express* in 1851. Greeley repeatedly denied that he had said it, and even reprinted the article in which Soule used the expression, but to no avail.

## 67. The Liberty Bell Legend

Although the Liberty Bell is now a hallowed part of American historical legend, no one cared about the bell until many years after its creation.

But in 1847, a man named George Lippard, a Philadelphia journalist, immortalized the Liberty Bell in his "Legends of the American Revolution." Lippard invented the whole story about the bell being used to ring in American independence. The bell did hang in the Philadelphia statehouse in 1776 when the founding fathers drafted the Declaration of Independence. But it occurred to no one to ring it.

The city of Philadelphia tried to sell the bell as scrap in 1828, but could find no buyers. No one believed the bell was worth the expense of removing it from the building.

The bell was first referred to as the "Liberty Bell" in 1839 when a pamphlet entitled "The Liberty Bell, by Friends of Freedom," was distributed at the Massachusetts Anti-Slavery Fair. In the pamphlet, the bell symbolized the freedom of black slaves, not the independence of Americans from Britain.

## 68. The American Dream

For many years the Fourth of July was a day awash with patriotic oratory. Clare Boothe Luce (1903-1987), a playwright, diplomat and a member of Congress, once complained that "the politicians were talking themselves red, white, and blue in the face."

One of the finest articulators of the American dream was a philosopher who never studied philosophy in college and who learned it from life as a longshoreman in San Francisco. His name was Eric Hoffer (1902-1983), who died in 1983 at the age of 81. During his long life, Hoffer wrote many insightful things about America. Here's a sample:

"History contrived an earth-shaking joke when it lifted by the nape of the neck lowly peasants, shopkeepers, laborers, paupers, jailbirds, and drunks from the midst of Europe, dumped them on a vast, virgin continent and said: 'Go to it; it is yours!'

"And the lowly were not awed by the magnitude of the task...They went to it with ax, pick, shovel, plow, and rifle; on foot, on horse, in wagons, and on flatboats. They went to it praying, howling, singing, brawling, drinking, and fighting. Make way for the people!

"Small wonder that we in this country have a deeply ingrained faith in human regeneration. We believe that, given a chance, even the degraded and apparently worthless are capable of constructive work and great deeds."

## 69. Fourth of July Essay

The following was written in 1955 by Otto Whittaker as a public relations advertisement for the Norfolk and Western Railway under the title "I Am the Nation." It was run as the front cover of the Norfolk and Western Railway Company Magazine on January 15, 1976. The year of America's bicentennial:

"I was born on July 4, 1776, and the Declaration of Independence is my birth certificate. The bloodlines of the world run in my veins, because I offered freedom to the oppressed. I am many things, and many people. I am the nation.

"I am 213 million living souls — and the ghost of millions who have lived and died for me.

"I am Nathan Hale and Paul Revere. I stood at Lexington and fired the shot heard around the world. I am Washington, Jefferson and Patrick Henry. I am John Paul Jones, the Green Mountain Boys and Davy Crockett. I am Lee and Grant and Abe Lincoln.

"I remember the Alamo, the Maine and Pearl Harbor. When freedom called I answered and stayed until it was over; over there. I left my heroic dead in Flanders Fields, on the rock of Corregidor, and on the bleak slopes of Korea.

"I am the Brooklyn Bridge, the wheat lands of Kansas and the granite hills of Vermont. I am the coal fields of the Virginias and Pennsylvania, the fertile lands of the West, the Golden Gate and the Grand Canyon. I am Independence Hall, the Monitor and the Merrimac.

"I am big. I sprawl from the Atlantic to the Pacific...my arms reach out to embrace Alaska and Hawaii...3 million square miles throbbing with industry. I am more than 5 million farms. I am forest, field, mountain and desert. I am quiet villages — and cities that never sleep.

"You can look at me and see Ben Franklin walking down the streets of Philadelphia with his bread loaf under his arm. You can see Betsy Ross with her needle. You can see the lights of Christmas, and hear the strains of 'Auld Lang Syne' as the calendar turns.

"I am Babe Ruth and the World Series. I am 110,000 schools and colleges, and 330 churches where my people worship God as they think best. I am a ballot dropped in a box, the roar of a crowd in a stadium and the voice of a choir in a cathedral. I am an editorial in a newspaper and a letter to a Congressman.

"I am Eli Whitney and Stephen Foster. I am Tom Edison, Albert Einstein and Billy Graham. I am Horace Greeley, Will Rogers and the Wright brothers. I am George Washington Carver, Jonas Salk, and Martin Luther King.

"I am Longfellow, Harriet Beecher Stowe, Walt Whitman and Thomas Paine.

"Yes, I am the nation, and these are the things that I am. I was conceived in freedom and, God willing, in freedom I will spend the rest of my days.

"May I possess always the integrity, the courage and the strength to keep myself unshackled, to remain a citadel of freedom and a beacon of hope to the world.

"This is my wish, my goal, my prayer in this year of 1976 — two hundred years after I was born."

## 70. Courage of Founding Fathers

The following information about America's founding fathers was taken from T. R. Fahrenbach's book, *Greatness to Spare*:

- Nine signers died of wounds or hardships during the Revolutionary War.

- Five were captured or imprisoned, in some cases with brutal treatment.

- The wives, sons and daughters of others were killed, jailed, mistreated, persecuted or left penniless. One was driven from his wife's deathbed and lost all his children.

- The houses of twelve signers were burned to the ground.

- Seventeen lost everything they owned.

- Every signer was proscribed as a traitor; every one was hunted. Most were driven into flight; most were at one time or another barred from their families or their homes.

- Most were offered immunity, freedom, rewards, their property or the lives and release of loved ones to break their pledged word or to take the king's protection. Their fortunes were forfeited, but their honor was not. No signer defected or changed his stand throughout the darkest hours.

The pledge of the men who signed the Declaration of Independence was not a perfunctory assent to a flourish of Thomas Jefferson's (1743-1826) pen: it was an earnest commitment entered into by thoughtful, pious, and intrepid men. Of the 56 signers, half of them went on to serve in the new nation as state or national legislators and two of them, John Adams and Thomas Jefferson, as President.

# ANGER

## 71. Burying the Hatchet

During the Civil War, the Union captured two English agents who were seeking to help the South, and President Lincoln ordered that they be released.

"This was a bitter pill for me to swallow," said Lincoln, "but I told myself that England's triumph would be short-lived, and that after our war was ended successfully, we would be so powerful that we could call England to account for all the embarrassments she had caused us."

Said Lincoln, "I feel a good deal like the sick man in Illinois who was told he probably hadn't many days longer to live, and that he ought to make peace with any enemies he might have.

"The sick man said the person he hated worst was a fellow named Brown who lived in the next village. The sick man said he had better begin with him first.

"So Brown was sent for, and when he came the sick man said in a voice as meek as Moses that he wanted to die at peace with all his fellow creatures and he hoped he and Brown could now bury all their animosity.

"Brown was so moved by this speech that he had to take out his handkerchief and wipe the tears from his eyes. It wasn't long before Brown melted and gave his hand to his neighbor in friendship."

Lincoln said that, "After a parting that would have softened the heart of a grindstone, Brown had about reached the bedroom door when the sick man rose up on his elbow and said, 'But see here, Brown, if I should happen to get well, that old grudge still stands.'"

## 72. Permanent Anger

Those who saw the Academy Award-winning movie *Forrest Gump*, starring Tom Hanks (1956- ), will never forget it. One memorable scene was Gump quoting his mother's observation to him that "Life is like a box of chocolates. You never know what you are gonna git."

One of the movie's most stirring scenes was when a love interest of Gump's returns to her girlhood home after her abusive father had died. As she remembers the sexual abuse she had endured as a child, she begins throwing rock after rock at the dilapidated, abandoned house. In a sobbing rage, she keeps on throwing rocks at the house until she falls down in exhaustion.

Looking on sympathetically, Gump says, almost to himself, "Sometimes there just aren't enough rocks."

There are a great many problems and inequities in life that make us feel exactly the same way.

## 73. Nails in the Fence

There was a little boy with a bad temper. His father gave him a bag of nails and told him that every time he lost his temper, to hammer a nail in the back fence.

The first day the boy had driven 37 nails into the fence. Then it gradually dwindled down. He discovered it was easier to hold his temper than to drive those nails into the fence.

Finally the day came when the boy didn't lose his temper at all. He told his father about it and the father suggested that the boy now pull out one nail for each day that he was able to hold his temper.

The days passed and the young boy was finally able to tell his father that all the nails were gone.

The father took his son by the hand and led him to the fence.

"You have done well, my son," said the father, "but look at the holes in the fence.

"The fence will never be the same. When you say things in anger, they leave a scar just like this one. You can put a knife in a man and draw it out, it won't matter how many times you say 'I'm sorry,' the wound is still there. A verbal wound is as bad as a physical one."

## 74. The Angry Letter

Edwin Stanton (1814-1869), Secretary of War in Abraham Lincoln's cabinet, was incensed that a Major General had accused him of favoritism.

Lincoln suggested that Stanton write the offending officer a strong letter.

This Stanton promptly did and he showed it to Lincoln, who asked Stanton what he planned to do with it.

"Why, send it of course," replied the surprised Stanton.

"You don't want to send that letter." Lincoln advised. "Put it in the stove. That's what I do when I have written a letter while angry. It's a good letter and you had a good time writing it. Now burn it, and write another."

# ANIMALS, LESSONS FROM

## 75. Fear of Failure

The African impala can jump to a height of over 10 feet and cover a distance of greater than 30 feet. Yet these magnificent creatures can be kept in an enclosure in any zoo with a 3 foot wall. The animals will not jump if they can not see where their feet will fall.

Some humans are like this, not true risk takers.

## 76. Barnacles

The barnacle is confronted with an existential decision about where it's going to live. After it decides...it spends the rest of its life with its head cemented to a rock."

Many of us humans make the same mistake.

## 77. Some Lessons from Insects

Sir Francis Bacon (1561-1626), an English lawyer, philosopher and essayist, wrote the following in 1620:

"The men of experiment are like the ant, they only collect and use; the reasoners resemble spiders, who make cobwebs out of their own substance. But the bee takes the middle course; it gathers its materials from the flowers of the garden and field, but transforms and digests it by a power of its own.

"Not unlike this is the true business of philosophy (science); for it neither relies solely or chiefly on the powers of the mind, nor does it take the matter which it gathers from natural history and mechanical experiments and lay up in the memory whole, as it finds it, but lays it up in the understanding altered and digested. Therefore, from a closer and purer league between these two faculties, the experimental and the rational (such as has never been made), much may be hoped."

## 78. A Love Letter from Jefferson

Thomas Jefferson (1743-1826), the third President of the United States wrote to a friend, Maria Cosway, in Paris the following on December 24, 1786. Mrs. Cosway reportedly stole Jefferson's heart during his stay in Paris as the American ambassador to France:

"I wish they had formed us like the birds of the air, able to fly where we please. I would have exchanged for this many of the boasted preeminencies of man. I was so unlucky when very young, as to read the history of Fortunatus. He had a cap of such virtues that when he put it on his head, and wished himself anywhere, he was there. I have been all my life sighing for this cap. Yet if I had it, I question if I should use it but once. I should wish myself with you, and not wish myself away again."

## 79. How Can Bumblebees Fly?

In the 1930s, a leading zoologist concluded, after careful study that, according to the laws of aerodynamics, it should be impossible for a bumblebee to fly. That is because its size, weight, and the shape of its body are all wrong in relation to its total wingspread.

Fortunately, no bumblebees have ever studied aerodynamics so they just naively keep on doing what they're incapable of doing.

## 80. Chickens' Social Order

In 1913, Thorlief Schieldorup-Ebbe, a Danish zoologist, discovered that the lowly barnyard chicken lived within a strict organizational structure. Inevitably there was a top chicken who could peck any other chicken in the yard to express its dominance, a second layer of chickens that could peck a third group of still lower-ranked chickens but could not peck the boss chicken, and so on down the hierarchy.

He called the phenomenon "the pecking order," a phrase that has become a part of our modern vocabulary.

## 81. How's Your Personal Effort?

Have you ever seen a duck move through water on a lake? You don't see its feet paddling under water, but let me tell you, the duck really moves.

What is impressive to look at is the wake the duck leaves behind as it moves forward. WOW! It opens up an angle of at least 40 degrees and the water rippled as far as...oh, say 40, 50 feet, maybe even more.

That's a lot. Think about it, that duck left a wake that's 600 times its actual size. That's a lot of effect from a duck that's only two feet long.

Now think about yourself. How big are you? What kind of effect do your actions bring about?

## 82. Helplessness Can Be Learned

In cultures that depend on elephants for labor and transportation, it's common to tie untrained elephants by their ankles to a bamboo tree, using heavy-duty rope.

After three or four days of trying to free themselves, the elephants give up. From that time on they can be restrained by tying one leg to a small peg in the ground — something they surely could escape from with minimal effort. But at the least resistance, the elephants don't try to get loose; they have learned helplessness.

## 83. Reaching Your Full Potential

Flea trainers have observed a predictable and strange habit of fleas while training them.

Fleas are trained by putting them in a cardboard box with a top on it. The fleas will jump up and hit the top of the cardboard box over and over and over again. As you watch them jump and hit the lid, something very interesting becomes obvious. The fleas continue to jump, but they are no longer jumping high enough to hit the top.

When you take off the lid, the fleas continue to jump, but they will not jump out of the box. They won't jump out because they can't jump out. Why? The reason is simple. They have conditioned themselves to jump just so high. After they have conditioned themselves to jump just so high, that's all they can do.

Many times, people do the same thing. They restrict themselves and never reach their full potential. Like the fleas, they think they are doing all they are capable of doing.

## 84. The Hedgehog and the Fox

An essay written many years ago by the philosopher Isaiah Berlin (1909-1997) was titled "The Hedgehog and the Fox." It contained some very interesting insights into human behavior.

Berlin divided the world into two types of people: foxes and hedgehogs. Foxes pursue many ends, often unrelated and contradictory.

Hedgehogs, on the other hand, relate everything to a single central vision, a single universal organizing principle that defines what they think and believe.

One can conclude that most people are foxes... and that leaders like Ronald Reagan (1911-2004) are hedgehogs. Reagan had some singular ideas and never departed from them.

## 85. Teamwork and Ego

The sin (and danger) of excessive pride (or an excessive ego) is admirably demonstrated in this simple fable:

A frog asked two geese to take him south with them. At first they resisted; they didn't see how it could be done. Finally, the frog suggested that the two geese hold a stick in their beaks and that he would hold on to it with his mouth.

So off the unlikely threesome went, flying southward over the countryside. It was really quite a sight. People looked up and expressed great admiration at this demonstration of creative teamwork.

Someone said, "It's wonderful! Who was so clever to discover such a fine way to travel?"

Whereupon the frog opened his mouth and said, "It was I," as it plummeted to the earth.

## 86. Unnoticed Change

If you place a frog in a pot of boiling water, it will immediately try to scramble out. But if you place the frog in room temperature water, it will stay put.

If the pot is placed on a heat source, and if you gradually turn up the temperature from 70 to 80 degrees F, the frog will still do nothing. As the temperature gradually increases, the frog will become groggier and groggier, until it is unable to climb out of the pot.

Though there is nothing restraining it, the frog will sit there and boil. Why? Because the frog's internal apparatus for sensing threats to survival is geared to sudden changes in his environment, not to slow, gradual changes.

## 87. The Synergy of Teamwork

Have you ever watched a flock of geese flying in their traditional "V" formation, heading for Canada?

Two engineers learned that each bird, by flapping its wings, creates an uplift for the bird that follows. Together, the whole flock gains something like 70 percent greater flying range than if they were journeying alone.

Whenever a goose falls out of formation, it suddenly feels the drag and resistance of trying to go it alone and quickly gets back into formation to take advantage of the lifting power of the birds immediately in front. When the lead goose gets tired, the goose rotates to the back and another goose flies the point.

## 88. Personal Growth

The Japanese carp, commonly known as the koi, is a favorite fish of many hobbyists. A fascinating thing about the koi is that if it is kept in a small fish bowl, it will only grow to be two or three inches long. But place the koi in a larger tank or small pond and it will grow to six or even 10 inches. Place it in a large pond and it may grow to as long as a foot and a half. Placed in a large lake, it has the potential to reach sizes up to three feet.

One could easily use the example of the carp to philosophize about reaching our own maximum potential. Our personal growth is dependent upon the size of the world we choose to inhabit. Key to our growth is the mental, spiritual, emotional, and other challenges to which we expose ourselves.

## 89. How the Kangaroo Got Its Name

The story goes that, when Captain James Cook (1728-1779) discovered Australia, his sailors brought a strange animal aboard ship whose name they didn't know.

Intrigued, Cook sent a sailor ashore to inquire of the natives the name of this strange creature. He returned and reported it was known as a "kangaroo."

Many years passed before it was learned that, when the natives were asked the name of the animal, they replied, "kangaroo," meaning "I don't know?"

Note: Although there is a record of this in Captain Cook's journal, the story, according to the *Oxford English Language Dictionary*, is probably apocryphal.

## 90. Taking Risks

If a lobster is left high and dry among the rocks, it does not have enough instinct and energy to work its way back to the sea, but waits for the sea to come to it.

If the sea does not come, the lobster remains where it is and dies, although the slightest effort would enable it to reach the waves, which could be as close as a yard away.

Unfortunately, the world is filled with human lobsters: people who are stranded on the rocks of procrastination and indecision. By using their own determination and energy, they could instead solve the problems facing them rather than waiting for some lucky break to do so.

## 91. Monkey at the Typewriter

In a paper delivered at the Aspen Design Conference, Dr. Jacob Bronowski (1908-1974), the famous British scientist, recalled that Arthur Eddington (1882-1944) had made the casual remark that, if you put a monkey in front of a typewriter and simply let him hit the keys, sooner or later he would write out in sequence all the plays and sonnets of Shakespeare.

Dr. Bronowski said, "It's a good statement for randomness or chance, and I thought I would calculate how long it would take a monkey to write part of Shakespeare's wonderful sonnet that starts, 'Shall I compare thee to a summer's day. Thou art more lovely and more temperate...'"

The British scientist then informed the audience that, by the known rules of probability, the monkey would not have gone as far as the tenth letter in the first line of the Shakespeare sonnet in the 15 billion years or so that the universe existed.

## 92. How Wild Geese Choose Leaders

While studying the migratory habits of wild geese, Professor Margaret Kuhn learned that these birds fly unerringly thousands of miles across whole continents.

In her research, Professor Kuhn discovered some interesting facts about the birds' ability to fly such long distances. One of these is that they rotate the leaders. Another factor is that they always choose the leaders — the up front birds — from the ones who can handle turbulence.

The other birds just honk along! This honking is not from discomfort. The birds behind the leader birds are honking encouragement to their leader.

## 93. Ability to Let Go of Problems

A story is told of an expedition of scientists who were on a mission to capture a particular species of monkeys in the jungles of Africa. It was important that the monkeys be brought back alive and unharmed.

Using their knowledge of monkey ways, the scientists devised a trap consisting of a small jar with a long, narrow neck. Into the jar was placed a handful of nuts. Several of these jars were staked out, while the scientists returned to their camp, confident of catching the monkeys.

Scenting the nuts in the bottle, a monkey would thrust his paw into the long neck of the jar and take a fistful of nuts. But when he tried to withdraw the prize, he discovered that his clenched fist would not pass through the narrow neck of the bottle. So he was trapped in the anchored bottle, unable to escape with his prize, and yet unwilling to let it go. When the scientists returned, they easily took the monkeys captive.

There is a moral here for those of us who refuse to let go from problems that do not have a workable solution.

## 94. Every Little Bit Helps

It was a chilly overcast day when the horseman spied the little sparrow lying on its back in the middle of the road. Reining in his mount, he looked down and inquired of the little creature, "Why are you lying upside down like that?"

"I heard the sky is going to fall today," replied the bird.

The horseman laughed, "And I suppose your spindly little legs can hold up the sky?"

"One does what one can," said the little sparrow.

## 95. A Poem about Accomplishment

The author of this instructive and inspiring poem is unknown:

There once was an oyster whose story I tell,
Who found that sand had got under his shell;
Just one little grain, but it gave him much pain,
For oysters have feelings although they're so plain.
Now, did he berate the working of fate,
Which had led him to such a deplorable state?
Did he curse out the government, call for an election?
No. As he lay on the shelf, he said to himself,
"If I cannot remove it, I'll try to improve it."
So the years rolled by as the years always do,
And he came to his ultimate destiny — stew.
But this small grain of sand which had bothered him so,
Was a beautiful pearl, all richly aglow.
Now this tale has a moral — for isn't it grand
What an oyster can do with a morsel of sand.
What couldn't we do if we'd only begin
With all of the things that get under our skin.

## 96. Competitiveness

Has anybody noticed how many dead squirrels you see on the roadside in summer and how few you see during the winter? Think about it.

In summer, the nuts are plentiful, and it's easy for even the slowest squirrel to survive. With easy living the squirrels get fat and lazy and cars pick them off one by one.

In winter, things are just the opposite. Nuts are few and far between and you must hustle to survive. The fat and lazy squirrels have all gone to their maker. The survivors are sleek, fast, and smart. No cars catch them unawares.

One could say the same thing about businesses that become complacent and stop trying real hard. This leaves them wide open to business predators that soon put an end to their prosperity.

## 97. Disarmament

The following anecdote has been attributed to Winston Churchill (1871-1947):

When the animals had gathered, the lion looked at the eagle and said gravely, "We must abolish talons."

The tiger looked at the elephant and said, "We must abolish tusks." The elephant looked back at the tiger and said, "We must abolish claws and jaws."

Thus each animal in turn proposed the abolition of the weapons he did not have, until at last the bear rose up and said in tones of sweet reasonableness, "Comrades, let us abolish everything — everything but the great universal embrace."

## 98. Danger of Greed

An old method of catching wild turkeys can be an excellent lesson to all of us.

To trap the turkeys, corn was scattered on the ground. Then a net was stretched about two feet high over the grain. When the wild turkeys sensed that no human was near, they would approach the corn and lower their heads to eat it. Never lifting their heads, they would nibble their way beneath the net.

When they became full and tried to leave, instead of keeping their heads down, they lifted their heads and were immediately caught in the net.

## 99. Conditioned for Failure

In an experiment, four monkeys were placed in a room. In the center of the room was a tall pole from whose top hung a bunch of bananas. Seeing the bananas, one hungry monkey eagerly climbed up the pole toward the bananas. But just as he reached out to grasp the bananas, the researchers hit him with a stream of cold water from an overhead shower. Uttering a frightened squeal, the monkey abandoned its attempt to reach the bananas and hurriedly slid down the pole.

One after another, the other three monkeys attempted to reach the bananas. And each one was drenched with an equally cold stream of water. Each one gave up without touching a single banana. After repeated efforts and cold showers, the monkeys finally gave up on trying to reach the bananas.

The researchers then removed one of the original four monkeys from the room, and a new monkey was added. No sooner had this new, innocent monkey started climbing the pole after the bananas than the original three monkeys reached up and pulled the new monkey back down the pole. The new monkey tried again to reach the bananas, but after a few attempts, and without being subjected to a cold shower, the new monkey also stopped trying to get to the enticing cluster of bananas.

There is a lesson here for individuals or businesses not to avoid seeking new opportunities just because others have failed or have warned them not to even try.

## 100. The Risk of Growing

An oceanographer was asked how a lobster is able to grow bigger when its shell is so hard. The only way, he explained, is for the lobster to shed its shell at regular intervals. When its body begins to feel cramped inside the shell, the lobster instinctively looks for a reasonably safe spot to rest while the hard shell comes off and the pink membrane just inside forms the basis of the new shell. The process takes about two days.

But no matter where a lobster goes for this shedding process, it is vulnerable. It can get tossed against a coral reef or eaten by a fish. In other words, the lobster has to risk its life in order to grow.

There is a lesson here for all of us when we resist trying new things or running calculated risks because of fear of failure. For the lobster, there seems to be no choice. For us, there is.

## 101. Wild Ducks

Thomas J. Watson, Jr., (1914-1993) who built IBM into a worldwide power in computers, loved to retell Kierkegaard's (1813-1855) tale about a man who relished watching the annual flight of wild ducks.

Each year the man left feed near a nearby lake so the ducks would stop to eat. However, this encouraged some of the ducks to give up flying south and they wintered at the lake instead.

In time these ducks grew fat and lazy. Why bother to fly when everything was laid out for them right there?

The moral: You can make wild ducks tame, but you can never make tame ducks wild again.

After telling the story, Tom Watson always said he wanted to encourage "wild ducks" in IBM as an antidote to conformity and bureaucratic self-satisfaction.

# ATTITUDE

## 102. Self-Image

There once was a Sioux Indian brave who found an eagle's egg high on a mountain. Not knowing what kind of egg it was, he carried the egg down to the prairie and placed it in the nest of a prairie chicken.

The eaglet hatched with the brood of prairie chicks and grew up with them. All his life, the changeling eagle, thinking he was a prairie chicken, did what his fellow prairie chickens did. He scratched in the dirt for seeds and insects to eat. He clucked and cackled as they did. And he flew no more than a few feet off the ground. After all, he told himself, that's how prairie chickens are supposed to fly.

One day, soon after the sun rose, the young eagle saw a magnificent bird flying high above in the cloudless prairie sky. Soaring high above the prairie on uplifting wind currents, the magnificent creature moved across the sky powered only by an occasional flap of its powerful wings.

"What a beautiful bird!" exclaimed the young eagle to one of his prairie chicken brothers. "I wonder what it is."

"That's an eagle, the king of birds," clucked his companion. "But don't get any ideas, you can never be like him."

So the young eagle never gave it another thought. And he died, close to the ground, thinking he was a prairie chicken.

## 103. Home Is What We Make It

An old man was tending his garden by a fork in the road on the edge of a town.

A traveler came by and said, "I'm thinking about moving to your town. Tell me, what is it like?"

The old man asked, "What is it like where you came from?" The traveler answered, "It was terrible. People were always bickering and arguing. No one could get along with his neighbor, and the town was full of gossip and jealousy."

The old man replied, "Well, it's just like that here."

A while later, a second traveler came by and questioned the old man, "What is this place like? I'm thinking of moving here."

Again, the old man asked, "What was it like where you came from?"

The traveler replied, "It was a wonderful place to live. The people were so kind and caring and all the neighbors were just like a loving family."

The old man said, "Well, it's just like that here," and he went back to tending his garden.

How could the town be "just like" each traveler's explanation of where he had been? Very simple. How things seem to you has a tremendous amount to do with your own attitude and outlook. You can find the good or dig up the ugly. The choice belongs to each and every one of us.

# BOOKS

## 104. Man's Most Valuable Creation

A well-known American writer, Clarence Day (1874-1935) wrote a valentine to books in 1920 on the subject of the Yale University Press. It went like this:

"The world of books is the most remarkable creation of man. Nothing else that he builds ever lasts. Monuments fall; nations perish; civilizations grow old and die out; and, after an era of darkness, new races build others. But in the world of books are volumes that have seen this happen again and again, and yet live on, still young, still as fresh as the day they were written, still telling men's hearts of the hearts of men centuries dead.

"And even the books that do not last long, penetrate their own times at least, sailing farther than Ulysses even dreamed of, like ships on the seas. It is the author's part to call into being their cargoes and passengers, living thoughts and rich bales of study and jeweled ideas. And as for the publishers, it is they who build the fleet, plan the voyage, and sail on, facing wreck, till they find every possible harbor that will value their burden."

## 105. Value of Books

Inscribed on the Thomas Jefferson Building at the Library of Congress are the first eight words of this quotation by Henry David Thoreau (1817-1862):

"Books are the treasured wealth of the world and the fit inheritance of generations and nations. Their authors are a natural and irresistible aristocracy in every society, and, more than kings or emperors, exert an influence on mankind."

## 106. Humanity in Print

The distinguished American historian Barbara W. Tuchman (1912-1989) wrote the following in the "Authors League Bulletin" in 1979:

"Books are the carriers of civilization. Without books, history is silent, literature dumb, science crippled, thought and speculation at a standstill. Without books, the development of civilization would have been impossible. They are engines of change, windows on the world, 'lighthouses,' (as a poet said) 'erected in the sea of time.' They are companions, teachers, magicians, bankers of the treasures of the mind. Books are humanity in print."

## 107. Books Increase Longevity

One of America's most famous editors was Norman Cousins (1912-1980). A scholarly man who ended his career teaching medical students, he wrote this about books:

"There is a simple non-medical technique for increasing longevity. This system goes by the name of 'book.' Through it, man can live hundreds of lifetimes in one. What is more, he may enjoy fabulous options. He can live in any age of his choosing. He can take possession of an experience. He can live inside the mind of any man who has recorded an interesting thought, any man who has opened up new sluices of knowledge, any man who has engaged in depths of feeling or awareness beyond the scope of most mortals. This is what good books are all about."

## 108. How to Pick a Gift Book

Mark Twain (1835-1910) was introduced to a young lady at a Christmas party and she asked him if he thought a book was the most useful gift one could give.

"Yes," said Twain, "but of course it depends on the book. A big leather-bound volume makes an ideal razor strap. A thin book is useful to stick under a table with a broken caster to steady it. A large, flat atlas can be used to cover a window with a broken pane. And a thick, old-fashioned heavy book with a clasp is the finest thing in the world to throw at a noisy cat."

## 109. Books Are Immortal

In an age when books were being burned by Hitler's Nazis, America's 32nd president, Franklin Delano Roosevelt (1882-1945) sent the following message to the American Booksellers Association in 1942:

"We all know that books burn — yet we have the greater knowledge that books cannot be killed by fire. People die, but books never die... no man and no force can put thought in a concentration camp forever. Books are weapons... weapons for man's freedom."

# BUREAUCRACY

## 110. The Boss Speaks!

The most famous FBI chief ever was J. Edgar Hoover (1895-1972), who ran the agency with an iron hand from 1924 to his death in 1972. He intimidated criminals and U.S. Presidents alike for the secret files he kept on them.

One day, Hoover received a memorandum whose margins were too small for his liking.

In big red letters he scrawled an angry warning across the top: "Watch the borders!"

The next morning, his frightened aides transferred 200 FBI agents to border stations in Canada and Mexico.

## 111. A Satirical Look at Bureaucracy

Physicists have just discovered the heaviest known element to date, which they have named "Administerium."

It has no electrons and no protons, giving it an atomic number of zero, but it does have one neutron, 75 vice neutrons and 111 assistants to the vice neutrons, giving it an atomic mass of 322. These particles are bound together in the nucleus by a force that involves the continuous exchange of subatomic particles called "memorandons."

Administerium occurs naturally in large corporate structures. Because it has no electrons, Administerium is totally inert. However, it prevents the formation of new and useful compounds, and it can be detected by its tendency to impede every reaction in which it is present. In one experiment, it extended one split-second reaction into a two-day continuum.

Administerium has a half-life of two years, after which it doesn't actually decay, but rather undergoes a mysterious reorganization involving vice neutrons exchanging places. The element's mass actually increases after each reorganization. The only known way of reducing its mass is by bombarding it with a stream of particles called "consultons" — an expensive procedure — which causes it to release redundant particles.

As yet, researchers have been unable to identify any practical use for Administerium.

## 112. Bureaucratic Reasoning

There is a story, which is perhaps apocryphal but which certainly could have happened, that the French police were chasing a criminal who fled into a building in Paris. Their first thought was that they would surround the building. But then they realized that the building was so large, and had so many exits, that they didn't have enough policemen on the scene to do that. So they surrounded the building next door, which was small and had fewer exits.

## 113. National Defense

The British created a civil service job in 1803 calling for a man to stand on the cliffs of Dover with a spyglass. He was supposed to ring a bell if he saw Napoleon coming. The job was abolished in 1945.

## 114. How Bureaucracy Is Born

One day, the CEO of a large meat packing company said to his senior advisers, "You know, I'm a little worried that someone might steal from the stockyard at night." So the advisers created a night watchman position, and the company hired a person for the job.

A month later, the CEO asked, "How does the watchman do his job without instruction?" So the advisers created a Planning Department and the company hired two people — one to write the instructions and one to do time studies.

The following month, the CEO asked, "How do we know if the night watchman is doing the tasks correctly?" So the advisers established a Quality Control Department and the company hired two more people — one to do the studies and one to write the reports.

A few months later, the CEO asked, "How are these people getting paid?" So the advisers created positions for a timekeeper and a payroll office — and the company hired two more people.

A few months later, the CEO asked, "Who will be accountable for all these people?" So the advisers created an administrative section — and the company hired an administrative officer, an assistant administrative officer, and a legal secretary.

Next month, the CEO said, "We've had this department in operation for one year and we're $18,000 over budget — we must cut back overall cost."

So the advisers fired the night watchman.

## 115. Filling out Forms

One of Great Britain's most famous actresses was Mrs. Patrick Campbell (1865-1940), who created the role of Eliza Doolittle in George Bernard Shaw's play *Pygmalion*.

Mrs. Campbell went to Hollywood in the early 1930s to pursue a film career and a studio functionary handed her the customary publicity form to fill out.

As the form requested, she filled in her name, the color of her hair and eyes, her height, her interests, etc. In the blank headed "Experience," she wrote in *Edward VII*.

## 116. It Is in the Rule Book

In the early days of World War II, according to technology and military historian Elting E. Morison (1910-1995), armaments of all kinds were in short supply, and the British made use of venerable field pieces that had come down to them from previous generations. Some stretched as far back as the Boer War.

There was a plan to use these guns in the coast defense. However, it was felt that the rapidity of fire could be increased. Therefore a time and motion expert was called in to study the firing procedures. He watched one of the gun crews of five men at practice in the field for some time, without spotting anything significant. However, puzzled by certain aspects of the procedures, he took some slow-motion pictures of the soldiers performing the loading, aiming and firing routines.

When he ran these pictures, he noticed something that appeared odd to him, but he couldn't make any sense out of it. A moment before the firing, two members of the gun crew ceased all activity and came to attention for a three-second interval, extending throughout the discharge of the gun.

Morison summoned an old colonel of artillery, showed him the pictures, and pointed out the strange behavior. What did it mean, he asked the colonel.

The colonel, too, was puzzled, and he asked to see the pictures once again. "Ah," he said, after the second viewing, "I have it. They are holding the horses."

## 117. Red Tape

Many years ago and long before today's threat of terrorism, a BBC commentator named Gilbert Harding (1907-1960) planned a visit to North America. He was greeted warmly in Canada, as you would expect, but before he could go on to New York he had to get a U.S. visa at the American consulate in Toronto.

There, he was called upon to fill out a long form with many bureaucratic questions, including one near the end that asked, in the most straightforward manner imaginable: "Is it your intention to overthrow the government of the United States by force?"

Suffice to say, by the time Harding got to that question, he was so irritated that he answered, "Sole purpose of my visit."

## 118. The Joys of Patronage

The British have always been good at the patronage system. For more than twenty years, an attendant stood for no apparent reason at the foot of the stairway leading to the House of Commons. At last someone checked and discovered that the job had been held in the attendant's family for three generations. It seemed it had originated when the stairs had been painted, and the grandfather had been assigned to stand at the foot of the stairs to warn people not to step on the wet paint.

## 119. Plain Talk from Washington

There is an oft-told tale about the clarity of written communications turned out by Washington bureaucracy that is as true today as it was years ago.

The story goes that a plumber wanted to use hydrochloric acid to clean out some drains. But before doing so, he wrote to the Bureau of Standards in Washington, D.C. to make sure this procedure was safe.

Within a few days, he received this reply in the mail:

"The efficacy of hydrochloric acid is indisputable, but chlorine residue is incompatible with metallic permanence."

The plumber fired off a return letter thanking the Bureau for its quick turnaround and thanked them for telling him the use of hydrochloric acid to clean out the pipes was OK.

By return mail, the Bureau sent another note which read: "We cannot assume responsibility for the production of toxic and noxious residues with hydrochloric acid, and suggest that you use an alternative procedure."

Reassured, the plumber responded with another letter thanking the Bureau for its help and expressing his pleasure that their experts agreed with him.

This time, the Bureau responded with a telegram which read as follows:

"Don't use hydrochloric acid; it eats hell out of the pipes."

## 120. "We Were Just Following Orders"

There is an ancient story of a Russian sentry who stood day after day at his post with no apparent reason for his being there. One day, a passerby asked him why he was standing in that particular place.

"I don't know," the sentry replied, "I'm just following orders." The passerby then went to the captain of the guard and asked him why the sentry was posted in that place.

"I don't know," the captain replied, "we're just following orders."

This prompted the captain of the guard to pose the question to higher authority. "Why do we post a sentry at that particular spot?" he asked a general. But the general didn't know either. So he summoned a group of military historians and asked them the question.

The answer came back that 100 years before, Catherine the Great (1729-1796) had planted a rosebush and had ordered a sentry placed there to protect it. The rosebush had been dead for eighty years, but the sentry still stood guard.

## 121. Full Employment

While in the process of checking employee records, a wealthy British landowner called a longtime employee into his study.

"Peter," asked the landowner, "how long have you been with us now?"

"Almost 25 years," replied the employee, at which his employer frowned.

"According to these records, you were hired to take care of the stables," said the landowner.

"That's correct, sir," said the veteran employee.

"But we haven't owned horses for more than 20 years," said the landowner.

"Right, sir," replied the old retainer. "What would you like me to do next?"

# BUSINESS, SERVICE

## 122. The Man Who Sold Hot Dogs

During the 1930s there was a man who lived by the side of the road and sold hot dogs. He was hard of hearing, so he had no radio. He had trouble with his eyes, so he read no newspapers. But he sold good hot dogs.

He stood at the side of the road and cried: "Buy a hot dog, mister?" and people bought. He increased his meat and bun orders. He bought a bigger stove to take care of his trade.

Business was so good he brought his son home from college early to help him out. And his son said: "Father, haven't you been listening to the radio? Haven't you been reading the newspapers? The European situation is terrible. The domestic situation is worse."

The father thought to himself, "Well, my son's been to college, he reads the papers and he listens to the radio — so he ought to know."

So the father cut down his meat and bun orders, took down his signs, and no longer bothered to stand out on the highway to sell his hot dogs. And his hot dog sales fell almost overnight.

The father said to the boy, "You're right, son, we certainly are in the middle of a great depression."

## 123. Ask for the Order

Some of us often search for complicated answers to problems when the truth is right under our nose.

The famous automobile pioneer Henry Ford (1863-1947) was once asked by an insurance agent, whom he had known for many years, why he never got any of Ford's business.

"You never asked me," Ford replied.

## 124. Ancient Chinese Consultants

In ancient China, scholars moved from one province to another offering guidance to sovereigns. But these early consultants were probably more careful with their advice than their counterparts of today. For, although they were richly rewarded if their recommendations were good, if their advice turned out not to work, they were cut in two, boiled, or tied between two chariots and ripped in half.

## 125. The Title of Chairman

Where do we get the word "chairman?" It comes from the custom during the Middle Ages when the master of the house and his lady were the only ones who owned and sat on chairs.

The rest of the household, although it shared a communal dining table, sat on stools or cushions at a lower level.

A guest of great importance was honored by being invited to "take the chair."

## 126. Customer Satisfaction

Few names in retail are more famous than that of Stanley Marcus (1905-2002), the man who built Neiman Marcus into one of the world's most famous department stores.

Marcus is fond of telling how it was his father, founder of the business, who gave him an unforgettable lesson in valuing a customer properly.

A woman customer had ruined a dress she had obviously worn once and was loudly demanding her money back. When Stanley seemed resistant, his father admonished him and told him to give the woman her money back, no questions asked.

Later, Stanley argued with his father that the woman had obviously worn and abused the dress and that the manufacturer would not help pay for it. His father replied that the woman wasn't doing business with the manufacturer, she was doing business with Neiman Marcus and that he didn't want to lose a customer over a $175 dress.

Many years later, someone calculated that the woman had spent more than $500,000 at Neiman Marcus.

## 127. Buyer Beware

The wisdom "Let the buyer beware" appeared in the Code of Hamurabi (c. 1750 B.C.E.), one of the oldest sets of human laws.

Known in Roman times as "caveat emptor," it was first rendered in English in *The Book of Husbandry* (1523), by John Fitzherbert (1870-1947).

## 128. Going against Size

Everyone advised David to forget about confronting the enormous giant Goliath, saying, "He's so big, there's no way you can win."

David replied, "He's so big, there's no way I can miss."

## 129. The Office in 1872

1. Office employees each day will fill lamps, clean chimneys, and trim wicks. Wash windows once a week.

2. Each clerk will bring in a bucket of water and a scuttle of coal for the day's business.

3. Make your pens carefully. You may whittle nibs to your individual taste.

4. Men employees will be given an evening off each week for courting purposes, or two evenings a week if they go regularly to church.

5. After thirteen hours of labor in the office, the employee should spend the remaining time reading the Bible and other good books.

6. Every employee should lay aside from each pay day a goodly sum of his earnings for his benefit during his declining years so that he will not become a burden on society.

7. Any employee who smokes Spanish cigars, uses liquor in any form, or frequents pool and public halls or gets shaved in a barber shop, will give good reason to suspect his worth, intentions, integrity, and honesty.

8. The employee who has performed his labor faithfully and without fault for five years, will be given an increase of five cents per day in his pay, providing profits from business permit it.

## 130. A Dot-Com Bubble of Yesteryear

We all remember the stock market craziness when dot-com businesses with no profits were making multi-millionaires out of 20-year-olds. Now that most of these phony businesses have gone broke, we say to ourselves, "How could people have been so gullible?"

It turns out that such manias grip the human race every so often. It happened in the Netherlands in the 1630s when tulip bulbs were selling at prices up to $4,000. Nobles, citizens, farmers, mechanics, seamen, footmen, maid servants, even chimney sweeps, not only grew bulbs but speculated in them.

A "Semper Augustus," white and red, tinted blue underneath, brought the record high: "a new and well-made carriage and two dappled-gray horses and accessories," plus enough cash to push the total up to more than $4,000.

And a century later, in 1836 – the mania struck again. A new bulb, "Citadel of Antwerp" brought $3,120. The solid, stolid Dutch? One wonders at humankind!

Though it is somewhat less well-known, the same thing happened to orchids in 19th-century England. A manic passion for these exotic plants gripped residents of the British Isles just as tulips had entranced their Dutch neighbors.

For example, orchids were in such demand that auctions in Liverpool and London saw prices soaring to ridiculous heights. Buyers often paid 500 British pounds for a single plant, and top prices were much higher. In today's money, 500 pounds would be worth more than $30,000!

Orchids have a long and exotic history. Because the bulbs of common European orchids looked like testicles, aphrodisial powers were attributed to them. Dried and pulverized orchid tubers were used in love potions. It was believed that potions made from the younger, firmer tubers would encourage the conception of male children, whereas potions made from the older, softer tubers would lead to the birth of female children.

## 131. Customer Gouging

The ancient Greeks knew how to handle "overruns" by building contractors. For example, they would have bidders submit estimates of the cost of constructing a public building. The winning bidder would then have to turn over his property and assets to a magistrate until the job was completed.

If the job was finished at or below the estimate, the bidder was awarded a commendation in his honor. If the work was up to 25 percent over budget, the state paid. But if costs went beyond 25 percent, assets equal to the overrun were taken from the contractor.

## 132. The Three Snake Rule

James Barksdale (1943- ), founder of Netscape, is a charismatic manager whose maxims have endeared him to his employees. One of his favorites was formulated at a management retreat soon after he took over Netscape.

It's known as his three-snake rule:

- The first rule: If you see a snake, kill it. Don't set up a snake committee. Don't set up a snake user group. Don't write snake memos. Kill it.
- The second rule: Don't play with dead snakes. (Don't revisit decisions.)
- The paradoxical third: All opportunities start out looking like snakes.

## 133. Abraham Lincoln on Trade Tariffs

Discussing trade tariffs with a visitor, President Lincoln recalled a time when he was a clerk in a grocery store in New Salem.

"A man came in," said Lincoln, "and said to the storekeeper, 'I want a nickel's worth of ginger snaps.'"

"When they were laid out on the counter, the customer changed his mind and said, 'I'll have a glass of cider instead.'"

"The man drank the cider and turned toward the door. 'Here, Bill,' said the storekeeper, 'ain't you going' to pay for that cider?'"

"The man replied: 'Didn't I give you the ginger snaps for it?'"

"'Well, then,' said the storekeeper, 'pay me for the ginger snaps.'"

"'But I never ate your ginger snaps,' said the customer."

"The storekeeper grudgingly admitted that the customer had told the truth, but added he had lost something, somehow, in the deal. "So it is with the tariff," said Lincoln. "Somebody loses, but I don't know as yet who it is."

## 134. Customer Satisfaction

One grocery shopper told a friend this story.

"There's a meat counter in the market I go to that has three or four clerks waiting on customers. But one of the clerks always has a line of customers waiting for him even if one of the other clerks isn't busy. The other day I asked him the reason for his popularity."

"'The other clerks,' he said, 'always put more meat on the scale and then take some away to arrive at what the customer ordered. I always put less on the scale and then add to it. It makes all the difference.'"

## 135. Who Invented the CEO Post?

In the last article he wrote for "The Wall Street Journal," the Austrian-born American management consultant and author Peter Drucker (1909-2005) told how the modern CEO post was invented.

"The CEO is an American invention," he said, "designed first by Alexander Hamilton (1755-1804) in the Constitution in the earliest years of the Republic, and then transferred into the private sector in the form of Hamilton's own Bank of New York and of the Second Bank of the United States in Philadelphia. There is no real counterpart to the CEO in the management of any other country. The German 'Sprecher des Vorstands,' the French 'Administrateur Delegue,' the British 'Chairman,' or the Japanese 'President' are all quite different in their powers and in the limitations thereon."

## 136. Modern Business Communications

A study commissioned by Pitney Bowes and the Institute for the Future turned up the following facts:

*   The average office worker communicates with 24 different people per day using eight different communications tools.

*   Incoming messages interrupt office workers between six and 20 times an hour.

- This is a global phenomenon. The average worker in the UK receives 48 phone calls, 23 e-mails, 11 voice mails, 20 letters, 15 internal memos, 11 faxes, 13 Post-it Notes, and 8 pager calls a day.

- It's worse in the U.S. where an average worker gets 190 messages a day.

All this suggests that by the time you finish a long meeting, you will be about 47 messages behind.

## 137. The Productivity Engineer Speaks

It is not easy working through the painful task known variously in modern business as "rightsizing" or "workplace reengineering."

A consultant was brought in to help remaining managers through the difficult process of reducing the workforce while maintaining productivity. In his first meeting with them, he added a contemporary twist to the old classic.

"What does the optimist say about the glass and the water?" he asked.

"It's half full," was the reply.

"And what does the pessimist say?" he queried.

"It's half empty."

"And what does an outside consultant like me have to say about it?"

The response was dead silence. Then the productivity consultant revealed the answer he had to give the employer who had brought him in for his opinion.

"Looks to me," he said, "like you've got twice as much glass as you need."

## 138. Some Good Business Advice

Asked by Fortune Magazine what was the best advice she had ever received in business, Anne Mulcahy (1952- ), chief executive officer of Xerox, said it occurred at a breakfast meeting in Dallas, to which she had invited a group of business leaders. One of them, a plainspoken, self-made, streetwise guy, came up to Mulcahy and said:

"When everything gets really complicated and you feel overwhelmed, think about it this way. You gotta do three things.

"First, get the cow out of the ditch.

"Second, find out how the cow got into the ditch.

"Third, make sure you do whatever it takes so the cow doesn't go into the ditch again."

Mulcahy says this bit of advice has become a mantra at Xerox.

## 139. One Way to Do Business

Thomas Hobson (1544-1631) was an Englishman living in Cambridge during the late 16th and early 17th centuries. He was well known during his time. His job was to carry people and mail between Cambridge and London. And to do the job correctly, he kept a stable of about 40 horses.

To earn extra money, he sometimes rented out the horses. After a while, though, it became apparent that some horses were being overworked. Customers were requesting only the best horses he had.

So Hobson came up with a new system giving every horse and every customer equal treatment. It worked like this: He constantly rotated his stable of horses and told his customers, "Either take the horse nearest the stable door...or take none at all."

His technique of presenting only one true choice has come to be known as Hobson's Choice.

# 140. How Not to Ride a Dead Horse

The following is from a syndicated column published by Harvey Mackay (1932- ), American businessman, author and lecturer:

Lakota Indian tribal wisdom says that when you discover you are riding a dead horse, the best strategy is to dismount.

However, in modern organizations, we often try other strategies with dead horses, including the following:

- Buying a stronger whip.
- Changing riders.
- Saying things like, "This is the way we have always ridden this horse."
- Appointing a committee to study the horse.
- Arranging to visit other sites to see how they ride dead horses.
- Appointing a tiger team to revive the dead horse.
- Creating a training session to increase our riding ability.
- Comparing the state of dead horses in today's environment.
- Changing the requirements, declaring that "This horse is not dead."
- Outsourcing contractors to ride the dead horse.
- Harnessing several dead horses together for increased speed.
- Declaring that "No horse is too dead to ride."
- Providing additional funding to increase the horse's performance.
- Doing a cost analysis study to see if contractors can ride it cheaper.
- Declaring the horse is "better, faster and cheaper" dead.
- Forming a quality circle to find uses for dead horses.
- Saying that the horse was procured at great cost.
- Promoting the dead horse to a supervisory position.

## 141. Encouraging Employees

Stanley Marcus (1905-2002) was a giant in retailing, having built up the famous Neiman Marcus Department Store. One of his secrets was an ability to inspire growth in his employees.

One of his favorite stories is as follows: "I once visited the bridge of a naval vessel where the brass gleamed like gold. I asked the captain how often they had to shine the brass. 'Every day,' he told me. 'The minute you stop polishing it, it starts to tarnish.'"

"This incident," said Marcus, "can be correlated to people. None of us is made of gold, we're all made of brass, but we can look like gold if we work hard at polishing ourselves as the sailor polishes the brass on his ship. We can be better than we really are if we will make the effort."

"That may sound trite," said Marcus, "but it must have made an impression on many people, because almost every week some member of our staff comes up to me and says, 'I'm sure polishing my brass today.'"

## 142. Some Stock Market Advice

Warren E. Buffett (1930- ), the Omaha billionaire and chairman of Berkshire, Hathaway, Inc. in Omaha, Nebraska, has what he calls the "cigar butt" approach to investing.

If you buy a stock at a sufficiently low price, he says, there will usually be some hiccup in the fortunes of the business that gives you a chance to unload at a decent profit, even though the long-term performance of the business may be terrible.

However, Buffett adds, a cigar butt found on the street that has only one puff left in it may not offer much of a smoke, but the "bargain" purchase will make that puff all profit.

## 143. About Meetings

An edict was issued in the 17th century by Lord Protector of England, Oliver Cromwell (1599-1658), whose purpose was to lessen the savage practices of some of his troops. These often ranged from rape to pillage and murder.

The edict described a new procedure to be initiated. The offending soldier and his entire company would assemble underneath the local gallows and hold a meeting.

This meeting would primarily consist of the rolling of dice. Everyone at the meeting would participate. The man who lost would die by hanging. This would not necessarily be the instigator of the crime, but simply the man who lost.

You will not be surprised that this new practice resulted in fewer crimes, fewer troops, and fewer meetings.

## 144. How to Run a Business

Profits of $137 million have been donated to charities by the unusual food business started in 1978 by Hollywood legend Paul Newman (1925-2008) and his author friend, A.E. Hotchner (1920- ).

Their business, whose products are marketed under the name of "Newman's Own," began with a whimsical project. They started filling empty wine bottles with Newman's homemade salad dressing as gifts for friends. They did the work in a converted horse barn in Newman's backyard in Westport, Connecticut.

As an experiment, the pair decided to sell their all-natural salad dressing to local stores. This was so successful that what began as a backyard project is now an empire with 77 products on the market, including spaghetti sauce, popcorn, and "Newman's Own Old Fashioned Roadside Virgin Lemonade."

The two men say they built the business "with no marketing survey, no business plan, no budget and no organized strategy."

In fact, there is a sign in the pair's office that reads: "There are three rules for running a business; fortunately we don't know any of them."

## 145. Fish Tale with a Moral

Codfish are a delicious treat in America's northeast region. But when attempts were made to ship them to markets far distant, the cod did not taste like they did when eaten closer to home.

In an attempt to deal with the problem, shippers froze the cod and then shipped it. However, the fish still didn't taste right. Then the fish dealers tried shipping the codfish in tanks filled with seawater. That proved even worse. Not only was the shipping more expensive, but the codfish lost their flavor and their flesh became soft and mushy.

Finally, some creative soul thought of a way to solve the problem in a most unusual way. The codfish were shipped in a tank along with their natural enemy — the catfish. From the time the codfish left the East Coast until the shipment arrived at far west destinations, those catfish had pursued the cod all over the tank! Guess what. Using this method, the cod arrived at the market as fresh tasting as if they had just been taken from the ocean. In fact, the flavor was better than ever.

The above is a clear demonstration of what keen competition and marketing challenges can do — for humans as well as codfish.

## 146. How to Avoid Meetings

The distinguished British molecular biologist Sydney Brenner (1927- ) hated wasting time in meetings, so this is what he did about it.

"I learned very quickly that the only reason that would be accepted for not attending a committee meeting was that one already had a previous commitment to attend a meeting of another organization on the same day.

"I therefore invented a society, the Orion Society, a highly secret and very exclusive society that spawned a multitude of committees, sub-committees, working parties, evaluation groups and so on that, regrettably, had a prior claim on my attention.

"Soon people wanted to know more about this club and some even decided that they would like to join it. However, it was always made clear to them that applications were never entertained and that if they were deemed to qualify for membership they would be discreetly approached at the appropriate time."

## 147. Sell What's on the Truck

It was the early days in New York City and an Italian fruit vendor was teaching his son the basics of salesmanship.

"Don't tell people we are out of peaches," the father said patiently, "ask them to buy some of our very fresh plums. Sell what's on the truck."

Many of today's salesmen could take the same advice.

Don't spend a lot of time complaining about the current state of the product line, or describing products you can't deliver right away.

"Sell what's on the truck." And your customers will be well served with the quality products you can deliver to them now in a timely fashion.

## 148. Meet Mr. Market

Many of you are familiar with what Warren Buffett (1930- ) has said about "Mr. Market," the invention of his mentor and friend, Ben Graham (1894-1976).

As Buffett wrote in a famous essay, Mr. Market is "a remarkably accommodating fellow who appears daily and names a price at which he will either buy your interest or sell you his," but "the poor fellow has incurable emotional problems. At times he feels euphoric, while at other times he is depressed and can see nothing but trouble ahead for the world."

On those occasions, Buffett says it's important to remember that Mr. Market doesn't mind being ignored — transactions are strictly at your option.

## 149. Skirts and the Stock Market

The following was printed by Financial World in 1979:

Early in the century, when skirts were unappealingly long, the Dow Jones industrials meandered disinterestedly below 100.

Then, in the 1920s, the era of the short-skirted flappers, the Dow floated merrily upward to over 300.

With the Great Crash, however, both the market and hemlines plunged back down again.

As skirts fluttered up to knee-level in the 1940s and 1950s, the market showed periodic signs of renewed liveliness.

But it wasn't until miniskirts and hot pants came along in the 1960s that the market really got into high gear, soaring about 100 points.

More recently, with minis but a memory, the market has plodded along a generally dispirited course.

## 150. Making a Sale

Harvey Mackay (1932- ), president of Mackay Envelope Corporation and a syndicated columnist and lecturer, once said, "I remember when I was first starting out and asking a colleague I respected how many calls he would make on a prospect before giving up.

"He told me, 'It depends on which one of us dies first.'"

## 151. Conservative Investing

The Tokyo stock market has a history even more volatile than the U.S. stock market.

One Japanese investment adviser tells his clients to participate, but with a smaller share of their investment portfolio.

He quotes an old Japanese saying: "Enjoy the party, but dance near the exit."

## 152. Sam Walton's Rules for Success

Sam Walton (1918-1992), the founder of Walmart, was a very innovative and competitive merchant. Here are some rules he passed on to colleagues:

1. Commit with a passion to your business.
2. Share profits with your employees. If you treat them as partners, they will treat you as a partner, and together you will perform beyond your wildest dreams.
3. Motivate your partners. Money and ownership are not enough. Set high goals, encourage competition, and then keep score.
4. Communicate everything you can to your employees. The more they know, the more they will understand. Information is power, and the gain you get from empowering your associates more than offsets any risk of informing your competitors.
5. Show appreciation for a job well-done.
6. Celebrate success, and in those inevitable failures, find some humor. Don't take it so seriously.
7. Listen to everyone in your company, especially the ones who actually talk to customers. They really know what's going on out there.
8. Exceed your customers' expectations and they'll always come back.
9. Control your expenses better than your competition.
10. Swim upstream. If everyone else is going it one way, there is a good chance you can find your niche by going in the opposite direction.

## 153. Unhappy Customers

In a survey conducted by the Travelers Home Equity Service, the following was discovered about unhappy customers:

The answer [to poor service] is unhappy customers. But what's worse is that we never hear from 96 percent of them! Listen to this: for every complaint received, there are 26 more unhappy people who simply remain silent about their complaints. And six of their problems are serious ones. What happens is that these people broadcast our poor service! The average unhappy customer tells 9 or 10 people about it. A tenth or so of them tell more than 20 people.

## 154. Description of a Salesman

During a convention of sales managers in Los Angeles, Harry G. Moock, then a Vice President at Chrysler Corporation, gave this description of the ideal salesman:

"He has the curiosity of a cat, the tenacity of a bulldog, the friendship of a little child, the diplomacy of a wayward husband, the patience of a self-sacrificing wife, the enthusiasm of a Sinatra fan, the assurance of a Harvard man, the good humor of a comedian, the simplicity of a jackass, and the tireless energy of a bill collector."

## 155. Patience Brings Rewards

Although Japan and the United States are extremely important to each other, the cultural differences which divide them are often enormous.

For example, there is a wonderful Japanese word, "nemawashi," whose rough translation is "to prepare the roots." Although the phrase was borrowed from infinitely patient Japanese gardeners, every Japanese businessman understands its meaning.

A gardener would use the term "nemawashi" to describe the infinite and time-consuming pains he might take preparatory to transplanting a small tree. The whole process might take several years — the time necessary to "prepare the roots" so that the little tree can stand the shock of being uprooted.

The same care and patience is necessary in many complex business tasks — opening up a new market, educating customers to additional uses for your product, even training your most promising young employees. Not everything important can be accomplished in a day, a month, or even a year.

The Japanese word "nemawashi" can be a valuable reminder that patience and care can accomplish things that sheer managerial drive cannot.

## 156. Tip for Service

The humorist Robert Benchley (1889-1945) was usually a generous tipper but on one occasion he was very upset with the service he was getting at a top luxury hotel.

When check-out time came, he pointedly ignored all the hotel employees lined up in the lobby expecting a big tip.

Going out the door, Benchley was greeted by the officious doorman who said, "You're not going to forget me, are you, sir?"

"Absolutely not," said Benchley, grasping the doorman's outstretched hand, "I will write to you."

# CAREER

## 157. Be Careful What You Wish for

Dwight D. Eisenhower (1890-1969), World War II hero and 34th President of the United States, reminisced about his boyhood career dreams in these words:

"When I was a small boy in Kansas, a friend of mine and I went fishing and as we sat there in the warmth of the summer afternoon on a river bank, we talked about what we wanted to do when we grew up.

"I told him that I wanted to be a real major league baseball player, a genuine professional like Honus Wagner (1874-1955). My friend said that he'd like to be president of the United States. Neither of us got our wish."

## 158. Management Development

America has always been the land of opportunity for immigrants from around the world. Here's a story that illustrates that fact:

Back in the 1920s and 1930s there was a country called Rumania and its ruler's name was King Carol.

He once told a British diplomat that, before his ouster from the throne, he had selected 14 of the brightest Rumanians for special training in government service.

He sent seven to England and seven to the United States to study their political and economic systems.

"The seven who went to England were very smart," King Carol recalled, "and on their return home they all achieved great success in the government in Bucharest."

"And what happened to the seven you sent to the United States?" asked the British diplomat.

"They were even smarter," King Carol replied, "they stayed there."

## 159. Late Bloomer

In 1860, a 38-year-old man was working as a handyman for his father, a leather merchant. He kept books, drove wagons, and handled hides for about $66 a month.

Prior to this menial job, the man had failed as a soldier, a farmer, and a real estate agent. Most of the people who knew him had written him off as a failure.

Eight years later, he was President of the United States. The man was Ulysses S. Grant (1822-1885).

## 160. Getting Fired Can Be an Opportunity

The famous British author Somerset Maugham (1874-1965) used to like to tell this story. It was about a young Vicar of St. Peter's Church in London, who, discovering that the church's janitor was illiterate, fired him.

Jobless, the man invested his meager savings in a tiny tobacco shop where he immediately prospered. He then bought another shop, then another, and still another until he owned a large chain of tobacco stores all over Britain. Altogether they were worth a lot of money.

One day, he dined in a fancy private club with his banker. After an elaborate meal, and over the cognac and cigars, the banker observed, "You've done quite well for an illiterate man. I wonder where you would be today if you could read and write."

"That's easy," replied the man, "I'd still be the janitor in St. Peter's Church in Neville Square."

# CHANGE

## 161. Avoiding Change

There is a wonderful story about an old dog that lay stretched out on the porch of a country general store, moaning and growling as he lay half-asleep in the sun.

"Why is your dog making all those noises?" a customer asked the store owner.

"Oh," answered the owner, "he's lying on a nail."

"Well then," said the customer, "why doesn't he move?"

"Because," said the owner, "it's not hurting him bad enough."

There is a lesson here for those of us who put up with things we dislike and that cause us pain such as an unsatisfying job, an unnecessary chore, a bad habit, or whatever — that we could change if we just had the gumption to make a change. "Lying on a nail" may work for an old dog in a general store but it is a habit human beings should certainly not emulate.

## 162. Changing One's Mind

The famous British economist John Maynard Keynes (1883-1946) was once approached after a lecture by a young man demanding an explanation for an apparent contradiction between something he had said that evening and something he had written in an article years before.

"When I'm wrong, I change my mind," Keynes replied. "What do you do?"

## 163. The Changing Workplace

If a stonecutter from ancient Greek days miraculously came to work today in a stone mason's yard, the only significant change would be the design he would be asked to carve on the grave stones. The tools he would use would be exactly the same, only now they might have been electrified in some way.

Throughout history, a craftsman who had learned his trade after five or seven years of apprenticeship would have learned everything he would ever need to use during his lifetime.

That would certainly not be so today. In today's world, any tradesman or professional will have to acquire new knowledge every four or five years or become obsolete.

## 164. Alice in Wonderland

In Lewis Carroll's (1832-1898) *Alice in Wonderland*, Alice goes through some remarkable changes in size after she falls down the rabbit hole. When she encounters a caterpillar, she is set back by the question.

"Who are you?"

Alice replies: "I - I hardly know, sir, just at present — at least I know who I was when I got up this morning. But I think I must have been changed several times since then."

"What do you mean by that?" said the Caterpillar sternly, "Explain yourself."

"I can't explain myself, I'm afraid sir," said Alice, "because I'm not myself, you see."

## 165. Doing It like Mother Did It

President Ronald Reagan (1911-2004) used to like to tell this story.

"We sure can't be like the fellow's wife who used to cut off both ends of the ham before she cooked it. When he asked her why she did that, she said because that's the way her mother always did it.

"One day, he got the chance to ask his mother-in-law why she cut off both ends of the ham before she cooked it. And she said because that's the way her mother did it.

"Came the holidays and Grandma was visiting and he told her about it and asked if that was true. Why did she cut off both ends of the ham before she cooked it? She said, 'That's simple. I never had a pan big enough to get the whole ham in it.'"

## 166. Technological Change

In 1829, Martin Van Buren (1782-1862), then the governor of New York, wrote this to the President of the United States:

"The canal system of this country is being threatened by the spread of a new form of transportation known as 'railroads.' The Federal government must preserve the canals for these reasons: If canal boats are supplanted by railroads, serious unemployment will result. Captains, cooks, drivers, hostlers, repairmen, and lock tenders will be left without means of livelihood. Canal boats are absolutely essential to the defense of the U.S. In the event of expected trouble with England, the Erie Canal could be the only means by which we could ever move the supplies so vital to waging modern war.

"As you may well know, railroad carriages are pulled at the enormous speed of 5 miles per hour by engines, which in addition to endangering life and limb of passengers, roar and snort their way through the countryside. The Almighty certainly never intended that people should travel at such breakneck speed."

# CHARACTER

### 167. Cheating Is an Old Trait

Once upon a time in a tiny French village, the peasants decided to honor their parish priest by each one bringing to the parish house the next Sunday a bottle of wine for the pastor's empty wine barrel.

The pastor was delighted, and he asked all in attendance to join him in a glass of wine from the now full barrel. But when the tap was opened, only water came out.

Each peasant had brought water instead of wine — thinking that all the others would bring wine and the one bottle of water would never be detected.

### 168. An Act of Conscience

Ralph Waldo Emerson (1803-1882), the distinguished American writer and philosopher, once visited his friend Henry David Thoreau (1817-1862) who had been jailed for civil disobedience.

According to Thoreau's aunt, Maria Thoreau, Emerson asked Thoreau, who was also a writer and philosopher, "Henry, why are you here?"

"Waldo," replied Thoreau, "why are you not here?"

### 169. Cost of Flattery

In ancient Greece, the politically crafty philosopher Aristippus had learned to get along in court by flattering the tyrant Denys. Aristippus looked down his nose at some of his less prosperous fellow philosophers and wise men who would not stoop that low.

One day he saw his old colleague, Diogenes, washing some vegetables, and he said to him disdainfully, "If you would only learn to flatter King Denys you would not have to be washing lentils."

Diogenes looked up slowly and in the same tone replied, "And you, if you had only learned to live on lentils, would not have to flatter King Denys."

## 170. Getting Credit

Indira Gandhi (1917-1984), an Indian stateswoman who was the granddaughter of Mahatma Gandhi (1869-1948) said her grandfather had once told her there are two kinds of people: those who do the work and those who take the credit. She said, "He told me to try to be in the first group; there was less competition there."

## 171. An Ancient Hawaiian Belief

Each child born has, at birth, a bowl of perfect light. If he tends to his light, it will grow in strength and he can do all things. Swim with the sharks, fly with the birds, know and understand all things. If, however, he becomes envious, jealous, angry, or fearful, he drops a stone into his bowl of light and some of the light goes out. Light and the stone cannot hold the same space.

If he continues to put stones in the bowl, the light will go out and he will become a stone himself. A stone does not grow, nor does it move. If at any time he tires of being a stone, all he needs to do is turn the bowl upside down and the stones will fall away and the light will grow once more.

## 172. A Hindu Legend

Long ago all men were divine, but mankind so abused the privilege that Brahma, the god of all gods, decided the godhead (the essential being of god) should be taken away from them. But he had to hide it where man would never find it again.

"Let us bury it deep in the earth," suggested one god.

Brahma said, "No, man will dig down until he finds it."

"Then let us throw it into the deepest part of the biggest ocean," proposed another god.

"Man will learn to dive and someday come across it," insisted Brahma.

"Then it can be hidden in the clouds atop the highest mountain of the Himalayas."

"Man will manage to climb that high some day," Brahma said and then added:

"I have a better idea. Let us hide it where he will never think to look: inside man himself."

## 173. A Miracle of Character

If you ever feel you are having to contend with difficulties almost beyond human endurance, listen to this story about a courageous man named Jean-Dominique Bauby (1952-1997) who refused to give up.

Jean-Dominique Bauby was the editor-in-chief of the popular French magazine *Elle*. He was 43 years old, happily married, the father of two young children, and loved by all who knew him for his wit, his style, and his passionate approach to life.

On the evening of December 8, 1995, Bauby was driving a new BMW in peak-hour Paris traffic accompanied by his son, Theophile, when he felt his eyes blur and all of his faculties seemed suddenly out of his control. Miraculously, he was able to reach the house of his sister-in-law, Diane, a trained nurse. But, by this stage, Bauby was half conscious and his head was bobbing about uncontrollably. Soon he sank into a coma that lasted for 20 days.

When he came out of the coma at the hospital, doctors told him he had suffered a sudden and severe stroke of the brain stem called "locked-in syndrome," a rare condition that leaves the patient mentally alert but almost totally paralyzed. In the hospital he was put on a respirator, an intravenous drip, and a gastric tube for giving him nourishment. His body had all but stopped working. Only his left eye functioned, allowing him to see and, by blinking it, to make clear his mind was unimpaired. Doctors give him no hope for recovery.

This is where the miracle of Bauby's courage and accomplishment begins. Unable to write or speak, Bauby began to write a book about his condition and his inner excursions into the realms of his memory, imagination, and dreams. He did it by composing each passage in his mind and then dictating it, letter by letter to a woman sent out by his publisher. His helper painstakingly recited from a frequency-ordered alphabet until Bauby chose a letter by blinking his left eyelid once to signify "yes". He did this letter after letter, after letter, after letter, for three months until his memoir was done.

He titled the book, *The Diving-Bell & The Butterfly*. In it, he wrote, "Through the frayed curtain at my window a wan glow announces the break of day. My heels hurt, my head weighs a ton, and something like a giant invisible diving-bell holds my whole body prisoner." A book critic said of the book, "It is the strength of his thoughts, memories and dreams that imbue this book with an astounding humanity that continually resounds in the face of desperation and fear."

Bauby's accomplishment was an heroic act of will and defiance to cruel adversity. He survived just long enough to see his book published in the spring of 1997. It received wonderful reviews and was an instant success.

Now what were those troubles you were complaining about?

## 174. Cure for a Terrible World

G. K. Chesterton (1874-1936), the famous English author and journalist, wrote a book early in the twentieth century called *What's Wrong With The World*.

He got the idea for the book's title from a letter to a London newspaper wanting to know the best answer to the world's problems.

Chesterton took his pen in hand and wrote this pungent reply: "What's wrong with the World? I am."

Signed: G.K. Chesterton

In drafting such a reply, Chesterton was expressing a belief often expressed by Greek philosophers and in the Bible: what is right or wrong in the world is directly connected to what is right and wrong with ourselves.

## 175. What Every Person Needs

Abraham Maslow's (1908-1970) hierarchy of needs is set forth in his 1954 book, *Motivation and Personality*.

In the book, he urges that before a person can even consider moving toward his own vision of excellence — something Maslow calls "self-actualization" — he first has to be assured of the physical needs for survival: food, air, sleep, water, shelter.

Then he has to feel secure from illness and danger. Next he needs a sense of "belongingness": acceptance, affection, understanding. Next, a sense of esteem, pride, self-respect, status. And having assured all those needs, he can then move toward achieving his full potential.

## 176. A Native American Legend

The Lakota tribe of Native Americans believed there was a spirit of creation, an awesome force which they called "Wakan Tanka," the Great Spirit. As one of the greatest of Lakota spiritual teachers, Black Elk, expressed it, "Everywhere is the center of the world."

The Lakota have a story they call "The Seventh Direction," and it goes like this:

After Wakan Tanka arranged the other six directions — East, South, West, North, Above (the sky) and Below (the earth), one direction was still left to be placed — the Seventh Direction. Since the Seventh Direction was the most powerful, the one containing the greatest wisdom and strength, Wakan Tanka wished to place it somewhere where it could not easily be found.

So the Seventh Direction was hidden in the last place humans usually think to look — in each person's heart.

## 177. The Three "Bones" of Success

A wise man was counseling a young graduate who was preparing to start a new life. He said, "Remember there are three bones, and you will never have any trouble."

"How will three bones keep me out of trouble?" asked the student.

Explained the elder, "There is a wishbone, a jawbone, and a backbone. The wishbone keeps you going after things. The jawbone helps you find out how to go after them if you are in doubt, and the backbone keeps you at it until you get there."

## 178. How Character Is Formed

The following "inspirational" message is brought to you by humorist Ed McMahon. He claims he heard it from an Irish missionary speaking in a London church.

"Consider the walnut: If you compare a walnut with some of the beautiful and exciting things which grow on our planet, it does not seem to be a marvelous creation. It is common, rough, not particularly attractive, and certainly not valuable in any monetary sense. Besides, it is small. Its growth is limited by the hard shell which surrounds it. The shell from which it never escapes during its lifetime.

"Of course, that's the wrong way to judge a walnut. Break one open and look inside. See how the walnut has grown to fill every nook and cranny available to it? It had no say in the size or shape of that shell but, given those limitations, it achieved its full potential of growth.

"How lucky we will be if, like the walnut, we find ways to blossom and bloom in every crevice of the life that is given us."

## 179. Where Character Comes from

The following is from a commencement address given to the Citadel Military College of South Carolina in 1993 by President Ronald W. Reagan (1911-2004):

"The character that takes command in moments of crucial choices has already been determined.

"It has been determined by a thousand other choices made earlier in seemingly unimportant moments.

"It has been determined by all the little choices of years past-by, all those times when the voice of conscience was at war with the voice of temptation, whispering the lie that it really doesn't matter.

"It has been determined by all the day-to-day decisions made when life seemed easy and crises seemed far away — the decisions that, piece by piece, bit by bit, developed habits of discipline or of laziness, habits of self-sacrifice or self-indulgence, habits of duty and honor and integrity — or dishonor and shame.

"Because, when life does get tough, and the crisis is undeniably at hand — when we must, in an instant, look inward for strength of character to see us through — we will find nothing inside ourselves that we have not already put there."

# CHILDREN

## 180. A Mother Who Knew What Was Important

This is an old story but one whose moral still rings true through all the years.

It involves a beautiful woman named Cornelia (c. 150BC). She had been married to a famous Roman general who had defeated Hannibal and the Carthaginians. However, he was killed and Cornelia had to sell most of her property and valuable possessions, just to live simply.

One day she said to her two young sons, "A friend is coming to dine today and she is very rich. She will most certainly want to show us her jewels."

When the visitor arrived, her fingers sparkled with rings and her arms glistened with gold bracelets. Chains of gold hung about her neck and strands of pearls gleamed in her hair.

The two boys gazed somewhat forlornly at their mother who was wearing a simple white robe, and her hands and arms were bare.

"Would you like to see more of my treasures?" asked the woman. And a servant brought in a box filled with blood-red rubies, sapphires as blue as the sky, emeralds as green as the sea, diamonds that flashed in the sunlight.

"If only our mother could have such beautiful things!" thought the boys.

"Tell me Cornelia," the rich woman said with a pitying smile, "is it true that you no longer have any jewels? And that you had to sell them to live?"

At this Cornelia smiled and answered: "Not at all. I have jewels far more valuable than any you might purchase."

"Then let me see them," said the skeptical visitor, and Cornelia called the two boys to her side.

"These are my jewels," she said smiling. "Are they not more precious than any gems?"

Cornelia's two sons grew up to become great statesmen in Rome. It was a moment in their lives when their mother taught them a lesson they would never forget.

## 181. An Angel's Way of Keeping a Secret

A Pennsylvania folktale says that before a baby is born, it knows all the secrets of life and death; but at the moment of its birth, an angel presses his forefinger against its upper lip, sealing it, and leaving the small vertical crease (philtrum) that we all carry for the rest of our lives.

## 182. Rachel Carson on Children

Rachel Carson (1907-1964), American biologist and author, penned the following about children: "A child's world is fresh and new and beautiful, full of wonder and excitement. It is our misfortune that for most of us that clear-eyed vision, that true instinct for what is beautiful and awe-inspiring, is dimmed and even lost before we reach adulthood. If I had influence with the good fairy who is supposed to preside over the christening of all children I would ask that her gift to each child in the world be a sense of wonder so indestructible that it would last throughout life, as an unfailing antidote against the boredom and disenchantments of later years, the sterile preoccupation with things that are artificial, the alienation from the sources of our strength."

## 183. Emerson on Children

Ralph Waldo Emerson (1803-1882), American essayist, poet and philosopher, said of children, "Every book is a quotation, and every house is a quotation out of all forests and mines and stone-quarries; and every man is a quotation from all his ancestors."

## 184. Erma Bombeck on Children

Few people wrote about daily home life more lovingly and with more humor than columnist Erma Bombeck (1927-1996). Here she writes about children. "Children are like kites. You spend a lifetime trying to get them off the ground. You run with them until you're both breathless... they crash... you add a longer tail... they hit the rooftop... you pluck them out of the spout... you patch and comfort, adjust and reach. You watch them lifted by the wind and assure them that someday they'll fly. Finally, they are airborne, but they need more string and you keep letting it out, and, with each twist of the ball of twine, there is a sadness that goes with the joy because the kite becomes more distant and somehow you know that it won't be long before that beautiful creature will snap the lifeline that bound you together and soar as it was meant to soar... free and alone. Only then do you know that you did your job."

# CITIES

## 185. Lincoln's Joke about Chicago

His friends said Abraham Lincoln (1809-1865) liked to tell this story about the biggest city in Illinois.

A businessman from St. Louis died in a Chicago hotel during a trip there and soon found himself outside Heaven's Golden Gates.

St. Peter was sitting in a small office by the gates. He had a pipe in his mouth and on the table before him was a steaming whisky toddy.

"Good morning," said the man tentatively, "I would like to come in if I can."

"Good morning," said St. Peter, taking down a huge ledger from a shelf. "Would you please tell me your name and where you are from?"

"My name is Johnson," the man said, "and before my death I lived in St. Louis in the State of Missouri."

"Thank you," said St. Peter, "and where did you die?"

"I died in Chicago, in Illinois," the man answered.

"Chicago?" said St. Peter shaking his head skeptically, "There is no such place as Chicago."

"I beg your pardon, St. Peter," said the applicant, somewhat frightened, "but do you have a map of the United States here? I will show you."

St. Peter pulled off the shelf a handsome atlas of the United States and Johnson politely pointed out to him where the city of Chicago was located on the map.

"By George, you're right," admitted St. Peter, "it's there sure enough."

Signing Johnson's admittance papers, St. Peter gave him a big smile and said, "Do walk right in, sir. But I must tell you that you are the first man ever to come here from Chicago."

## 186. Love of New England

Mark Twain wrote this in his notebook in the late 1800s:

"A man down south from New England said, 'if I had heaven or home placed before me, I wouldn't know which to choose' — [he] reflected and added, 'I Would take home – I can go to heaven any time.'"

## 187. Personal Resumes

Mark Twain (Samuel Clemens)(1835-1910), talking about the residents of three well-known American cities, said, "In Boston they ask, 'How much does he know?' In New York, 'How much is he worth?' In Philadelphia, 'Who were his parents?'"

## 188. Description of Manhattan

Jacques Barzun (1907- ), French-born American historian, educator and author, described Manhattan Island in these words, "Manhattan, except for its harbor the least likely site for a modern metropolis, is an island tucked away on the map like an appendage on an anatomical chart. A hilly tract of mud, ledge, and fill, thirteen miles long and two miles wide, it is said to have been bought from the Indians for twenty-four dollars and a bottle of whiskey. Only now, after three centuries' experience, can one begin to appreciate the Indians' long view."

## 189. Eager for Money

Fletcher Knebel (1911-1993), a well-traveled American journalist, had this view of four U.S. cities, "In Dallas, they take away your money with gusto; in New Orleans with a bow; in San Francisco with a wink and a grin. In New York, you're lucky if you get a grunt."

## 190. Great American Cities

Norman Mailer (1923-2007), noted American author, wrote this about American cities, "Chicago is the great American city. New York is one of the capitals of the world, and Los Angeles is a constellation of plastic, San Francisco is a lady, Boston has become Urban Renewal, Philadelphia and Baltimore and Washington blink like dull diamonds in the smog of Eastern Megalopolis, and New Orleans is unremarkable past the French Quarter. Detroit is a one-trade town. Pittsburgh has lost its golden triangle, St. Louis has become the golden arch of the corporation, and nights in Kansas City close early. The oil depletion allowance makes Houston and Dallas naught but checkerboards for this sort of game. But Chicago is a great American city. Perhaps it is the last of the great American cities."

# CLOTHING

## 191. Clothing History

Men's shirts have the buttons on the right, but women's blouses have the buttons on the left. This is more than just a way to tell whether a shirt is for men or women. There is a historical reason for it.

During the Victorian period, buttons were quite expensive and were mostly worn by rich people. Because proper, well-to-do ladies were dressed by their servants, and most people are right-handed, their buttons were placed on the servant's right, which is the wearer's left side. However, most gentlemen dressed themselves, so their buttons were placed on the wearer's right side.

Those who could not afford servants copied the style of the wealthy, and women's buttons thereafter remained on the left.

## 192. New Clothes for Einstein

The famous scientist Albert Einstein (1879-1955) was not a man to be interested in new clothes.

For example, he absolutely forbid his faithful assistant, Helen Dukas, to throw out a very shabby raincoat he had worn for years.

"All it needs," said Einstein stubbornly, "is a trip to the dry cleaners and it will be good as new."

Next day Miss Dukas arrived at a men's clothing store in Princeton, New Jersey, where Einstein lived, and asked them to find her a new raincoat EXACTLY like Einstein's old one. And together, the store's owner and Miss Dukas removed the tags from the new coat and slipped it into a dry-cleaner's bag.

When the garment was returned to Einstein, he exclaimed, "See, I told you dry-cleaning would make this coat as good as new."

## 193. Gandhi on Fashion

More and more office workers are enjoying special days (usually Fridays) when they are allowed to doff their usual neckties and (many ladies say) their pantyhose for real working comfort on the job.

In a way, this trend is reminiscent of when the famous Indian spiritual leader Gandhi (1869-1948) visited England's King George wearing only a loincloth, shawl, and sandals.

When questioned later about the propriety of his attire, Gandhi replied, "The King was wearing enough for both of us."

The trend toward more informal clothing in the workplace seems certain to continue.

## 194. Inaugural Dress

How American presidents dress for their inaugurals and other important occasions has changed a bit over the years.

For example, at his second inaugural on March 4, 1793, George Washington (1732-1799) wore a black velvet suit trimmed with silver lace, an embroidered white satin vest, black silk stockings, diamond-studded knee and shoe buckles, and yellow kid gloves. Over his powdered hair, he wore a cocked hat, and he carried a dress sword with a jeweled hilt sheathed in a white leather scabbard. He arrived at the Philadelphia State House in a cream-colored coach with cherubs painted on the door panels and drawn by six pure-white horses.

For many years, newly-elected American Presidents wore top hats to the event. Today, American presidents are partial to dark blue business suits and a bright-colored tie.

As for transportation to the ceremony, as contrasted to Washington's coach and horses, George W. Bush (1946- ) at his second inaugural on January 20, 2005, rode in a specially-built, heavily armored Cadillac limousine equipped with all kinds of communications equipment. It even had a built-in desk in case the President wanted to work on his speech.

## 195. How Neckties Came to Be

Neckties began their history when a band of Croatian soldiers marched into France in the mid-1600s. Part of their uniforms were fancy scarves made of linen or muslin. These scarves so impressed the French that they began wearing fancy linen scarves themselves. The French called these scarves "cravats."

Meanwhile, the fashion was picked up by King Charles II (1630-1685) of England. When cravats became part of his daily wear, the rest of England followed. Over the next 100 years, the cravat evolved into the modern tie.

## 196. Who Invented the Tuxedo?

Have you ever wondered how and why the tuxedo was invented and where it got its name?

We owe it all to the Algonquin Indians and to the wolf they called "p'tuksit" (pronounced tuck-sit). It means "round-footed animal" and there's a lake in New York State that used to be called Tuk-sit — only now they call it Tuxedo Lake.

Several generations ago, a man named Pierre Lorillard (1833-1901) decided to develop a tony summer resort on the lake and he named it Tuxedo Park.

At a party hosted by the wealthy Astor family, a guest who balked at wearing the traditional tailcoat that was expected in those days cut off the tails on his coat and went that way. It started a fashion that swept the nation and came to be called a Tuxedo Jacket, later shortened to just plain Tuxedo.

So, if you don't like Tuxedos, you can blame the round-footed wolves and not the poor little penguins.

## 197. How Was Velcro Discovered?

In the beginning was the button. Then came the zipper. And then came velcro. How did it happen?

The ubiquitous "touch fastener" was invented in 1941 by a Swiss engineer named George de Mestral (1907-1990), who based his idea on his observation, after a walk in the woods, of the way burrs stuck to the fur of his hunting dogs.

# COMMITMENT

### 198. Building a Cathedral

This is a story told to a group of Andover students by the well-known minister William Sloan Coffin (1924-2006) to a group of Andover students in November of 2003. Said Coffin:

"Heinrich Heine (1797-1856), the 19th century German Jewish poet, was standing with a French friend before the great cathedral of Amiens in northern France. Said his friend, 'Heinrich, why can't people build piles like this anymore?'"

"To which Heine replied, 'Because, in those days, people had convictions. We moderns have opinions, and it takes more than an opinion to build a Gothic cathedral.'"

### 199. Total Commitment

General Dwight Eisenhower (1890-1969) was raised on a Kansas farm and he never forgot its lessons. In response to a difficult question put to him at the National Press Club, Eisenhower said it reminded him of an incident in his boyhood.

"An old farmer had a cow that we wanted to buy," Eisenhower recalled, "so we went to visit him and asked about the cow's pedigree.

"The old farmer didn't know what the word pedigree meant so we asked him about the cow's butterfat production. His answer was that he didn't have the foggiest idea.

"Finally we asked him if he knew how many pounds of milk the cow produced each year.

"The farmer shook his head and said, 'I don't know. But she's an honest cow and she'll give you all the milk she has!'"

"Well," concluded Ike, "I'm like that cow. I'll give you everything I have."

## 200. Lincoln's Commitment

Asked by a friend what it felt like to be president, Abraham Lincoln (1809-1865), replied, "It is my ambition and desire to so administer the affairs of the government while I remain President that if at the end I have lost every other friend on earth I shall at least have one friend remaining and that one shall be down inside me."

# COMMUNICATIONS

## 201. Confucius on Good Communications

The Chinese sage Confucius (551 BC-479 BC) was once asked his views on the importance of good communications in getting things done.

"What," asked his questioner, "is the first thing to be done if good work is to be accomplished?"

Confucius replied, "Getting the definitions right, using the right words."

Asked to elaborate, Confucius explained, in effect, that "when words are improperly applied, issues are misunderstood.

"When issues are misunderstood, the wrong plans are devised.

"When the wrong plans are devised, wrong commands are given.

"When wrong commands are given, the wrong work is performed.

"When the wrong work is performed, organizations fail.

"When organizations fail, the people suffer."

And so, he concluded, "the first thing is to achieve the proper naming of things."

## 202. Motivating Employees

The founder and president of Misawa Homes, Chiyoshi Misawa, **heads** a company that is the largest home builder in Japan. To combat the momentum of out-of-date assumptions and policies within the company, Mr. Misawa "dies" at least once every decade. His method is to periodically write a memo to his employees that formally announces "the death of your president."

In this manner, he forces the entire company to rethink everything. When employees resist change because they are used to the old way of doing things, Misawa says: "That was the way things were done under Mr. Misawa. He is now dead. Now, how shall we proceed?"

## 203. How the Word "Amen" Came to Be

Amen. This powerful little word is now used in more languages (perhaps over 1,000) than any other single word in human speech. Here is how the word came to be:

It is believed that in Alexandria, Egypt, around 250 B.C.E., King Ptolemy (308 BC-246 BC) wanted a translation of the Hebrew Bible. He assigned 70 or 72 scholars, chosen from the Jewish community, to work on the translation. They came across the word "Amen," first cousin of "emet" (truth). Amen meant "So be it"; or, "May this prayer come true."

There was no single Greek word expressing this thought, so they turned it into a Greek word — Amen. When the Bible was translated into Latin, "Amen" became a Latin word. And so its wide use began.

## 204. Hatred of Bad News

For years people have been trying to determine just how the expression "Don't kill the messenger who brings bad news" got started. Here are some of the leading theories.

Greeks, Persians and the Babylonian King Nebuchadnezzar (c. 605 BC-562 BC) have all been candidates but the actual first source seems elusive.

Plutarch's *Lives of the Noble Grecians and Romans* has this line: "The first messenger that gave notice of Lucullus's coming was so far from pleasing Tigranes that he had his head cut off for his pains."

There is an engraving titled *The Bearers of Evil Tidings Slain by Pharaoh* by J. J. A. Lecomte-du-Nouy which seems to have been inspired by the act of an all-powerful Egyptian Pharaoh who took the life of three messengers who brought him bad news. Some say the engraving was inspired by lines in Theophile Gautier's *Mummy*.

There is a Biblical story of King David killing the man who brought him the news of Saul's death (2 Samuel 1:1-15). However the actual reason that the messenger was killed is that he boasted of having killed Saul himself.

Sophocles (c. 496 BC-406 BC), the Greek playwright, wrote in *Antigone* (c. 442 BC), lines 276-77): "I well believe it, to unwilling ears; None love the messenger who brings bad news." The lines are spoken by a sentinel speaking to Creon.

In the standard edition of the complete psychological works of Sigmund Freud, edited by Strachey, vol. XXII, p.246, Freud writes of a "famous lament of the Spanish Moors...which tells how King Boabdil (the last Moorish king of Granada) received the news of the fall of his city..." The translated verse: "Letters had reached him telling him that Alhama [sic] was taken. He threw the letters in the fire and killed the messenger."

In a book, *Television and the Real World* by William Small (c.1970), he refers to a historical anecdote about Alexander the Great's policy to "kill the messenger" who brought bad news."

Shakespeare took a swing or two at it also. In *Antony and Cleopatra*, Cleopatra threatens a messenger with a knife and the messenger says, "It is never good to bring bad news."

Russian Czar Peter the Great (1672-1725) in 1700 ordered by strangling the death of messengers who came to St. Petersburg to announce the defeat of the Russian fleet by the Swedes at Narva.

On a much lighter note, there was a cartoon in the *New Yorker* magazine that went like this:

The king is seated on his throne after just reading a message from the battlefront. At his feet, the cowering messenger is held by two of the king's guards.

Whereupon the king says to the guards: "Don't kill him. This news is neither good nor bad. Just take him outside and rough him up a little."

## 205. Why Lincoln Used Stories to Communicate

Abraham Lincoln (1809-1865) became famous for his ability to use a humorous story or anecdote to make a point. To explain why he used stories so frequently, Lincoln said:

"I believe I have the popular reputation of being a story-teller, but I do not deserve the name in its general sense, for it is not the story itself, but its purpose, or effect, that interests me.

"I often avoid a long and useless discussion by others or a laborious explanation on my own part by a short story that illustrates my point of view. So, too, the sharpness of a refusal or the edge of a rebuke may be blunted by an appropriate story, so as to save wounded feelings and yet serve the purpose. No, I am not simply a story-teller, but story-telling as an emollient saves me much friction and distress."

## 206. The Power of Communications

When Johnny Carson (1925-2005) was host of the NBC *Tonight Show*, he made a joke during the program to the effect that there was a toilet paper shortage in the United States.

Carson then went on to describe what some of the consequences of this shortage could be. The implication was that viewers should stock up on toilet paper right away if they did not want to put up with such consequences.

The subject made for a good laugh as there was, in fact, no toilet paper shortage. However, in a few days a real shortage did develop.

Viewers all over the nation concluded there was a real toilet paper shortage and they rushed out to buy up all the stocks they could find. As a result, they disrupted the normal flow of toilet paper distribution and a shortage was born.

Never underestimate the power of a television show — or for that matter a good joke!

## 207. Semantics

The same word may have quite different meanings to different hearers. This is not surprising when you realize that the 500 most commonly used words in English have 14,070 dictionary meanings.

In the Second World War, Winston Churchill (1874-1965) tells of a long argument in a meeting of the British and American Chiefs of Staff Committee. The British brought in a memo on an important point and proposed to "table" it - which to them meant to discuss it right away. The Americans protested the matter must not be tabled, and the debate grew quite hot before the participants realized they all wanted the same thing.

## 208. A Tragic Result of Poor Communications

A Japanese word, "mokusatsu," may have changed all our lives. It has two meanings: (1) to ignore, and (2) to refrain from comment. Historians says the release of a press statement using the second meaning, in July 1945, might have ended the war then.

The Japanese Emperor was ready to end it, and had the power to do so. The cabinet was ready to accede to the Potsdam ultimatum of the Allies – unconditional surrender — but they wanted a little more time to discuss the terms.

A press release was prepared announcing the policy of "mokusatsu", with the "no comment" interpretation. But it got on the foreign wires with the "ignores" interpretation through a mixup in translation: "The cabinet ignores the demand to surrender."

To recall the release would have entailed an unthinkable loss of face. Had the intended meaning been publicized, the cabinet might have backed up the Emperor's decision to surrender. In which event, there might have been no atomic bombs over Hiroshima and Nagasaki.

Tens of thousands of Japanese might have been saved. One word, misinterpreted made all the difference.

## 209. History of the U.S. Mail Service

(Part of Daniel Webster's (1782-1852) speech in the U.S. Congress in 1844 against an appropriation of $50,000 to establish mail communications with the Pacific Coast.)

"What do we want of the vast worthless area, this region of savages and wild beasts, of deserts of shifting sands and whirlwinds of dust, cactus and prairie dogs? To what use could we ever hope to put these deserts, or these endless mountain ranges, impenetrable and covered to their bases with eternal snow? What can we ever hope to do with the western coast of three thousand miles, rockbound, cheerless and uninviting, with not a harbor in it? What use have we for such a country? Mr. President, I will never vote one cent from the public treasury to place the Pacific Coast one inch nearer Boston than it is today."

## 210. The New Order

On his first day as President of Yale University, in 1978, the late Bartlett Giamatti (1938-1989) issued a memo to everyone in the university, saying:

"I wish to announce that henceforth, as a matter of university policy, evil is abolished and paradise is restored. I trust all of us to do whatever possible to achieve this policy."

## 211. Some Words about Communication

- The Lord's Prayer has 56 words.

- The Ten Commandments have 297 words.

- The American Declaration of Independence has 300 words.

- The directive of the European Economic Community (EEC) on the import of caramel and caramel products has 26,911 words.

## 212. Beautiful Words

What are the most beautiful words in the English language?

Wilfred J. Funk (1883-1965), lexicographer and poet, has said that the ten most beautiful words, in meaning and in the musical arrangement of their letters, are: dawn, hush, lullaby, murmuring, tranquil, mist, luminous, chimes, golden, and melody.

Here are a few more for the list: soothe, purr, mother, dreaming, marmalade, memories, home, meadow, heaven, miracle, comfort, giving, pray, others, and divine.

What are some of the most beautiful statements in the English language — those we most enjoy hearing? Here are some nominees:

- I love you.

- You are wonderful.

- It's benign — not malignant.

- The war is over.

- It's a boy! It's a girl!

- No cavities.

- Thank you.

- All is forgiven.

- God bless you.

- Welcome home.
- Good morning!
- Merry Christmas!
- Your car is ready.
- You passed the examination.
- Your child is beautiful.
- You were right.
- I'm ready to sign.

## 213. Speed of Gossip

Someone has calculated that, if a rumor was started at midday in the office, and was repeated within two seconds by everyone who heard it to two other people, who repeated it — and so on, by about six-thirty the same day, everyone on earth would have heard it.

# COMMUNITY SERVICE

## 214. Mental Health

Dr. Karl Menninger (1893-1990), the famous psychiatrist, was once asked what action he would recommend if a person were to feel a nervous breakdown coming on.

"Lock up your house," he said, "go across the railroad tracks, and find someone in need and do something for him."

## 215. The Visiting Philanthropist

In the early 1920s, the pioneer auto pioneer Henry Ford (1863-1947) paid a visit to the city of Cork in Ireland. His father, William, had emigrated from a nearby village 70 years earlier. Another reason for the trip was that the Ford Motor Company was opening there for its first time outside the United States.

Ford had no sooner arrived than he was called upon by a delegation from the local Hospital Building Fund, and he pledged 5,000 Irish pounds. The local paper headlined the pledge the next day as "Henry Ford Gives 10,000 Pounds to Hospital."

The delegation returned the next day with deep apologies for the "error" and offered to arrange with the paper for another headline, "Henry Ford Did Not Give 10,000 Pounds to Hospital."

Ford smiled knowingly and said he would make it 10,000 if he could specify a Biblical quotation to be inscribed on a plaque at the hospital.

The Irish delegation quickly agreed and asked Ford what would it be. Ford replied, "I came among mine own and they took me in."

## 216. The Secret of Happiness

There is a fable about a little orphan who was feeling particularly lonely and blue when she happened across a gorgeous butterfly trapped in the thorns of a blackberry bush.

Taking great care not to tear its fragile wings, the girl's nimble fingers finally worked the insect free, whereupon, instead of fluttering away, it turned into a golden fairy who offered to grant her any wish.

"I want to be happy!" the orphan cried.

The fairy smiled, leaned forward, whispered something in her ear, and vanished. And from that day forward there was no more happy spirit in the land than that child, who grew into a merry woman and a contented old lady. On her deathbed, her neighbors crowded around, desperate that the secret of happiness not die with her.

"Tell us, please tell us, what the fairy said to you," they pleaded.

The old woman smiled benevolently, and whispered, "She told me that everyone, no matter how rich or secure or self-contained or successful they might appear, had need of me."

## 217. For the Next Generation

Leo Tolstoy (1828-1910), the Russian writer, reportedly liked to tell this story.

A very old farmer was planting apple trees. Watching him, a young man asked, "Why are you planting apple trees? It will be a long time before they bear fruit, and you may not live to eat a single apple."

The old man replied, "It's true, I may never live to eat the apples, but others will, and they will thank me."

## 218. A Call to Service

During World War II, a much-prized statue of Christ was shattered by German artillery when they departed from a little town located in Southern Italy.

Afterward, the local priest called the men in the town together and asked them to search for the arms, legs, head and other parts of the statue so that they might be reassembled. At the same time, he asked the town's women to prepare a celebration feast in anticipation of the statue's rejuvenation.

But at nightfall the townsmen came to the priest in despair. "Father," they said, "we have tried to put it back together, but we have been unable to find hands for Jesus. They are totally missing."

"Children," said the priest, "Don't you realize, you are His hands."

## 219. The City of God

Socrates (473 BC-399 BC) had been going on for a while about how humans ought to order their lives and about how they ought to behave toward each other, and he called his description "the city of God." At this point, his down-to-earth friend, Glaucon, had had enough. This whole discussion to him was so up in the clouds, so idealistic as to be useless.

"Socrates," he said, "I do not believe that there is such a city anywhere on this earth," implying "forget it."

To this Socrates had an answer. "Whether such a city exists in heaven or ever will exist on earth, the wise man will live after the manner of that city, having nothing to do with any other, and in so doing he will set his own house in order."

# COMPROMISE

## 220. Marital Disagreement

Abraham Lincoln was a man who believed in compromise.

When he was practicing law in Illinois, a farmer asked Lincoln's help in getting a divorce from his wife.

"Just what has been the trouble?" asked Lincoln.

"It is our house," said the farmer angrily, "I want to paint it brown and she wants to paint it white. We got into a big argument about it. She threw pots and pans at me, used abusive language, and even poured scalding tea down my back. I want you to get me a divorce!"

After calming the man down, Lincoln suggested that he go back to his wife and try to work out a compromise.

"After all," said Lincoln, "you have lived together a long time and you should try to work things out if only for the children's sake."

The farmer was very doubtful that any such solution was possible but he agreed to try. Lincoln told him to come back in four weeks.

After the four weeks had passed, the farmer returned to Lincoln's office saying, "There's no need to start proceedings against my wife. We've made up — compromise is how we did it."

"How did you manage it?" said the pleased Lincoln.

"Well," said the farmer, "we decided to paint the house white."

# 221. Ben Franklin's View of the Constitution

Benjamin Franklin (1706-1790), statesman, diplomat, scientist, publisher and philosopher, played a key role in the drafting of the U.S. Constitution. He wrote the following about it on September 17, 1787:

"I confess that there are several parts of this Constitution which I do not at present approve, but I am not sure I shall never approve them. For, having lived long, I have experienced many instances of being obliged, by better information or fuller consideration, to change opinions, even on important subjects, which I once thought right, to be found otherwise.

"It is therefore that, the older I grow, the more apt I am to doubt my own judgment, and to pay more respect to the judgment of others. Most men, indeed, as well as most sects in religion, think themselves in possession of all truth, and that whenever others differ from them it is so far error. Steele, a Protestant, in a dedication, tells the Pope, that the only difference between our churches, in their opinions of the certainty of their doctrines, is 'the Church of Rome is infallible, and the Church of England is never in the wrong.'

"But though many private persons think almost as highly of their own infallibility as of that of their sect, few express it so naturally as a certain French lady, who, in a dispute with her sister, said, 'I don't know how it happens, sister, but I meet with nobody but myself that is always in the right.'

"In these sentiments, Sir, I agree to this Constitution, with all its faults, if they are such...I doubt, too, whether any other Convention we can obtain may be able to make a better Constitution. For, when you assemble a number of men to have the advantage of their joint wisdom, you inevitable assemble with those men all their prejudices, their passions, their errors of opinion, their local interests, and their selfish views. From such an assembly can a perfect production ever be expected?

"It therefore astonishes me, Sir, to find this system approaching so near to perfection as it does...Thus I consent, Sir, to this Constitution because I expect no better, and because I am not sure that it is not the best. The opinions I have had of its errors I sacrifice to the public good. I have never whispered a syllable of them abroad. Within these walls they were born, and here they shall die."

# CONFORMITY

## 222. Trying to Please Everybody

A man in ancient times had a disobedient son. Whenever the son was asked by his father to do something he always refused, saying, "what would people say?"

Deciding to teach his son a lesson, the man climbed on the back of his donkey and asked his son to follow him. No sooner had they gone a few paces when they passed by a woman who exclaimed, "Isn't there any mercy in your heart? You ride and let that poor little boy walk behind?"

The father then dismounted and told his son to ride. They went a little further and were passing some elderly people. One of them nudged the other and said, "Look at that fool! See how children are being brought up these days." They said to the father, "You, an old man, are walking while letting your son ride, yet you hope to educate him in the ways of life?"

"Did you hear that?" said the man to his son. "Let us now both ride for a change." In no time they came upon a group of people who shouted at them, "Don't you even fear God? You two ride this poor creature with all your fleshy bulk that weighs more than the beast does."

Then the man told his son, "Let us both walk and lead the beast behind us." They soon passed some people who mocked them saying, "Why don't you carry the donkey and relieve it from the burden of the road!"

So the frustrated father stopped at a tree, cut off a thick branch, tied the donkey to its middle and set off with his son, both of them raising the stick to their shoulders and carrying the poor animal.

Walking together in this manner they soon attracted a crowd. Then along came the sultan's guards, who dispersed the crowd and led the two men to the madhouse. On their way there, the father turned to his son and said,

"Such, my son, is the end of one who does a deed in the hope of winning the approval of others."

Moral: Trying to please everybody never works.

## 223. Where Conformity Can Lead You

There is a strange insect called the Processionary Caterpillar. This insect bears this unusual name because of its unusual method of navigation.

A number of Processionary Caterpillars will attach themselves front to back in a single line. The leader seeks the mulberry leaf, the main food of this caterpillar. Wherever the leader goes, the other Processionary Caterpillars are sure to follow. Off they go in one continuous line of five or more caterpillars looking for mulberry leaves.

Several years ago John Henry Fabre (1823-1915), the noted French naturalist, conducted an experiment by taking a line of Processionary Caterpillars and arranging them in a circle around the rim of a flowerpot. What had been the leader caterpillar was attached to what had been the last caterpillar in the line. Now there was no "leader" and no "follower" caterpillars.

In the center of the circle of caterpillars he placed a bowl of mulberry leaves. Fabre wanted to know how long they would maintain the circle with no leader and no objective. He knew that eventually they must break the circle to eat the mulberry leaves or they would starve.

The result of this experiment surprised him. The caterpillars continued in a circle until they were so weak that they couldn't reach the mulberry leaves. Though food was only inches away, they continued to follow the caterpillar in front. They continued to go forward with no objective at all.

## 224. Danger of Conformity

Thomas J. Watson, Jr. (1914-1993) took over from his father the leadership of IBM while he was still a young man and he built it into a giant corporation that girdled the globe. Here are his thoughts on conformity.

"If you stand up and be counted, from time to time you may get yourself knocked down. But remember this: A man flattened by an opponent can get up again. A man flattened by conformity stays down for good."

# COURAGE

## 225. Two Men of Courage

Sir Winston Churchill (1874-1965) lay dying in London's King Edward VII Hospital in August of 1964. Churchill, the fearless leader of Britain during World War II, was in his ninetieth year.

General Dwight Eisenhower (1890-1969) (by now a former President of the United States) had just attended the 20th anniversary of the D-Day invasion of Normandy in France, and he had come to visit Churchill at his bedside.

The failing Churchill did not speak when Eisenhower entered his suite but instead reached out a frail pink hand to clasp Eisenhower's. The two hands joined on the bedside table.

No words were spoken, just two old warriors sharing silently the memories of their struggles in war and peace for the principles they both cherished. Ten minutes passed in silence. Then Churchill unclasped his right hand and slowly raised it upward in his famous "V for Victory" sign.

Eisenhower, his eyes moist, left the room and said to an aide.

"I just said goodbye to Winston, but you never say farewell to courage."

## 226. The Courage to Keep Fighting

James J. Corbett (1866-1933) was one of America's great prize fighters. Known as "Gentleman Jim," he defeated John L. Sullivan (1858-1918) for the heavyweight crown in 1892. Here is what he had to say about what it takes to be a champion:

"Fight one more round. When your feet are so tired that you have to shuffle back to the center of the ring, fight one more round. When your arms are so tired that you can hardly lift your hands to come on guard, fight one more round. When your nose is bleeding and your eyes are black and you are so tired that you wish your opponent would crack you one on the jaw and put you to sleep, fight one more round — remembering that the man who always fights one more round is never whipped."

## 227. Robert Kennedy on Courage

The following words by Robert Francis Kennedy (1925-1968) are inscribed at his grave at Arlington National Cemetery in Washington, D.C. They are from an address he made at the University of Cape Town, South Africa, on June 6, in 1966:

"It is from numberless diverse acts of courage and belief that human history is shaped. Each time a man stands up for an ideal, or acts to improve the lot of others, or strikes out against injustice, he sends forth a tiny ripple of hope, and crossing each other from a million different centers of energy and daring those ripples build a current which can sweep down the mightiest walls of oppression and resistance."

## 228. The Cowardly Lion Speaks

One of the most lovable characters in the movie, *The Wizard of Oz*, is the Cowardly Lion. With Dorothy, he travels to see the Wizard in the hope that the all-powerful Wizard will give him something he badly lacks, Courage. Here are the Cowardly Lion's words on the importance of courage:

"Courage. What makes a King out of a slave? Courage.

"What makes the flag on the mast wave? Courage.

"What makes the elephant charge his tusk in the misty mist or the dusky dusk? Courage.

"What makes the muskrat guard his musk? Courage.

"What makes the Sphinx the 7th Wonder? Courage.

"What makes the dawn come up like THUNDER? Courage.

"What makes the Hottentot so hot?

"What puts the "ape" in ape-ricot?

"Whatta they got that I ain't got? Courage."

## 229. Churchill's Advice to Schoolboys

On October 29, 1941, with Britain facing an almost certain defeat by expected German invaders, Winston Churchill (1874-1963) said the following words to students at Britain's Harrow School:

"Never give in, never give in, never, never, never, never – in nothing, great or small, large or petty – never give in except to convictions of honor and good sense."

## 230. A Formula for Courage

Judy Garland (1922-1969) was a movie star when she was a very young girl and she grew up to be a world-famous popular singer. She had a troubled life, had bouts with drugs and failure, but through it all, she remained a star whose memory still lives on. Here is how she described dealing with depression:

"What do I do when I'm down? I put on my lipstick, see my stockings are straight, and go out there and sing 'Over the Rainbow.'"

## 231. Courage of Life

In his book, *Profiles of Courage*, published in 1956 and which was awarded a Pulitzer Prize, John F. Kennedy (1917-1963), who later became the 35th President of the United States, wrote eloquently about courage. The following is an excerpt:

"Courage, the universal virtue, is comprehended by us all. For without belittling the courage with which men have died, we should not forget those acts of courage with which men have lived.

"The courage of life is often a less dramatic spectacle than the courage of a final moment; but it is no less a magnificent mixture of triumph and tragedy."

## 232. Final Sacrifice

The following words are inscribed on a tablet at the Arlington National Cemetery in Washington, D.C.:

"Not for fame or reward, not for place or for rank, not lured by ambition or goaded by necessity, but in simple obedience to duty as they understood it, these men suffered all, sacrificed all, dared all, and died.

# CREATIVITY

## 233. Ingredients

There are only three pure colors — red, yellow, and blue — but look at what Michelangelo (1475-1564) did with those three colors.

There are only seven musical notes, but look what Chopin (1810-1849), Beethoven (1770-1827), and Vivaldi (1678-1741) did with those seven notes.

Lincoln's Gettysburg Address contained only 262 words, and 202 of them had one syllable. Think of the impact those simple, direct words have had on our society.

## 234. How to Tell Real Art

A friend of the famous artist Marc Chagall (1887-1985) once asked him how he knew a painting of his represented true art.

Chagall replied, "When I judge art, I take my painting and put it next to a God-made object like a tree or flower. If it clashes, it is not art."

## 235. Michelangelo's Masterpiece

Agostino d'Antonio, one of the best sculptors of his day, worked diligently on a large piece of marble. Unable to produce his desired masterpiece, he declared, "I can do nothing with it."

Other sculptors — masters of the craft — also tried to work this difficult piece of marble, but to no avail. Then Michelangelo (1475-1564) visualized the possibilities in the stone. The result? One of the world's masterpieces — the statue of *David*, on display in Florence, Italy.

Visualization drives reality. Victory is all about people's belief in a higher vision fueling the courage and commitment to carry it through.

## 236. Trust Yourself

During the filming of his movie *Blazing Saddles*, Mel Brooks (1926- ) became worried that a scene he was working on might be in bad taste and not appreciated by movie audiences.

Assisting Brooks was a senior production executive who said to him, "Mel, if you're going to step up to the bell, RING IT."

The scene was shot and people thought it was one of the movie's funniest moments.

Brooks, whose movie and Broadway productions of *The Producers* are considered by critics to be among the great comedy classics, was so impressed with the advice he had been given that he had it framed and hung on his office wall. It reads:

"If you are going to step up to the bell, RING IT."

# CRITICISM

### 237. Critics

Brendan Behan (1923-1964), the famous Irish playwright, was once asked what he thought of drama critics.

"Critics," he said, "are like eunuchs in a harem. They're there every night, they see it done every night, they see how it should be done every night, but they can't do it themselves."

### 238. Controlling One's Temper

One day in Britain's House of Commons, a Socialist poured out abusive words against Prime Minister Churchill.

Churchill's face remained passive — almost bored.

When the critic's harangue was over, Churchill rose and said, "If I valued the opinion of the honorable gentleman, I might get angry."

### 239. Defending an Associate

Lincoln received many complaints about the arbitrary actions of his Secretary of War Stanton. In reply to the critics, Lincoln reportedly said:

"We may have to treat Stanton as they are sometimes obliged to treat a Methodist minister I know out West. He gets wrought up to so high a pitch of excitement in his prayers and exhortations that they put bricks in his pockets to keep him down. But I guess we'll let our man jump awhile first."

### 240. Leaving a Bad Performance

In Budapest, they tell this story about Ferenc Molnar (1848-1907), the great Hungarian playwright.

Molnar and his lady friend had been given two free tickets to a play, but early in the first act Molnar suddenly got up to leave.

"But you can't just walk out," his lady friend objected. "We are guests of the management. You will offend everybody."

The playwright sat down but after hearing a few more lines of poorly-written dialogue, he jumped to his feet again.

"Where are you going now?" asked his female companion.

Replied Molnar, "I'm going to the box office to buy some tickets so we can leave."

Moral: sometimes one has to go to some expense to get out of an intolerable situation.

## 241. Staving off Criticism

A delegation of politicians were badgering President Abraham Lincoln about his handling of various issues. When they started criticizing the direction of his administration, Lincoln cut them off by telling them this story.

"Gentlemen, suppose all the property you were worth was in gold, and you had placed it in the hands of a man to carry across the Niagara River on a rope.

"Would you shake the cable and keep shouting at him; 'Stand up a little straighter, stoop a little more, go a little faster, go a little slower, lean a little more to the south?'

"No, you would hold your breath as well as your tongue and keep your hands off until he got safely across."

Then Lincoln added, "The Government is carrying an enormous weight. Untold treasure is in our hands. Don't badger us. Keep silent and we will get you safely across."

## 242. A Churchill Rejoinder

Nancy Astor (1879-1964), an American-born British Conservative politician, once said to Winston Churchill, "If you were my husband, I would put poison in your coffee."

Without hesitation, Churchill responded, "And if I were your husband, I would drink it."

## 243. Reply to a Snob

A snobbish Bostonian approached the famous painter James Whistler (1834-1903) at a party one evening.

"And where were you born, Mr. Whistler?" she asked.

"Lowell, Massachusetts," replied the painter.

"Whatever possessed you to be born in a place like that?" exclaimed the lady.

"The explanation is quite simple," said Whistler. "I wished to be near my mother."

## 244. A Chinese Editor Rejects a Manuscript

"Illustrious brother of the sun and moon — Behold thy servant prostrate before thy feet. I kow-tow to thee and beg of thy graciousness thou mayest grant that I may speak and live.

"Thy honored manuscript has deigned to cast the light of its august countenance upon me. With raptures I have pursued it. By the bones of my ancestors, never have I encountered such wit, such pathos, such lofty thoughts.

"With fear and trembling I return the writing. Were I to publish the treasure you sent me, the Emperor would order that it should be made the standard, and that none be published except such as equaled it. Knowing literature as I do, and that it would be impossible in ten thousand years to equal what you have done, I send your writing back. Ten thousand times I crave your pardon. Behold my head is at your feet. Do what you will."

Your servant's servant,

The Editor

### 245. Lincoln Wasn't Handsome

At a meeting of newspaper editors, Abraham Lincoln for some reason felt uncomfortable.

Said Lincoln, "I feel like I did once when I met a woman riding horseback in the woods. As I stopped to let her pass, she also stopped and looking at me intently, said, 'I do believe you are the ugliest man I ever saw.'"

Replied Lincoln, "You are probably right, Madam, but I can't help it."

"No," she answered, "you can't help it, but you might stay at home."

### 246. Accused of Lying

Winston Churchill once squashed a critic in the House of Commons by replying thus to one of his questions:

"I should think it hardly possible to state the opposite of the truth with more precision."

# CULTURAL DECLINE

### 247. Why Rome Fell

In 1788 Edward Gibbon (1737-1794) set forth in his famous book *Decline and Fall of the Roman Empire* five basic reasons why that great civilization withered and died. They were:

1.  The undermining of the dignity and sanctity of the home, which is the basis for human society.

2.  Higher and higher taxes: the spending of public money for free bread and circuses for the populace.

3.  The mad craze for pleasure, with sports and plays becoming more exciting, more brutal and more immoral.

4.  The building of great armaments when the real enemy was within - decay of individual responsibility.

5.  The decay of religion, whose leaders lost touch with life and their power to guide.

# CURIOSITY

## 248. Everything Interested Him

Luther Burbank (1849-1926), the famed horticulturist, invited every guest who visited his home to sign the guest book. Each line in the book had a space for the guest's name, address, and special interests.

When inventor Thomas Edison (1847-1931) visited Burbank, he signed the book and in the space marked "Interested in," Edison wrote in the word, "Everything," followed by a large exclamation point.

That was almost an understatement. In his lifetime, Edison invented the incandescent light, the phonograph, the wax recording and the hideaway bed.

He also invented wax paper, a variety of Portland cement, underground electrical wires, an electric railway car, an electric railroad signal, the light socket and light switch, a method for making synthetic rubber from goldenrod plants, the chemical phenol, and the motion picture camera.

He also found time to start the first electric company and gave us the quadruplex telegraph.

If there is a moral here, it is that curiosity about the world around us can open up opportunities for us that would be undreamed of otherwise.

## 249. Secret of Youth

When the poet Henry Wadsworth Longfellow (1807-1882) was well along in years his hair was white as snow, but his cheeks were as red as a rose. An admirer asked him how he was able to keep so vigorous and yet have time to write so beautifully.

Pointing to a blossoming apple tree, the poet said, "That tree is very old, but I never saw prettier blossoms on it than those which it now bears. That tree grows new wood each year. Like that apple tree, I try to grow a little new wood each year."

Longfellow knew the secret of remaining young was developing new interests.

## 250. Serving Men

Rudyard Kipling (1865-1936), one of Britain's most beloved authors and poets, wrote this wonderful poem about the curious nature of man.

I keep six honest serving men
(They taught me all I knew);
Their names are What and Why and When
and How and Where and Who.

I send them over land and sea,
I send them east and west;
But after they have worked for me,
I give them all a rest.

I let them rest from nine till five,
For I am busy then,
As well as breakfast, lunch, and tea,
For they are hungry men.
But different folk have different views,
I know a person small —
She keeps ten million serving-men,
Who get no rest at all!
She sends 'em abroad on her own affairs,
From the second she opens her eyes —
One million Hows, two million Wheres,
And seven million Whys!

## 251. Einstein on Curiosity

One of the world's greatest scientists, Albert Einstein (1879-1955) described the value of curiosity this way: "The important thing is not to stop questioning. Curiosity has its own reason for existing. One cannot help but be in awe when he contemplates the mysteries of eternity, of life, of the marvelous structure of reality. It is enough if one tries merely to comprehend a little of this mystery every day. Never lose a holy curiosity."

## 252. A Mother's Wish

Eleanor Roosevelt (1884-1982), author, diplomat, humanitarian, and wife of President Franklin D. Roosevelt. said of curiosity, "I think, at a child's birth, if a mother could ask a fairy godmother to endow it with the most useful gift, that gift would be curiosity."

# DEATH

## 253. The End of Innocence

When President John Kennedy was killed, the *Washington Post* editor Mary McGrory (1918-2004) said to her friend, Patrick Moynihan (1927-2003), a member of the Kennedy administration, "We'll never laugh again."

And Moynihan, who later became U.S. Senator from New York, replied, "Mary, we'll laugh again, but we'll never be young again."

## 254. Last Words

When President Franklin Roosevelt died in Warm Springs, Georgia, in April of 1945, he was posing for a portrait and was also working on a speech for the upcoming Jefferson/Jackson Day dinner.

The President suddenly slumped over and died, the victim of a cerebral hemorrhage at the age of 63. The last words he had written were, "The only limit to our realization of tomorrow is our doubts of today."

### 255. Life and Nature

Henry David Thoreau (1817-1862), American naturalist and philosopher, said of life and death, "Every part of nature teaches that the passing away of one life is the making room for another. The oak dies down to the ground, leaving within its rind a rich virgin mold, which will impart a vigorous life to an infant forest."

### 256. Meaning of Life

Charles A. Beard (1874-1948), one of America's most respected historians, wrote about life in these words, "I am convinced that the world is not a mere bog in which men and women trample themselves in the mire and die. Something magnificent is taking place here amid the cruelties and tragedies, and the supreme change to intelligence is that of making the noblest and best in our curious heritage prevail."

### 257. A Meaningful Life

While hoeing his garden, St. Francis of Assisi (1182-1226), Italian friar and founder of the Franciscan Order, was asked what he would do if he were suddenly informed that he would die at sunset. His reply was. "I should finish hoeing my garden."

# DECISION MAKING

### 258. One Is a Majority

The trouble presidents encounter in consensus-building is reminiscent of the dilemma Abraham Lincoln faced when he presided over a nation that was split down the middle on the issue of slavery.

In 1863 Lincoln, perplexed and worried about the future of a nation breaking apart at the seams, made a bold decision to take charge, take risks, and move ahead. He wrote one of the most profound statements about human rights of all time, the Emancipation Proclamation.

He took these ideas to his cabinet, which then numbered only six. After reading the Proclamation to them, he asked for their consensus and support. The vote was two "ayes," and five "nays."

Lincoln announced the vote as recorded, two "ayes," five "nays."

And he said, 'the' ayes" have it."

## 259. Making Decisions on Your Own

Abraham Lincoln liked to tell this story designed to encourage people to take action on their own initiative without waiting for orders.

Lincoln said there was a Colonel, who while organizing his regiment in Missouri, told his men that he would do all the swearing for the regiment. The men promised to obey, and for months there was no violation of the Colonel's order concerning profanity.

The regiment had a mule driver named John Todd, who, as roads were not always the best, had some difficulty in controlling his temper. One day, John was driving a mule team through a series of mud holes that were worse than usual when he suddenly filled the air with a volley of all-out profanity.

The Colonel heard about the transgression and he brought John to account for his violation of the profanity order.

"John," said the Colonel, "didn't you promise to let me do all the swearing for this regiment?"

"Yes, I did, sir," said the mule driver, "but the fact was that the swearing had to be done then or not at all, and you weren't there to do it."

# DENIAL

### 260. The Fox and the Grapes

There is an old Aesop fable about pretending that you didn't want something desperately in the first place, but only after it was denied you.

One summer's day a fox was passing through a vineyard. He was thirsty and hungry when suddenly his eye fell upon a delicious bunch of grapes hanging above a wall.

"Ha!" he said to himself. "Just the thing! Who could resist it!" He eyed the plump purple cluster for a moment and jumped to reach it. But he failed.

Shaking his head and his mouth watering, he said to himself again, "This time I'll take more careful aim."

He lunged upward again, putting all his strength into the jump. But the result was just the same. The grapes still hung there temptingly just out of his reach.

He jumped again and again, each time with more desperation, but each time he failed as before.

Finally, in total frustration, he said to himself wistfully, "I'll bet those grapes are sour anyway" and he went on his way, leaving them behind.

### 261. Repetitive Error

Nomi Whalen (1932- ), Canadian family therapist and political advisor, says "The definition of insanity is doing the same thing over and over, and expecting a different result."

### 262. Self-Delusion

John W. Gardner (1912-2002), American educator and public official, said of denial, "Self-knowledge, the beginning of wisdom, is ruled out for many people by the increasingly effective self-deception they practice as they grow older. By middle age many of us are accomplished fugitives from ourselves."

# DIPLOMACY

## 263. A Diplomatic Fib

While serving in London as Pennsylvania's lobbyist to the British Parliament, Benjamin Franklin (1706-1790) was frequently both amused and exasperated at the bizarre impressions Londoners had of colonial America.

To the average Englishman, the colonies were one vast unsettled continent occupied only by exiled convicts and dangerous Indians. Once at dinner, Franklin's English host asked him if he had ever seen the Niagara Falls and inquired as to what were they like.

"Of course, I have seen them," replied Franklin with a mischievous smile, and added, "it's quite a sight to see the killer whales shooting up the falls."

## 264. Disagreement

People rarely want to take any responsibility for their part in a dispute.

Adlai Stevenson (1900-1965), the one-time Democratic Presidential candidate and United Nations diplomat, explained it this way:

"This confusion over who is doing what to whom makes me think of the schoolboy who came home with his face damaged and his clothes torn. When his mother asked him how the fight had started, he said, 'It started when the other guy hit me back.'"

## 265. A Diplomatic Toast

At one diplomatic affair in Versailles soon after the formation of the United States, a group of dignitaries were offering toasts to their respective sovereigns.

The British ambassador toasted King George III (1738-1820) and likened him to the sun.

The French foreign minister then proposed a toast to King Louis XVI (1754-1793) and compared him to the moon.

One-upping them, Benjamin Franklin raised his glass and proposed a toast to: "George Washington, commander of the American armies, who, like Joshua of old, commanded the sun and the moon to stand still, and they obeyed him."

Note: many authorities believe this story to be apocryphal.

## 266. French Aid to the American Revolution

We had to get France to support us in the American Revolution. Even back then the French were a little bit of a handful. So they sent old Benjamin Franklin, now in his 70s, over to France with instructions to woo them.

He built a printing press at his house near Paris, and printed the Declaration of Independence so that all the people in France could see what we were fighting for; the idea of liberty, and an aversion to tyranny and inequality.

Franklin did a lot to get France caught up in the appeal of America's value and they joined our cause. Without them, we would not have won the Revolution. They supplied 90 percent of the gunpowder. The Marquis de Lafayette (1757-1834) had as many troops at Yorktown as General Washington did.

It was the appeal of America's values and the vision of statesmen like Thomas Jefferson (1743-1826) and Franklin who were willing to engage in a war of ideas that won our freedom. They realized that ideas have power, and that the power of America's ideals and values would prove stronger even than our weapons.

## 267. Air Can Be Valuable

"Diplomacy is nothing but a lot of hot air," said an aide to Georges Clemenceau (1841-1929), the famous French statesman, as they rode together to an international meeting.

"Perhaps," said Clemenceau, but air is what is in our automobile tires and notice how it eases the bumps."

## 268. Divine Assistance

"Mr. Prime Minister, I don't resent your having a card up your sleeve, but I do resent your thinking that God put it there."

Ascribed to a French diplomat in conversation with the British Prime Minister William Gladstone (1809-1898), c. 1885

## 269. The English Empire

Abraham Lincoln had a story about the English that went like this.

"John Bull," said Lincoln, "met with a North American Indian and was anxious to impress him with the greatness of the British Empire."

"The sun," said Mr. Bull, "never sets on English dominion. Do you understand how that is?"

"Oh, yes," replied the Indian, "that is because God is afraid to trust them in the dark."

## 270. Language of Flirtation

Prince von Bismarck (1815-1898) was a famous German statesman and the first chancellor of the German Empire (1871-1890).

At a ball in St. Petersburg, Russia, Bismarck entertained his attractive young dance partner with the usual pleasant flatteries. But she would have none of it, exclaiming, "One can't believe a word you diplomats say."

"What do you mean?" asked Bismarck.

"Well," she said, "when a diplomat says, 'Yes,' he means 'perhaps.' When he says 'perhaps,' he means 'no.' And if he should say 'no' — well, he's no diplomat."

To which Bismarck replied, "Madam, you are quite right, it's part of our profession, I fear. But with you ladies the exact opposite is the case."

"How so," said the young lady.

With a twinkle in his eye, Bismarck replied, "When she says 'no,' she means 'perhaps.' When she says 'perhaps,' she means 'yes.' And if she says 'yes' — well, she's no lady."

## 271. The Indispensable Man

In 1777, our Minister to France, Benjamin Franklin, had resigned to return to his home in Philadelphia. His successor at the court of Versailles was Thomas Jefferson.

In greeting the new American minister, the French prime minister, Count Vergennes, said, "Mr. Jefferson, have you come to replace Dr. Franklin?"

Jefferson replied, "No one can ever replace Benjamin Franklin. I am only succeeding him."

## 272. Consummate Diplomat

When Adlai Stevenson was U.S. Ambassador to the United Nations he was a constant target for autograph seekers. Once he was surrounded by a group of young people clamoring for his signature when he noticed a small, elderly woman on the edge of the crowd.

He made his way through the group and the woman held out a piece of paper.

"Please, Mr. Ambassador," she said, "your autograph for a very, very old lady."

Right there, Stevenson showed his diplomatic skill. "I'd be delighted," he said. "Where is she?"

## 273. Diplomatic Romance

Even rather late in life, Benjamin Franklin had a wit and charm that attracted women of all ages.

When he was serving as U.S. minister to France, an attractive lady complained to him that he hadn't paid a visit to her all summer.

With a twinkle in his eye, Franklin replied, "I was waiting until the nights were longer."

# DISCOURAGEMENT

### 274. Devil's Secret Weapon

There is an old-time fable that the devil once held a sale and offered all the tools of his trade to anyone who would pay their price.

They were spread out on the table, each one labeled — hatred, malice, envy, despair, sickness, sensuality — all the weapons that everyone knows so well.

But off on one side, apart from the rest, lay a harmless looking, wedge-shaped instrument marked "DISCOURAGEMENT." It was old and worn looking, but it was priced far above all the rest.

When asked the reason why, the devil explained: "Because I can use this one so much more easily than the others. No one knows that it belongs to me, so with it I can open doors that are tight bolted against the others. Once I get inside, I can use any tool that suits me best."

### 275. Experimentation by Edison

Two dejected assistants of Thomas Edison (1847-1931), the famous inventor, said, "We've just completed our seven hundredth experiment and we still don't have the answer. We have failed."

"No, my friends, you haven't failed," replied Edison, "It's just that we know more about this subject than anyone else alive. And you're closer to finding the answer, because now we know seven hundred things not to do. Don't call it a mistake. Call it an education."

### 276. News of the Day

The following newspaper editorial could have been written today, but, in fact, it appeared more than 150 years ago on June 16, 1833, in the *Atlantic Journal*, back "in the good old days."

"The world is too big for us. Too much going on, too many crimes, too much violence and excitement. Try as you will you get behind in the race, in spite of yourself. It's an incessant string, to keep pace... and still, you lose ground. Science empties its discoveries on you so fast that you stagger beneath them in hopeless bewilderment. The political world is news seen so rapidly you're out of breath trying to keep pace with who's in and who's out. Everything is high pressure. Human nature can't endure much more!"

# DIVERSITY

### 277. Building Diversity

There is a wonderful fable about a giraffe who wants to befriend an elephant and who invites the elephant into his house. After some quick carpentry to enlarge the basement door in order to admit the elephant, the giraffe goes off to answer a phone call, telling the elephant, "Please make yourself at home."

But every time the elephant moves, there is a large crashing sound. When the giraffe returns, he is amazed at the damage that the elephant has done and is quick to offer advice.

"Sign up for weight-watchers," he urges the elephant. "And it wouldn't hurt," he adds helpfully, "if you'd go to ballet class at night. In order to become lighter on your feet."

There are three clear morals to be drawn from the interaction between the giraffe, as the insider, and the elephant, as the outsider. The first is the silliness of expecting an elephant to assume the same dimensions as a giraffe. If you are serious about diversity, you should build your house with that in mind. But that is not the easiest of tasks.

As a second moral to the story, you should expect a certain amount of tension and complexity. And finally, each of us must be prepared to move outside our original comfort zone if we want to embrace and promote diversity. That's the third and biggest moral from the story. There is no such thing as a diverse organization created by executive dictate. It is something that will come into being only through the willing and active behavior of supervisors, managers, and people at all levels.

## 278. About Diversity

According to the dictionary, "diversity" simply means difference, unlikeness, or variety. Like the proverbial snowflake, each of us is different — in some way, unique.

However, again like the snowflake, we are also incredibly alike. For all of the differences between people, far less than 1 percent of our DNA separates any one human being from any other.

The true test of diversity within an organization, or across a whole society is whether people build upon their differences, or whether they are divided or even destroyed by them. Part of the greatness of our country is contained in the motto that is stamped on our coinage, "E Pluribus Unum, Out of Many One." Conversely, in a place like Yugoslavia, the tragedy has been the failure of a people who are racially and in other ways the same to bridge their differences in religion and history.

Skin color, gender, age, and sexual orientation are some of the obvious and important differences between people. But there are many other differences in background, history, and habit that are also profoundly important and that must be addressed in any organization that wants to reap the benefits of diversity.

# ECOLOGY

## 279. Native Americans' View of Nature

The North American Indian stressed the web of life, the interconnectedness of land and man and creature. One of their famous leaders, Chief Luther Standing Bear of the Ogalala Sioux, put it this way:

"Only to the white man was nature a wilderness and only to him was the land 'infested' with 'wild' animals and 'savage' people. To us it was tame. Earth was bountiful and we were surrounded with the blessings of the Great Mystery."

## 280. Unforeseen Consequences

Garrett Hardin (1915-2003), the famous ecologist, formulated what he calls "The First Law of Ecology."

"We can never do merely one thing."

"This law," says Hardin, "warns us that any human intervention in the order of things will likely have unforeseen consequences; and that many, perhaps most — perhaps all — will be contrary to our expectations and desires."

He gives as an example the building of the High Aswan Dam in Egypt, which produced electricity and water for year-round irrigation — and which also increased the incidence of disease-bearing parasites, decimated shrimp fisheries in the eastern Mediterranean, and disrupted the five-thousand-year flow of silt nutrients into delta farmland.

# ECONOMICS

## 281. Great Wisdom

When a plague of poverty decimated an ancient land, the King called in his wisest economic advisors and demanded to be shown a short textbook on economics so that he might devise a remedy.

A full year later the king's advisors returned bearing not one but 87 volumes. Enraged at having his orders ignored, the King ordered his guards to execute half of the advisors.

Fearful for their lives, the remaining advisors edited the economics texts down to four volumes. To this, the angry King responded by ordering his guards to execute all but one of the remaining economic experts.

Finally, and with trembling, the last royal economist prostrated himself before the king and said: "Sire, in five words I will reveal to you all the wisdom that I have distilled through all these years from all the writings of all the economists who once practiced their science in your kingdom."

"Quick," said the impatient King, "what are they?"

Answered the counselor, "There ain't no free lunch."

NOTE: the above fable was inspired by an article in the *San Francisco News* by Walter Morrow published on June 1, 1949. Actually, the real-life economist most generally credited with the free lunch line is the noted American economist Milton Friedman (1912-2006).

## 282. Price Controls

The Roman Emperor Diocletian (245-313), who is remembered as the last great persecutor of the Christians, also is credited with directing the first well-documented attempt to control prices.

Diocletian and his fiscally irresponsible predecessors reduced the silver content of Roman coins, creating what we would recognize as consumer price inflation. But Diocletian blamed the "avarice" of merchants and speculators, and promulgated the Edict of 301, which set maximum prices for more than 1,000 goods and services.

The penalty for evading the controls was death, but even that didn't make them work. One reason, according to a contemporary account, was that "the people brought provisions no more to markets, since they could not get a reasonable price for them." The edict was revoked after much bloodshed and suffering. Diocletian abdicated in 305.

## 283. Description of Soviet Economics

A leading Russian reform economist, Gregory Yavlinsky, was giving a television interview in 1991. Asked by the interviewer to evaluate the state of the then-Soviet economy, Yavlinsky thought for a moment, and said,

"It reminds me of the anecdote about the two men who were walking along on the edge of a cliff. One of them fell off. The other one waited a minute or so, looked over the edge and said, 'Are you alright?'

"A voice came back up, 'Yes, I'm okay.'

"'Anything broken?' asked the man above.

"A voice came back up saying, 'No, nothing is broken.'

"The fellow up top said, 'Well, come on back up then.'

"The climber below replied, 'I can't. I'm still falling.'"

# EDUCATION

## 284. Harvard Admission

The following is an excerpt from an article published by *Atlantic Monthly* in 1892 on Harvard's entrance requirements of that day. The article stated:

"Without going into troublesome details, it may be said that the examinations in the elementary studies test the following acquirements: an elementary working knowledge of four languages, two ancient, Latin and Greek, and two modern, French and German; some acquaintance with English classical literature, and the ability to write clearly and intelligently about the books which have been read; a knowledge of elementary algebra and plane geometry; an acquaintance with the laws and phenomena of physics obtained from experiments performed by the pupil in a laboratory, or a knowledge of descriptive physics and elemental astronomy, and last, a knowledge of the history and geography either of ancient Greece and Rome or modern England and America.

"In addition to examinations in these prescribed elementary studies the candidate must be examined on two more subjects, chosen, according to his tastes and natural aptitudes, from the following list of nine advanced studies: Latin Translation, Greek Translation, Latin and Greek Composition, French, German, Trigonometry and Solid Geometry, or Trigonometry and Analytical Geometry, Advanced Algebra and Analytical Geometry, Physics, Chemistry."

## 285. Education of Youth

The aboriginal people of Australia had a unique way of instilling responsibility in the young people of their tribe.

At a predetermined time, a young person would be solemnly entrusted with a secret piece of knowledge vital to the tribe's survival. For example, it might be the location of a hidden spring on their territory or a secret cave which could be a hiding place if the tribe were suddenly attacked.

No one else in the tribe would be trusted with that particular piece of information and the young person would be expected to contribute it for the welfare of all when the right occasion presented itself. Imagine what a sense of importance and belonging this custom gave to each of the tribe's young people. Each of them had a unique and important role to play in the tribe's well-being.

How much richer in self-esteem and mental health today's young people would be if we could find modern ways to emulate this ancient tribal custom.

## 286. What Made Athens Great

The ancient city of Athens, Greece, may well have been the birthplace of what we call civic spirit. When he reached voting age, it was the obligation of every Athenian to stand in the public square — before his family and neighbors — and take this oath:

"We will strive unceasingly to quicken the public sense of duty — so that we will make this city greater, better, and more beautiful than it was when we took this oath."

## 287. How to Raise a Genius

There is a story that a mother once asked Albert Einstein (1879-1955) how to raise a child to become a genius.

Einstein's advice was to read the child fairy tales.

"And after that?" the mother asked.

"Read the child more fairy tales," Einstein replied, adding that what a scientist most needs is a curious imagination.

## 288. Books and Education

At a meeting attended by Benjamin Franklin, the people attending were discussing what was the most pitiful sight each of them had ever seen. When it came Franklin's turn, he said, "The sorriest sight is the lonely man on a rainy day who cannot read."

## 289. Rules for Teachers in 1872

The following rules for teachers in 1872 are on record at the Washakie County Museum and Cultural Center in Worland, Wyoming:

1. Teachers each day will fill lamps, clean chimneys.

2. Each teacher will bring a bucket of water and a scuttle of coal for the day's session.

3. Make your pens carefully. You may whittle nibs to the individual taste of the pupils.

4. Men teachers may take one evening each week for courting purposes, or two evenings a week if they go to church regularly.

5. After ten hours in school, the teachers may spend the remaining time reading the Bible or other good books.

6. Women teachers who marry or engage in unseemly conduct will be dismissed.

7. Every teacher should lay aside from each pay a goodly sum of his earnings for his benefit during his declining years so that he will not become a burden to society.

8. Any teacher who smokes, uses liquor in any form, frequents pool or public halls, or gets shaved in a barber shop will give good reason to suspect his worth, intention, integrity and honesty.

9. The teacher who performs his labor faithfully and without fault for five years will be given an increase of twenty-five cents per week in his pay, providing the Board of Education approves.

## 290. Introduction to Manhood

The early American Indians had a unique practice of training young braves. On the night of a boy's thirteenth birthday, after learning hunting, scouting, and fishing skills, he was put to one final test.

He was placed in a dense forest to spend the entire night alone. Until then, he had never been away from the security of the family and tribe. But on this night, he was blindfolded and taken several miles away. When he took off the blindfold, he was in the middle of a thick woods, and he was terrified.

Every time a twig snapped, he visualized a wild animal ready to pounce. After what seemed like an eternity, dawn broke and the first rays of sunlight entered the interior of the forest. Looking around, the boy saw flowers, trees, and the outline of a path. Then to his utter astonishment, he beheld the figure of a man standing just a few feet away, armed with bow and arrow.

It was his father. He had been there all night long.

## 291. Honorary Degrees

Mark Twain (Samuel Clemens) (1835-1910) was awarded an honorary degree in 1907 by Oxford University.

A friend described Twain at the event as "a wonderful personage, his white hair glistening in the sun, and the Oxford gown with its brilliant hood setting off his fine head and face."

Asked later about his memory of the event, Twain said, "I like the degree well enough, but I'm crazy about the clothes! I wish I could wear 'em all day and all night."

## 292. Teacher Expectations

The first day of school began on a bright note for a teacher who was glancing over the class roll. After each student's name was a number such as 138, 140, 154, and so on.

"Look at these IQs," she thought excitedly. "They've given me a terrific class!"

As a result, the elated teacher worked harder with this class than with her others. She tried new innovations that she thought would challenge them and hold their interest.

And it worked! The class did much better than any of the other classes she had taught in the usual way.

Only later did she find out that the figures after each pupil's name stood for their locker number, not their IQs.

## 293. The Way to Education

Isidor Rabi (1898-1988), the famous physicist who won a Nobel Prize for inventing a technique that permitted scientists to probe the structure of atoms and molecules, gave credit for his success to the way his mother used to greet him each day on coming home from school.

"Did you ask any good questions today, Izzy?" she would ask him as soon as he was in the door.

"Asking good questions," said Rabi, "helped me become a scientist."

## 294. Education Standards

In 1785, the entrance criteria for Columbia College declared:

"No candidate shall be admitted into the College unless he shall be able to render in English Caesar's *Commentaries of the Gallic War*; the four *Orations* of Cicero against Catiline; the first four books of Virgil's *Aeneid*; and the Gospels from the Greek; and to explain the government and connections of the words, and to turn English into grammatical Latin, and shall understand the four first rules of Arithmetic, with the rule of three."

## 295. A Frontier Story

Learning is good in and of itself. The mothers of the Jewish ghettoes in Europe would pour honey on a book so the children would know that learning is sweet. And the parents who settled hungry Kansas in homestead days would take their children in from the fields when a teacher came.

## 296. Constant Learning

There is a famous story about Oliver Wendell Holmes, Jr. (1841-1935), one of America's most distinguished Supreme Court Justices.

 Holmes was in the hospital one time, when he was over ninety, and President Roosevelt came to visit him. As the President was ushered into the hospital room, there was Justice Holmes reading a Greek grammar.

President Roosevelt said, "Why are you reading a Greek grammar, Mr. Holmes?"

And Holmes replied, "To improve my mind, Mr. President."

## 297. Guarantee Wanted

An anxious mother was questioning Princeton University President Woodrow Wilson (1856-1924) (later to become President of the United States) about what Princeton could do for her son.

"Madam," the exasperated Wilson replied, "We guarantee satisfaction or you will get your child back."

## 298. Raising Useful Citizens

The following is a message to the Commissioner of Virginia from representatives of the Native American "Six Nations" as recorded by Benjamin Franklin:

"Several of our young (Native American Indian) people were formerly brought up in the colleges of the northern provinces. They were instructed in all your sciences. But when they came back to us, they were bad runners, ignorant of every means of living in the woods, unable to bear either cold or hunger, knew neither how to build a cabin, take a deer, and spoke our language imperfectly.

"They were therefore neither fit for hunters, warriors, nor counselors. They were totally good for nothing. We are, however, nonetheless obliged by your kind offer, though we decline it.

"And to show our grateful sense of it, if the gentlemen of Virginia will send us a dozen of their sons, we will take great care of their education, instruct them in all we know, and make men of them."

## 299. Real Importance

An anthropologist studying the native society on a small South Pacific Island decided one day that he wanted to meet their leader.

He had become good friends with the tribe's medical healer and he asked him if he would take him to meet with the tribe's most important man — assuming that this would be their king.

Instead the healer took him to a small clearing in the jungle where an old man was teaching a group of children.

"Is that your king?" asked the anthropologist.

"No," said the healer, "the King is the most powerful man on the island, but you said you wanted to meet the most important, so I brought you to our teacher."

## 300. A Holiday Message

William Lyon Phelps (1865-1943) was a storied U.S. scholar and critic who taught at Yale University.

When marking an examination paper written shortly before Christmas, Phelps came across a note written by a student on the margin: "God only knows the answer to this question. Merry Christmas"

Phelps returned the paper with the annotation, "God gets an A. You get an F. Happy New Year!"

## 301. A Mother's Confidence

The boy was hopeless, the schoolmaster decided. Restless, inattentive and seemingly incapable of learning anything. "You're addled," he curtly informed the 7-year-old, and sent him home in tears. But the boy's mother was a tigress. No sooner had he sobbed out the schoolmaster's cruel verdict than she whipped off her apron, put on her bonnet, and marched her son back to school to confront the boy's tormentor.

"This boy is destined for greatness," she stormed at the cowed teacher. "One day, he will be famous and respected, while you will be remembered only as the dolt who couldn't recognize a budding genius when you saw one."

With that, the mother, who had been a schoolteacher herself, took charge of her son's education and tutored him at home.

Most mothers have made equally extravagant predictions about their offspring at one time or other. But in this case, the mother's fondest hopes were to be surpassed. Because the boy's name was Thomas Alva Edison (1847-1931), and he never forgot the enormous debt he owed his mother.

"My mother was the making of me," he declared in his later years. "She was so true, so sure of me, and I felt I had someone to live for, someone I must not disappoint."

During his amazing career, Thomas Edison was awarded more than 1,300 U.S. and foreign patents for his inventions.

## 302. Dinner at the White House

The noted American novelist James Michener (1907-1997) received an invitation to a dinner at the White House during the Eisenhower administration, and he declined it. As his reason for turning down such an unusual opportunity, Michener wrote:

"Dear Mr. President, I received your invitation three days after I had agreed to speak a few words at a dinner honoring the wonderful high school teacher who taught me how to write. I know you will not miss me at your dinner, but she might at hers."

Michener promptly received this reply from an understanding President Eisenhower, who wrote, "In this lifetime a man lives under fifteen or sixteen presidents, but a really fine teacher comes into his life but rarely."

# EGO

### 303. A Good Story Anyway

During World War II and after, British and American leaders were driven to great heights of frustration by the stubbornness of General Charles De Gaulle (1890-1970), who led France during and after the war, first as head of a French government in exile and later as President. Though surely apocryphal, this story certainly captures his egocentric personality:

As President of France in his last years, De Gaulle instructed an aide to purchase a monument or burial crypt suitable to the majesty of the Great Charles. After much study the aide brought back a plan for a magnificent mausoleum.

De Gaulle studied it, then rejected it. "Impossible , much too costly," he said.

The aide went back to the architects, who after some months came up with a new plan, an elegant obelisk. This plan was shown by the aide to De Gaulle and again he objected.

So the aide consulted the architects once more, and another plan was prepared. This design showed a simple tall memorial shaft with a place for entombment. De Gaulle was apparently satisfied until he asked the aide for the price.

"Mr. President," said the aide, "it will cost five hundred thousand francs."

Drawing himself up to his considerable height, De Gaulle said: "Isn't that a bit expensive? I only need it for three days."

## 304. Presidential Self-Esteem

Students of American presidents and their personalities are fond of telling this story about President Lyndon Johnson (1908-1973), who was famous for his well-developed ego.

For relaxation, Johnson liked to drive himself around his ranch in Texas and vicinity. One day he was stopped by a Texas patrolman for speeding. When the patrolman came closer to Johnson's car and saw who was driving, he reportedly exclaimed, "Oh, my God!"

Looking straight at the patrolman, Johnson replied, "And don't you forget it!"

# ENGINEERING

## 305. Unbelievable Courage

The Brooklyn Bridge that spans the river tying Manhattan Island to Brooklyn is truly a miracle bridge. In 1863, a creative engineer named John Roebling (1806-1869) was inspired by an idea for this spectacular bridge. However, bridge building experts throughout the world told him to forget it; it could not be done.

Roebling convinced his son, Washington (1837-1926), who was a young up and coming engineer, that the bridge could be built. The two of them developed the concepts of how it could be accomplished and how the obstacles could be overcome. With unharnessed excitement and inspiration, they hired their crew and began to build their dream bridge.

The project was only a few months under construction when a tragic accident on the site took the life of John Roebling and severely injured his son, Washington. Washington was left with permanent brain damage and was unable to talk or walk. Everyone felt that the project would have to be scrapped since the Roeblings were the only ones who knew how the bridge could be built.

Even though Washington was unable to move or talk, his mind was as sharp as ever, and he still had a burning desire to complete the bridge. An idea hit him as he lay in his hospital bed, and he developed a code for communication. All he could move was one finger, so he touched the arm of his wife with that finger, tapping out the code to communicate to her what to tell the engineers who were building the bridge.

For thirteen years, Washington tapped out his instructions with his finger until the spectacular Brooklyn Bridge was finally completed.

## 306. Hiring Engineers

Thomas Edison had a unique method for screening engineering applicants. He would hand the applicant a light bulb and ask, "How much water will it hold?"

There were two ways to find the answer. The first choice was to use gauges to measure all the angles of the bulb. With these measurements in hand, the engineer could then calculate the surface area. This approach could take as long as twenty minutes.

The second choice was to fill the bulb with water and then pour the contents into a measuring cup. Total elapsed time: about a minute.

Engineers who took the first route, and performed their measurements by the book, were politely thanked for coming and sent on their way.

Applicants who took the second route heard Edison say, "You're hired."

## 307. Origin of Murphy's Law

In 1949, Edward A. Murphy was an engineer at the Wright Field Aircraft Lab in Ohio. When a gauge he designed wouldn't work, Murphy traced the problem to improper wiring by a technician.

"If there's a way to do it wrong, he will," Murphy said.

The remark, repeated and modified over time, was to become the pessimist's favorite challenge to order in the universe, Murphy's Law: "If anything can go wrong, it will."

## 308. Doing the Impossible

In the early days of World War II (May 30, 1942, to be exact), Britain's Prime Minister Winston Churchill sent a memo to Lord Louis Mountbatten (1900-1979), Chief of Combined Operations, requesting that research begin immediately to determine how a temporary harbor could be constructed on a coastline where no good harbor existed.

In other words, how do you build an artificial harbor off the coast of France where an invading army could unload all its troops, supplies, tanks, jeeps, ammunition and other materiel for the invasion of Europe. Remember, this invasion did not take place until 1945 but Churchill was already thinking about what would be necessary for victory.

The memo goes like this:

"They (the supply ships) must float up and down with the tide. The anchor problem must be mastered. The ships must have a side flap cut in them and a drawbridge long enough to overreach the moorings of the piers. Let me have the best solution worked out."

Then Churchill added this zinger: "Don't argue the matter. The difficulties will argue for themselves."

In other words, Churchill was saying to Britain's best engineers, "Don't bother me with all the reasons this project cannot be done. Just tell me how we can do it."

As history knows, such a huge temporary harbor was successfully installed in the surf off Omaha Beach in Normandy, France. And millions of tons of war materiel were successfully unloaded there under heavy fire. The Germans had paid special attention to building defenses around the natural harbors located on the coastline facing Britain. They did not consider Omaha Beach a prime landing place because it had no major harbor.

Today, a copy of Churchill's memo is framed in a museum located near Omaha Beach, a written testament to a far-seeing executive who demanded that a solution be found to a complex problem he saw was going to develop in the future.

NOTE: The development described above was called the Mulberry Harbors project. Text of Churchill's memorandum can be found on page 718 of Churchill's *Memoirs of the Second World War* (Houghton & Mifflin, Boston, 1959) which is an authorized condensation of Churchill's six-volume: *The Second World War*." The museum where the memorandum is framed is the Musee du Debarquement in Arromanches-les-Bains in Normandy, France.

# ETHICS

### 309. Code of Ethics

Years ago, after a few modest little scandals, President Harry Truman (1884-1972) was asked if Washington officials shouldn't sign a code of ethics.

He said no, that the Ten Commandments and the Sermon on the Mount were all the code of ethics anybody needed. So he signed nothing and never needed to.

### 310. What Socrates Held Sacred

When Athenians gathered in 399 BC to sit in judgment over the 70-year-old self-proclaimed gadfly Socrates (469 BC-399 BC), what they heard was not a plea for forgiveness but a proud, dignified accusation of the verdict.

Socrates declared that what he deserved was not the death sentence but rather a reward for attempting to force his fellow citizens to face truth, justice, and beauty. In words that would inspire for centuries thereafter, Socrates refused to stoop to a genuine defense of his actions and what he saw as begging for forgiveness and life.

He dismissed such an option with the words, "The difficulty, my friends, is not to avoid death, but to avoid unrighteousness."

### 311. Changing Journalism Ethics

In the 1987 movie *Broadcast News*, the subject of journalism ethics played a key role in its plot.

Holly Hunter, whose character was an idealistic television editor, accused a highly successful television reporter (played by William Hurt) with violating journalistic ethics by faking tears in a reaction shot while doing an emotional interview.

"You've crossed the line of journalistic ethics!" screamed Hunter, who previously had had a romantic interest in Hurt's character.

"Is that right?" said Hurt coolly, "But they do keep moving that little sucker don't they?"

### 312. Doing What's Right

Once, when Lincoln was censured for his unwavering policy, he gave this answer to his critics:

"I am not bound to win, but I am bound to be true. I am not bound to succeed, but I am bound to live up to what light I have. I must stand with anybody that stands right; stand with him while he is right and part with him when he goes wrong."

# ETIQUETTE, MANNERS

### 313. Etiquette Lesson

At ceremonies commemorating the hundredth anniversary of President Harry Truman's birth, the White House counsel during the Truman Administration was reminiscing. He recalled being at a White House banquet one night when one of the guests turned to the woman seated next to him.

"Did I get your name correctly?" he asked. "Is your name Post?"

"Yes, it is." the woman answered.

"Is it Emily Post (1873-1980)?"

"Yes," she replied.

"Are you the world-renowned authority on manners?" the man asked.

"Yes," Mrs. Post said. "Why do you ask?"

"Because," said the man, "you have just eaten my salad."

## 314. How the Handshake Came to Be

Historians say that for centuries a handshake signified the conferring of power from a god to an earthly ruler.

Around 1800 B.C., in Babylonia, it was required that the king grasp the hands of a statue of Marduk, the country's chief god. This ceremony took place annually during the New Year's festival and served to transfer authority to the king for another year.

So persuasive was this ceremonial custom that when the Assyrians defeated and occupied Babylonia, Assyrian kings felt compelled to adopt the ritual, for fear they might otherwise offend a major heavenly being.

## 315. Cultural Manners

In America, a male brought up in the Northeast is brought up to stand 18 to 20 inches away when talking face to face to a man he does not know very well.

Talking to a woman under similar circumstances, he increases the distance about four inches.

Anthropologists say a distance of only 8 to 13 inches between males is considered either very aggressive or indicative of a closeness of a type we do not ordinarily want to think about.

Yet, in many parts of Latin America and the Middle East, distances which are almost sexual in connotation are the only ones at which people can talk comfortably.

## 316. Invitations

The Irish playwright and critic George Bernard Shaw (1856-1950) once sent Winston Churchill a note inviting him to the opening-night performance of Shaw's play *Saint Joan*.

He enclosed two tickets with a note saying, "One for yourself and one for a friend, if you have one."

Churchill sent a reply expressing his regret at being unable to attend. In his note, Churchill asked if it would be possible to have tickets for the second night. Then he added, "If there is one."

## 317. Excuse Me

When in 1747 the adventurer Blackwell was to be decapitated, he put his head on the wrong side of the chopping block.

When the axman advised him of his mistake, Blackwell apologized, explaining that this was the first time he had been beheaded.

## 318. A Way of Saying Thank You

The Masai tribe in West Africa has an unusual way of saying thank you.

Anthropologists say that, when the Masai want to say thank you to someone, they bow, put their foreheads on the ground, and say, "My head is in the dirt."

When members of another African tribe want to express gratitude, they sit for a long time in front of the hut of the person who did the favor and literally say, "I sit on the ground before you."

## 319. Symbol of Hospitality

A pineapple isn't just a fruit. It is a symbol of fertility and hospitality.

In parts of early America, sailors would place a pineapple on the gatepost to let neighbors know they were home from the sea.

Caribbean Indians hung pineapples or pineapple crowns at the entrances to their huts as a promise of welcome and refreshment to all comers. On the other hand, they planted thick hedges of pineapple plants around their villages to keep strangers out. The plant's sharp, spiky leaf edges could inflict nasty cuts on intruders.

The pineapple frequently served as a motif in colonial America for such items as quilt designs and bedstead carvings.

## 320. Shaking the President's Hand

George Washington, America's first president, avoided physical contact at presidential receptions. Instead, he greeted guests by bowing. To thwart those angling for a handshake, Washington rested one hand on the hilt of a dress sword; in his other hand he held a special hat that consisted of a fake front and feathers.

John Adams (1735-1826), America's second president, honored Washington's tradition of bowing to guests, but his successor, Thomas Jefferson (1743-1826), instituted what he thought was a more democratic custom, shaking hands. To Jefferson, bowing smacked too much of monarchy. He also began the tradition of throwing the White House doors open on New Year's Day and personally shaking the hand of anyone who came by.

From that day until 1930, all presidents welcomed the new year by thus greeting their public. The practice was discontinued in 1930 by President Herbert Hoover (1874-1964), who felt the number of visitors, which had grown into the thousands, had become too unwieldy.

## 321. History of the Toast

In medieval times, a common way to kill an enemy was to offer him a poisoned drink. To prove to the guest that a drink was safe, the host would receive a small amount of the guest's drink in his own glass, and both would drink at the same time.

If the guest trusted the host, rather than pouring some of his drink into the host's glass, he would simply clink his glass against it. Although offering a poisoned drink is no longer a popular way to kill someone, the custom of clinking glasses still remains.

The ancient Romans placed toasted bread in wine to collect the impurities and heighten the effect of the drink. They called the wine-soaked bread by the inelegant name, "the sop." The more apt word, "the toast," not only referred to the content of the cup, but by implication to the act of a spoken blessing or a word of honor to the person or occasion rather than merely to the drink itself.

# EXCELLENCE

## 322. Importance of Details

Michelangelo (1475-1564) was putting what appeared to be the finishing touches on a sculpture when a friend dropped in for a visit. Days later, the friend dropped by again and was surprised to find the artist still working on the same statue.

To the friend, the statue looked the same as it had days earlier, so he said, "You haven't been working on this statue all this time, have you?"

"I have," Michelangelo replied. "I've been busy retouching this part, and polishing that part; I've softened this feature, and brought out that muscle; I've given more expression to the lips, and more energy to that arm."

"But all those things are so insignificant," said the friend. "They're mere trifles."

"That may be so," replied Michelangelo, "but trifles make perfection, and perfection is no trifle."

## 323. Pride in One's Work

There are markets in South America where they sell rope and native residents can tell you, just by looking at it, who made each particular piece. The rope reflects the character and style of the person who made it.

Residents in a rural village in England also say they can look at a field where ten people had plowed and tell you the name of the man who had done each furrow.

The farmers were asked why they took such care to make their furrows so precise. Such precision would not yield a bigger crop. Their answer is that it was not because they were paid more, it was because it was their work and they did it as best they could. It belonged to them. It was their personal signature.

## 324. How to Make a Speech Perfect

The famous dancer Fred Astaire (1899-1987) once said something about his dance routines that are applicable to preparing any speech.

He said, "Work on it until it's perfect. Then cut two minutes."

## 325. Nature's Symmetry

In his lectures on physics, the noted American physicist Richard P. Feynman (1918-1988) made the following comments:

"Why is nature so nearly symmetrical? No one has any idea why. The only thing we might suggest is something like this: There is a gate in Japan, a gate in Neiko, which is sometimes called by the Japanese the most beautiful gate in all of Japan; it was built in a time when there was great influence from Chinese art.

"The gate is very elaborate, with lots of gables and beautiful carvings and lots of columns and dragon heads and princes carved into the pillars, and so on. But when one looks closely he sees that in the elaborate and complex design along one of the pillars, one of the small design elements is carved upside down; otherwise the thing is completely symmetrical. If one asks why this is, the story is that it was carved upside down so that the gods will not be jealous of the perfection of man. So they purposely put the error in there, so that the gods would not be jealous and get angry with human beings.

"We might like to turn the idea around and think that the true explanation of the near symmetry of nature is this: that God made the laws only nearly symmetrical so that we should not be jealous of His perfection!"

## 326. Artistic Pride

The Greek sculptor, Phidias (c. 490 BC-430 BC), had high standards when he was carving the statue of "Athenia" for the Acropolis.

He was busy chiseling the strands of her hair at the back of her head when an onlooker commented, "That figure is to stand 100 feet high, with its back to a marble wall. Who will ever know what details you are putting behind there?"

Phidias replied, "I will."

## 327. Another Phidias Story

On the roof of the Parthenon in Athens stand statues created by the greatest sculptor of ancient Greece, Phidias. They were carved around 440 B.C., more than 2,400 years ago.

When Phidias submitted the bill for his work to the city, the city accountant of Athens refused to pay it saying, "These statues stand on the roof of the temple, and on the highest hill in Athens. Nobody can see anything but their fronts. Yet, you have charged us for sculpturing them in the round, that is, for doing the backsides, which nobody can see."

"You are wrong," Phidias retorted. "The gods can see them."

## 328. Statue of Liberty

When Frederic Auguste Bartholdi (1834-1904) completed his 152-foot-high Statue of Liberty in 1884, there were no airplanes or helicopters to inspect its detail from the air. It was installed in New York harbor two years later as a gift from the people of France to commemorate 100 years of American independence.

Yet many years later, when helicopters can hover close overhead, it is clearly evident that the sculptor meticulously finished every detail of the lady's coiffure and crown without "cheating" in any area that could not be seen from the ground.

Many years later the famous lyrist Oscar Hammerstein (1895-1960) mentioned the statue in his book, *Lyrics* and said, "When you are creating a work of art, or any other kind of work, finish the job off perfectly. You never know when a helicopter, or some other instrument not at the moment invented, may come along and find you out."

Clearly, Bartholdi was a perfectionist who needed no such advice. He wanted to create a thing of beauty that was perfect from every point of view and over any period of time. That's a good principle to follow when creating anything of lasting worth.

# EXPLORATION

### 329. Men Crave Adventure

In the early 1900s, the following classified ad was placed in the London *Times*.

"Men wanted for hazardous journey. Low wages, bitter cold, long hours of complete darkness. Safe return doubtful. Honour and recognition in the event of success."

The advertisement was signed by "E. Shackleton."

Ernest Shackleton (1874-1922) was preparing an expedition to discover the South Pole and was looking for adventurous crew members.

Did the ad pull?

The next morning, more than 5,000 men were waiting outside the *Times'* offices wanting to brave the rigors of Shackleton's dangerous mission.

Shackleton and his crew reached the pole in 1907. The unprecedented response to his advertisement was proof that people will respond to almost any challenge when they are approached in the right way.

## 330. Discovering the Pacific Ocean

Nearly five hundred years ago, as Balboa (1475-1519) stood on the Pacific shores of Panama looking out at that expanse of water he had just discovered, he didn't have the faintest idea of how large the Pacific Ocean really was.

Most of us are like Balboa. We don't have any idea of how large our potential is.

## 331. Invasion Strategy

When Spanish explorer Hernando Cortes (1486-1547) landed at Veracruz on the Gulf of Mexico in 1519, one of the first things he did was to burn his fleet of 11 ships.

His goal was to conquer this new land by pushing west to the Pacific. By burning his ships he eliminated the possibility that his men would lose heart and sail back to Spain. Two previous Spanish expeditions had been unable to establish a settlement in Mexico.

With such zeal, Cortes led 110 sailors and 553 soldiers to conquer 5 million people. If the ships had not been burned, the Cortes forces would have had an alternative if they lost the fight that lay ahead. Burning the ships gave the men a powerful motive to win.

Convinced that they could not turn back, they were better able to focus on the goal and do what had to be done to reach it.

## 332. Fear of the Unknown

Browsing through marine book stores containing the lore of the sea, you can come across old ocean charts done in ancient times. When the map makers of that day ran out of known world before they ran out of parchment, they often placed a sketch of a dragon accompanied by the printed warning, "Here be dragons." This was their way of telling explorers they would be entering unknown territory at their own risk.

Unfortunately, some explorers took this symbol literally and were afraid to push on to new worlds. Other more adventurous explorers saw the dragons as a sign of opportunity, a door to virgin territory.

## 333. He Showed Them the Way

When Columbus (1451-1506) returned to Spain after reaching America, his well-earned fame made many of his contemporaries quite jealous.

One night at a fabulous dinner given in his honor, some of his critics conspired to poke fun at his achievements.

"It is true you found strange lands beyond the seas," they said contemptuously, "but why should there be so much said about it? We now know that anybody can sail across the ocean just as you have done. It is the simplest thing in the world."

The great admiral made no answer but he reached out to take an egg from a nearby dish.

"Who among you, sirs, can make this egg stand on end?" he asked his tormentors.

One by one those at the table tried unsuccessfully to make the egg stand on its end without falling.

"It cannot be done," said all of them at last.

At this Columbus took the egg and struck its small end gently upon the table so as to break the shell a little at one end. Then he easily made the egg stand upright without any difficulty.

There was a hush around the table.

"My dear sirs," said Columbus, "like discovering new lands, anything is simple once you have been shown how!"

## 334. The Least Successful Explorer

Thomas Nuttail (1786-1859) was a pioneer botanist whose main field of study was the flora of remote parts of Northwest America. As an explorer, however, his work was characterized by the fact that he was almost permanently lost.

During his expedition of 1812 his colleagues frequently had to light beacons in the evening to help him find his way back to camp.

One night, he completely failed to return and a search party was sent out. As it approached him in the darkness, Nuttail assumed they were Indians and tried to escape. The annoyed rescuers pursued him for three days through bush and river until he accidentally wandered back into the camp.

On another occasion, Nuttail was lost again and lay down exhausted. He looked so pathetic that a passing Indian, instead of scalping him, picked him up, carried him three miles to the river and paddled him home in a canoe.

## 335. Setting

In the fifteenth century, Spain considered itself the western-most point of civilization. Evidence of that was the motto emblazoned on its coat of arms "ne plus ultra," or "nothing more beyond."

But when Columbus returned from his voyage in 1493, Queen Isabella (1451-1504) decided to have the motto changed.

On her orders, the word "ne" was eliminated from the motto, leaving it to read "plus ultra," or, "more beyond."

## 336. Double Bookkeeping

On his first voyage to the New World, in 1492, the members of Columbus's crew were extremely uneasy about taking such a long journey through unknown waters — and for an unknown destination.

To reassure the sailors and to disguise the true length of the journey, Columbus kept two logs:

One was a secret log in which he put the true distances they had sailed that day as best he could calculate them.

The second log, which he shared with the crew, contained shorter distances so that the sailors would think they were closer to home than they actually were.

The irony is that the falsified figures turned out to be more accurate than those Columbus kept in his "secret" log.

# FAILURE

## 337. Don't Let Failure Discourage You

Many of those who have risen from failure to real achievement have rejected the rejection of this world.

In 1902, the poetry editor of *The Atlantic Monthly* returned a sheaf of poems to a 28-year-old poet with this curt note: "Our magazine has no room for your vigorous verse." The poet was Robert Frost (1874-1963), who rejected the rejection.

In 1905, the University of Bern turned down a Ph.D. dissertation as being irrelevant and fanciful. The young physics student who wrote the dissertation was Albert Einstein (1879-1955), who rejected the rejection.

In 1894, the rhetoric teacher at Harrow in England wrote on the 16-year-old's report card, "a conspicuous lack of success." The 16-year-old was Winston Churchill (1874-1965), who rejected the rejection.

## 338. Don't Let Failure Scare You

From time to time, life as a leader can look hopeless. After taking a hard look in the mirror at your leadership, you may be overwhelmed by the focus on what's needed. To help you, consider a man who lived through this:

Failed in business in '31
Defeated for the legislature in '32

Again failed in business in '34
Sweetheart died in '35
Had a nervous breakdown in '36
Defeated in election in '38
Broken marriage engagement in '41
Defeated for Congress in '43
Defeated for Congress in '48
Defeated for Senate in '55
Defeated for Vice-President in '56
Defeated for Senate in '58
Elected President in '60
This man was Abraham Lincoln (1809-1865).

## 339. Famous People Who Refused to Be Failures

LOUISA MAY ALCOTT (1832-1888): author of *Little Women*, was advised by her family to find work as a servant or as a seamstress.

FRED ASTAIRE (Frederich Austerlitz) (1899-1987): after his first screen test, a 1933 memo about Astaire from the MGM testing director said, "Can't act. Slightly bald. Can dance a little." Astaire kept that memo over the fireplace in his Beverly Hills home.

LUCILLE BALL (1911-1989): began studying to be an actress in 1927 and was told by the head instructor of the John Murray Anderson Drama School, "Try any other profession. Any other."

THE BEATLES: in 1962, four nervous young musicians played their first record audition for the executives of the Decca Recording Company, and the executives were not impressed. While turning down this British rock group, one executive said, "We don't like their sound. Groups of guitars are on the way out."

LUDWIG VAN BEETHOVEN (1770-1827): handled the violin awkwardly and preferred playing his own compositions instead of improving his technique. His teacher called him hopeless as a composer.

ALEXANDER GRAHAM BELL (1847-1922): when Bell invented the telephone in 1876, it did not ring off the hook with calls from potential backers. After making a demonstration call, President Rutherford Hayes (1822-1893) said, "That's an amazing invention, but who would ever want to use one of them?"

CHESTER CARLSON (1906-1988): in the 1940s, this young inventor took his idea to twenty corporations, including some of the biggest in the country. They all turned him down. In 1947 — after seven long years of rejections — he finally got a tiny company in Rochester, New York, the Haloid Company, to purchase the rights to his electrostatic paper-copying process. Haloid became Xerox Corporation, and both it and Carlson became very rich.

ENRICO CARUSO (1873-1921): the first vocal teacher to evaluate Caruso said Caruso had no voice at all and could not sing. The teacher said "your voice sounds like wind whistling through a window."

JULIA CHILD (1912-2004): In 1953, Child and her two collaborators signed a publishing contract to produce a book tentatively titled *French Cooking for the American Kitchen*. Julia and her colleagues worked on the book for five years. The publisher rejected the 850-page manuscript. Child and her partners worked for another year totally revising the manuscript. Again the publisher rejected it. But Julia Child did not give up. She and her collaborators went back to work again, found a new publisher, and in 1961 — eight years after beginning — they published *Mastering the Art of French Cooking*, which has sold more than 1 million copies.

WALT DISNEY (1901-1966): was fired by a newspaper for lacking ideas; he also went bankrupt several times before he built Disneyland.

BOB DYLAN (Robert Allen Zimmerman)(1941- ): when this famous musician-singer performed at a high school talent show, his classmates booed him off the stage.

CLINT EASTWOOD (1930- ) AND BURT REYNOLDS (1936- ): In 1959, a Universal Pictures executive dismissed them at the same meeting with the following statements. To Burt Reynolds: "You have no talent." To Clint Eastwood: "You have a chip on your tooth, your Adam's apple sticks out too far and you talk too slow."

THOMAS A. EDISON (1847-1931): was probably the greatest inventor in American history. When he first attended school in Port Huron, Michigan, his teachers complained that he was "too slow" and hard to handle. As a result, Edison's mother decided to take her son out of school and teach him at home. In his lifetime, Edison produced more than 1,300 inventions.

ALBERT EINSTEIN (1879-1931): was four years old before he could speak and seven before he could read. The University of Bern turned down a Ph.D. dissertation by Einstein as being irrelevant and too fanciful.

HENRY FORD (1863-1947): this famous auto pioneer forgot to put a reverse gear in his first car. Ford went broke five times before experiencing success.

ROBERT FROST (1874-1963): the poetry editor of the *The Atlantic Monthly* sent a sheaf of poems by Frost back to the 28-year-old poet with this curt note, "Our magazine has no room for your vigorous verse."

JAMES EARL JONES (1931- ): this famous actor stuttered so badly as a youth he communicated with friends and teachers using written notes. Today, he is acclaimed for the richness and power of his voice.

VINCE LOMBARDI (1913-1970): when he was starting out, an expert said of Lombardi, "He possesses minimal football knowledge. Lacks motivation." Lombardi, of course, became one of the greatest football coaches of all-time.

R. H. MACY (1822-1877): this famous merchant failed seven times before the store in New York bearing his name caught on.

MARILYN MONROE (Norma Jean Mortenson) (1926-1962): in 1944, Emmeline Snively, director of the Blue Book Modeling Agency, told modeling hopeful Norma Jean, "You'd better learn secretarial work or else get married."

IGNACE JAN PADEREWSKI (1860-1941): this great Polish pianist was once told by his music teacher that his hands were much too small to master the keyboard.

ELVIS PRESLEY (1935-1977): in 1954, Jimmy Denny, manager of the Grand Ole Opry, fired Elvis after one performance. He told Presley, "You ain't goin' nowhere son. You ought to go back to drivin' a truck."

AUGUSTE RODIN (1840-1917): this famous sculptor's father said, "I have an idiot for a son." Described as the worst pupil in the school, Rodin failed three times to secure admittance to the school of art. His uncle called him uneducable.

FRANKLIN DELANO ROOSEVELT (1882-1945): paralyzed by polio at the age of 39, Roosevelt went on to become one of America's most beloved and influential leaders. He was elected President of the United States four times.

HARRY S. TRUMAN (1884-1972): as a young man, Truman went broke in the men's clothing store he had started. He later became a distinguished U.S. Senator and the 33rd President of the United States.

# FAME

## 340. Why We Call Big Shots "Big Wigs"

Many years ago, men and women took baths only twice a year! (May and October). Women kept their hair covered, while men shaved their heads, because of lice and bugs, and wore wigs.

Wealthy men could afford good wigs made from wool. The wigs couldn't be washed, so to clean them they could carve out a loaf of bread, put the wig in the shell, and bake it for thirty minutes. The heat would make the wig big and fluffy, hence the term, "big wig."

Today we often use the term "here comes the Big Wig" because someone appears to be or is powerful and wealthy.

## 341. Personal Ego

After President Calvin Coolidge (1872-1933) retired, a newspaper reporter went to see him at his home in Vermont.

As they sat talking, the reporter said, "It must make you proud to see all these people coming by here just to look at you sitting on the porch. It shows that although you are a former president, you are not forgotten. Just look at those cars going by!"

"Not as many as yesterday," replied Coolidge. "There were 163 then."

## 342. Such Is Fame

Red Adair (1915-2004) was probably the world's most famous oil well fire fighter. When oil fields exploded anywhere in the world, they called for Red to do his magic and his fees made him a wealthy man. He was a Texan and John Wayne played him in a movie.

After subduing a particularly dangerous oil well fire, Red stopped at a Texas tavern to have a beer. He looked disheveled and his clothes were soaked with oil.

The bartender asked him to pay before getting the beer. Red said, "I have been fighting an oil fire and I don't have any money on me."

Belatedly recognizing Red, the bartender said to the other bar patrons, "Will anybody here buy a beer for Red Adair?"

One slightly tipsy patron said, "I'd be honored to buy a beer for Red Adair."

Red thanked him and was enjoying the beer when the tipsy patron came over and said in a conspiratorial tone, "Red, do you mind if I ask you a personal question?"

"Sure," said Red, "ask away."

"Well," said the tipsy patron, "Tell me, did you ever make it with Ginger Rogers?"

## 343. Public Recognition

One of America's greatest football coaches was Vince Lombardi (1913-1970), under whose command the Green Bay Packers of Green Bay, Wisconsin, won five national championships in the 1960s.

Even such famous people sometimes are put in their place, and this happened to Lombardi. He was at a restaurant, and a little boy approached his table. Lombardi reached for a menu and autographed it for the kid, but the boy said, "I don't want a menu. I want to borrow the ketchup."

# FATE

### 344. Does Fate Exist?

Mark Twain (Samuel Clemens) (1835-1910) was visiting Springfield, Illinois, and a Congressman was visiting there at the same time. The Congressman said to him:

"Mr. Clemens, I have often thought what a pity it was that fate did not intend that Lincoln should marry the true love of his life, Ann Rutledge. It seems that fate governs our lives and plans history in advance."

Twain responded, "Yes, had Lincoln married the dear one of his heart's love he might have a led a happy but obscure life and the world would never have heard of him. Happiness seeks obscurity to enjoy itself."

"Doesn't that prove," asked the Congressman, "that what is to be will be?"

"The only thing it proves to me," replied Twain, "is that what has been was."

### 345. Our Future

Albert Einstein (1879-1955), one of the world's great scientists and philosophers, said, "Everything is determined...by forces over which we have no control. It is determined for the insect as well as for the star. Human beings, vegetables, or cosmic dust — we all dance to a mysterious tune, intoned in the distance by an invisible piper."

### 346. Happiness and Pain

Arthur Schopenhauer (1788-1800), German philosopher, wrote, "We came into the world full of claims to happiness and pleasure and cherish the foolish hope of having them fulfilled.

"But as a rule, fate soon comes along, takes rough hold of us and teaches us that nothing belongs to us but everything to it. That it has an uncontested right not only to all we own and earn, to wife and child, but even to our arms and legs, eyes and ears, and the nose in the middle of our faces.

"In any event, experience comes after a while to teach us that happiness and pleasure are a will o' the wisp visible only from a distance but vanishing when we approach; that on the other hand suffering and pain are real and anything but illusions."

## 347. Fate Is Not Controllable

From the pen of Emily Dickinson (1830-1886) came this bittersweet description of fate:

We never know when we are going
We jest and shut the door,
Fate, following us, bolts it,
And we accost no more...

# FEAR

## 348. Assumption Is the Father of Error

In a discussion concerning elaborate preparations that were being made for an important project, Abraham Lincoln told this story:

"Once, there was a man on foot who came to a running stream that he had to get across. Fearing that the stream was deep and not wanting to get wet, the man made elaborate preparations to cross over.

"He stripped off all his garments, added them to a bundle he was already carrying, and tied them all to the top of a stick. He knew this would enable him to raise the bundle high above his head to keep them dry during the crossing.

"He then fearlessly waded into the stream and carefully made his way across, finding the water at no place higher than his ankles."

## 349. False Alarms

There is a famous Aesop fable that dramatically illustrates how important it is to preserve the absolute credibility of alarms warning of danger. It goes like this:

A certain shepherd's boy kept his sheep upon a common, and in sport and deviltry would often cry out in an irresponsible manner, "The wolf! The wolf!"

By this means he several times drew the husbandmen in an adjoining field from their work. Finding themselves deluded, the husbandmen resolved for the future to take no notice of his alarm.

Soon after, the wolf came indeed. The boy cried out in earnest; but no heed was given to his cries. With no help coming, the sheep were devoured by the wolf.

## 350. The Power of Fear

Legend has it that one day a man was walking in the desert when he met Fear and Plague.

They said they were on their way to a city to kill 10,000 people.

The man asked Plague if he was going to do all the work.

Plague smiled and said, "No, I'll take care of only a few hundred. I'll let my friend Fear do the rest."

## 351. Fear of the Unknown

When a spy was captured and sentenced to death in the Persian army, the commanding general would go through a rather unusual ritual. He would give the criminal a choice between the firing squad or going through "the big, black door."

A captured spy was given the usual choice. The prisoner would deliberate for a long time, then finally would decide on the firing squad. Moments later his life was extinguished.

Turning to his aide, the General said, "They always prefer the known way to the unknown. It is characteristic of people to be afraid of the undefined. Yet, we gave him a choice."

The aide asked the General what lay behind the big, black door.

"Freedom," replied the General, "and I've only known a few brave enough to take it."

## 352. How to Combat Panic

Once upon a time, a young donkey asked his grandpa, "How do I grow up to be just like you?"

"Oh, that's simple," the elder donkey said. "All you have to do is remember to shake if off and step up."

"What does that mean?" asked the youngster.

The grandfather replied, "Let me tell you a story...

"Once, when I was your age, I was out walking. I wasn't paying attention and fell deep into an old abandoned well. I started braying and braying. Finally an old farmer came by and saw me. I was scared to death. But then he left. I stayed in that well all night.

"The next morning he came back with a whole group of people, and they looked down at me. Some of them even laughed. Then the old farmer said, 'The well's abandoned and that donkey isn't worth saving, so let's get to work.' And believe it or not, they started to shovel dirt into the well. Well, I panicked. I was going to be buried alive!

"After the first shovels of dirt came down on me, I realized something. Every time dirt landed on my back, I could shake it off and use it to step up a bit higher! They kept shoveling, and I kept shaking the dirt off and stepping up. This went on for some time.

"'Shake it off and step up...shake it off and step up...' I kept repeating to myself for encouragement. I fought the panic by shaking it off and stepping up. And it wasn't long before I stepped out of the well, exhausted but triumphant.

"So no matter how difficult the situation, no matter how bad things get, no matter how much dirt gets dumped on you, just remember – shake it off and step up. You'll be alright."

# FOOD AND UTENSILS

## 353. Coffee Hater

Gustav III (1746-1792), the 18th century king of Sweden, believed that coffee was poisonous. In order to prove his theory, he commissioned a long-term experiment on two murderers who had been sentenced to death.

Each murderer was pardoned, one on the condition that he drink tea every day for the rest of his life, and the other on the condition that he drink coffee. Gustav then appointed two doctors to oversee the experiment and to see which of the subjects died first.

The doctors died first. Then King Gustav was assassinated in 1792 at the age of 46. Many years later, one of the murderers died at the age of 83. He was the tea drinker.

## 354. How Dinner Plates Were Invented

Plates for serving food were not used in Europe until the fifteenth century. Before that, food was usually served on thick, hollowed-out slabs of stale bread called trenchers, which were specially baked and allowed to harden so they could hold more food without falling apart.

The food's juices would soak into the bread, and after the meal the soggy trenchers might be fed to the dogs or offered to poor peasants waiting outside for leftovers.

The evolution of modern plates began when trenchers were carved out of wood, sometimes with special compartments for spices and condiments. Wooden trenchers were later replaced by clay or ceramic plates, which did not rot under long use.

This explains why today we call a heavy eater a "trencherman."

## 355. History of the Fork

The fork, a common dining utensil today, was not always so popular.

Its first ancestor appeared in Tuscany during the 11th century, but these tiny forks were very rare.

In 1611, Thomas Coryate (1577-1617) brought several of these oddities to England after he ran across them in Italy. People were not interested. In fact, they were vehemently opposed to using forks. They preferred using their fingers.

As a matter of fact, it was not unusual for ministers to preach against the use of forks, and they often used funerals to declare death was God's way of showing displeasure over the use of such a novelty.

It was not until the end of the 18th century that forks found favor. French nobility began using forks as a statement of refinement, and the use of fingers started getting frowns.

## 356. History of Spoons

To some, a spoon may be a shovel used to scoop nourishment through a hole in one's face. But, if you think about it, a spoon is never less than an elegant tool, a utensil cited in Exodus, crafted by the Egyptians of ivory, with pointed edges by the Romans (for spiking the tips of eggs, where evil spirits were believed to dwell), fashioned from silver as early as the fourth century, and in the Middle Ages of rock crystal for the rich, the poor being forced to use horn.

## 357. Preserving Food

The fact that French currency became almost worthless during Napoleon's (1769-1821) repeated wars was ultimately responsible for the invention of a method to preserve food without refrigeration.

Seeking to restore French industry, Napoleon established prizes of up to 100,000 francs for new ideas. An early winner was Nicholas Appert (1750-1841), a champagne bottler and cook.

Appert placed food to be preserved in champagne bottles, sealed them with corks, and placed them in boiling water for varying lengths of time. The French innovator had inadvertently discovered what no one was to verify until half a century later: that heat sterilizes food.

Preserved by Appert's method were meat stew, soup, milk, peas, beans, cherries, asparagus, artichokes, spinach, tomatoes, prunes and many more.

In March of 1809 the French Society for the Encouragement of Industry awarded Appert a prize of 12,000 francs on condition that he make his methods known by publishing them.

Thus was born our capability to can and preserve all manner of foodstuffs for easy transport and use in a variety of conditions.

## 358. History of the Hamburger

The hamburger originated with the warring Mongolian and Turkish tribes known as Tatars who shredded low-quality beef before cooking to make it taste better.

The dish was introduced to Germany sometime before the 14th century where it was spiced and prepared cooked or raw, from the town of Hamburg. The dish became known as "Hamburg steak."

In the 1880s, German immigrants brought the Hamburg specialty to America where it became known as "hamburger steak." It was also known as "Salisbury Steak," named after the English Dr. J. H. Salisbury, who recommended to his patients that they eat beef three times a day.

The "hamburg" began its ascent to unparalleled popularity when it was served as a sandwich at the 1904 St. Louis World's Fair. Unfortunately, no one knows exactly how its association with ketchup started, or who thought of serving it on a bun.

Today, the hamburger is the most popular entree in American restaurants.

## 359. Diamond Jim Brady

Diamond Jim Brady (1856-1917), a flamboyant character who lived in New York City around the turn of the century, was a prodigious eater.

His average breakfast, as recorded by a New York restaurateur, went like this:

A gallon of orange juice, three eggs, a quarter of a loaf of corn bread, sirloin steak with fried potatoes, hominy grits and bacon, two muffins, and several pancakes.

For dinner, Diamond Jim's consumption might include three dozen oysters, two bowls of turtle soup, and six crabs as an appetizer. Restaurant owners referred to him as the best twenty-five customers they ever had.

## 360. The Wonderful Hot Dog

Although no one can agree on just how or when it was invented, the hot dog is a long-time food treat for Americans.

The National Hot Dog & Sausage Council reports that Americans consume more than 20 billion hot dogs in a year's time, nine billion of which are purchased in retail stores.

A total of 26 million hot dogs are consumed annually in major league baseball parks. Los Angeles's Dodgers' Stadium won the baseball hot dog derby in 2001 by selling 1.5 million hot dogs, tops among ball parks.

It is estimated that Americans will down 150 million hot dogs during Fourth of July celebrations. The Southeast eats more hot dogs than the rest of the country. Thirty-eight percent of annual hot dog consumption takes place between Memorial Day and Labor Day.

No one is quite sure when the hot dog in a bun originated but it is certain that the frankfurter was invented in the German city of Frankfurt in 1484, five years before Christopher Columbus set sail for the New World.

Mustard is the favorite hot dog topping of 30 percent of Americans; ketchup is second at 22 percent; chili is next at 12 percent; and 10 percent favor relish.

## 361. How the Hot Dog Got Its Name

The name "Hot Dog" was coined in 1906. A syndicated cartoonist named Tad Dorgan was enjoying a baseball game at New York's Polo Grounds. Inspired by the vendors' call of "Get your red hot dachshund dogs!" he went back to his office and began sketching a cartoon based on the notion of a real dachschund in a bun, covered with mustard.

When he couldn't come up with the correct spelling of dachschund, he supposedly just settled for "hot dog." The name stuck. Ironically, although Dorgan is clearly given credit for the name, the original cartoon has never been found.

## 362. Julia Child on Food

Julia Child (1912-2004) was probably the most widely-known authority on food preparation than anybody else on the planet. But throughout her long career, she was hounded by people she often referred to as "food police" — people who thought her recipes and culinary edicts were too high in fat and unhealthy.

To one of these critics, Childs sent the following recipe for a healthy life:

• Small helpings,

• no seconds,

• eat a little bit of everything,

• no snacking,

• have a good time,

• and pick your grandparents.

## 363. Mark Twain Food Memories

In an autobiographical sketch written in 1897-98, Mark Twain (Samuel Clemens) wrote down his memories of the food served at the Missouri farm owned by his uncle and aunt, John and Patsy Quarles, where he used to spend summers.

"It was a heavenly place for a boy, that farm of my uncle John's. The house was a double log one, with a spacious floor (roofed in) connecting it with the kitchen. In the summer the table was set in the middle of that shady and breezy floor, and the sumptuous meals — well, it makes me cry to think of them.

"Fried chicken, roast pig, wild and tame turkeys, ducks, and geese; venison just killed; squirrels, rabbits, pheasants, partridges, prairie chickens, home-made bacon and ham, hot biscuits, hot batter-cakes, hot buckwheat cakes, hot wheat-bread, hot rolls, hot corn pone; fresh corn boiled on the ear, succotash, butter-beans, string beans, tomatoes, peas, Irish potatoes, sweet potatoes, butter-milk, sweet milk, 'clabber', watermelons, musk melons, canteloups (sic) — all fresh from the garden — apple pie, peach pie, pumpkin pie, apple dumplings, peach cobbler — I can't remember the rest."

## 364. A True Story about Potatoes

It is hard to believe but potatoes were once believed to be poison. In eighteenth century France, people believed that potatoes caused leprosy.

A promoter of the potato was a French farmer named Parmentier. Parmentier believed the humble potato could be the salvation of French agriculture, but his efforts to get farmers to grow them met with great resistance. That is, until Benjamin Franklin came to his rescue.

Franklin, on diplomatic duty in Paris from the struggling American colonies, heard of Parmentier's problem and offered to help. He suggested to Parmentier that he stage a lavish banquet in which every course would be made of potatoes. And Franklin, who was then a most popular and famous man in Paris, agreed to attend as an honored guest.

At the banquet, Franklin gave every course a rave review. He gave particularly high praise to the bread which was made out of ground flour from potatoes. He even topped off the meal with a fermented potato drink that was not unlike vodka.

When news of the exclusive event swept France, including Franklin's rare remarks, farmers were soon stealing and planting potatoes grown in Parmentier's experimental gardens. It was not long before potatoes became a Parisian culinary passion.

## 365. Restaurant Advertising

"Le patron mange ici"

The translation is "The owner eats here."

Such signs are hung outside quality French restaurants to imply that, if the owner eats here, the food must be good.

## 366. History of the Sandwich

Whether it is totally true or not, the credit for inventing the sandwich is generally given to John Montagu (1718-1792), the fourth Earl of Sandwich. The year was 1762 and the location was London's Beef Steak Club.

An inveterate gambler, the 44-year-old Montagu reportedly did not want to leave the club's gambling table. So he requested his manservant to bring him meat between bread to satisfy his hunger.

Presto chango — the sandwich was born. At least that is the legend.

However, this account comes from the famous *Larousse Gastronomique* (1961):

Since the most faraway times it has been the custom in the French countryside to give workers in the fields meat for their meal enclosed between two pieces of wholemeal or black bread. Moreover, in all the southwest districts, it was customary to provide people setting out on a journey with slices of meat, mostly pork or veal cooked in the pot, enclosed, sprinkled with their succulent juices, between two pieces of bread. Sandwiches made with sardines, tuna fish, anchovies, sliced chicken and even with flat omelettes were known in France well before the word, coming from England, had entered into French culinary terminology.

# FREEDOM

### 367. Loss of Freedom

A bitter quarrel arose between the horse and the stag in the days when both creatures roamed wild in the forest. The horse came to the hunter to ask him to take his side in the feud.

The hunter agreed, but added: "If I am to help you punish the stag, you must let me place this iron bit in your mouth and this saddle upon your back."

The horse was agreeable to the man's conditions and he soon was bridled and saddled. The hunter sprang into the saddle, and together they soon had put the stag to flight.

When they returned, the horse said to the hunter: "Now if you will get off my back and remove the bit and saddle, I won't require your help any longer."

"Not so fast, friend horse," replied the hunter. "I have you under bit and spur, and from now on you shall remain the slave of man."

And that is how the wild horse lost his freedom.

Moral: Freedom is too high a price to pay for revenge or to get one's way.

### 368. The Four Freedoms

Franklin Delano Roosevelt (1882-1945), the 32nd President of the United States, spelled out in a speech to Congress on January 6, 1941, the freedoms he hoped would be achieved by the world in the near future. Here they are:

"In the future days, which we seek to make secure, we look forward to a world founded upon four essential human freedoms.

"The first is freedom of speech and expression — everywhere in the world.

"The second is freedom of every person to worship God in his own way — everywhere in the world.

"The third is freedom from want — which, translated into world terms, means economic understandings which will secure to every nation a healthy peacetime life for its inhabitants — everywhere in the world.

"The fourth is freedom from fear — which translated into world terms, means a world-wide reduction of armaments to such a point and in such a thorough fashion that no nation will be in a position to commit an act of physical aggression against any neighbor – anywhere in the world."

## 369. Freedom and Athens

Sir Edward Gibbon (1737-1794), author of *The Decline and Fall of the Roman Empire*, wrote of the collapse of Athens, which was the birthplace of democracy. He judged that, in the end, more than they wanted freedom, the Athenians wanted security. Yet they lost everything — security, comfort and freedom. This was because they wanted not to give to society, but for society to give to them. The freedom they were seeking was freedom from responsibility.

## 370. Frederick Douglass on Freedom

Frederick Douglass (1817-1895), an early African-American abolitionist and gifted writer, said of freedom, "If there is no struggle, there is no progress. Those who profess to favor freedom, and yet deprecate agitation, are men who want crops without plowing up the ground. They want rain without thunder and lightning. They want the ocean without the awful roar of its many waters. This struggle may be a moral one; or it may be a physical one; or it may be both moral and physical; but it must be a struggle. Power concedes nothing without a demand."

## 371. Martin Luther King on Freedom

Martin Luther King Jr. (1929-1968) the revered American civil rights reformer, and for which he gave his life, was given the Nobel Peace Prize in 1964. He said of freedom, "When we let freedom ring, when we let it ring from every village and every hamlet, from every state and every city, we will be able to speed up that day when all of God's children, black men and white men, Jews and Gentiles, Protestants and Catholics, will be able to join hands and sing in the words of the old Negro spiritual, 'Free at last! Free at last! Thank God Almighty, we are free at last!'"

## 372. Drucker on Freedom

Peter Drucker (1909-2005), the Austrian-born American management consultant whose insights did much to change the business world, said this of freedom, "Freedom is not fun. It is not the same as individual happiness, nor is it security or peace or progress. It is a responsible choice. Freedom is not so much a right as a duty.

"Real freedom is not freedom from something; that would be license. It is freedom to choose between doing or not doing something, to act one way or another, to hold one belief or the opposite. It is not 'fun' but the heaviest burden laid on man; to decide his own individual conduct as well as the conduct of society and to be responsible for both decisions."

## 373. Servitude Is Man's Natural Condition

Adlai Stevenson (1900-1965), an eloquent American politician and diplomat who once ran for presidential office, said, "If freedom had been the happy, simple, relaxed state of ordinary humanity, man would have everywhere been free — whereas through most of time and space he has been in chains. Do not let us make any mistake about this. The natural government of man is servitude. Tyranny is the normal pattern of government."

# FRIENDSHIP

## 374. Three Kinds of Friendship

Aristotle (384-322 B.C.), a pupil of Plato, viewed friendship among the highest virtues. It was an essential element in a full, virtuous, and worthwhile life. For Aristotle, there were three kinds of friendship:

1.  Friendship of pleasure: two people are wonderfully happy in one another's company.
2.  Friendship of utility: two people assist one another in everyday aspects of life.
3.  Friendship of virtue: two people mutually admire one another and will be on their best behavior in order not to jeopardize their relationship.

## 375. Washington on Friendship

George Washington (1732-1799), the first President of the United States wrote the following advice on friendship to his nephew, Bushrod Washington on January 15, 1783:

"Be courteous to all, but intimate with few; and let those few be well tried before you give them your confidence. True friendship is a plant of slow growth, and must undergo and withstand the shocks of adversity before it is entitled to the appellation. Let your heart feel for the afflictions and distress of every one, and let your hand give in proportion to your purse, remembering always the estimation of the widow's mite, that it is not everyone that asketh that deserveth charity; all, however, are worthy of the inquiry, or the deserving may suffer."

## 376. Thoreau on Friendship

Henry David Thoreau (1817-1862) was one of America's most famous and articulate naturalists, as well as a philosopher whose thoughts and writings are still cherished today. Below is his definition of friendship:

"A friend is one who incessantly pays us the compliment of expecting from us all the virtues, and who can appreciate them in us.

"The friend asks no return but that his friend will religiously accept and wear and not disgrace his apotheosis of him. They cherish each other's hopes. They are kind to each other's dreams.

"That kindness which has so good a reputation elsewhere can least of all consist with this relation, and no such affront can be offered to a friend, as a conscious good-will, a friendliness which is not a necessity of the friend's nature.

"Friendship is never established as an understood relation. It is a miracle which requires constant proofs. It is an exercise of the purest imagination and of the rarest faith.

"We do not wish for friends to feed and clothe our bodies – neighbors are kind enough for that — but to do the life office to our spirit. For this, few are rich enough, however well disposed they may be...

"The language of friendship is not words, but meanings. It is an intelligence above language."

## 377. An Arabian Proverb about Friendship

A friend is one to whom one may pour out all the contents of one's heart, chaff and grain together, knowing that the gentlest of hands will take and sift it, keep what is worth keeping and with the breath of kindness blow the rest away.

## 378. What Is a Friend?

The following description of friendship was discovered on the wall of a doctor's office. It was attributed to C. Raymond Beran, who was not otherwise identified:

"Friends are people with whom you care to be yourself. Your soul can be naked with them. They ask you to put on nothing, only to be what you are.

"They do not want you to be better or worse. When you are with them, you feel like a prisoner feels who has been declared innocent. You do not have to be on your guard. You can say what you think, as long as it is genuinely you.

"Friends understand those contradictions in your nature that lead others to misjudge you. With them you breathe freely. You can avow your little vanities and envies and hates and vicious sparks, your meannesses and absurdities, and in opening them up to friends, they are lost, dissolved on the white ocean of their loyalty.

"They understand. You do not have to be careful. You can abuse them, neglect them, tolerate them. Best of all, you can keep still with them. It does not matter. They like you. They understand. You can weep with them, sing with them, laugh with them, pray with them. Through it all — and underneath — they see, know, and love you."

"What is a friend? Just one, I repeat, with whom you dare to be yourself."

### 379. Oscar Wilde on Friendship

Oscar Wilde (1854-1900), the Irish poet, wit and dramatist, was a major literary talent in every way. Here are some his quite different thoughts on what he expected of friendship:

"If a friend of mine gave a feast, and did not invite me to it, I should not mind a bit. But if a friend of mine had a sorrow and refused to allow me to share it, I should feel it most bitterly.

"If a friend shut the doors of the house of mourning against me, I would move back again and again and beg to be admitted so that I might share in what I was entitled to share. If my friend thought me unworthy, unfit to weep with him, I should feel it as the most poignant humiliation..."

### 380. Victor Hugo on Friendship

Victor Hugo (1802-1885), a distinguished French writer and novelist, composed this unusual analogy between his favorite old coat and friendship:

"My coat and I live comfortably together. It has assumed all my wrinkles, does not hurt me anywhere, has moulded itself on my deformities, and is complacent to all my movements, and I only feel its presence because it keeps me warm. Old coats and old friends are the same thing."

# FUTURE

### 381. Read This and Cheer Up

"The world is too big for us. Too much going on, too many crimes, too much violence and excitement. Try as you will, you get behind in the race, in spite of yourself. It's an incessant strain to keep pace...And still, you lose ground. Science empties its discoveries on you so fast that you stagger beneath them in hopeless bewilderment. The political world is news seen so rapidly you're out of breath trying to keep pace with who's in and who's out. Everything is high pressure. Human nature can't endure much more!"

Note: This editorial appeared on June 16, 1833, in the *Atlantic Journal*.

Some things never change.

## 382. Keep Looking Forward

A farmer famed for his agricultural know-how once hired a neighbor's teenage boy to help him do the spring plowing.

The farmer believed in letting people do their work without undue supervision, so he placed the boy on the tractor and went over the hill to work on another field.

Anxious to plow straight furrows, the inexperienced, teenager kept looking over his shoulder to check how he was doing.

Despite this precaution, he was dismayed to find that, by the time he reached the edge of the field, the row he was plowing was noticeably crooked. He tried and tried but he was unable to keep the rows straight.

When the farmer came back to see how the young man was doing, he instantly saw what was the problem.

Taking the boy aside, the farmer told him in a calm voice, "You can't plow a straight row if you continually look back. You must keep your eyes focused straight ahead. And always remember where you've been."

So it is with a lot of important tasks in life.

## 383. Politics and the Future

A journalist once asked Winston Churchill what were the desirable qualifications for a young man who wanted to enter politics.

Churchill scowled first at the question, then answered thoughtfully:
"It is the ability to foretell what is going to happen tomorrow, next week, next month and next year."

Then he stopped to gauge the effect of this statement on the surrounding journalists. Then he added:

"And to have the ability afterwards to explain why it didn't happen."

# GENIUS

### 384. Franklin the Innovator

Benjamin Franklin (1706-1790) was the youngest son of a youngest son of a youngest son of a youngest son.

He was the first American philosopher. He was the first American ambassador.

He invented the harmonica. He invented the rocking chair. He invented the street lamp. He was the first political cartoonist. He was the best swimmer of his time. He originated the first circulating library. He discovered the Gulf Stream. He is the originator of Daylight Saving Time. He is the father of modern dentistry. He organized the first fire department. He originated the first street cleaning department of his city. He invented the lightning conductor. He established the modern post office system. And, lastly, he was a printer.

### 385. Disabilities Didn't Stop Him

Charles Steinmetz (1865-1923), the electrical genius, and one of the founding fathers of General Electric, was crippled from birth. His body was grotesque; he was so short in stature that he looked like a dwarf; he was a hunchback.

His mother had died before he was one year old. His father was comparatively poor, but was determined that, as far as possible, young Charles would have a thorough education. As for Charles, he couldn't run and play games as normal boys did, so he made up his mind that he would devote himself to science. He set this goal: "I will make discoveries that will help other people."

When he immigrated to the U.S., he could not speak a word of English. The port authorities were tempted to return him to his native Switzerland. His face was swollen from the cold he had endured on the boat passage across the Atlantic.

He was dwarfed and misshapen in body. His sight was defective. His clothes were shabby.

But Charles stayed, and even found a job that paid him twelve dollars a week. And he showed amazing abilities. The infant company, General Electric, quickly realized that in Charles Steinmetz they had one of the greatest experts in the world in the field of electricity. His career was marked by unparalleled research and development.

When Steinmetz died in 1923, one writer said, "This deformed hunchback had the mind of an angel and the soul of a seer." Though he was twisted and dwarfed in body, Charles Steinmetz was a giant in mind and spirit.

## 386. Youthful Genius

Spectacular achievements accomplished at young ages abound.

WOLFGANG AMADEUS MOZART (1756-1797) wrote his first musical composition at age 4; LUDWIG VAN BEETHOVEN (1770-1827) at age 13; ALEXANDER THE GREAT (356 B.C.-323 B.C.), the great Macedonian leader, conquered most of the civilized world by 27 years of age; NAPOLEON (1769-1821) defeated Italy by age 26; SAMUEL COLT (1914-1962) devised a wooden model of his revolver at 16 years; ELI WHITNEY (1765-1825) invented the cotton gin at age 28; MICHAEL FARADAY (1791-1867) developed the electric motor at age 21, perhaps the single most important invention of the Industrial Era; ALBERT EINSTEIN (1879-1955) began work on his space-time relativity theory at 26 years of age and suggested that mass could be converted into energy, stepping-stones leading to inauguration of the Atomic Age and space travel; CHARLES DARWIN (1809-1882) began work on his revolutionary theory of evolution at age 27, laying the foundation for the impending Bio-Tech/Life Science Era that looms ahead in this century.

## 387. Inventor Extraordinaire

As if the electric light, the phonograph, and the motion-picture camera weren't enough, Thomas Edison (1847-1931) also invented the following: wax paper, the mimeograph machine, the dictating machine, a variety of Portland cement, an electric vote recorder, the chemical phenol, an electric pen, and a version of the stock ticker.

He also gave us the light socket and light switch, and when he died he was working on a machine that, in his words, was "so sensitive that if there is life after death, it will pick up the evidence."

Thomas Edison averaged one new patent every two weeks of his adult life. He was quoted in *Harper's Monthly Magazine* as saying, "Genius is one per cent inspiration and ninety-nine percent perspiration."

## 388. Nepotism Not Spoken Here

When the famous scientist Albert Einstein (1979-1955) paid a visit to Hollywood's Warner Brothers Studios, all the brass turned out to greet him.

"This is the great Professor Einstein," said an executive introducing Einstein to studio head Jack Warner. "He invented the theory of relativity."

"Professor," said Warner, "I have developed a theory about relativity of my own."

"Really?" said Einstein.

"Yes," said Warner in all seriousness. "I don't hire them!"

## 389. Bernard Shaw's Regrets

About a year before his death, George Bernard Shaw (1856-1950), the Irish-born playwright and critic, granted a rare interview to a well-known journalist.

The reporter's questions were designed to lead the famous English playwright to reminisce.

One of the journalist's probing questions was, "Mr. Shaw, you have known some of the greatest men of our time — statesmen, artists, philosophers, and writers — and you've outlived most of them. Suppose it were possible for you to talk with one of them again, whom would it be? Which man do you miss the most?"

Without hesitation, Shaw, whose biting wit had made him internationally known, retorted, "The man I miss most is the man I could have been."

## 390. Einstein's Sense of Humor

Albert Einstein's driver used to sit at the back of the hall during each of his lectures. After a period of time, the driver remarked to the famous scientist that he could probably give the lecture himself, having heard it so many times.

So at the next lecture stop, Einstein and the driver switched places, with Einstein sitting at the back, dressed in the driver's uniform. The driver gave the lecture, flawlessly.

At lecture's end, a member of the audience asked a detailed scientific question about some of the subject matter. Without missing a beat, the "lecturer" replied, "Well, the answer to that question is so simple, I'll let my driver, sitting at the back there, answer it."

And he did.

## 391. One Secret of Genius

Although many critics of his day thought Ludwig van Beethoven's (1770-1827) music was radical, the public absolutely adored his work.

After the performance of one of his compositions, a group of well-wishers gathered around Beethoven to congratulate him. One woman said to him, "I wish God had bestowed on me such genius."

Beethoven replied, "It isn't genius, madam, nor is it magic. All you have to do is practice on your piano eight hours a day for 40 years."

## 392. Einstein's Research Laboratory

When Albert Einstein (1879-1855) was in residence at the Institute for Advanced Studies at Princeton during his later years, a guest asked him if Einstein would show him his laboratory.

The famous scientist and mathematician smiled, held up his fountain pen and pointed to his head.

# GLOBAL

### 393. Geography Lessons

Jigsaw puzzles were first made to teach geography in England in the late 18th century. They were called "dissected maps," and were made by drawing a map on a sheet of wood and sawing it into irregular pieces with a saw.

Later, different kinds of pictures were made into puzzles, with topics like history, alphabets, botany, and zoology.

Jigsaw puzzles reached a peak of popularity in the 1860s in Great Britain and the United States. During the Great Depression, their relative cheapness made them popular again as gifts.

### 394. The Global Village

According to a report issued by the World Development Forum in the 1990s, if you lived in a representative global village of 1,000 people:

- 565 would be Asians
- 210 Europeans
- 86 Africans
- 80 South Americans
- 60 North Americans

There would be:

- 300 Christians (183 Catholics, 84 Protestants and 33 Orthodox)
- 175 Moslems
- 138 Hindus
- 55 Buddhists
- 47 Animists
- 210 without any religion or confessed atheists

Of this group:

- 60 would control half the total income

- 500 would be hungry

- 600 would live in shantytowns

- 700 would be illiterate

## 395. A Second Global Village Report

The following is a report issued by the Trilateral Commission, also in the 1990s. If we could shrink the Earth's population to a village of precisely 100 people with all existing human ratios remaining the same, it would look like this:

There would be 57 Asians, 21 Europeans, 14 from the Western Hemisphere (North and South) and 8 Africans.

- 51 would be female; 49 would be male.

- 70 would be non-white; 30 white.

- 70 would be non-Christian; 30 Christian.

- 50 percent of the entire world's wealth would be in the hands of only

- 6 people and all 6 would be citizens of the United States.

- 80 would live in substandard housing.

- 70 would be unable to read.

- 50 would suffer from malnutrition. 1 would be near death. 1 would be near birth. Only 1 would have a college education; and no one would own a computer.

## 396. Growth of Cities

If Marco Polo's (1254-1324) writings can be trusted, Kinsai in China — on the site of today's Hankow — may have had three million inhabitants in the thirteenth century. Edo — as Tokyo was first called — seems to have reached a million by the eighteenth century.

However, the concept of what constituted a "big city" did not go much beyond 100,000 until the beginnings of the nineteenth century. At the time of the American Revolution, only two American cities, Boston and Philadelphia, had even reached 50,000.

As industrialization and worldwide trade spread, the city of a million became more common. London reached the mark in the 1820s. By 1900, there were 11 "million-cities," six of them in Europe. But the jump from two to 11 in the nineteenth century was followed by an infinitely more formidable acceleration in our own time. By 1950, there were 75 "million-cities," 51 of them in developed regions, 24 in the developing world.

## 397. History of Roads

Of all the world's ancient civilizations, only two ever produced a complete network of roads. The first such system was organized by the Romans. Their roads covered 56,000 miles, linking countries in Europe, the Near East and parts of Africa.

Second only to the Romans were the Incas. Like the Romans, the Incas themselves did not create anything new. Thus, a road network begun by the Chimus was improved and extended. At its peak, the Inca empire could boast 10,000 miles of highway extending from present day Argentina to Colombia.

## 398. How the Earth Was First Measured

Twenty-two hundred years ago, a geographer by the name of Eratosthenes (276 BC-194 BC), who was the chief librarian at the University of Alexandria in Egypt, did something extraordinary. With the equivalent of a simple stick, he measured the diameter of the earth.

From information in the library, Eratosthenes knew that at noon on June 22, the sun would be directly overhead of the town of Syene, 800 kilometers due south of Alexandria, and thus cast no shadow. At the exact same time, Eratosthenes measured the shadow cast by a vertical pillar in Alexandria and found it to be one-eighth of the height of the pillar. From that, and the use of simple geometry, he was able to calculate the diameter of the globe as a multiple of the distance between two cities.

Twenty-two hundred years later, we have more sophisticated tools. Our sticks have become gamma-ray and x-ray telescopes, hyper-spectral imaging, and the Mars rovers. Our simple geometry has become advanced physics coupled with complex computer programs.

## 399. Global Water

The same glass of water you drink today could also have been drunk by Napoleon (1761-1821) or Cleopatra (69 BC-30 BC) or Julius Caesar (100 BC-44 BC). In fact, no new water has been created since the beginning of time; 72% of the earth's surface is covered by water that is constantly recycling itself.

## 400. Population Growth

The following is according to the *Encyclopedia Britannica*.

At the time of King David (1000 BC), there were approximately 150 million people on earth.

By the time of Christ, the figure had doubled to 300 million.

Due to wars and plagues, the population increased very little for the next 1,500 years.

By the 1600s, when the Pilgrims emigrated to the New World, there were about 500 million people on the planet — (one-half billion).

By 1750, conventionally the beginning of the Industrial Revolution in Britain, world population may have been as high as 800,000,000.

The world reached 1 billion about 1800.

By 1930, the population reached 2 billion.

By 1960, 3 billion.

By 1974, 4 billion.

In 1999, 6 billion.

By 2025, the world's population is projected to be 7.8 billion.

By 2050, nearly 9 billion.

According to the Population Reference Bureau, every minute 101 people in the world die — and 261 people are born.

## 401. World's First Map

The first map of all the known lands was probably drawn by the Greek philosopher Anaximander of Miletus (610 BC-ca. 546 BC). He may have been the first person to attempt such a map, although in several places there were people who could draw local maps.

Anaximander collected information from voyagers stopping at Miletus, and tried to construct a full picture of the entire world, as it was known at the time. He drew the Mediterranean Sea surrounded by land, with a larger ocean around the land.

He conceived of the Earth as a cylinder, suspended in empty space, with the sphere of the heavens rotating around it once each day. He said that the curvature of the cylinder explained the variation in the angle of the sun with latitude.

## 402. How the Continents Were Formed

Throughout Earth's history the continents have been moving around, pushed by deep currents of semi-liquid rock. About 400 million years ago all the land masses came together to form one single continent. In those days plants had just started coming on to land, along with primitive scorpion-like creatures.

The huge mass called Pangea formed when the two smaller continents Gondwana and Laurasia slowly merged, a process which took millions of years. After more millions of years, Pangea began to break apart and some of the continents we have today were formed.

About 95 million years ago, today's continents of Africa and South America split apart, forming the Atlantic Ocean. About 55 million years ago, the subcontinent of India pushed up against southern Asia forming the magnificent Himalaya Mountains.

# GOOD LUCK

### 403. Silver Pine Cones

Years ago there lived a poor family with barely enough to eat and little wood for a fire to keep warm. In desperation the mother went to the woods to gather pine cones, some to burn, some to sell to buy food.

Suddenly she heard a voice, "Why are you stealing my pine cones?" Beside her was an elf, to whom she told her sad story. With a smile he said, "Go into the next forest. The pine cones there will serve you much better."

When she reached the next forest she was very tired. She let her basket drop to the ground and down fell dozens of pine cones! She gathered them and returned home. When she reached her doorstep she discovered every cone had turned to silver! The family would never be poor again.

To this day the people of the Harz Mountains in Germany keep a silver pine cone on the dresser. For, as legend has it, a silver pine cone will bring good fortune your way!

### 404. Accidental Discovery

That we often stumble onto good things when we are looking for something else is aptly dramatized in this story written by Horace Walpole:

"The Three Princes of Serendip went out searching for treasure. They didn't find what they were looking for, but they kept finding things just as valuable." It is from this legend that we get the word "serendipity."

### 405. Chinese Formula

"Feng Shui" — the two Chinese characters that stand for "wind" and "water" – is a 4,000-year-old technique for improving your chances in life by arranging furniture, travel dates, choice of mistress, and so on in a way that takes best advantage of luck and natural forces.

## 406. FDR's View of Good Luck

Franklin Delano Roosevelt (1882-1945), the 32nd President of the United States, had both good and bad luck in his life. He was born into a wealthy, distinguished family and was blessed with personal charm and good looks. Yet, as a young man, he was stricken by polio and spent the rest of his life with his legs encased in steel braces, able to walk only with assistance.

However, he never lost his sense of humor. About luck, he once said, "I think we consider too much the good luck of the early bird, and not enough the bad luck of the early worm."

# GREED

## 407. Whose House Are You Building?

There is a story of a wealthy man who called his servant in and told him that he was leaving the country for a year and that while he was gone, he wanted the servant to build him a new house. The wealthy man told him to build it well, and that when he returned, he would pay all the bills for material and for his labor.

Shortly after the employer left, the servant decided that he was foolish to work so hard, so he started cutting corners and began to squander the money he saved on personal extravagances.

When his employer came back, he paid all the bills, and then asked the servant, "Are you satisfied with the house?" When the servant said he was, his employer said, "Good, because the house is yours. You can live in it the rest of your life."

Question: If your life could be compared to a house, are you building the kind of house that you will be proud to live in forever? Are you cutting corners and squandering time, commitment, and effort? Are you giving it your best?

## 408. A Lesson in Greed

Leo Tolstoy (1828-1910), the famous Russian novelist, tells a legend of Pakhom, a rich peasant who was never satisfied. He always wanted more.

Pakhom heard of a wonderful chance to get land cheap. For a thousand rubles he could have all the land he could walk around in a day.

He arose at dawn and set out. He walked on, and on, and on, and went so far that he realized he must walk very fast if he was to get back on time to claim the land. He quickened his pace; he ran, and ran, and ran.

As he came within sight of the starting place, Pakhom exerted his last energies, plunged over the line, fell to the ground, and collapsed. A stream of blood poured out of his mouth and he lay dead.

A worker took a hoe, dug a grave, made it just long enough and wide enough, and buried him.

This, after all, was all the land Pakhom really needed.

## 409. Be Careful of What You Wish for

There once lived a stonecutter who was content with his life and work. That is until the day he delivered a piece of stone to a client who was a merchant.

As the stonecutter gazed at the merchant's lavish home and belongings, he was overcome with envy. "I wish I were a merchant with such fine things," he thought to himself.

Amazingly, the stonecutter suddenly found that he had indeed become a merchant, and possessed with a luxurious home and rich furnishings. He was quite happy until one day he saw the local Prince passing through town, followed by a cheering crowd.

"How much better it would be if I were a Prince," he said to himself. And suddenly he found himself dressed in regal garb and riding a fine stallion. But guess what, as he rode under the hot sun wearing such heavy clothing, he soon grew weary and cranky.

"If I were indeed the sun," he said to himself, "then I could have a profound effect on the entire universe, not just one little town." At that moment, he was indeed magically turned into the sun. But it was not long before he soon became irritated that clouds were blocking the rays he was sending to earth.

So he wished he was a "cloud" instead of the sun and soon he found himself floating over a mighty mountain dominating a green valley. The "cloud" showered the area with rain day after day and in no time sprigs of green began sprouting on the landscape. But the mountain itself never changed and he was again frustrated.

So the "cloud" wished it could be a "mountain." "Certainly nothing could be more powerful than that," he said to himself. And, for a while, he was content to be a "mountain." That is until one day a young stonecutter came along and began to chisel away part of him.

As the young stonecutter chiseled away to create a block of stone for a client, the "mountain" suddenly yearned to be a man again and a stonecutter at that. After all, he remembered enjoying the stonecutter profession and he had not found fulfillment in wishing he could be something or someone else.

The happy ending to the story is that, as before, he suddenly got his wish. He found himself again to be a simple stonecutter.

As the old saying goes, "Be careful what you wish for, you may get it."

## 410. Buried Treasure

Once upon a time, there was an old farmer who had a rich farm and three sons. There was only one problem — all three boys were bone lazy and outdid each other in shirking their duties.

Because of this, and despite their father's hard work from sunup to sundown, the farm went down hill year after year. Tired and discouraged after years of overwork, the farmer finally became seriously ill. From his deathbed, the farmer sent for his sons, telling them that he had an important secret to tell them.

"My sons," said the old man, "I have never told you before but a great treasure lies hidden on this farm which I am about to leave you in my will. If you can find it, you will all be wealthy beyond your wildest dreams."

"Where is it hidden?" asked the three sons, greed shining in their eyes.

"I am about to tell you," wheezed the old man, "you will have to dig for it..." And with a sudden gasp, he died before he could tell them.

Immediately, the sons went to work with spades and plows up and down the long-neglected fields. Even the little garden in back of the farm house was thoroughly tilled. Every piece of earth on the estate was turned over, not once but several times.

The three boys were angry at first when no treasure was found. But after a while, they discovered they enjoyed working the rich, fertile soil. And when seeds were scattered over the fields, a bumper crop sprung up and was sold in the market for top prices. The yield was especially great because the soil had been cultivated so thoroughly.

Thus it was that the three lazy sons discovered the treasure that was buried on the farm all along. Finding it had only required some diligent effort to bring it forth.

## 411. The Golden Goose

An ancient Aesop fable tells the story of a man who had a goose which laid him a golden egg every day.

But, not contented with this, which increased rather than lessened his avarice, he decided to kill the goose and cut up her belly. In that way he would possess in its entirety the inexhaustible treasure which he fancied she had within her.

He did so and, to his great sorrow and disappointment, found nothing.

## 412. Helping Others

In a far away kingdom many years ago lived a young man whose official title was "Server of the Kingdom." Specifically, his duty was cup bearer for the King.

One day, while he was out walking in a nearby forest, he was approached by a genie. As so often happens in tales like this, the genie offered to grant the young man a wish.

"Any wish?" he exclaimed.

"Anything," replied the genie.

The young man thought for a moment, then told the genie how all of his life he had served others. "I know what I want," he blurted out. "I want people to serve me for a change!"

The genie said, "Granted!" and vanished into the forest.

Eager to test his newfound power, the young man walked back to his quarters in the castle. As he approached the gate of the royal palace, a servant bowed to him and opened the gate for him.

That night after he finished his dinner, a servant stepped forward with a linen napkin to wipe his mouth while the servant cleared his table. When the young man prepared for bed that evening, a servant appeared to turn down the bed covers.

The next morning he was greeted by still another servant who retrieved his slippers and prepared a breakfast for him fit for a king.

Though the young man valiantly tried to perform his duties as the King's cup bearer, somebody was always there to perform the chore for him.

Throughout his life all he had ever done was serve others. It wasn't long before he realized that he was no longer allowed to do anything for anyone, and he didn't like how this made him feel.

Wisdom Well Said ❖ 193

For the first thirty days the novelty of his good fortune was interesting; for the next thirty days it began to be irritating, and by the last thirty days, he couldn't stand it any longer. In a growing rage, he went out into the forest again looking for the genie. After a three-day search, he found him near where they had first met.

In tears, the young man told the genie, "I am so glad I found you. I've changed my mind. I want to go back to serving others."

Without any emotion, the genie shook its head and said, "I can't help you."

But the young man angrily persisted, "You don't understand. I am willing to do anything to dedicate my life to my fellow man." Again the genie stated, "There's nothing I can do."

But the king's young servant wouldn't quit. He pleaded, "Kind sir, I would rather be in hell than not be able to serve my fellow man!"

And to this the genie replied, "My dear young man, where do you think you've been for the past ninety days?"

## 413. Acre of Diamonds

The following story was used by Dr. Russell H. Conwell to raise millions of dollars to help fund the formation of Temple University in Philadelphia. He used the story to fire the imagination of listeners during more than 6,000 fund-raising lectures. The story goes like this:

Many years ago a young American was traveling down the Tigris and Euphrates rivers in the Middle East and was accompanied by an old Arab guide he had hired in Baghdad.

During the trip, the old guide told him a story about an ancient Persian named Ali Hafed. Hafed owned a very large farm, orchards, grain fields, gardens, and money coming in from loans made. He was a wealthy and contented man.

But one day Hafed was visited by an ancient Buddhist priest who told him how the earth was created and, particularly, about the most valuable thing in the world — diamonds!

Said the priest, "A diamond is a congealed drop of sunlight." The priest told Hafed that, if he had one diamond the size of his thumb, he could purchase the entire county, and if he had a mine of diamonds he could place his children upon thrones through the influence of his great wealth.

This set Hafed's mind ablaze with a lust for such great wealth. So he sold his farm, left his family in charge of a neighbor, and began a search for diamonds in places the priest had said might contain them. Hafed spent all his money on his lifelong, unsuccessful search and died, far from home, a penniless, suffering, disappointed old man.

The man who purchased Hafed's farm one day led his camel into the garden to drink, and as that camel put its nose into the shallow water of the garden brook, Hafed's successor noticed a curious flash of light emanating from a black stone in the stream. He pulled out the black stone and placed it on the mantel of his home, and forgot all about it.

A few days later the same Buddhist priest who had taught Hafed about diamonds came to meet the new owner and saw the black stone. "That is a diamond!" he shouted. When his host said it was just a pebble he had picked up in the garden, the priest replied, "I tell you I know a diamond when I see it. I know positively that is a diamond."

It turns out that the farm became the famed diamond mine of Golconda, the richest diamond mine in all history. The Kohinoor diamond and the crown jewels of England and Russia came from that mine.

The moral, of course, is that, if Hafed had spent the time and energy to explore his own farm, he would have discovered riches beyond his wildest dreams.

This story should teach us all that, if you wish to find greatness, and even wealth, you must first begin where you are — NOW. If you serve your community well, if you are an honest person, if you are a good provider for your family, whether you work in a shop or in a factory, whatever your occupation, you can find happiness and recognition if you do it well. To find success in any endeavor, you must first look for your "acre of diamonds" right where you live.

# GRIEF, LOSS

## 414. Dealing with Grief

One of the most common questions that family and friends ask is how long does it take to "get over" the death of a loved one.

Native American culture holds many lessons about grief and its duration. The Native American legend of the Caterpillar People holds lessons for us all in grief. This legend is traditionally told during funeral services of the Shoshone tribe.

"Long ago, there were two caterpillar people who loved each other very much. When the caterpillar man died the caterpillar woman was overcome by her grief. In her remorse, she withdrew into herself and pulled her sorrow around her like a shawl. She walked and mourned for a year and because the world is a circle she ended up where she had started.

"The Creator looked down upon her and told her that she had suffered too long.

"'Now,' He told her, 'is the time for you to step into a new world of beauty.' He clapped his hands and the caterpillar woman burst forth as a butterfly. Her world was now full of beauty and color."

## 415. Mourning Diana

The following poem by Henry Van Dyke (1852-1933), American clergyman poet and educator, was read at the funeral of Princess Diana in Westminster Abbey in London on September 6, 1997, by one of Diana's sisters, Lady Jane Fellowes:

Time is
Too Slow for those who Wait,
Too Swift for those who Fear,
Too Long for those who Grieve,
Too Short for those who Rejoice,
But for those who Love
Time is not

### 416. Test of Courage

Daphne du Maurier (1907-1989), English writer, wrote this of loss, "I would say to those who mourn — and I can only speak from my own experience — look upon each day that comes as a challenge, as a test of courage. The pain will come in waves, some days worse than others, for no apparent reason. Accept the pain. Do not suppress it. Never attempt to hide grief from yourself. Little by little, just as the deaf, the blind, the handicapped develop with time an extra sense to balance disability, so the bereaved, the widowed, will find new strength, new vision, born of the very pain and loneliness which seem, at first, impossible to master.

### 417. The Emotions

Zane Grey (1872-1939) American author of western novels, wrote of human emotions, "To bear up under loss, to fight the bitterness of defeat and the weakness of grief, to be victor over anger, to smile when tears are close, to resist evil men and base instincts, to hate hate and to love love, to go on when it would seem good to die, to seek ever after the glory and the dream, to look up with unquenchable faith in something evermore about to be, that is what any man can do, and so be great."

# HELPING OTHERS

### 418. Kindness to Strangers

When he was President of the United States, Thomas Jefferson (1743-1826) was riding across the country on horseback with a group of companions.

The mounted party arrived at a river which had flooded its banks during unusually heavy rains. The resulting flood had even washed the bridge away, so that the only possible way to cross the swollen river was on horseback. This would be an extremely dangerous maneuver that could even result in death by drowning one or more of the riders.

As the men in Jefferson's party struggled to ford the stream against the raging waters, an unmounted man stood on the riverbank and watched them with grave concern for how he was going to get across the river with no bridge and no horse. After several of Jefferson's group had successfully made it to the other side on horseback, the man asked President Jefferson if he could ride behind him when he and his horse tried to ford the river. Jefferson agreed and the two men, with some difficulty, made it safely across the raging river.

As the man slid off Jefferson's horse, one of Jefferson's party asked the stranger if he knew who Jefferson was. And he asked also why the stranger had chosen him to ask for help on the dangerous crossing.

On learning that his good Samaritan was the President of the United States, the man was shocked and embarrassed. Then he added, "All I know is that on some of your faces was written the answer 'No' and on some of your faces was written the answer 'Yes.' His was a 'Yes' face."

## 419. The Boy and the Starfish

There is a story about an old man and a boy who were walking along a deserted beach.

The boy kept picking up living starfish which had been washed up by the surf. Once he saw a starfish, the boy would pick it up and fling it back into the waves so that it would not die on the beach.

After the pair had walked a mile or so, and the boy had flung several dozen starfishes back into the ocean, the old man asked him why he was doing it.

"To save their lives," the boy said.

"But", said the old man, "there are thousands, even hundreds of thousands of starfish on the beach, mile after mile after mile. Does it really matter?"

The boy picked up still another starfish and flung it back into the life-giving water. "It does to this one," he said.

## 420. Love One Another

A great Amazon legend tells of a priest who was speaking with God about heaven and hell.

"I will show you hell," said God. They went into a room that had a delicious beef stew on the table, around which sat people chained to their benches who looked desperately famished. They held spoons with long handles that reached into the pot, but were too long to put the stew back into their mouths. Their suffering was terrible.

"Now, I will show you heaven," said God. They then went into an identical room with the savory stew on the table, around which sat people with identical spoons and handles, but they were well nourished and joyous.

The priest was baffled until God said, "Quite simply, you see, these people have learned to feed each other."

## 421. Kindness to Others

There is an old Chinese story about a woman who lost her only son and went to the holy man in her village and said, "What mystic powers do you have that will lift the ache from my heart?"

"Dear woman," he said gently, "there is a wonderful thing you can do. I want you to go and get me a mustard seed from a home that has no problems. Such a mustard seed can ward off your own problems."

So she traveled to a beautiful mansion. Nothing could possibly be wrong here, she thought. She knocked at the door and said, "I am looking for a mustard seed from a home where there are no problems. It's very important to me."

"Oh," they said, "you have come to the wrong house." They began listing all of their family problems, and the list went on and on.

The woman thought to herself, "Well, I certainly know something about problems, for I have my own. Maybe I can be of help to them." And she was. She listened and comforted them. The fact that she listened and cared helped them.

She then went on in her search to find the magic mustard seed. She went from house to house. But no matter where she went, to the wealthy or to the poor, she could not find such a seed. It simply was not to be found.

The woman found that troubles are universal and she learned that in giving of herself in love and compassion to others, her own pain vanished.

## 422. Caring for Others

Someone once asked the anthropologist Margaret Mead (1901-1978), "What is the first sign you look for to tell you of an ancient civilization?"

The interviewer had in mind a tool or article of clothing. But Margaret Mead surprised him by answering, "a healed femur" (thigh bone, for those of you who didn't study anatomy).

Explained the famous anthropologist, "When someone breaks a femur, they can't survive to hunt, fish or escape enemies unless they have help from someone else."

"Thus," she said, "a healed thigh bone indicates that someone else helped that person, rather than abandoning them and saving themselves."

## 423. Serving One's Neighbors

Once upon a time there was a blacksmith who worked hard at his trade. When the time came for him to die, an angel was sent to him and much to the angel's surprise he refused to go.

He pleaded with the angel that he was the only blacksmith in the area and it was time for all his neighbors to begin their planting and sowing. He was badly needed by his neighbors.

So the angel pleaded his case before God. The angel argued that the man didn't want to appear ungrateful, and that he was glad to have a place in the kingdom, but could he put off going for a while? The angel made his case and the blacksmith was allowed to continue working.

About a year or two later the angel came back again with the same message: the Lord was ready to share the fullness of the kingdom with him. But again the man was reluctant to go and said: "A neighbor of mine is seriously ill, and it's time for the harvest. A number of us are trying to save his crops so that his family won't become destitute. Can you please come back later." Persuaded, the angel left again, his mission unfulfilled.

Well, it got to be a pattern. Every time the angel came, the blacksmith had one excuse or another. The blacksmith would just shake his head and tell the angel where and why he was needed and decline.

Finally, the blacksmith grew very old, weary and tired. He decided it was time, and so he prayed: "God, if you'd like to send your angel again, I'd be glad to come home now."

Immediately the angel appeared at the man's bedside. The blacksmith said: "If you still want to take me home, I'm ready to live forever in the kingdom of heaven."

And the angel laughed and, looking at the blacksmith with delight, said: "Where do you think you've been all these years?" He was home.

## 424. Brotherly Love

There once were two brothers whose father had died and left them the family farm. One was married and had a large family to support. The other was single. The agreement was that the two brothers would share everything equally.

However, one day the single brother said to himself, "It's not right that we should share equally. I'm alone and my needs are simple." So every night he took a sack of grain from his bin and secretly dumped it into his brother's bin.

Meanwhile, the married brother said to himself, "It's not right that we should share the produce and the farm's profit equally. After all, I am married and I will have my wife and grown children to look after me in the years ahead. My brother has no one." So each night he took a sack of grain and dumped it secretly into his single brother's bin.

For years both men were puzzled as to why their personal supply of grain never dwindled. Then one dark night the two brothers bumped into each other and it suddenly dawned on them what had been happening.

With a cry of deep affection, the two brothers dropped their sacks of grain and embraced one another.

# HOLIDAYS

### 425. Definition of the Word "Holiday"

The word "holiday" comes from the Anglo-Saxon "halig daeg," or "holy day." At first, holidays honored some sacred event or holy person.

Today, a holiday is any day on which people lay aside their ordinary duties and cares.

# HOLIDAYS – JANUARY

### 426. (January 1) How New Year's Day Was Selected

It is perfectly natural for us to accept without thinking that the new year has always began on January 1. Actually the new year for ancient Romans began in March. January and February had not been invented yet. The old Roman year totaled 304 days until, in 153 B.C., a Roman emperor added January and February to better align the tally of the moon's phases with the sun's cycle. Our present beginning date of January 1 and the length of our months (including an extra day on leap year) was established by Pope Gregory, XIII in 1582. However, believe it or not, staid old England and her colonies refused to adapt the new Gregorian calendar and continued to designate New Year's Day as March 25 until 1751.

As you may know, the month of January is named after Janus, the Roman god of doorways, a mythological character with two faces who could look in opposite directions at the same time. He was considered to be a special patron of all new undertakings, certainly a happy symbol of hope for the days to come.

# 427. New Year's Celebrations around the World

Not all countries celebrate the new year at the same time or in the same way because of different calendars and customs.

The Jewish New Year, Rosh Hashanah, is a holy time when people consider things they have done wrong in the past and promise to do better in the future. Special services are held in synagogues and the Shofar is blown.

The Muslim calendar is based on the movements of the moon, so the date of New Year is eleven days earlier each year. In some Islamic nations, people put grains of wheat or barley in a little dish to grow. By New Year's the grains have produced shoots, reminding the people of a new year of life.

Hindus do not all celebrate New Year in the same way or at the same time. The people of West Bengal wear flowers of pink, red, purple or white. In Kerala, mothers put food, flowers, and little gifts on a special tray to surprise their children. In central India, orange flags are flown from buildings. In Gujarat in western India, small oil lamps are lit along the roofs of buildings.

In Thailand, people throw water playfully at one another.

In Peru, it is the custom for women to wear yellow underwear.

In Vietnam, the New Year is called Tet Nguyen Dan, or Tet for short. It begins between January 21 and February 19, the exact date changing from year to year. The Vietnamese believe there is a god in every home who travels to heaven, traditionally on a carp, to report how good or bad each family member has been in the past year. Live carp are often purchased and set free in a river.

In Shinto families in Japan, a rope of straw is often placed across the front of houses to keep out evil spirits and bring happiness during the coming year.

The Chinese New Year is celebrated some time between January 17 and February 19, at the time of the new moon, and is called Yuan Tan. It is a time of parades and street processions involving large costumes and thousands of lanterns which light the way for the New Year. Firecrackers are used to frighten bad spirits away.

In Greece, New Year's Day is also the Festival of Saint Basil, who was famous for his kindness. Greek children leave their shoes by the fire on New Year's Day with the hope that he will come and fill them with gifts.

In some villages in Scotland, barrels of tar are set afire and rolled through the streets, signifying the burning of the old year.

In the United States, New Year's Eve is celebrated with parties and champagne by some, and by prayer and worship by others in traditional "watch night" services. January 1st is devoted to parades, football games, and for some, black-eyed peas.

All over the world, Robert Burns' poem, "Auld Lang Syne," is sung at midnight on New Year's Eve. The words "auld lang syne" mean "old, long time."

## 428. Japanese New Year

New Year's Day is the most important day of the whole calendar in Japan.

On New Year's Eve, houses are cleaned thoroughly from top to bottom, and are decorated for the morrow. When everything has been made clean and neat, the people of the house dress themselves in their finest clothes. Then the father of the household marches through the house, followed by all the family, and drives the evil spirits out. He throws dried beans in every corner, bidding the evil spirits to withdraw and good luck to enter.

## 429. (January 21) Martin Luther King, Jr.'s Birthday

The birthday of this great American civil rights leader is celebrated as a national holiday in the U.S. every January 21. Killed by an assassin's bullet in 1968, King (1929-1968) was a life-long advocate of non-violence and was awarded a Nobel Peace Prize on December 11, 1964.

Few people realize how King's devotion to the principle of non-violence was inspired by a visit to India in 1959 whose purpose was to learn from, and pay tribute to the works of that nation's great spiritual leader Mahatma Gandhi (1869-1948). King visited there with his wife, Coretta, from February 1 to March 10, and he made no secret of why he was there.

"He told the press, "To other countries I may go as a tourist, but to India I come as a pilgrim."

During his visit, King walked the very ground that the Mahatma had trod and he spoke personally with many of Gandhi's relatives and close friends. During the visit, King became convinced that true pacifism was "not simply non-violent resistance to evil," but that Gandhi had "resisted with love instead of hate."

After his lengthy visit, King wrote that he came away convinced "that the Christian doctrine of love, operating through the Gandhian method of non-violence is one of the most potent weapons available to an oppressed people in their struggle for freedom."

# HOLIDAYS – FEBRUARY

### 430. (February 2) Groundhog Day

This day is a holiday celebrated on February 2. In weather lore, if a groundhog, also known as a woodchuck, marmot or ground squirrel, emerges from its burrow on this day and fails to see its shadow because the weather is cloudy, winter will soon end. If the groundhog sees its shadow, it will return into its burrow and the winter will continue for six more weeks.

Groundhog Day proponents state that the forecasts are accurate 75 to 90 percent of the time. A Canadian study for 13 cities in the past 30 to 40 years puts the success rate level at 37 percent. Random chance at a correct guess would be about 50 percent.

### 431. (February 14) Valentine's Day

The origin of this popular holiday is shrouded in mystery. There were two early Christian martyrs named Valentine but any possible connection with the holiday remains vague. Another theory dating back to the Middle Ages is that birds begin to mate on February 14. Closer to home may be an ancient practice in which the names of young women were placed in a box from which was drawn by chance the name of a young man. The young man so matched then became the suitor of a young woman for the next year, or at least became her partner for a festival being held on

February 14. This custom continued for centuries. The young men and women who were paired by this method were expected to give presents to each other. In modern times, only the male is expected to give a gift or present flowers.

Today, Valentine's Day is big business. According to *The New York Times*, more than $1 billion is spent on Valentine's Day candy and 900 million valentines are exchanged each year. The Italian city of Verona, where Shakespeare's Romeo and Juliet lived, receives about 1,000 letters addressed to Juliet every Valentine's Day.

# HOLIDAYS – MARCH

### 432. (March 17) St. Patrick's Legend

President John Kennedy (1917-1963) was of Irish descent and a 10-year-old boy wrote him to ask what he knew about the "little people" of Irish legend. Here is the President's reply dated March, 1963:

"Dear Mark:

"I want to thank you for your nice letter. I enjoyed hearing from you and hearing about your school.

"Your questions are quite pertinent, coming as they do just before St. Patrick's Day. There are many legends about the 'little people,' but what they all add up to is this: if you really believe, you will see them.

"My 'little people' are very small, wear tall black stovepipe hats, green coats and pants, and have long white beards. They do not have horses. I have never been able to determine where they live. They are most friendly and their message is that all the people of the world should live in peace and friendship.

"Since you are interested in the Irish, I want to wish you a happy St. Patrick's Day.

"Sincerely,

John F. Kennedy"

## 433. The Irish and St. Patrick

Almost every one knows that St. Patrick is Ireland's patron saint. Few, however, know that he was British. He came to Ireland first, not as a priest but as a young slave who had been kidnapped.

He worked as a shepherd for seven years before he managed to make his escape to France. No one knows what made him return to Ireland as a priest to convert the Irish.

Here is where the legend of St. Patrick becomes quite unbelievable, but it is still fun to talk about. The folklore is that, before St. Patrick drove out all the snakes from the Emerald Isle, all animals there could talk. Not only that, they could predict the future. Irish animals, like the Irish people, were extremely good at it.

Some people say that St. Patrick drove the snakes out of Ireland with a shamrock. Some say he used the shamrock to teach the Holy Trinity. At any rate, regardless of its use, the shamrock became the Irish national symbol in the 17th century.

## 434. To Be Irish

Hal Boyle (1911-1974), an American newspaper man who was of Irish lineage, once wrote down what he thought it meant to be Irish. It went like this:

"...It is to have an angel in your mouth, turning your prose to poetry. It is to have the gift of tongues, to know the language of all living things...

"...On this day it is music. Not just the cornet in the parading high school band, but the deep, deep music of living, the low, sad rhythms of eternity. The Irishman hears the high song of the turning spheres, the dim lullaby of the worm in its cocoon. All the world is in tune, a tune that only he can hear.

"...It is to live the whole history of his race between a dawn and a dawn — the long wrongs, the bird-swift joys, the endless hurt of his ancestors since the morning of time in a forgotten forest, the knock-at-his-heart that is part of his religion.

"...Why, on Saint Patrick's Day, to be Irish is to know more glory, adventure, magic, victory, exultation, gratitude and gladness than any other man can experience in a lifetime..."

## 435. (date varies) History of Easter

Although to Christians, Easter is the celebration of the Resurrection of Christ, the name "Easter" derives from "Eostre," the dawn goddess of Anglo-Saxon myth who was traditionally honored with an annual festival at the beginning of spring.

This celebration coincided with Christian holy days, and so was co-opted by that religion. Easter was largely ignored in America until immediately after the Civil War. The battle-scarred nation needed a holiday which stressed rebirth, so observance of Easter became important.

Easter used to call for buying new clothes (a new "Easter outfit") and there even is a parade down New York's Fifth Avenue with people showing off their new spring apparel. There was even a song written about it, "The Easter Parade." The Easter lily is the floral symbol of Easter because its shape resembles a trumpet heralding the resurrection of Christ.

## 436. Easter Eggs

Which came first, the bunny, the chicken or the egg?

When it comes to Easter customs, this is more than a mere philosophical question.

First, take the egg. Whether you paint it or dye it, you are following the lead of ancient Egyptians and Persians who produced similar feats of artistry with these delicate ovals. In antiquity, the egg was a religious symbol of fertility and rebirth.

## 437. Jokes after Easter Sunday

In the tradition of the ancient Russian Orthodox church, the day after Easter was devoted to telling jokes. Priests would join with people in unveiling their best jokes for one another.

It was an interesting tradition of imitating the cosmic joke that God pulled on Satan in the Resurrection. Satan thought he won on Friday but God had the last laugh on Easter Sunday. We would do well to laugh more often about the joyous victory.

# HOLIDAYS – APRIL

### 438. (April 1) History of April Fool's Day

April Fool's Day, or All Fools day, takes its name from a centuries-old tradition among the English, Scots, and French of playing practical jokes on April 1.

Until 1564, it was traditional to launch the New Year with a week of celebration, culminating with a big party. But the calendar was different then, and the New Year began on March 25, which meant that the annual party was held on April 1.

A new calendar was adopted in 1564, making January 1 the beginning of the New Year. Some people forgot, or didn't realize, what had happened, and still showed up to celebrate on April 1. They were dubbed "April fools."

In earlier times, the most popular form of April fooling was the "fool's errand," in which an unsuspecting person is sent on an absurd mission, for example, to buy some pigeon's milk or a stick with one end. Today, it is common for people to play practical jokes on friends and members of the family on April Fool's Day. This can range from putting sugar in the salt shaker to putting some big object on top of a neighbor's roof. The victim of a practical joke is called a "fish" in France and a "cukoo" in Scotland.

Mark Twain wisely observed that "April 1 is the day upon which we are reminded of what we are on the other 364."

# HOLIDAYS – MAY

## 439. (May 1) May Day

Although it is not an official holiday in either the U.S. or Canada, May Day ranks as one of the oldest holidays in the world. Many pre-Christian civilizations used the day to express their thankfulness to the gods for the arrival of spring and the rebirth of nature. In Elizabethan England, May Day with its maypole and general merriment was one of the most significant holidays of the year.

May Day is celebrated as Labor Day in Mexico and several other countries. For years the Soviet Union used the day to parade their armed might in front of the crowds gathered near the Kremlin. A gentler celebration of the day takes place in Hawaii where it is observed as "Lei Day." Residents and tourists alike take part in making, wearing and displaying "leis," colorful garlands made from fresh flowers.

May is a lovely month full of springtime rewards. In Tudor England, all classes of people, even royalty, rose at dawn to go "a-maying." Women rose before sunrise to wash their faces with the dew, a custom believed to beautify the skin.

In the United States, May Day has never enjoyed quite the same kind of tradition and ceremony that it enjoyed in England and Europe. For one thing, the Puritans were against it and overtly discouraged any observance. However, for many years young people used to mark the day by giving each other gaily decorated baskets of candy as tokens of affection.

## 440. (date varies) How Mother's Day Came to Be

Both the ancient Greeks and Romans held festivals to pay tribute to mothers, and Christians during the Middle Ages honored Mary, the mother of Jesus, with appropriate observances every year.

In England during the 1600s, young men and women who were apprentices or servants returned home on "Mothering Sunday," bringing to their mothers small gifts like trinkets or a "mothering cake."

However, Mother's Day, as most of us know it, can be credited to the tireless efforts of a woman named Anna May Jarvis (1864-1948).

Unmarried and left on her mother's death with a blind sister, Elsinore, Anna missed her mother greatly. She also believed that there should be a national day honoring the contribution of mothers. Two years after her mother's death in 1907, she and her friends began a letter-writing campaign to gain the support of influential ministers, businessmen and congressmen in declaring a national Mother's Day to honor mothers everywhere.

Her campaign paid off when the U.S. Congress passed a joint resolution on May 8, 1914, establishing the second Sunday in May as Mother's Day. On the next day, President Woodrow Wilson issued a proclamation officially establishing the day as a national holiday in the U.S.

Mother's Day is now officially celebrated in many other countries around the world.

## 441. (May 17) Armed Forces Day

Armed Forces Day is celebrated all over the world by countries wishing to honor the men and woman in their military forces. In the United States, the day is celebrated on the third Sunday in May. The day was created in 1949, and was a result of the consolidation of the military services in the Department of Defense. It was intended to replace the separate Army, Navy, Air Force, Marine Corps, and Coast Guard Days.

## 442. (date varies) Memorial Day

In the United States, the dead veterans of the nation's various wars have been honored on a secular holiday known as Memorial Day since the time of the Civil War. In 1968, President Lyndon Johnson (1908-1973) signed legislation stating that Memorial Day would be a national holiday to be observed on the last Monday of May every year.

Memorial Day is observed in hundreds of cities and towns in the U.S. but the most elaborate ceremonies are held at the Arlington National Cemetery in Washington, D.C. On Memorial Day in 1958 the bodies of unknown servicemen who had died in World War II and the Korean War were interred next to the Unknown Soldier of World War I and every year the President of the United States or his representative places a wreath at the Tomb of the Unknown Soldier.

In communities large and small, the day is marked by parades and other appropriate ceremonies which include decorating the graves of veterans with flowers. There is an inscription at Arlington National Cemetery which reads:

"Not for fame or reward, not for place or for rank, not lured by ambition or goaded by necessity, but in simple obedience to duty as they understood it, these men suffered all, sacrificed all, dared all, and died."

# HOLIDAYS – JUNE

## 443. (June 14) U.S. Flag Day

The American flag has not always had thirteen stripes. When Vermont and Kentucky came into the Union in the 1790s, Congress adopted a flag of fifteen stars and fifteen stripes. In 1818 Congress, not wanting to crowd the flag, voted to indicate the admission of new states by the addition of stars only. On May 1, 1795, the Congress also voted to revert to a flag of thirteen stripes.

## 444. (Flag Day) Who Designed the First U.S. Flag

The popular legend is that Betsy Ross, a Philadelphia seamstress, designed and sewed the first U.S. flag. We know that George Washington knew her and that she used to embroider the ruffles on his shirts.

The Betsy Ross legend became so firmly established that President Woodrow Wilson, when asked about its authenticity, said, "Would that it were true!"

However, it has been quite firmly established that the first U.S. flag was designed by Francis Hopkinson (1737-1791), a lawyer, a Congressman from New Jersey, and a signer of the Declaration of Independence. He was also a poet and artist.

Hopkinson was appointed to the Continental Navy Board on November 7, 1776, and it was while serving there that he turned his attention to designing the flag of the United States. In a letter to the Board of Admiralty in 1780, Hopkinson asserted that he had designed "the flag of the United States of America" and asked whether a "Quarter Cask of the public wine" would not be a reasonable and proper reward for his labors.

Though Hopkinson's political adversaries blocked all attempts to have him paid for his services, they never denied that he made the design. The journals of the Continental Congress clearly show that he designed the flag.

## 445. (Flag Day) The Pledge of Allegiance

Each of us has recited its words a thousand times. But who composed the Pledge of Allegiance in the first place?

Our country's pledge was written especially for children in 1892 as part of a celebration for Columbus Day in public schools across the United States.

The original verse first appeared in an educational publication called "The Youth's Companion" on September 8, 1892. It then read, "I pledge allegiance to my Flag and the Republic for which it stands —one nation indivisible — with liberty and justice for all."

The author, Francis Bellamy (1855-1931), was an assistant editor for the *Companion*. It was intended to be used just for the 400th anniversary of Columbus's discovery, but its popularity led to an annual tradition.

The pledge later became a daily ritual in schoolrooms throughout the U.S. In 1923, the first revision was made. "My Flag" was replaced by "the Flag of the United States of America." Then in 1954, President Eisenhower signed a bill that added the words, "under God."

## 446. (date varies) How Father's Day Was Born

Contrary to popular misconception, Father's Day was not established as a holiday to help greeting card manufacturers sell more cards. In fact, when a "Father's Day" was first proposed there were no Father's Day cards.

It was Mrs. John B. Dodd (1882-1978), of the state of Washington, who first proposed the idea of a day to honor fathers in 1909. Mrs. Dodd wanted a special day to honor her father, William Smart, a Civil War veteran who became a widower when his wife died in childbirth with their sixth child.

Mr. Smart was left to raise the newborn and his other five children by himself on a farm in eastern Washington State. After Mrs. Dodd became an adult, she realized what strength and selflessness her father had shown in raising his children as a single parent.

The first Father's Day was observed on June 19, 1910, in Spokane, Washington, under the sponsorship of the Spokane (Washington) Ministerial Association and the YMCA. At about the same time in various towns and cities across America, other people were beginning to celebrate a "father's day" as well.

In 1924, President Calvin Coolidge supported the idea of a national Father's Day. Finally in 1966, President Lyndon Johnson (1908-1973) signed a presidential proclamation declaring the third Sunday of June as Father's Day.

Father's Day has become a day to honor all men who act as a father figure, including stepfathers, uncles, grandfathers, and other significant male members of the household.

# HOLIDAYS – JULY

### 447. (July 1) Canada Day

Canada Day, formerly known as Dominion Day, is Canada's national holiday, marking the establishment of Canada as a self-governing country on July 1, 1867. It is a federal holiday generally celebrated on July 1 annually by all provincial governments and most businesses across the country.

A day off from work for most citizens and residents, Canada Day is Canada's most patriotic holiday, often a time for outdoor activities in the early Canadian summer. Frequently referred to as "Canada's birthday," the holiday celebrates the anniversary of Canada's creation as the first Dominion, through the 1867 British North America Act, which joined several British colonies into one self-governing organization. The name was officially changed to Canada Day on October 27, 1982, a move largely inspired by the adoption of the Canada Act, 1982, earlier in the year.

The day is celebrated with parades, carnivals, festivals, barbecues, air and maritime shows, fireworks and free musical concerts.

## 448. (July 4) Independence Day

One wonders how many Americans would be able to say exactly why the nation chose July 4, 1776, as the date to mark the nation's founding. The reason is that the Declaration of Independence was approved on that day by the Continental Congress meeting in Philadelphia. It is an amazing document and, in eloquent language, it announced the Colonies' determination to free themselves of British rule.

The only person to sign the Declaration on July 4 was John Hancock (1737-1793) of Massachusetts, an extremely wealthy man who risked his life and fortune on the success of the Revolution. He was president of the Continental Congress. When the Continental Congress adjourned on July 4 after debating the Declaration for three days and having voted to adopt the document with some revisions, Hancock was charged with authenticating the revised document, signing it, and sending copies to the colonial legislatures for approval. When Hancock affixed his boldly-written signature to the Declaration, he did so in an empty chamber. The only other person present was Charles Thomson (1729-1824), a Pennsylvanian serving as secretary of Congress. Thomson was never a signatory. His name appeared on printed copies of the document due to his position as secretary of Congress.

Thus, it is apocryphal that, on signing the Declaration with a flourish and in big letters, Hancock declared, "There, I guess King George will be able to read that without his spectacles." Like many great historical legends, it apparently never happened.

Most of the other delegates signed the Declaration on August 2, 1776, and the last of 56 signatures would not be added until five years later.

A little-known fact is that the first signed copy of the Declaration was printed by a woman in January of 1777. Members of the Continental Congress were in hiding from the British (remember they were considered traitors) and apparently all the male printers had made themselves scarce. So the Congress engaged Mary Katherine Goddard (1738-1816) of Baltimore to publish the official signed copy. She risked arrest by the British, but her courage was such that she placed at the bottom of the Declaration, "Printed by Mary Katherine Goddard." All the signers were men.

## 449. Adams and Jefferson

Even casual students of American history know that two of its most famous founding fathers, John Adams (1735-1826) and Thomas Jefferson (1743-1826), both died on the Fourth of July, 1826, the fiftieth anniversary of the Declaration of Independence.

Adams passed away quietly at his home in Quincy, Massachusetts, and his last words were, "Thomas Jefferson still survives." But Jefferson had already died earlier in the day at his home in Virginia.

This letter from Adams to his talented wife, Abigail (1744-1818), written on July 3, 1776, shows how strongly he felt about Americans celebrating the nation's birthday. Here is an excerpt from his letter:

"I am well aware of the toil, and blood, and treasure that it will cost us to maintain this declaration and support and defend these States. Yet, through all the gloom, I can see the rays of ravishing light and glory...I am apt to believe that it will be celebrated in succeeding generations as the great anniversary festival...It ought to be solemnized with pomp and parades, with shows, games, sports, guns, bells, bonfires, and illuminations, from one end of the continent to the other, from this time forward for ever more."

# HOLIDAYS – OCTOBER

### 450. (October 31) History of Halloween

Halloween is an ancient celebration combining Druid autumn festival and Christian customs.

Hallowe'en (All Hallow's Eve) is the beginning of Hallowtide, a season that embraces the Feast of All Saints (November 1) and the Feast of Souls (November 2).

The observance, dating from the sixth or seventh centuries, has long been associated with thoughts of the dead, spirits, witches, ghosts and devils. In fact, the ancient Celtic Feast of Samhain, the festival that marked the beginning of winter and of the New Year, was observed on November 1.

### 451. Halloween and the Irish

Many hundreds of years ago, Halloween was a festival for witches, goblins, and ghosts, as well as for lighting bonfires and playing devilish pranks.

Irish immigrants escaping from their country's potato famine in the 1840s brought with them to America the Halloween customs of costume and mischief. On "mischief night" the favorite pranks played by Irish youths in New England were overturning outhouses and unhinging front gates.

What has changed over the years are the reasons we have for dressing up ghoulishly, lighting fires, and doing mischievous things. We do these things now for pure fun – usually by children. In ancient times, they were done in deathly earnest — and by adults.

Named "All Hallows Eve," the festival was first celebrated by the ancient Celts in Ireland in the fifth century BC.

On the night of October 31, then the official end of summer, Celtic households extinguished the fires on their hearths to deliberately make their homes cold and undesirable to disembodied spirits. They then gathered outside the village, where a Druid priest kindled a huge bonfire to simultaneously honor the sun god for the past summer's harvest and to frighten away dangerous spirits.

The Celts believed that on October 31, all persons who had died in the previous year, assembled to choose the body of the person or animal they would inhabit for the next twelve months, before they could pass peacefully into the afterlife.

To frighten roving souls, Celtic family members dressed themselves as demons, hobgoblins, and witches. They paraded first inside, then outside, the fireless house, always as noisy and destructive as possible.

In time, as belief in spirit possession waned, the dire portents of many Halloween practices lightened to ritualized amusement.

## 452. Halloween Customs

Apples have long played an important role in Halloween activities. Apples were thought by magic to bring fullness and fruitfulness to their recipients.

A custom once common in the north of England and in Wales was to bite at apples with the mouth, the apple being suspended on a string. Another version has an apple attached to one end of a suspended beam with a lighted candle at the other end.

Apples and nuts were the feature of the evening feast, hence the name "Nutcrack Night."

Apples were also used to forecast the future. The apples were roasted and the parings thrown over the left shoulder. The parings are then analyzed to see which paring most resembles the initial letter of the Christian name of the man or woman "whom you will marry."

In Ireland, when young women want to know if their lovers are faithful, it is the custom on Halloween to put three nuts upon the bars of a grate, naming the nuts after the lovers.

If a nut cracks or jumps, the lover will prove unfaithful; if it begins to blaze or burn, he has a regard for the person making the trial. If the nuts named after the girl and her lover are burned together, they will be married.

## 453. Jack O'Lanterns

Can you guess how the practice of turning pumpkins into scary Jack O'Lanterns was born? The origin is an unusual one.

The term O'Lantern is Irish of course. The scary, carved pumpkin faces that are familiar sights on Halloween have their origin in an old Irish custom of creating crude lanterns from vegetables.

The Halloween flashlight for an Irish child was a hollowed-out turnip or potato with a lighted candle inside. And when the Irish landed in America in the nineteenth century, they were quick to spot the possibilities of hollowing out a pumpkin instead of a turnip.

The legend upon which the Jack O'Lantern is based is too long to tell in detail. But suffice to say, it is about a stingy Irish tippler named Jack who nearly lost his soul by borrowing money from the Devil to buy "just one more drink."

After many attempts by the Devil to collect the drinking debt, Jack played still another trick on the Devil and made him promise to never again ask for his soul. However, when Jack died, he was turned away from Heaven for his sins, and he was also rejected by Hell because the Devil had to live up to the promise he had made to not own Jack's soul. This rejection by both Heaven and Hell, left the old tippler more or less "stateless."

"Give me at least a light to find my way," Jack pleaded, and the Devil obliged him by hurling in his direction a coal from the fires of Hades.

According to the legend, Jack placed it inside a turnip he had been munching on and the Jack O'Lantern was born.

## 454. Black Cats

Why so many people dislike and fear black cats is a direct descendant of the witch-hunting era. This prejudice may continue because elderly women still keep cats and, it might be added, "old" women are still ranted at by the dim-witted as "crones" and "witches."

Although black cats are pretty widely feared, that is not always so. In England, for example, black cats are considered lucky.

## 455. Trick or Treat Origins

The most commonly accepted theory on the origins of trick-or-treating is based on the practice of the ninth-century European custom of "souling."

On All Soul's Day, Christians walked from village to village begging for square biscuits with currants, called soul cakes. The beggars promised to offer up prayers for the dead relatives of the donors, the number of prayers to be proportional to the donors' generosity.

# HOLIDAYS – NOVEMBER

## 456. (date varies) History of Thanksgiving Day

Thanksgiving Day proclamations were issued in America on numerous occasions during its earliest days. Governor William Bradford (1590-1657) in 1621 proclaimed a day for the Massachusetts colonists to offer thanks to God for their lives, their food, their clothing, etc.

During the Revolutionary War, numerous days of thanksgiving were appointed for prayer and fasting by the Continental Congress. November 26, 1789, was set aside by President Washington (1732-1799) to thank God for the newly formed government and the blessings which accompanied it.

Other Thanksgiving days were set aside to commemorate special occasions such as the conclusion of war.

The first of the national Thanksgiving Day proclamations was issued by Abraham Lincoln (1809-1865) in 1863, on October 3, the month and day of George Washington's first Thanksgiving Day proclamation.

President Andrew Johnson (1808-1875) continued the custom, which was followed by the succeeding Presidents until President Franklin Delano Roosevelt (1882-1945) made a change.

An extract from Lincoln's Thanksgiving Day proclamation of October 3, 1863, follows:

"I do, therefore, invite my fellow citizens in every part of the United States, and also those who are at sea and those who are sojourning in foreign lands, to set apart and observe the last Thursday of November next (November 26) as a day of thanksgiving and praise to our beneficent Father who dwelleth in the heavens. And I recommend to them that, while offering up the ascriptions justly due to Him for singular deliverances and blessings, they do also, with humble penitence for our national perverseness and disobedience, commend to His tender care all those who have become widows, orphans, mourners, or sufferers in the lamentable civil strife in which we are unavoidably engaged, and fervently implore the interposition of the almighty hand to heal the wounds of the nation, and to restore it, as soon as may be consistent with the Divine purposes, to the full enjoyment of peace, harmony, tranquility, and union."

## 457. Washington and Thanksgiving

Americans don't know it and children aren't taught it, but George Washington (1732-1799) is responsible for our Thanksgiving holiday. It was our first President who led the charge to make this day of thanks a truly national event, not the pilgrims and not Abraham Lincoln (1809-1865).

On October 3, 1789, George Washington issued his Thanksgiving Proclamation, designating for "the People of the United States a day of public thanksgiving to be held on "Thursday the 26th day of November," 1789," marking the first national celebration of a holiday that has become commonplace in today's households.

Though subsequent Presidents failed to maintain this tradition, it was Washington's original Proclamation that guided Abraham Lincoln's 1863 Thanksgiving Proclamation. In fact, Lincoln issued his proclamation on the same day, October 3, and marked the same Thanksgiving Day, Thursday, November 26 as Washington, setting Thanksgiving as the last Thursday in November after our first President's example. The proclamation was printed in newspapers, including the October 9, 1789, issue of the *Pennsylvania Packet and Daily Advertiser*.

George Washington first mentioned the possibility of a national Thanksgiving Day in a confidential letter to James Madison (1751-1836) in August, 1789 (just months after taking office), asking for his advice on approaching the Senate for their opinion on "a day of thanksgiving." By the end of September, 1789, a resolution had been introduced to the House of Representatives requesting that "a joint committee of both Houses be directed to wait upon the President of the United States, to request that he would recommend to the people of the United States a day of public thanksgiving."

The committee put the resolution before the President, and George Washington issued the first national Thanksgiving Proclamation within days.

Washington knew the value of a thanksgiving day long before becoming our first President. During the Revolutionary War, he would order special thanksgiving services for his troops after successful battles, as well as publicly endorse efforts by the Continental Congress to proclaim days of thanks, usually in recognition of military victories and alliances.

The concept of thanksgiving was not new to the citizens of the new United States. Colonists, even before the pilgrims, often established Thank Days to mark certain occasions. These one-time events could occur at any time of the year and were usually more solemn than the Thanksgiving we observe today, emphasizing prayer and spiritual reflection.

Thanksgiving was not made a legal holiday until 1941 when Congress named the fourth Thursday in November as our national day of thanks in answer to public outcry over President Franklin Roosevelt's (1882-1945) attempt to prolong the Christmas shopping season by moving Thanksgiving from the traditional last Thursday to the third Thursday in November.

## 458. Thanksgiving Myths

Samuel Eliot Morison (1887-1976), the American historian, has written that "more bunk has been written about Pilgrims than any other American subjects except Columbus (1451-1506) and John Paul Jones (1747-1792)." Here are some of the myths and the facts as we know them:

Myth: Thanksgiving for the Pilgrims was a solemn, religious occasion.

Fact: First of all, these Massachusetts settlers didn't call themselves "Pilgrims." They called themselves "Saints." Hardly saint-like, their three-day harvest festival included drinking, gambling, even target shooting with English muskets. A by-product of the latter was a friendly warning to nearby Indians that the "Saints" were prepared to defend themselves if necessary.

Myth: The Thanksgiving celebration took place in November.

Fact: Usually, it was some time between late September and the middle of October, after the harvest had been completed.

Myth: At their Thanksgiving celebrations, the Pilgrims ate turkey.

Fact: The Pilgrims ate deer (venison), not turkey. If wild turkey was served, it was an inconsequential side dish. Other foods that were probably on the menu included cod, bass, clams, oysters, Indian corn, native berries and plums. The meal was washed down with beer made from corn. There was no pumpkin pie either. In those days, the Pilgrims boiled their pumpkin and ate it plain. There was no bread other than corn bread, and no beef, milk, or cheese.

Myth: The Pilgrims wore large hats with buckles on them.

Fact: Pilgrims didn't dress in black, didn't wear buckles on their hats or shoes, and didn't wear tall hats. The 19th century artists who pictured them that way did so because they associated black clothing and buckles with being old-fashioned.

Note: The above facts have been verified by the Research Department of the Pilgrim Museum in Plymouth, Massachusetts.

## 459. Why We Eat Turkey on Thanksgiving

The Pilgrims aren't responsible for making turkey the center of the Thanksgiving feast, so who is? Business historian Thomas DiBacco believes that poultry companies deserve the credit.

"There is no rhyme or reason for us to have turkeys on Thanksgiving, except that business promoted it," he says, adding that poultry producers in New Jersey, Pennsylvania, and Maryland began promoting turkey as Thanksgiving food after the Civil War. Why? Because at 10 cents a pound, it was more profitable than any other bird.

Illustrators followed their lead and painted Pilgrim dinners with roast turkey on the table. Soon a brand new "tradition" was born.

The next group of businesses to cash in on Thanksgiving were turn-of-the-century retailers, who used the holiday to jump-start Christmas sales. Newspaper ads began counting down the number of shopping days until Christmas, and, in 1921, Gimbel's department store in Philadelphia came up with a retailer's tour-de-force: they held the first Thanksgiving Day parade, designed to kick off the shopping season. By 1930, department stores all over the country sponsored parades to get shoppers into their stores.

# HOLIDAYS – DECEMBER

## 460. (December 25) History of Christmas

During the early days of Christianity, different parts of the world celebrated Christmas on different dates. If you traveled widely in the Roman world, you could conceivably enjoy six different Christmases in the span of a single year.

It was Pope Julius I in the mid-fourth century who appointed a monk named Dionysius to set up a calendar standardizing a universal date, which came to be December 25.

Christmas was outlawed in England by the Puritans under Oliver Cromwell (1599-1658) who thought of it as a "heathen celebration." It was illegal to celebrate the holiday until the British monarchy was restored in 1660.

Christmas was also outlawed by the Puritans in New England. The following law was passed in Massachusetts in 1659: "Whoever shall be found observing any such day as Christmas and the like, either by forbearing labor, feasting or any other way, shall pay for any such offense five shillings as a fine to the country." The law remained on the books for 22 years, and Christmas was not made a legal holiday in Massachusetts until just before the Civil War.

In Spain, Christmas gifts are not exchanged until January 6 — for a very good reason. That is the date commemorating the visit of the Magi, who were the first to offer Christmas gifts - gold, frankincense, and myrrh. On that night, children set their shoes outside on the doorstep, filling them with straw. They believe the wise men will use the straw to feed their camels and in return fill the shoes with gifts and candy.

The custom of sending Christmas cards began in 1843 when a wealthy Englishman, Sir Henry Cole, ran out of time to write personal letters to his friends at Christmas. He commissioned an artist, John Calcott Horsley, to design a card instead. Horsley drew a picture of a group of merry wishers raising their glasses in a toast. Underneath were the words, "A Merry Christmas and a Happy New Year to You." The card created much controversy, as critics complained it encouraged holiday drinking. But the custom of sending cards at Christmas caught on nonetheless. In the nineteenth century, the British post office used to deliver cards on Christmas morning.

The Poinsettia is a Christmas tradition harkening from Mexico. According to legend, a boy named Pablo was headed to his village church to see its nativity scene. Realizing he had no gift for the Christ child, he hurriedly gathered some branches and weeds from the roadside. When he laid them before the manger, the other children laughed at him. But suddenly there appeared on each branch the brilliant, star-shaped flower of the Poinsettia.

Candy canes were reportedly developed by a Christian candymaker in Indiana who built the story of Christmas into each piece. The hardness of the candy represents the solid rock of the Christian faith. The white represents the sinlessness of Christ, and the red stripes symbolize the bloody wounds caused by his flogging. The shape of the candy is that of a shepherd's staff, representing Christ as the Good Shepherd. Turned upside down, it forms the letter "J" for Jesus.

Our word Christmas comes from the English observance of the birth of Christ called "Christes masse" (Christ's mass), because a special mass was celebrated on that day. In France, it's known as Noel; in Spain, Navidad, and in Italy, Natale — all words meaning " birthday." The Germans use the word "Weihnachten," meaning holy night.

The word Yule comes from the Teutonic tribes of northern Europe. Because their winters were so long and harsh and their days so short, they always celebrated the winter solstice on December 22, the shortest day of the year. It was a time of great joy for them. From that point each year the days began to lengthen. They called the month Yule, or Jol, from which we get our English word jolly.

The day after Christmas is commonly called "Boxing Day" in England because of the custom of giving Christmas boxes containing gifts and money to the servants.

## 461. Interesting Facts about Christmas

In 1647 the English parliament passed a law that made Christmas illegal. Christmas festivities were banned by Puritan leader Oliver Cromwell (1599-1658), who considered feasting and revelry on what was supposed to be a holy day to be immoral. Anybody caught celebrating Christmas was arrested. The ban was lifted only when the Puritans lost power in 1660.

There is some confusion about who first used electric lights on Christmas trees. One version is that electric tree lights were first used just three years after Thomas Edison (1847-1931) had his first mass public demonstration of electric lights back in 1879. Thomas Edison's assistant, Edward Johnson, came up with the idea of electric lights for Christmas trees in 1882. He had them made especially for his home.

A second version credits a man named Ralph Morris, an American telephone technician. Some say in 1895 Morris used actual strings of lights that had already been manufactured for use in telephone switchboards. Morris reportedly looked at the tiny bulbs on switchboards and had the idea of using them on his tree. Although electric tree lights caused a sensation, it wasn't until 1903 that the Ever-Ready company made strings of lights, and they were expensive. In 1927, GE introduced tiny lights that didn't get too hot, and if one went out, the others stayed lit.

Christmas crackers were invented by Thomas Smith. He had imported some French novelties to sell as Christmas gifts, but these were not popular until he wrapped them up and added a snapper.

St. Francis of Assisi introduced Christmas carols to formal church services.

The popular Christmas song "Jingle Bells" was composed in 1857 by James Pierpont (1822-1893), and was originally called "One-Horse Open Sleigh." It was actually written for Thanksgiving, not Christmas.

## 462. Additional Facts about Christmas

Where did Christmas come from in the first place? Look back centuries and you will find that the holiday is a combination of influences — German, Dutch, English, American, and other traditions, both religious and pagan — that emerged over the millennia.

Even today, Christmas-time activities are far from a homogeneous phenomenon, taking place alongside Kwanzaa, an African-American harvest holiday, and the eight-day Jewish celebration of Hanukkah. Together they make up the annual December celebrations.

Part of the reason winter festivities went global began 150 years ago at the tail end of the Industrial Revolution. It was then that "Christ's Mass" (Cristes maesse in Old English), the church service that celebrates the birth of Jesus Christ, along with a wealth of other traditions, entered the scientific age of mass communications, transport, and other technologies.

## 463. Origin of Christmas Ornaments

Early Christmas ornaments were homemade paper flowers, fruit, nuts, and the like.

Later, decorations that could be purchased came from Germany, famous for its blown-glass ornaments, or "Kugles."

In 1880, F.W. Woolworth brought back a few to the United States and sold out within a day. The next year they brought in 200,000 of them!

During World War I the supply from Germany ceased, so American manufacturers began making their own. With new technologies and materials, many ornaments of any shape and size could be made in minutes for much less money than ever before.

## 464. How Santa Claus Got His Name

Legend says [Saint] Nicholas, born in Patara [Turkey] around A.D. 300, achieved fame by resurrecting three children whom a butcher had cut up and put in brine.

His association with children was matched by a reputation for gift-giving. Hearing of a man, once wealthy, but now fallen on hard times, who was unable to fund dowries for his three daughters, Nicholas entered the house secretly by night and left three purses of gold. With this gift, the three daughters were able to contract suitable marriages and thus avoided a disagreeable public fate.

Many stories are told of Nicholas's miraculous powers in rescuing prisoners, shipwrecked sailors, lost travelers, recovering lost property, and generally answering the prayers of those in distress.

St. Nicholas was buried in the crypt of his church at Myra, in Turkey, but in 1087 his bones were stolen by some Italian sailors, who reburied them at Bari, on the east coast of Italy. They are still there.

Now, 1700 years after his birth, belief in Santa Claus has reached mystical proportions among children, who await his beneficence each Christmas morning.

## 465. How Santa Claus Got His Current Look

Dutch settlers brought the myth of Santa Claus to America in the seventeenth century. But the Santa Claus they brought did not look anything like the jolly figure we know today.

The Dutch Santa was tall, slender, and very dignified. Around the beginning of the nineteenth century, Santa took on the appearance of a jolly figure. Washington Irving (1783-1859) in 1809 pictured Santa as a bulky man who smoked a pipe and wore a Dutch broad-brimmed hat and baggy breeches. Later in the century, artists pictured Santa as a fat man, with brown hair and a big smile.

Finally, in 1863, illustrator Thomas Nast (1840-1902) drew a picture of Santa as a jolly old man with a white beard and wide girth, the first picture of Santa as he looks today.

## 466. The Origin of Christmas Stockings

The tradition of hanging stockings from the fireplace originated from one of the most famous stories of St. Nicholas.

The story goes that there was a very poor man who could not afford a dowry for his three young daughters to be married. St. Nicholas heard of the man's misfortune, and having just inherited his parents' fortune, he secretly dropped three bags of gold coins down the poor man's chimney.

The coins landed in the girl's stockings that were hanging by the fireplace to dry. And thus a tradition was born!

## 467. Santa's Christmas Eve Journey

A physicist named Roger Highfield once did some calculations of the speeds and times that Santa Claus would have to achieve to visit everyone's home on Christmas Eve. His calculations were published in a book, *The Physics of Christmas*, by Little, Brown and Company. Here are some excerpts:

- No known species of reindeer can fly.

- There are approximately two billion children under 18 in the world. However, since Santa does not visit children of Muslim, Hindu, Jewish or Buddhist religions, this reduces the workload for Christmas night to 15 percent of the total, or 278 million. At an average rate of 3.5 children per household, that comes to 108 million homes, presuming there is at least one good child in each.

- Santa has about 31 hours of Christmas to work with, thanks to the different time zones and the rotation of the earth, assuming he travels east to west. This works out to 967.7 visits per second. According to Roger Highfield, this works out that, for each Christian household with a good child, Santa has around 1/1000th of a second to park the sleigh, hop out, jump down the chimney, fill the stockings, distribute the remaining presents under the tree, eat whatever snacks have been left for him, get back up the chimney, jump back into the sleigh and get on to the next house.

- Assuming that each of these 108 million stops is evenly distributed around the earth, we are now talking about 0.78 miles per household, making the total trip 75.5 million miles. This means Santa's sleigh is moving at 750 miles per second – 3,000 times the speed of sound.

- Assuming that each child gets nothing more than a medium-sized Lego set (two pounds), the sleigh would therefore be carrying over 500 thousand tons.

## 468. Christmas and Mistletoe

Mistletoe was sacred to ancient druids and became widely used at Christmas time, among others. It has always been associated with romance.

Long ago it was imagined that mistletoe in the boughs of an oak tree held the juice of immortality, or Love. The plant was said to bloom on Midsummer Eve.

A girl would spread a white cloth under the tree that night, take the flower dust found there and sprinkle it under her pillow to see her future bridegroom in her dream.

## 469. The Magic Pickle

A tale of the pickle tells of two Spanish boys traveling home for the holidays from boarding school. Tired from their travels, they stopped at an inn to rest. The mean and evil innkeeper stole all their belongings and stuffed the boys in a pickle barrel.

Late that evening, St. Nicholas stopped to rest at the same inn. Aware of the boys' plight, he tapped the pickle barrel with his staff, and magically the boys were restored.

Through time the Victorian tradition has been celebrated by hiding a hand-blown glass pickle on the Christmas tree. It is the last ornament placed on the tree and is put there after all the children are in bed. Whoever finds the pickle on Christmas morning receives a special gift.

## 470. An Old German Christmas Custom

On Christmas Eve, in the old duchy of Swabia in southwest Germany, village maidens would blindfold a goose and form a circle around it. The girl whom the goose touched with its beak would be the first one to get married.

## 471. An Old Scandinavian Christmas Custom

In Scandinavian countries, it is customary on Christmas Eve for members of families to place all their shoes side by side. This will guarantee peace and harmony in the household throughout the coming year.

## 472. Puritans Outlawed Christmas

The Puritans have been blamed for many things in American life but they certainly cannot be blamed for making Christmas too commercial.

In colonial Massachusetts, a law was passed in 1659 making it illegal to observe Christmas. Anybody "found observing, by abstinence from labor, feasting or any other way, any such days as Christmas day" was to be fined five shillings for each offense. In 1681 the law was repealed, but only because the Puritans were sure no one would celebrate the holiday.

In 1685, Judge Samuel Sewall noted in his famous diary that on Christmas everyone went to work as usual. Not until the middle of the nineteenth century did Christmas become a major holiday.

## 473. He Didn't Like Christmas

The famous actor and comic W.C. Fields (1880-1946) always referred to Death as "that fellow in the bright nightgown," and he always hated and dreaded Christmas.

It is ironic that when "that fellow" came for him in 1946, it was indeed on Christmas Day.

## 474. (December 26) Boxing Day

In England, Boxing Day takes place on the day after Christmas, and is an additional holiday following the festivities of December 25th; but how did the name "Boxing Day" evolve and why?

The 26th of December has been called Boxing Day in Britain since the Middle Ages. The name refers to the alms boxes that were placed in churches at Christmas time to collect money to provide food for the poor. The Church opened these boxes on Christmas Day and distributed their contents on the following day — December 26th.

This custom of the "dole of the Christmas Box" or "the Box money" continued until the 16th century when the Protestant Reformation brought it to an end. After that, the poor, in hopes of reviving the custom, continued to collect for themselves on December 26th by visiting the houses of the rich and asking for money.

Another long-established custom was for apprentices and servants to request money from their masters and their master's customers at Christmas. These gifts of money were kept in an earthenware "box" with a slit in the top. The boxes were not broken open until the day after Christmas, allowing as much time as possible for everyone to give generously during Christmas time.

A similar tradition associated with December 26th involved tradesmen who had provided services throughout the year (dustmen, lamplighters, watchmen, parish beadles, etc.) coming to the house to ask for recognition in appreciation of their services. This tradition continues today when we give monetary gifts during the week proceeding Christmas Day to those who provide similar services.

## 475. (December 26) Kwanzaa

Kwanzaa is a cultural festival during which African-Americans celebrate and reflect upon their rich heritage as the products of two worlds. It begins December 26 and lasts for seven days.

Kwanzaa was founded in 1966 by Dr. Maulana "Ron" Karenga (1941- ), a college professor and African-American leader, who believed that a special holiday could help African-Americans meet their goals of building strong families, learning about their history, and creating a sense of unity.

After conducting extensive research in which he studied the festivals of many African groups of people, he decided that the new holiday should be a harvest or "first fruits" celebration, incorporating ideas from many different harvest traditions. Kwanzaa is a Kiswahili word meaning "the first fruits of the harvest."

The East African language of Kiswahili was chosen as the official language of Kwanzaa because it is a non-tribal language spoken by a large portion of the African population. Also, its pronunciation is easy — the vowels are pronounced like those in Spanish, and the consonants, for the most part, like those in English.

Kwanzaa is based on seven principles which are called Nguzo Saba. The principles are Umoja (Unity), Kujichagulia (self-determination), Ujima (collective work and responsibility), Ujamaa (cooperative economics), Nia (purpose), Kuumba (creativity), and Imani (faith). One principle is highlighted each day of the holiday.

In preparation for the celebration, a straw mat (Mkeka) is placed on the table, along with a seven-candle holder (Kinara) with seven candles, one black (placed in the center), three red (on the right), and three green (on the left). The black candle represents the African-American people, the red is for their struggles, and the green represents their hopes for the future.

Other items placed on the table are a variety of fruit (Mazao), ears of corn (Vibunzi) representing the number of children in the family, gifts (Zawadi), and a communal unity cup (Kikombe Cha Umoja) for pouring and sharing libations.

Each day of Kwanzaa, usually before the evening meal, family and friends gather around the table and someone lights a candle, beginning with the black. After that, candles are lit alternately from left to right. While the candle is being lit, a principle is recited; then each person present takes a turn to speak about the importance that principle has to him or herself.

Next the ceremony focuses on remembering those who have died. A selected person pours water or juice from the unity cup into a bowl. That person then drinks from the cup and raises it high saying "Harambee" which means "Let's all pull together." All repeat "Harambee!" seven times and each person drinks from the cup. Then names of African-American leaders and heroes are called out, and everyone reflects upon the great things these people did. The ceremony is followed by a meal, and then singing and perhaps listening to African music.

# HOLLYWOOD

### 476. Candid Interview

A Hollywood journalist asked Marilyn Monroe about her famous nude calendar photo.

"Didn't you have anything on?"

"I had the radio on," she answered.

Note: Marilyn Monroe's birthday was June 1, 1926; born Norma Jean Mortenson; later used surname Baker. She died in 1962.

### 477. Goldwyn Straight Talk

Simon Bessie was a young publisher at Harper and Row. He had sent a forthcoming novel to movie producer Sam Goldwyn (1879 or 1882-1974) and was impatiently waiting for an answer.

Hearing nothing after several weeks, Bessie finally got Goldwyn on the phone and pressed him for a decision about the novel's movie rights.

"I'll give it to you straight, Simon," said the famous Hollywood mogul. "About that property, I can't give you a positive 'yes' and I don't want to give you a positive 'no.' But I will give you a positive 'maybe.'"

### 478. Who Named Oscar

The movie star Bette Davis had (1908-1989) an interesting story about how Hollywood's "Oscar" got its name.

"I received my prized Academy Award statuette," Bette Davis said, "at about the same time I finally wheedled out of my husband, Harmon O. Nelson, Jr., the closely guarded secret of his middle name.

"It was 'Oscar.'

"To tease him, I began to call my statuette 'Oscar.' "Soon 'Oscar' was adopted by the industry, and that's how the Academy Award statuettes got their nickname."

## 479. Hedging One's Bet

The legendary film and vaudeville comedian stone-faced Buster Keaton (1895-1966) was one of Hollywood's biggest stars in the 1920s.

When he died in 1966, he was buried with a rosary in one pocket and a deck of cards in the other so he would be prepared, whichever direction he was headed.

## 480. What's In a Name?

A young actor went up to the movie producer Sam Goldwyn (1879 or 1882-1974) and told him excitedly that he had just become the father of a brand new baby boy.

"Wonderful," said Goldwyn. "What are you going to call him."

"Ronald," said the actor.

"Ronald," exclaimed Goldwyn, "What kind of name is that? Today every Tom, Dick and Harry is named Ronald."

## 481. A Poem to Clowns

Dick Van Dyke (1925- ), a famous "clown" himself, admired the poem below so much that he sent it as a Christmas card to his friend and fellow "clown", Stan Laurel (1890-1965), the famous comedy star of early motion pictures.

Laurel died of a heart attack at age 74, after warning his friends, "If anyone at my funeral has a long face, I'll never speak to him again."

Van Dyke read this poem at Laurel's funeral, February 26, 1965, in tribute to his personal idol and good friend. The poem goes this:

God Bless All Clowns

God bless all clowns
Who star in the world with laughter
Who ring the rafters with flying jest,
Who make the world spin merry on its way
and somehow add more beauty to each day.

God bless all clowns
So poor the world would be
Lacking their piquant touch, hilarity,
The belly laughs, the ringing lovely mirth
That makes a friendly place of this earth.

God bless all clowns —
Give them a long good life.
Make bright their ways — they're a race apart!
Alchemists most, who turn their hearts' pain
Into a dazzling jest to lift the heart.
God bless all clowns.

## 482. Settling a Dispute

The famous movie producer Samuel Goldwyn (1879 or 1882-1974) had gotten into a severe wrangle with another producer about a female star Goldwyn wanted and that the other producer had under contract. The negotiations between the lawyers got nowhere, and the producer finally picked up the phone and called Goldwyn.

"Look, Sam," he said, "We're getting nowhere. Why not submit the whole mess to arbitration?"

"Fine! Great!" said Goldwyn. "I agree, just so it's understood that I get her."

# HUMILITY

### 483. Help from Others

In the office of the late Alex Haley (1921-1992), author of *Roots*, hung a picture of a turtle sitting on a fence. When Haley looked at it, he would be reminded of a lesson taught to him by his friend John Gaines: "If you see a turtle on top of a fence post, you know he had some help."

Said Haley, "Any time I start thinking, 'Wow, isn't this marvelous what I've done!', I look at that picture and remember how this turtle , me, got up on that post."

### 484. Lesson in Humility

George Washington Carver (1864-1943), the scientist who achieved wonders with the humble peanut, used to tell this story: When I was young I said to God, "God, tell me the mystery of the universe."

But God answered, "That knowledge is reserved for Me alone."

So I said, "Then God, tell me the mystery of the peanut."

And God said, "George, that's more nearly your size."

"And so he told me."

Note: Carver during his distinguished career discovered more than 300 uses for the lowly peanut and 100 uses for the sweet potato.

### 485. The Mark of Greatness

Dr. Charles Mayo (1865-1939) and his brother William (1861-1939) are remembered for founding the famous Mayo Clinic.

Dr. Charlie, as he was called, once was host to an English visitor in his home at Rochester, Minnesota, for several days.

Before retiring for the night, the visitor put his shoes outside the door, expecting a servant to shine them.

Dr. Charlie shined them himself. That's the kind of man he was!

## 486. Taking Credit

On the desk of President Ronald Reagan (1911-2004) was a small bronze desk plaque bearing these words: "The way to get things done is not to mind who gets the credit of doing them." The author of these words was Benjamin Jowett (1817-1893), Master of Balliol College at Oxford.

## 487. Indispensable Man

The following poem was written by a truly humble man or woman because we do not know who the author was:

Some day when you're feeling important -
Some day when your ego's in bloom,
Some day when you take it for granted
You're the best-qualified man in the room —
Take a bucket and fill it with water,
Put your hands in it, up to the wrist,
Pull them out and the hole that remains
Is a measure of how you'll be missed!
The moral of this is quite simple,
You must do the best that you can.
Be proud of yourself — but remember!
There is no indispensable man.

## 488. True Humility

Thomas J. Watson, Jr. (1918-1993), former chairman of the IBM Corporation and Ambassador to Russia, said his father frequently used to say, "Everyone should take a step backwards every once in a while and watch himself walk by."

# INCOMPETENCE

### 489. A Judgment

Henry Ford II (1917-1987) loved stories and told this one when people encouraged him to venture outside the field he knew so well:

The town pharmacist died, Ford said, and his colleagues were eulogizing him.

"He certainly knew his compounds," said one. "Yes," agreed the other, "and he was loyal to his customers."

"Perhaps," said the third, "but he wasn't much of a pharmacist."

The others were horrified at this observation.

"Why not?" they demanded.

"Because," said the third, "he always put too much mayo in the tuna salad."

### 490. Spelling Test

Mark Twain (1835-1910) in 1888 gave some free advice to the administrators at Johns Hopkins University in Baltimore. It went like this:

"I told them I believed they were perfectly competent to run a college, as far as the higher branches of education are concerned, but what they needed was a little help here and there from a practical commercial mind. I said the public are sensitive to little things, and they wouldn't ever have full confidence in a college that didn't know how to spell "John."

### 491. A Lesson from the *Titanic*

The *Titanic* was state-of-the-art. No expense had been spared to make sure that it would be unsinkable. The officers were unconcerned by their inability to get accurate information on possible hazards which might lie in its course.

She had two lookouts on her masts, but the lookouts had no binoculars. The crew couldn't see far enough ahead to react to danger, and they had no way to get their information to the captain if they did see a problem approaching.

And we all know what happened. The unsinkable ocean liner went to her death, along with most of her passengers, on her maiden voyage from New York to Europe — the victim of a disastrous collision with an iceberg.

Disasters like that can happen in business too if we aren't careful to make sure vital intelligence doesn't get swallowed up by internal bureaucracy and inattention to what the competitor is doing.

## 492. Absence of Wisdom

Pope Julius III (1487-1555), who was Pope from 1550 to 1555, made the following comment about incompetence to a Portuguese monk commiserating with him upon the responsibilities of his position: "Do you not know my son, with what little understanding the world is ruled?"

## 493. The Peter Principle

Lawrence J. Peter (1919-1990), a Canadian writer, wrote a book about incompetence in 1969 (*The Peter Principle*) which added a new word and definition to the English language. Here is an excerpt:

In a hierarchy, every employee tends to rise to his level of incompetence.

There follow two sub-principles:

1. In time, every post tends to be occupied by an employee who is incompetent to carry out its duties.
2. Work is accomplished by those employees who have not yet reached their level of incompetence.

## 494. Lincoln's Useless General

Of all Abraham Lincoln's generals during the Civil War, none proved to be more incompetent than General George B. McClellan (1826-1885). Popular with the public, he had an enormous Army compared to the Confederates, yet he was always asking for more. He put the Union Army through countless training exercises and kept delaying engaging with the enemy. Lincoln had a habit of writing angry letters and then not sending them. The following letter, never sent, clearly shows the desperate impatience Lincoln had with McClellan. After McClellan was eventually relieved of command, he actually disloyally ran against Lincoln for president. Here is the letter, written in 1862: "My dear McClellan: If you don't want to use the Army I should like to borrow it for a while. A. Lincoln."

## 495. Incompetent Teachers

C. Emily Feistritzer, Director of the National Center for Education Research, wrote the following to the Washington Post in 1987: "If the nation has incompetent teachers, it is because it hired them in the first place, then not only tolerated them but protected them. The way to get rid of incompetents in teaching should be no different than it is in any other workplace — provide them assistance for improvement, and if that fails, replace them with competent people."

# INFERIORITY COMPLEX

## 496. Short in Height

Oliver Wendell Holmes Senior (1809-1894), who was a successful physician and literary man as well, once attended a meeting in which he was the shortest man present.

"Dr. Holmes," quipped a friend, "I should think you'd feel rather small among us big fellows."

"I do," replied Holmes coolly, "I feel like a dime among a collection of pennies."

## 497. Not Appreciating One's Worth

A water bearer in China had two large pots, each hung on the end of a pole which he carried across his neck. One of the pots was perfectly made and never leaked. The other pot had a crack in it and by the time the water bearer reached his master's house it had leaked much of its water and was only half full.

For a full two years this went on daily, with the bearer delivering only one and a half pots full of water to his master's house. Of course, the perfect pot was proud of its accomplishments. But the poor cracked pot was ashamed of its own imperfection, and miserable that it was able to accomplish only half of what it had been made to do.

After two years of what it perceived to be its bitter failure, the cracked pot spoke to the water bearer one day by the stream.

"I am ashamed of myself, and I want to apologize to you."

"Why?" asked the bearer. "What are you ashamed of?"

"I have been able, for these past two years, to deliver only half my load because this crack in my side causes water to leak out all the way back to your master's house. Because of my flaws, you have to do all of this work, and you don't get full value from your efforts," the pot said.

The water bearer felt sorry for the old cracked pot, and in his compassion he said, "As we return to the master's house, I want you to notice the beautiful flowers along the path."

Indeed, as they went up the hill, the old cracked pot took notice of the sun warming the beautiful wild flowers on the side of the path and this cheered it some. But at the end of the trail, it still felt bad because it had leaked out half its load, and so again the cracked pot apologized to the bearer for its failure.

The bearer said to the pot, "Did you notice that there were flowers only on your side of the path, but not on the other pot's side? That's because I have always known about your flaw, and I took advantage of it. I planted flower seeds on your side of the path, and every day while we walk back from the stream, you've watered them.

"For two years I have been able to pick these beautiful flowers to decorate my master's table. Without you being just the way you are, he would not have this beauty to grace his house."

# INVENTION, TECHNOLOGY

## 498. Air Conditioning

Who do we really blame for Washington, D.C. bureaucracy? Some people claim it's Willis Carrier (1876-1950) who, in 1902, invented the air conditioner.

Until then Federal workers used to be sent home whenever the temperature humidity index topped 90 degrees. But after air conditioning invaded our nation's capitol, keeping the city's famously hot summers at bay, federal bureaucracy mushroomed.

## 499. Invention of Alphabetizing

A young Greek librarian in the second century B.C., was trying to think of an efficient way to order and retrieve the thousands of manuscripts that he had in his library.

"How should I order these?" he wonders. "By subject? By author? By color?"

Then he thinks of using the alphabet. His fellow librarians think of the alphabet as simply a series of phonetic symbols — alpha, beta, gamma, delta, epsilon. When joined together, these symbols create words.

This librarian decides to use the Greek alphabet in a very unusual way. He puts all the documents beginning with "gamma" after those beginning with "beta" but in front of those beginning with "delta."

In the process, the inventive young librarian created alphabetization, a means still widely used to categorize and store information around the world.

## 500. The Origin of Bifocals

Like many other things, bifocals were invented by Benjamin Franklin (1706-1790), one of America's founding fathers and an early scientist. The following is based on this letter he wrote from Passy, France, on May 23, 1785:

"I had formerly two pair of spectacles, which I shifted occasionally, as in traveling I sometimes read, and often wanted to regard the prospects. Finding this change troublesome, and not always sufficiently ready, I had the glasses cut, and half of each kind associated in the same circle.

"By this means, as I wear my spectacles constantly, I have only to move my eyes up or down, as I want to see distinctly far or near, the proper glasses being always ready. This I find more particularly convenient since my being in France, the glasses that serve me best at table to see what I eat, not being the best to see the faces of those on the other side of the table who speak to me; and when one's ears are not well accustomed to the sounds of a language, a sight of the movements in the features of him that speaks helps to explain; so that I understand French better by the help of my spectacles..."

## 501. China and Technology Leadership

Consider China at the outset of the fifteenth century. Its curiosity, its instinct for exploration, and its drive to build had created all the technologies necessary to launch the Industrial Revolution, something that would not actually occur for another 400 years.

China had the last furnace and piston bellows for making steel (the amount of pig iron that China had produced annually in the late eleventh century would not be matched anywhere in the world for 700 years); gunpowder and the cannon for military conquest; the compass and the rudder for exploration; paper and movable type for printing; the iron plough, the horse collar, rotary threshing machines, and mechanical seeders to generate agricultural surpluses; the ability to drill for natural gas; and in mathematics the decimal system, negative numbers, and the concept of zero, which put the Chinese far ahead of the Europeans.

Large Chinese armadas — carrying as many as 28,000 men — were exploring Africa's east coast at about the same time that Portugal and Spain were sending much smaller expeditions down the west coast of Africa. Seven major Chinese expeditions explored the Indian Ocean with ships four times as large as those of Columbus.

But the geographic conquests and the industrial revolution that were possible did not happen. The Chinese rejected and ultimately forgot the technologies that could have given them world dominance. New technologies were perceived as threats rather than opportunities.

## 502. Chinese Dictator Mao on Technology

Mao Zedong (1893-1976) was the founder of the People's Republic of China and chairman of the Chinese Communist Party. He was an absolute dictator in every way.

He had a little set speech he was fond of giving to visitors. It went like this:

"Our fathers were indeed wise. They invented printing, but not newspapers. They invented gunpowder, but used it only for fireworks. Finally, they invented the compass, but took care not to use it to discover America."

## 503. Computer History

The following consists of excerpts from the text of a letter sent to Thomas Watson, Jr., (1914-1993) chairman of IBM, by Charles W. Springer of Bellerose, New York; the year it was received was 1968. The Hollerith machines mentioned in the letter were manufactured by IBM, then under the chairmanship of Thomas J. Watson, Sr. The Hollerith machines used punched cards and were ancestors of today's computers.

In the letter, Springer said he had worked for the early Hollerith company and had operated a tabulator at the Inter-Ocean building during the census of 1890.

The 92-year-old Springer wrote:

"Mechanics were there frequently...to get the ailing machines back in operation. The trouble was usually that somebody had extracted the mercury (which made the necessary electrical contacts) from one of the little cups with an eye-dropper and squirted it into a spittoon, just to get some un-needed rest.

"My immediate superior was a Mr. Shaw, and it was a saying in the office that 'Shaw does nothing and Springer helps him.' This was not true...Much of the time I didn't help him at all...

"Shaw was a remarkable man. With a drink or two, he could add three columns of figures simultaneously and get the right answer faster than any machine before or since. If he could have been kept in just the right amount of liquor, Hollerith's machines might now be no more of a memory than the Inter-Ocean Building and what would you, Mr. Watson, be doing now?"

## 504. Hay as Technology

The technologies which have had the most important effect on civilization are usually simple. Dr. Freeman J. Dyson (1923- ), a distinguished English-born physicist and educator, believes that a good example of a simple technology with great historical consequences is hay.

Whoever he was, the person who first discovered hay was the person who first had the idea to cut grass in the autumn and to store it in large enough quantities to keep horses and cows alive through the winter. We know that the technology of hay was unknown to the Roman Empire but was known to every village of medieval Europe.

Like many other crucially important technologies, the practice of cutting and storing hay emerged silently during the Dark Ages. According to the Hay Theory of History, the invention of hay was the decisive event which moved the center of gravity of urban civilization from the Mediterranean basin to Northern and Western Europe.

The Roman Empire did not need hay because in a Mediterranean climate grass grew well enough in winter so that animals could graze. That was not so north of the Alps. For large cities to grow there, it was necessary for them to have supplies of hay to feed the horse and oxen on which they were dependent for motive power. So it was hay that allowed populations to grow and civilizations to flourish among the forests of Northern Europe. Although it is hard to believe, it was hay that was responsible for moving the greatness of Rome to Paris and London, and later to Berlin and Moscow and New York.

## 505. The "First" Computer Bug

The first computer bug was an actual bug, a 2-inch long moth that got into the circuits of a Mark II computer at Harvard University in 1945. It was discovered by Grace Murray Hopper (1906-1992) and her assistant and it was removed with a tweezer.

"From then on," said Hopper, "when anything went wrong with a computer, we said it had bugs in it."

Hopper went on to become a Rear Admiral in the Navy and, for her many other endeavors, won fame in the early history of computing.

The moth is preserved today in the Naval Museum at Dahlgren, Virginia.

Note: According to some computer historians, the computer term, "bug", to describe a defect in a computer program, did not derive from this incident. The use of "bug" to refer to a defect in an apparatus or its operation dates from the early 1800s.

## 506. Highway Innovation

Paved highways have lines painted down their middle today because of an innovation made by Dr. June A. Carroll of Indio, California. Back in 1912 good roads were few and certainly none had lines painted down their middle to divide lanes. Automobiles themselves were still a novelty then.

Dr. Carroll did have an automobile and when she visited patients from her office near Palm Springs, California, she could often barely tell which side of the desert road she was on, especially at night.

So she bought a can of white paint and painted a line down the middle of a one-mile stretch of treacherous highway to help uncertain travelers find their way. Shortly afterward, the California Highway Commission adopted the idea and you know what happened from there.

## 507. Bad Predictions

- In 10 A.D., the esteemed Roman engineer Julius Sextus Frontinus (ca. 40 BC-103 AD) proclaimed, "Inventions have long since reached their limit, and I see no hope for further developments."

- In 1899, the Director of the U.S. Patent Office did it again. He advised President William McKinley (1843-1901) to close the Office, saying that everything that can be invented has been invented.

- In 1896, an English journal predicted that the idea of the wireless transmission of the human voice would be forgotten by the end of the year.

- When the automobile appeared, a number of American physicians solemnly declared that the human body could never withstand velocities exceeding 15 miles per hour.

- In 1925, a French journal of surgery warned that blood transfusions would prove fatal.

- In 1888, University of California Professor Joseph Le Conte (1823-1901) wrote, "One: There is a low limit of weight (of about) 50 pounds beyond which it is impossible for an animal to fly. Two: The animal machine is far more effective than any we can hope to make. Three: The weight of any machine constructed for flying, including fuel and engineer, cannot be less than three or four hundred pounds. Therefore is it not demonstrated that a true flying machine, self-raising, self-sustaining, self-propelling, is physically impossible?"

- Thomas Edison (1847-1931) once predicted, "Fooling around with alternating current is just a waste of time. Nobody will use it, ever."

- Albert Einstein (1879-1955) stated, "There is not the slightest indication that nuclear energy will be obtainable."

## 508. Our Cloudy Crystal Ball

In March of 1949, Popular Mechanics magazine looked as far into the future as it dared, and wrote this about the future of computing:

"Where a calculator on the ENIAC is equipped with 18,000 vacuum tubes and weighs 30 tons, computers in the future may have only 1,000 vacuum tubes and perhaps only weigh 1 1/2 tons."

## 509. Computer History

The first punched data cards were invented before there were any computers in the world. They were used in the Jacquard Loom, a weaving machine invented in 1801 by Joseph-Marie Jacquard (1752-1834).

The cards were carried in linked chains, and they controlled the weaving pattern by influencing the position of the needles. Small sensing pins detected the presence or absence of holes in the cards, and determined whether or not a needle would pick up a thread.

On seeing Jacquard's punched card system, the English mathematician Charles Babbage (1791-1871) was inspired to use the same principles to design a mechanical calculating machine, the forerunner of modern computers.

## 510. The Invention of Ear Muffs

Thomas Edison (1847-1931) gets all the credit for inventing things but the facts are America has had plenty of much younger innovators who had plenty of great ideas too.

Consider the case of 15-year-old Chester Greenwood (1858-1937) who, in 1873, invented ear muffs to keep his ears from freezing while he was ice skating near his home in Farmington, Maine.

Chester's ears itched fiercely at the touch of a wool scarf, so he had his Grandmother sew together what he called "ear mufflers" made of beaver fur on the outside and black velvet on the inside. The "ear mufflers" proved so popular he was able to patent them on March 13, 1877.

Before he died in 1937 at the age of 79, Greenwood had been granted more than 130 other patents. And by 1936 he had a factory turning out more than 400,000 pairs of ear muffs each year.

Edison would have loved the boy.

## 511. Friction Matches

The first friction matches were invented in England in the 1820s.

To be lit, they had to be pulled through a folded strip of sandpaper. These early matches were less convenient and more dangerous than the ones we use today.

The modern safety match, which can be lit easily only when struck on a specific surface, was invented in Sweden in 1855 by J.E. Lundstrom (1815-1888). It works because one of the chemicals needed to start the fire is in the striking surface.

Another curious (and dangerous) early match consisted of a glass bulb wrapped in paper, filled with sulfuric acid. The user had to bite the paper, breaking the bulb and setting the paper on fire.

## 512. Why Your Keyboard Is Arranged the Way It Is

Almost every alphabetic keyboard in the world has the letters in an arrangement called "qwerty," after the first six letters in the top row. There are several popular myths about the origin of today's standard keyboard arrangement. Some say it was deliberately designed to slow down typists. What is the truth?

When inventor C. L. Sholes (1819-1890) built his first typewriter in 1868, he arranged the keys in alphabetical order. But the clumsy mechanical linkages inside the machine would tangle if certain pairs of keys were struck quickly.

The "qwerty" arrangement fixed the tangling problem by separating the internal links for frequently paired letters, making the machines more reliable.

After a historic typing contest, "qwerty" became the standard way to arrange the keys.

## 513. Divine Inspiration

Arthur Fry (1941- ) sang in a choir in St. Paul, Minnesota. It bugged him when the bits of paper marking his place in the hymnal kept falling out.
One Sunday, during this weekly annoyance, he remembered an adhesive a 3M colleague had invented. Unlike most adhesives, this adhesive could be easily detached.

Using this information, Fry went on to invent "Post-it" notepads at the 3M company. The notepads became one of the five best-selling office products in the world.

"I don't know if it was a dull sermon or divine inspiration that gave me the idea," says Fry.

## 514. Negative Thinking

Robert Fulton (1765-1815) in 1807 attracted a large crowd to witness the first full-scale demonstration of the steamboat on the Hudson River.

When he tried to get the engine started, the crowd shouted, "It will never start! It will never start!"

When the engine finally did start and the steamboat took off with a flurry of sparks and heavy smoke, the crowd was silent for a moment — but only for a moment.

Then it began screaming, "It will never stop! It will never stop!"

## 515. The Greatest Generation Fires Back

Ronald Reagan (1911-2004) was speaking to a student audience at the University of California at Berkeley when a student got up to say that it was impossible for people of his generation to understand the next generation of young people.

"You grew up in a different world," the student said, "Today, we have television, jet planes, space travel, nuclear energy, computers..."

When the student paused for breath, Reagan said, "You're right. We didn't have those things when we were young. We invented them."

## 516. How Your Car Gets Painted

Charles F. Kettering (1876-1958) was the first head of research at General Motors and he was struggling with a problem – slow drying paint.

It was around 1919 and painting cars then was a terribly slow process done by hand. It could take as long as thirty-seven days to paint a car. Finding this totally unacceptable, Kettering met with paint manufacturers to see if they could devise a faster-drying finish. He was told that at best the time could be cut to a month. "An hour would be more like it," he responded.

One day while on a trip to New York, Kettering saw in a store window a wooden tray with a lacquer finish he did not recognize. He purchased the tray, located its manufacturer, and bought a few cans of the lacquer. Then he asked DuPont to analyze it. The result was a new kind of pyroxylin lacquer that would dry in minutes.

Despite this, the paint men remained skeptical. Kettering took one of them to lunch and afterward accompanied him to the parking lot. The man couldn't find his car.

"Isn't that yours?" asked Kettering, pointing.

"It looks like mine, but my car isn't that color," said the man.

"It is now," Kettering said.

## 517. Invention of the Sewing Machine

Elias Howe (1819-1867), who for years had been trying to invent a practical sewing machine, fell asleep one night and had a nightmare.

He dreamed that primitive tribesmen had captured him and were threatening to run him through with their spears. Howe noticed that the natives' spears all had holes through them at their pointed ends.

When he suddenly awoke, he realized the idea that would lead to a perfected sewing machine: use a needle with a hole not through its base or middle but through its tip.

## 518. How the @ Sign Was Born

Everyone who uses email knows the "at sign," the little "a" with a circle around it. It separates the user's online name from his or her mail server address. Before it was used in email addresses, the "at sign" was used in invoices to show how much each item cost, and in a few other places.

Like its relative, the ampersand, the "at sign" was invented in the days before printing presses, to shorten the task of transcribing documents. As short as the word "at" might be, it was still common enough in texts that medieval monks thought it would be worthwhile to shorten it even more. So they looped the "t" around and made it into a circle, saving one stroke of the pen.

The "at sign" has no official one-word name, even though many names have been proposed. Among the proposed names, arobase, vortex, and snail.

## 519. The Perfect Automobile

Once upon a time there was an enterprising businessman who had a fantastic idea. He figured out a way to build the perfect automobile.

He hired a team of young engineers and told them to buy one of every model car in the world and dismantle them.

He instructed them to pick out the best part from every car and to place it in a special room. Soon the room was filled with parts judged by the group to be the best engineered in the world — the best carburetor, the best set of brakes, the best steering wheel, the best transmission, and so on. It was an impressive collection — more than 5,000 parts in all.

Then he had all the parts assembled into one automobile — the pick of the world so to speak.

There was only one problem. The automobile refused to function — the parts would not work together.

One could draw a number of morals from this fictitious story. But one of them is that a group of people or things with a common objective and harmony about them can be superior to a team of individualistic "all stars" any day.

## 520. Next Generation of the Internet

In a speech given in 2006 in Las Vegas, Ivan Seidenberg (1946- ), the chairman and CEO of Verizon, gave his version of what he thought the next generation of the Internet would bring. Here is a summation of his remarks.

The next generation of broadband experiences won't be text-based or verbal, as they are today. They'll be visual. High-definition. Three-dimensional. Like the holograms in *Star Wars* — that come to life.

Nobody quite knows how all of this comes together, but what it does mean is that all of the applications we've been predicting for years will be compelling in a very new and more powerful way. With widespread deployment of 100-megabit networks.

- Doctors will "see" their patients.
- Students will be "in" the classroom.
- Business partners will negotiate "face to face" across the conference room.
- People with disabilities will "go" to work.
- E-Bay shoppers will "touch and feel" the merchandise.
- On-line gamers will "become" the game.
- And grandparents will practically be able to blow out the candles and taste the cake at their grandkids' birthday party.

All of this will be possible, no matter if you're across the street, across the country, or across the globe.

## 521. Space Invention

During the heat of the space race in the 1960s, the U.S. National Aeronautics and Space Administration decided it needed a ball point pen to write in the zero gravity confines of its space capsules.

After considerable research and development, the Astronaut Pen was developed at a cost of approximately $1 million. The pen worked and also enjoyed some modest success as a novelty item back here on earth. The Soviet Union, faced with the same problem, used a pencil.

The other part of the story is sharpening a pencil in space creates pencil shavings and graphite dust floating in the air. So when the U.S. and Russians had their first link-up in space, one of the first things the Russians requested from the orbiting U.S. astronauts was their pressurized pens.

## 522. Answering the Telephone

In the early days of the telephone, people didn't like the idea of picking up a strange electronic instrument and talking to a total stranger. They also were confused as to what they might use as a standard greeting at the beginning of a conversation.

Alexander Graham Bell (1847-1922), who invented the telephone, suggested that people use the nautical term "Ahoy" to greet someone at the other end of the line.

But the famous inventor Thomas Edison (1847-1931) had a better idea. He coined a brand new word: "hello." The term first appeared in American literature in 1880 when Mark Twain described the first telephone operators as "hello girls."

In 1883, the new word was published in the *Oxford English Dictionary* for the first time.

## 523. Invention of the Stirrup

One of the most decisive battles in world history was fought in 1066. William, Duke of Normandy (1027-1087), invaded England in the face of England's formidable forces. What gave William the confidence to launch such a risky undertaking was that he possessed a recently-invented technological edge that the English did not. That edge was the stirrup.

Although the English rode by horseback to the battlefield, they fought on foot. They believed the horse was too unstable a platform from which to fight.

However, standing secure in their stirrups, the Norman cavalry were able to ride down the English, letting the weight of their charging horses drive their lances home.

William's technological edge made possible the conquest of Britain. Without it, he might never have attempted such a perilous war. Advanced technology has been helping win battles ever since, both on the battlefield and in business as well.

## 524. Accepting the Telephone

According to Peter F. Drucker (1909-2005), noted Austrian-born American management consultant and author, the first management conference we know of was called in 1882 by the German Post Office. Only chief executive officers were invited and the topic was how not to be afraid of the telephone.

Nobody showed up. The invitees were insulted. The idea that they should use telephones was unthinkable. The telephone was for underlings.

## 525. More about Telephones

The telephone may be the most important communication tool of our time. Here are some interesting, unexpected, and thought-provoking facts about the telephone, its history and its impact on our world:

When telephones were first introduced into the White House, presidents made their phone calls in a booth outside their office. In 1929 Herbert Hoover (1874-1964) was the first U.S. president to have a phone installed on his desk. Prior to 1929, he used a telephone booth outside his office.

Eighty-eight million households in the U.S. have at least one telephone.

More than one-third of owners of answering machines use them to screen calls.

## 526. Suspicion of Technology

The following news item appeared in an 1868 New York City paper:

A man has been arrested in New York for attempting to extort funds from ignorant and superstitious people by exhibiting a device which he says will convey the human voice any distance over metallic wires so that it will be heard by the listener at the other end. He calls the instrument a telephone. Well-informed people know that it is impossible to transmit the human voice over wires.

## 527. A True Story about Standards

Joseph D. Malone, then Massachusetts state treasurer, is the source of the following item:

"At the heart of my procurement system is THE SPEC. Government specs are notoriously difficult to change, no matter how outdated they become.

"I have a friend who deals with government contracts all the time. He loves to explain how specs live forever. Have you ever wondered, he asks, why the distance between rails on the American railroad system is exactly four feet, eight and a half inches? Turns out, it was chosen because that's the gauge of the English railroad system and expatriate English railroad engineers built the American railroad.

"So why did the English use that gauge? Because their railroad was built by the same people who built the English tramways, and that was the distance between tramway rails. The reason for that, it seems, was that the people who built the tramways used the same jigs and tools that were used for building wagons, and the wheels on English wagons all had to have exactly that spacing.

"What was so special, then, about that spacing? Apparently, all of the ruts on the old English long distance roads were exactly four feet eight and a half inches apart and unless the wagon wheels fit into those ruts, they'd break.

"So where did the ruts come from? Well, the first long distance roads in Europe were built by Imperial Rome for the benefit of their legions and the ruts were made by Roman war chariots, which all had exactly that wheel spacing. And as it turns out, there was actually a very straightforward engineering reason that Roman chariots had that particular wheel spacing. They were built just wide enough to accommodate the rear ends of two Roman horses.

"So you may not be too far off the mark the next time you see a particularly odd government spec and ask, "What horse's ass came up with this?"

Note: This may be hard to believe but, after reading the above, an engineer connected with the U.S. space effort wrote the following:

"When we see a Space Shuttle sitting on its launch pad, there are two big booster rockets attached to the sides of the main fuel tank. These are solid rocket boosters, or SRBs. Thiokol makes the SRBs at their factory at Utah.

"The engineers who designed the SRBs might have preferred to make them a bit wider, but the SRBs had to be shipped by train from the factory to the launch site. The railroad line from the factory had to run through a tunnel in the mountains. Therefore, the SRBs had to fit through that tunnel. The tunnel is slightly wider than the railroad track, and the railroad track is about as wide as two horses' behinds."

"So, the major design feature of what is arguably the world's most advanced transportation system was determined by the width of a horse's rear end."

## 528. When Telephones Were an Oddity

We take the telephone so for granted today it is hard to comprehend what a scientific oddity it seemed at the time.

Its creator — Alexander Graham Bell (1847-1922) — invented the telephone in 1876 and patented it the same year. And a few months later, it was the hit of the centenary's celebrations of the Declaration of Independence.

Even so, people did not foresee how pervasive the telephone would become within the space of a generation.

An American mayor was thought daring when he predicted that, "One day there will be one in every city."

And in Britain, Sir William Preece, chief engineer of the Post Office, told a House of Commons committee, "The Americans have need of the telephone, but we do not. We have plenty of messenger boys."

## 529. Where New Ideas Come From

A news reporter once complimented Thomas Edison (1847-1931) on his inventive genius.

"I am not a great inventor," said Edison.

"But you have over 1,000 patents to your credit," protested the reporter.

"Yes," replied Edison, "but about the only invention I can really claim as absolutely original is the phonograph. I'm an awfully good sponge. I absorb ideas from every source I can and put them to practical use. Then I improve them until they become of some value."

Then Edison added, "The ideas I use are mostly the ideas of other people who don't develop them themselves."

## 530. The Eye of Inventors

GALILEO (1564-1642), Italian astronomer, saw the lenses in the eye of an ox and copied them into his telescope.

JOHANN WOLFGANG VON GOETHE (1749-1832), German author, saw that the core of the apple repeated the blossom, and that the leaf of the tree was a miniature of the oak and elm.

PIERRE LAPLACE (1749-1827), French astronomer, saw the Milky Way in the heavens and the rings around Saturn, and with his telescope broke up the milky whiteness into myriads of suns and stars and cosmic systems.

## 531. Busman's Holiday

One evening after inventor Thomas Edison (1847-1931) came home from a long day at work, his wife said to him, "You've worked long enough without a rest. You must go on a vacation."

"But where on earth would I go?" asked Edison.

"Just decide where you would rather be than anywhere else on earth," suggested his wife.

"Very well," said Edison, "I'll go tomorrow."

The next morning he was back at work in his laboratory.

# 532. New Inventions Are Suspected

New inventions are often suspected and resisted by the public. Here are some examples:

1.  The first successful cast-iron plow, invented in the United States in 1797 was rejected by New Jersey farmers under the theory that cast iron poisoned the land and stimulated the growth of weeds.

2.  An eloquent authority in the United States declared that the introduction of the railroad would require the building of many insane asylums, since people would be driven mad with terror at the sight of locomotives rushing across the country.

3.  In Germany it was proved by "experts" that if trains went at the frightful speed of 15 miles an hour, blood would spurt from the travelers' noses and passengers would suffocate when going through tunnels.

4.  Commodore Cornelius Vanderbilt (1794-1877) dismissed Westinghouse and his new air brakes for trains, saying, "I have no time to waste on fools."

5.  Those who loaned Robert Fulton (1765-1815) money for his steamboat project stipulated that their names be withheld for fear of ridicule were it known they supported anything so "foolhardy."

6.  In 1881, when the New York YWCA announced typing lessons for women, vigorous protests were made on the grounds that the female constitution would break down under the strain.

7.  Men insisted that iron ships would not float, that they would damage more easily than wooden ships when grounded, that it would be difficult to preserve the iron bottom from rust, and that iron would deflect the compass.

8.  Joshua Coppersmith was arrested in Boston for trying to sell stock in the telephone. "All well-informed people know that it is impossible to transmit the human voice over a wire."

9.  The editor of the Springfield Republican refused an invitation to ride in an early automobile, claiming that it was incompatible with the dignity of his position.

10. When Adam Thompson of Cincinnati, Ohio, filled the first bathtub in the United States in 1842, doctors predicted rheumatism and inflammation of the lungs would result.

11. Edward Jenner (1749-1823), who discovered vaccine used against small pox in 1796, was jeered. Some serious-minded critics went so far as to say that vaccinations would cause animal diseases to be transferred to the human race. Some said horns had actually been grown out of the foreheads of innocent people. Despite these fears, the dreaded smallpox was eliminated by using his vaccine.

## 533. Unwanted Inventions

Few people in history have been more creative than the famous inventor Thomas Edison. Nevertheless, he didn't always succeed.

Early in his career, Edison invented a vote-recording machine for use in legislatures. By moving an electric switch to the right or left, a legislator could vote for or against a proposal without leaving his desk. The machine would replace the tedious business of marking and counting ballots.

Excited about the prospects of his new invention, Edison obtained a patent (his first) and headed for Washington, D.C. to demonstrate the device before the chairman of a powerful Congressional committee.

After complimenting the young inventor on his ingenuity, the chairman promptly turned it down with this explanation.

"Filibustering and delay in the tabulation of votes," said the chairman," are often the only means we have for defeating bad or improper legislation."

Edison was crestfallen. He knew his invention was good and he knew that the Congressman knew that it was good also. Still, it wasn't wanted.

Edison said later, "Right there and then I made a vow that I would never again invent anything that no one wanted."

## 534. Skepticism about New Inventions

William Ewart Gladstone (1809-1898), then Chancellor of the Exchequer in Great Britain, interrupted Michael Faraday (1791-1867) as he was describing his work on electricity.

"But, after all," said Gladstone impatiently, "what use is it?"

In a flash came Faraday's response: "Why, sir, there is every probability that you will soon be able to tax it!"

Benjamin Franklin (1706-1790) was asked a similar question about the use of a new invention he was describing.

Franklin quickly replied, "What is the use of a newborn child?"

## 535. Inventions of the Twentieth Century

Here is a list of the top inventions that changed the way we lived and worked in the 20th century. The list was compiled by Martin C. Jischke (1941- ), president of Purdue University.

- electrification
- automobiles
- airplanes
- water supply
- electronics
- radio and television
- agricultural mechanization
- computers
- telephones
- air conditioning
- interstate highways

- the Internet
- imaging
- health technologies
- petrochemical technologies
- lasers and fiber optics
- nuclear technologies
- high-performance materials

Close your eyes and try to imagine our world today without these contributions from engineers as well as those from scientists. These are advancements that took us from the horse-and-buggy age at the dawn of the 20th century to the space age and the exploration of Mars and other planets at the dawn of the 21st.

## 536. Pushing the Envelope

As many of you know, "pushing the envelope" is a phrase that originated with American test pilots in the 1940s. Each aircraft they flew was said to have an "envelope" of performance. In other words, it was designed to fly safely up to a certain speed for a certain distance at a certain altitude. The job of test pilots was to "push the envelope" by making the plane go faster, farther, higher.

## 537. Always Something New

At a friend's luxurious estate in Connecticut, the colorful movie producer Sam Goldwyn noticed a curious metal object on a pedestal in the center of the garden.

"What's that?" he asked.

"That's a sundial, Sam," said his host.

"A sundial," said Goldwyn, "what does it do?"

Slowly and carefully, the host explained how "the vertical part casts a shadow, and the place that shadow falls on marks the time."

"Amazing," said Goldwyn. "What won't they think of next!"

# IRISH

## 538. How the Word Blarney Was Born

The person credited with first using the word "blarney" is Queen Elizabeth the First (1533-1603). One of her deputies in Ireland was trying, with no results, to persuade the owner of Blarney Castle to give up his ancient right to ownership of the castle. All he delivered to the Queen was excuses, excuses, excuses.

When the agent reported to the Queen, she went into a rage screaming, "Blarney, Blarney — it's all Blarney. What he says he does not mean. What he means he does not say."

What is the actual definition of the word blarney? Maybe the queen was right. Blarney is not the same as insincerity. It may deceive or flatter you but people using it properly do it without offending you. It is the Irish only who possess the perfect sixth sense on how to dispense blarney properly. It is the gift of saying the right thing rather than the wrong thing. The Irish believe over reliance on facts should not be allowed to get in the way of expressing the truth.

## 539. The Legend of Ireland's Blarney Stone

For many centuries, as everyone knows, English monarchs tried to impose their will on Ireland. Queen Elizabeth I, eager to extend the influence of her government, sent a deputy to Cormac MacDermot MacCarthy who was Lord of Blarney and demanded that he take the tenure of his lands from the Crown.

Cormac set out to visit the Queen and plead for his traditional right to his land, but he despaired of success for he was not fluent of speech.

Legend has it that, shortly after starting his journey, he met an old woman who asked him why he looked so forlorn. He told her his story and she said, "Cormac, when Blarney Castle was built, one stone was put in place by a man who predicted no one would ever be able to touch it again. If you can kiss that stone, the gift of eloquence will be conferred upon you."

Cormac succeeded in kissing the stone and was able to address the Queen with speech so soft and words so fair that, as long as he lived, he never had to renounce his right to his land.

Each year some 70,000 believers visit Blarney Castle in County Cork and climb 120 feet to kiss the Blarney Stone. To do this, you have to hang upside down. The touchstone of eloquence is a nondescript block of limestone about four feet long, one foot wide and nine inches high.

As usual with the Irish, there are many stories surrounding the stone. One is that it is Jacob's Pillow brought back from the Holy Land after the Crusades.

# KINDNESS

### 540. Kindness Is Powerful

Dale Carnegie (1888-1955), who made a fortune writing about how to make friends and influence people, liked to tell the following story:

"Years ago, when I was a barefoot boy walking through the woods to a country school out in northwest Missouri, I read a fable about the sun and the wind.

"They quarreled about which was the stronger, and the wind said, 'I'll prove I am. See the old man down there with a coat? I bet I can get his coat off him quicker than you can.'

"So the sun went behind a cloud, and the wind blew until it was almost a tornado, but the harder it blew, the tighter the old man clutched his coat to him.

"Finally, the wind calmed down and gave up, and then the sun came out from behind the clouds and smiled kindly on the old man. Presently, he mopped his brow and pulled off his coat.

"The sun then told the wind that gentleness and friendliness were always stronger than fury and force."

## 541. The Wisdom of St. Francis

The people of the little Italian city of Gubbio are understandably very proud of their beautiful home. It is both beautiful and peaceful. Then one night a shadow came out of the nearby woods and prowled the streets.

In the morning the townspeople were horrified to find on the street a mangled and gnawed dead body. This happened again and again. Finally an old woman said she had seen a wolf on the streets at night. The terrified people decided to ask a holy man who had a reputation for being able to talk to animals for his help. They sent a delegation to get St. Francis of Assisi.

They had very specific ideas on what St. Francis should tell the wolf. They demanded that he should preach to the wolf and remind him to obey the commandment against killing and to follow Christ's commandment about loving God and neighbors. Then, just in case, since a wolf is, after all, a wolf, he should tell the wolf to move to someone else's city.

St. Francis went into the forest and was able to meet "the strange shadow," which, of course, was a wolf. He addressed it as "Brother Wolf" and they had a brief conversation.

Then he returned to the town square. "My good people," said St. Francis to the assembled people of the town, "the answer to your problem is very simple. You must feed your wolf."

The townspeople were furious, especially at St. Francis's suggestion that this uninvited beast in their midst was somehow to be regarded as "their wolf." But, after much argument, they did feed it, and the killing stopped.

## 542. Three Ways to Be Kind

Fred Rogers (1928-2003), a revered television personality whose programs for children are still remembered, said this about kindness:

"There are three ways to ultimate success:

The first way is to be kind.

The second way is to be kind.

The third way is to be kind.

## 543. About Life

The following words about kindness are widely attributed to Stephen Grellet (1773-1855), a French-born Quaker clergyman who came to the U.S. in 1795, although they have not been found in his writings:

"I expect to pass through this world but once; any good thing, therefore, that I can do, or any kindness that I can show to any fellow creature, let me do it now, let me not defer nor neglect it, for I shall not pass this way again."

## 544. Audrey Hepburn on Kindness

Audrey Hepburn (1929-1993) was a famous actor whose elfin charm was known around the world. Born in Brussels, Belgium, she was a special ambassador for the United Nations International Children's Emergency Fund from 1988 to 1992: Here are some unusual beauty tips she once gave out:

"For attractive lips, speak words of kindness.
For lovely eyes, seek out the good in people.
For a slim figure, share your food with the hungry.
For beautiful hair, let a child run his fingers through it once a day.
For poise walk with the knowledge that you will never walk alone."

## 545. About Kindness

The following poem by Adam Lindsay Gordon (1833-1870), a 19th century Australian poet, was used by Princess Diana of Great Britain (1961-1997) at a 1996 cancer benefit in Washington, D.C.:

"Life is mostly froth and bubble.
Two things stand like stone,
Kindness is another's trouble,
Courage is your own."

# LANGUAGE

## 546. Define Your Words

Benjamin Disraeli (1804-1881), the famously articulate British prime minister, meticulously corrected himself during a parliamentary debate by substituting the word "misfortune" for "calamity."

Questioned afterward about his reason for drawing a distinction between the two words, Disraeli invoked the name of his great political rival William Gladstone (1809-1898) to explain in this manner.

"If, for example," Disraeli said, "Mr. Gladstone were to fall accidentally into the Thames, that would be a misfortune. But if anyone were then to pull him out, that would be a calamity."

## 547. Naming Something Doesn't Make It So

Failing to convince an opponent that his reasoning was faulty, Abraham Lincoln asked him, "Well, tell me how many legs has a cow?"

"Four, of course," was the quick reply.

"That's right," said Lincoln. "Now suppose we call the cow's tail a leg, how many legs would the cow have?"

"Why, five, obviously."

"That's where you are wrong," replied Lincoln. "Simply calling a cow's tail a leg doesn't make it a leg."

## 548. A Moving Library

The following is an excerpt from a speech made by Dr. Joseph Hankin, president of Westchester Community College to the Westchester Library Association, Bronxville, New York:

"In the 10th century, Abdul Kassem Ismael, the scholarly grand-vizier of Persia, had a library of 117,000 volumes. On his many travels as a warrior and statesman, he never parted with his beloved books. They were carried about by 400 camels trained to walk in alphabetical order!

"Today's speech is about the need to change. If we utilized the camel caravan, in order to hold the 6 million books in the Pals-Waldo consortium collection, we would need more than 20,000; if the WLS libraries were to join in, we would need another 7,000 camels! We cannot carry our books about by camel today, but we can by computer, and they are more versatile and less hungry, and cleaner!"

## 549. Slippers

Have you ever wondered why on earth poor Cinderella had to wear glass slippers? Dancing with a prince must have been nerve-wracking enough without worrying about your shoes breaking into a million pieces if the prince happened to step on your foot.

The story was written by a Frenchman named Charles Perrault (1628-1703) who lived in the 17th century. The story is that Perrault wrote that Cinderella's slippers were made of "vair" which is ermine. The slippers therefore were made of fur.

One version of how the mistake was made is that a proofreader thought that "vair" was a spelling error and that the author had meant to write "verre" or glass. And the rest is history.

## 550. Funny TV Mistakes

Lawrence Welk (1903-1992) was a fabulously successful orchestra leader and accordionist whose dance orchestra was a favorite of the nation for decades. All his life, he retained a Middle-European accent and in 1971 even titled his autobiography, "Wunnerful, Wunnerful."

When television came in, Welk became just as popular on TV as he had been on radio, but he occasionally had trouble reading the "idiot boards" held up off-camera to help him with his lines.

On one occasion, he announced he was going to play a selection of music made famous during the years 1939-1945 — or as he put it, reading the cue cards, "During the years of World War Eye-Eye."

## 551. A Queen's Displeasure

Malarkey is an old expression for bunk or baloney. It is based on the Queen of England's displeasure with an Irishman named Malarkey who persisted in stalling on something he was supposed to do — all he did was talk and talk some more.

Whereupon the Queen exclaimed, "That's all Malarkey!" So what had been a fine Irish family name suddenly became a noun — a synonym for insincere or foolish talk.

## 552. A Maxim for Hard Work

"No pain, no gain." One version or another of this popular saying has been in use for centuries by people endeavoring to get in better physical shape by working out, by pursuing hard-to-achieve goals, and other forms of difficult tasks requiring self-denial and self-discipline.

The earliest published version of this saying dates from 1577 in John Grange's *The Golden Aphroditis*; "Who wants the fruit that harvest yields, must take the pain."

A similar saying appeared the same year in Nicholas Berton's "Works of a Young Wit;" "There are no gains without pains."

A version even closer to the modern wording appeared in *A Display of Duty*, a book about responsibility written by Leonard Wright in 1589. His wording was, "No gain without pain."

In America, Benjamin Franklin combined the saying with other maxims in *Poor Richard's Almanack*, published in 1745.

## 553. Churchill on Jargon

Winston Churchill had a lifelong hatred of bureaucratic jargon.
As head of Britain's Conservative Party following World War II, he battled the incumbent Socialist administration. Their jargon, he said, was as bad as their policies.

The poor were called "marginal stipend maintainers."
A cap on wages was called "incremental arrests."

The worst, Churchill said, was their calling a house or home a "local accommodation unit."

"I suppose now," said Churchill in a speech, "we will have to change that old and favorite song, 'Home, Sweet Home' to 'Local Accommodation Unit, Sweet Local Accommodation Unit!'"

## 554. Political Mud-Slinging

The 1950 political contest between Senator Claude Pepper (1900-1989) of Florida and his opponent, George A. Smathers (1913-2007), for a U.S. Senate seat set a high water mark in the "dirty tricks" department.

Smathers's campaign messages cleverly played on the public's limited vocabulary and bigoted tendencies. Pepper, he said, was guilty of indulging in celibacy, practicing nepotism, having a thespian sister and having a latent tendency toward overt extraversion.

Smathers won in a landslide.

Note: However, Pepper (1900-1989) went on to a long and illustrious career in the U.S. House of Representatives.

## 555. Government Mumbo-Jumbo

Looking back the danger now seems remote, but in February of 1942, early in World War II, American officials seriously believed it might be possible for Japan or Germany to bomb the United States.

An official of the General Services Administration presented President Franklin Roosevelt (1882-1945) with a copy of a notice that was to be placed in every room of every government office across the nation. Before it was approved, the President asked the official to read the notice aloud. It went like this:

"It is obligatory that all illumination be extinguished before the premises are vacated."

The President replied, "Why in hell don't you just say, 'Put out the lights when you leave'?"

# LAUGHTER

## 556. Gift of Laughter

There is an Apache legend that the Creator gave human beings the ability to talk, to run, and to look at things. But in addition, the legend says He was not satisfied until He also gave them the ability to laugh. After giving man the ability to laugh, the Creator said, "Now you are fit to live."

## 557. Laughter Insurance

Believe it or not, the comedy team of Bud Abbott (1895-1974) and Lou Costello (1906-1959), once bought a $100,000 insurance policy from Lloyds of London that guaranteed payment to them if any of their audiences should die of laughter.

## 558. Use of Humor to Soften Tension

During his years in the White House, Abraham Lincoln's use of stories to alleviate the strain of his office during the terrible Civil War years became so legendary that amusing tales began to circulate about him.

One he was fond of telling on himself was about two Quaker women in a railway coach who were overheard in a conversation about Lincoln and Jefferson Davis (1808-1889), president of the Confederacy.

"I think Jefferson [Davis] will succeed," said the first.

"Why does thee think so?" asked the second.

"Because Jefferson is a praying man."

"And so is Abraham a praying man."

"Yes," said the other woman, "but the Lord will think Abraham is joking."

"When I tell a funny story," said Lincoln to a friend, "it has the same effect on me that I suppose a good square drink of whiskey has on an old toper. It puts new life into me. The fact is, I have always believed that a good laugh was good for both the mental and the physical digestion."

Another time, Lincoln said simply, "I laugh because I must not weep. That's all."

## 559. The Riverman

Mark Twain (1835-1910) spent his early years as a river boat pilot on the Mississippi. One day some rivermen were sitting around swapping stories about the river and how high its banks had risen at floodtide.

Each of the men was trying to top the others. A man named Jake Anders said he had seen the Mississippi fifty miles wide at Natchez. Another named Bill Sharp said some tall pines on top of a hill on his property still bore the river's high-water marks on their topmost limbs.

Mark Twain listened to each man's boast patiently. Then he said with a chuckle, "Gentlemen, you don't know what a wide river is. I've seen this river so wide it had only one bank."

## 560. Comedy Is Hard

Edmund Gwenn (1875-1959) was a talented character actor who appeared in many movies. One part still remembered by millions was his role as "Santa Claus" in "Miracle on 34th Street." The movie is still played frequently on television during the Christmas holidays.

The story goes that, when Gwenn became old and sick, his best friend, George Seaton (1911-1979), was visiting Gwenn at the Actor's Home, a retirement home for actors that Gwenn had resisted entering even though he was in financial difficulty.

Seaton, who had directed Gwenn in the famous movie, went to see Gwenn when he heard that the actor's condition was worsening. On arriving at the Actor's Home, Seaton took a chair next to the bed of the old actor and waited quietly.

After Seaton had been there for some time, Gwenn opened his eyes and immediately recognized his friend of so many years.

"George," the old actor whispered, "I think I'm going to die."

"Yes," said Seaton, understandingly, "I know."

"George," said Gwenn, "I don't like it a bit. It's frightening and I hate it."

Not knowing what to say, Seaton replied, "Yes, old friend, I guess dying can be very hard."

Gwenn thought about this for a moment and then replied to Seaton saying, "Yes, but not as hard as playing comedy!"

Reportedly, these were Gwenn's last words.

# LAW ENFORCEMENT

## 561. Deep in the Heart of Texas

An early Captain of the storied Texas Rangers was a man named Bill MacDonald.

One day he received an urgent request that a company of Rangers was needed in a nearby town to suppress a riot. When MacDonald showed up all by himself, the frantic townspeople asked him, "Are you the only Ranger coming."

"Of course," said MacDonald, "you ain't got more than one riot have you?"

# LEADERSHIP

### 562. By Example

They tell this story of leadership about the famous general and Macedonian king Alexander the Great (356 BC-323 BC).

Once, while he was leading his thirsty army across the desert, a soldier came up to him, knelt down, and offered him a helmet filled with precious water.

"Is there enough there for 10,000 men?" asked Alexander.

When the soldier shook his head, Alexander poured the water out on the desert sands, refusing to take even a sip.

### 563. Not Always Popular

Former U.S. Secretary of State Colin Powell (1937- ) has some strong views on what it takes to be an effective leader.

In his book, *My American Journey*, Powell writes, "I learned...you cannot let the mission suffer, or make the majority pay to spare the feelings of an individual.

"I kept a saying under the glass of my desk at the Pentagon that made the point succinctly if inelegantly: 'Being responsible sometimes means pissing people off.'"

### 564. People Need Praise

The Duke of Wellington (1769-1852), Britain's brilliant military leader who defeated Napoleon at Waterloo, was a great commander but he was a difficult man to serve under. He was a perfectionist, demanding, and complimented his subordinates only on rare occasions.

In retirement, Wellington was asked by a visitor what, if anything, he would do differently if he had his life to live over again.

The old Duke thought for a moment and then said, "I'd give people I worked with more praise."

## 565. A Piece of String

General Dwight D. Eisenhower (1890-1969) used a simple device to illustrate the art of leadership. Laying an ordinary piece of string on a table, he'd illustrate how you could easily pull it in any direction.

"However, try and push it," he cautioned, "and it won't go anywhere. It's just that way when it comes to leading people."

## 566. George Washington

George Washington (1732-1799) knew a thing or two about being a leader. The following passage, taken from a letter to William Woodford in 1775, talks about how to treat the people who have to follow you into battle. The advice holds up well when put into a corporate setting.

"Be strict in your discipline; that is, to require nothing unreasonable of your officers and men, but see that whatever is required be punctually complied with.

"Reward and punish every man according to his merit, without partiality or prejudice; hear his complaints; if well founded, redress them; if otherwise, discourage them, in order to prevent frivolous ones.

"Discourage vice in every shape, and impress upon the mind of every man, from first to the lowest, the importance of the cause, and what it is they are contending for."

## 567. Alcohol

Abraham Lincoln was quoted as saying the following to a Congressional delegation in 1863 in answer to an allegation that General Ulysses S. Grant (1822-1885) was drinking while in the field.

"If I knew what brand of whiskey he drinks, I would send a barrel or so to some other generals."

Lincoln's remark was reportedly recorded by Chaplain John Eaton, who Lincoln told about the meeting with the Congressmen. However, Lincoln denied saying it and said he thought the story might have been inspired by a similar story about George II (1683-1760) of Great Britain and a General James Wolfe.

## 568. Make Haste Slowly

Titus (39-81), the emperor of Rome, had a symbol of a dolphin wound around an anchor inscribed on coins minted in his reign.

The dolphin was regarded as the swiftest and most mercurial of fish. The anchor represented delay and unchanging conviction. Together, they symbolized the failure that comes from rushing into something and the failure that is the result of hesitation or undue caution.

Through the years the dolphin and anchor have been used as a family crest with the explanatory motto "Festina lente," "Hasten slowly." It expresses moderation between two opposing ideas.

In leadership, it means the middle way between acting too quickly and waiting too long.

## 569. Leadership Garden

The following are remarks made by Betty DeVinney of the Eastman Chemical Company to a conference on Leadership at Kingsport, Tennessee:

"Let me leave you with a thought one of my colleagues shared with me the other day. Although we're on the verge of winter now, I believe it's a good analogy for you to carry with you. He said he encourages leaders to plant a garden when they're young so they can reap the harvest later. And in that garden, he tells you to plant 13 rows.

"First, leaders must plant three rows of peas:
Patience
Promptness
Prayer

"Then three rows of squash:
Squash gossip
Squash indifference
Squash criticism

"Then there should be three rows of lettuce:
Let us be true to our obligations
Let us be unselfish, and
Let us be loyal

"And, finally, leaders should plant four rows of turnips:
Turn up when needed
Turn up with determination
Turn up with a vision
And most of all, turn up with a smile"

"If you do that, and you're careful with how you communicate, you'll not only achieve results, but you'll have a fun time doing it."

## 570. Lincoln on Reform

Abraham Lincoln used to say that the pioneer in any movement is not generally the best man to carry that movement to a successful conclusion.

"Moses," he said, "began the emancipation of the Jews, but didn't take Israel to the Promised Land after all. He had to make way for Joshua to complete the work.

"It looks as if the first reformer of a thing has to meet such a hard opposition, and get so battered and bespattered that, afterward, when people find they have to accept his reform, they will accept it more easily from another man."

## 571. A Leadership Odyssey

The story of Homer's *Odyssey* is about a king named Odysseus. He and his men spent 10 years fighting the Trojan War, and they won!

Then they spent another 10 years trying to get home. Ten years at war; 10 years trying to get home. Sounds like a typical day at the office!

During those 10 years of trying to get home, Odysseus and his men are on a journey. There were successes, and there were failures.

There were experiences, and there were lessons learned.

All of those stories can tell us a lot about leadership, and we can apply them to our business today.

On their travels home, Odysseus and his men stopped at an island to get provisions. While on the island, his men met people who sit around all day and eat the sweet fruit of the lotus trees.

The fruit was so delicious these lotus eaters spend all their time eating it. They were addicted.

Odysseus' men tried the fruit and soon, they were addicted too. They had no interest in going home. They forgot all about it. They became totally complacent.

Odysseus had a goal. He had a vision. He wanted to get back home. So he forced his men to get on the ship by tying them up and making them leave.

In this story, Odysseus shows great leadership. He has a vision and a purpose, and he is focused on his goal.

## 572. Leaders Must Be a Bridge

There is an old Welsh story about a prince who was leading an army to free his sister. The forces fleeing from him cross a river and then break all the bridges. The prince, a giant of a man, laid himself across the river and his soldiers used him as their bridge. This story gives us the words:

"He who would lead let him be a bridge."

These words are wise, inspiring and humbling for any who aspire to leadership.

## 573. A Need for Leadership

A tale is told of a man in Paris during the upheaval in 1848, who saw a friend marching after a crowd toward the barricades. He warned his friend that the demonstrators could not be successful against the government's troops, and that he had better keep away. He received this reply:

"I must follow them. I am their leader."

## 574. The Frogs Seek a Leader

One of Aesop's tales was about frogs who wanted a leader. Over and over again they kept asking the god, Zeus, to send them one. Zeus finally responded by putting a log into their pond.

"Here is your leader," he said.

For a time the frogs were placated. But then they found they could jump all over their new leader. He offered no resistance. He just floated around without purpose or direction. This soon exasperated the frogs. They were looking for a strong leader.

The frogs went back to Zeus and complained about the aimlessness of their leader.

This time Zeus gave them a stork. The stork looked like a leader. He stood tall and had a certain dignity about him. The frogs were delighted as the great bird stalked around the pond, preening itself. It didn't really communicate with the frogs, but it did impress them as it made a clatter with its bill and especially when it rose in flight and soared overhead.

But then one day the stork began eating the frogs and panic set in. Only then did the frogs realize that leadership was more than looks and charisma. A good leader, they learned, had to have more purpose and direction than a log, but be less self-seeking than a stork. A good leader had to be sensitive to the needs of all the frogs in the pond.

## 575. Churchill on Lincoln

Winston Churchill (1874-1965), the great British leader who was often highly controversial, had this quotation from Abraham Lincoln (1809-1865) framed on the wall of his office:

"I do the best I can, I mean to keep going. If the end brings me out all right, then what is said against me won't matter. If I'm wrong, ten angels swearing I was right won't make a difference."

# LEGAL

### 576. The Magic Cigar

It couldn't happen today with tough no-smoking rules in our courtrooms. But there is a legend that the great trial lawyer Clarence Darrow (1857-1938) would sometimes light up a cigar just as the prosecution would begin its argument to the jury. Darrow would sit forward in rapt attention, and pulling quietly on his cigar.

As the cigar's ash began to grow longer and longer, the jury's attention often became more focused on when the lengthening cigar ash might fall than on the prosecuting attorney's argument.

Courtroom regulars claimed Darrow had cigars especially made, with a wire running through them to hold up the ash, and those who knew Darrow's competitive spirit best had no reason to doubt it.

### 577. Lincoln the Joke Teller

During the circuit court term in 1850, Abraham Lincoln and another lawyer friend were spectators at a trial. During the testimony, Mr. Lincoln heard something that made him think of a funny story. He started telling his friend the story, and the friend began laughing out loud.

This made the judge angry and he said to Mr. Lincoln, "Is this your court or mine?" He fined Mr. Lincoln's friend $5.00 for contempt of court.

Later, the judge called Lincoln's friend up to the bench and asked him to tell him the funny story Lincoln had related. After hearing the story, the judge started laughing, too. He changed his mind about the fine and gave the money back.

### 578. Disappearing Democrats

Justice in the Old West was swift and sometimes was even administered with a sense of humor.

In 1874, a man named Alfred G. Packer (1842-1907) took on the assignment of guiding five homesteaders along the Mormon Trail through the San Juan Mountains in Colorado.

It was mid-winter and the party disappeared in terrible snow storms. When Spring came, only Packer emerged from the mountains, looking sleek and well-fed. He was charged with cannibalism and found guilty. During his sentencing by Judge Melville G. Gerry, Gerry reportedly shouted at Packer:

"Stand up, yah voracious man-eatin' son-of-a-bitch and receive your sentence! There were only seven Dimocrats in all of Hinsdale County and you et five of them!"

Note: The cafeteria at the University of Colorado at Boulder is known as the Alfred G. Packer Grill.

## 579. Expert Witnesses

Abraham Lincoln began his career as a country lawyer. In most of his trial work, Lincoln's voice was usually calm and controlled. However, when he thought an injustice was about to be done his client, he could be quite inspired.

At one of his trials, the entire case hinged on the testimony of a celebrated surgeon.

Lincoln refused to examine any of the witnesses except the surgeon, who had made some very extreme statements. At the end of his cross-examination, Lincoln asked the surgeon, "Doctor, how much money are you going to receive for testifying in this case?"

The surgeon hesitated and then asked the judge, "Your honor, do I have to answer that question?" "Yes," said the judge, "it is proper."

The surgeon named a fee so large that the audience and the jury gasped.

Lincoln rose to his full height of six feet four inches, and stretching out his long right arm and forefinger, he said in a loud voice filled with indignation:

"Gentlemen of the jury, big fee, big swear!"

That was all Lincoln said to the jury. He won the case.

## 580. Human Justice

Fiorello La Guardia (1882-1947), New York City's flamboyant mayor during the thirties and forties, was a tough, two-fisted crusader for what he thought was right. But he was also a very human man.

One bitter cold day they brought a trembling old man before La Guardia, when he was presiding at the police court. The charge was stealing a loaf of bread. And the old man's excuse was that his family was starving.

"I've got to punish you," declared La Guardia. "The law makes no exception. I can do nothing but sentence you to a fine of ten dollars."

But the Little Flower, which was La Guardia's nickname, was reaching into his pocket as he added, "Well, here's the ten dollars to pay your fine. And now I remit the fine." And he tossed a ten-dollar bill into his famous sombrero.

"Furthermore," he declared, "I'm going to fine everybody in this courtroom fifty cents for living in a town where a man has to steal bread in order to eat. Mr. Bailiff, collect the fines and give them to this defendant!"

The hat was passed and an incredulous old man, with a light of heaven in his eyes, left the courtroom with a stake of forty-seven dollars and fifty cents.

## 581. Facts and Conclusions

For a brief period in his career, Abraham Lincoln was notably successful as a corporation lawyer. In one case he defended a railroad in a suit involving hundreds of thousands of dollars. The opposing attorney's summation to the jury was long, detailed, and eloquent and took more than two hours.

When it came Lincoln's turn to address the jury in rebuttal, he arose and said only: "My opponent's facts are right, but his conclusion is wrong." The jury burst out in laughter and brought in a verdict favoring Lincoln's client.

After Lincoln had won this stunning court victory following his one-sentence summation to the jury, several attorneys asked him how he was able to do it.

Lincoln told his colleagues that the night before the case went to the jury, he had a few drinks with the judge and the gentlemen of the jury, and during the evening he told them about the little farm boy who came running to his father one night and said, "Father, the hired hand is out in the barn with the new serving maid, and they're keeping the hay warm."

The farmer said, "Son, your facts are right but your conclusion is wrong."

That, Lincoln said, was just what he told the jury in rebutting his opponent's argument, and he suggested that the jury the next morning may have remembered the story of the previous evening.

## 582. Lawyers

Viewing lawyers as convenient scapegoats for some of the ills of society is not a new phenomenon.

Dorothy Parker (1893-1967), a luminary in New York literary circles during the heyday of the famous Algonquin Round Table, once was asked for a donation of $25 toward the burial of someone with whom she was not acquainted.

"Was he a writer?" she asked.

"No, he was a lawyer," was the reply.

Whereupon she produced $50 and gave it to the collector.

"Here," she said. "Go bury two."

## 583. Lincoln's View of Lawyers

After a long trip across country, in the coldest kind of weather to appear in court, Lincoln tarried at a town tavern. The fire was surrounded by numerous other attorneys interested in the case. The host decided to create a little conversation with Lincoln.

"Pretty cold tonight," he said.

"Colder than hell," Lincoln replied.

One of the lawyers turned at this and asked: "You've been there, too, have you Mr. Lincoln?"

"Oh, yes," he replied, "and the funny thing is that it's much like it is here. All the lawyers are nearest the fire."

## 584. Taft and Judges

William Howard Taft (1857-1930) was the only man ever to serve both as President of the United States (1909-1913 - a Republican) and Chief Justice of the U.S. Supreme Court (appointed in 1921)

Once Taft was in a discussion with Robert Hutchins (1899-1977), dean of the Yale Law School and who later became the youthful president of the University of Chicago.

"I suppose, Professor Hutchins," said Taft, "that you teach your students that the judges are all fools."

"No, Mr. Chief Justice," replied Hutchins, "we let them discover that for themselves."

## 585. Testimony

When someone asks you what somebody is really like, you might want to remember this little story about Abraham Lincoln.

In a trial of a man who was charged with mistreating a livery horse, a witness for the defendant testified that "when his companion rides fast, he rides fast, and when his companion rides slow, he rides slow."

The prosecuting attorney then asked how the man rode when he was alone.

"I don't know," said the witness, "I never was with him when he was alone."

# LISTENING

## 586. Listening Is a Critical Skill

In the 3rd century A.D., King Ts'ao sent his son, Prince T'ai, to the temple with instructions to study under the great master Pan Ku. Since T'ai was to succeed his father as king, it was desired that Pan Ku teach the boy how to become a good ruler.

When the prince arrived at the temple, Pan Ku sent him to live alone in the Ming-Li Forest. After a year, the prince was to return to the temple and describe the sound of the forest.

When Prince T'ai returned, the great master asked the boy to describe all he could hear in the forest. "Master," replied the prince, "I could hear the cuckoos sing, the leaves rustle, the hum of hummingbirds, the chirping of crickets, the grass blow, the buzzing of bees, and the wind whisper."

When the prince finished his account, the master told him to go back to the forest to listen to what more he could hear. This request by the master puzzled the prince. Had he not heard every available sound already?

For many days and nights, the young prince sat alone in the forest listening. But he heard no sounds other than those with which he was already familiar. Then one morning, as the prince sat sitting silently beneath the trees, he started to hear faint sounds unlike those he had ever heard before. The more carefully he listened, the clearer the sounds became.

A feeling of enlightenment enveloped the prince. "These must be the sounds the master wished me to discover," he thought.

When Prince T'ai returned to the temple, the master asked him what more he had heard. "Master," said the prince with great respect, "when I listened more closely, I could hear the unheard — the sound of flowers opening, the sound of the sun warming the earth, and the sound of the grass drinking the morning dew."

286 ❖ Wisdom Well Said

The master nodded approvingly. "To hear the unheard," said Pan Ku, "is a necessary discipline to be a good ruler. For only when a ruler has learned to listen closely to the people's hearts, hearing their uncommunicated feelings, unexpressed pains, and unspoken complaints, can he hope to inspire confidence in his people, understand when something is wrong, and meet the citizens' true needs. The demise of states comes when leaders listen only to superficial words and do not penetrate deeply into the souls of the people to hear their true opinions, feelings, and desires."

## 587. Picture Language for Listening

Teamwork provides an opportunity to enlarge the caring-side of our nature. A critical part of teamwork is the ability to listen.

It is interesting that the ancient Chinese character for the word "listen" pictures both a big ear, ten eyes, and a heart. To listen with one's ears, eyes, and heart is the essential element needed for good human relations and teamwork.

## 588. People Don't Listen

Communications is tough because people don't do a good job of listening.

The famed editor Maxwell Perkins (1884-1947), who helped make Ernest Hemingway famous, decided to test his hypothesis that no one really listens to what others say at most social events.

Arriving late to a cocktail party, Perkins grasped his hostess's hand and said, "I'm sorry I'm late, but it took me longer to strangle my aunt than I had expected."

"Oh, I completely understand," said the hostess smiling sweetly. "I'm so happy you could come."

# LOVE, MARRIAGE

## 589. An Ancient Wedding Custom

Why does the bride stand to the groom's left?

In western marriage ceremonies, the bride always stands to the groom's left. This tradition is extremely ancient. But how did this custom begin?

In medieval times, humans lived mostly in small, isolated villages, and there were not many young brides to choose from. Men who wanted to marry sometimes had to go to neighboring villages and do what essentially amounted to kidnapping a young maiden.

Naturally, the maiden's relatives often objected to this practice. Just in case of trouble, the groom would keep his sword at hand, even during the wedding itself. Since he might be attacked at any time, he kept the bride on his left, so that his good right sword arm would be free.

## 590. A Love Story

The German philosopher and scholar Moses Mendelssohn (1729-1786) was born a hunchback. Despite this deformity, which could have soured him on life forever, Mendelssohn achieved a maturity and wisdom few people ever achieve.

While on a trip to Hamburg as a young man, Mendelssohn met a rich merchant who had a beautiful young daughter, Frumtje. The young man fell hopelessly in love with her. She, too, was mature beyond her years, and despite his obvious physical defect, she was attracted to his gentleness, his charm, and his brilliant mind.

Mendelssohn stayed several weeks in Hamburg, spending much of his time with this lovely young woman he had fallen in love with at first sight.

When it finally came time to leave, he worked up enough nerve to speak to her father. It was either that or lose her forever.

The rich and powerful merchant hesitated for a long time. Mendelssohn finally asked him to speak his thoughts frankly.

"Well," said the older man, "you are known throughout Germany as a brilliant young man. And yet...I must tell you my child was a bit frightened when she first saw you."

"Because I am a hunchback?" asked Mendelssohn knowingly.

The merchant nodded, sadly.

Downcast, but not defeated, Mendelssohn asked only one last favor, the privilege of seeing her once more before he left. Admitted to her room, he found her busy with needlework. He spoke at first of various matters, then carefully and gradually, he led the conversation to the subject that was nearest to his heart.

"Do you believe," he asked, "that marriages are made in heaven?"

"Yes," she said, "for that is our faith."

"And it is true," he said gently. "Now let me tell you about something strange that happened when I was born. As you know, at a child's birth, according to our tradition, they call out in heaven that the birth has occurred. And when it is a boy, they announce, 'such-and-such boy will have this-or-that-girl for a wife.'

"Well, there I was, just born, and I heard the name of my future wife announced. At the same time, I heard a great far-off voice say, 'Unfortunately, the poor little girl, Frumtje, will have a terrible hump on her back.'

"Quick as a flash, I cried out, 'O Lord God, if a girl is hunchbacked, she will grow up bitter and hard. Please give her hump to me and let her develop into a well-formed lovely, and charming young lady.'"

Mendelssohn waited for her reaction. Slowly, Frumtje looked up. She dropped her needlework, rose, and approached him with arms outstretched.

The merchant gave his consent and they were soon married, living a long and fruitful life together.

## 591. Origin of Honeymoon

It was the accepted practice in Babylonia 4,000 years ago that for a month after the wedding, the bride's father would supply his son-in-law with all the mead he could drink. Mead is a honey beer, and because their calendar was lunar based, this period was called the "honey month," or what we know today as the "honeymoon."

Another version: In ancient times, Teuton couples would marry beneath a full moon, then drink honey wine for thirty days after; hence the term "honeymoon."

## 592. Secret of a Successful Marriage

Henry Ford (1863-1947), who founded the Ford Motor Company and introduced mass manufacturing techniques to America, was asked on the occasion of his 50th wedding anniversary, "What is the formula for a good marriage?"

He replied, "The formula is the same as in car manufacturing. Stick to one model."

## 593. How to Pick a Wife

All of us at one time or another get depressed about the mass of paperwork that piles up around us.

A journalist was interviewing Fiorello La Guardia (1882-1947), the flamboyant mayor of New York City during the thirties and forties, and remarked about the large collection of files in La Guardia's office.

"I'll tell you a little story," said La Guardia. "Files are the curse of modern civilization. I had a young secretary once. Just out of school. I told her, 'If you can keep these files straight, I'll marry you.'

"She did, and so I married her."

## 594. Lincoln the Dancer

When Abraham Lincoln was introduced at a party to Mary Todd the woman he would someday marry, he said he wanted to dance with her in the worst way.

Miss Todd accepted his invitation but after a few turns around the floor she asked to sit down.

A friend who had heard Lincoln's invitation to dance said to Mary, "Well, did he dance with you in the worst way?"

"Yes," replied Mary, "the very worst."

## 595. Japanese Love Custom

It was the custom in ancient Japan that, after a night of making love, the man was supposed to compose a poem so that when his lover awakened she would find the poem next to her sleeping mat.

This charming Japanese custom was intended to bring together sensuality and love. The poem and the consideration behind its creation was tangible reassurance that the sexual exchange was a fruit of love and not just a "taking."

The gift of the poem was assurance to the woman that she was truly loved.

## 596. Pakistan Custom

In villages in Pakistan, a prospective bridegroom is brought before relatives of the bride, who insult him with every known invective.

The theory is that, if he can take that, he has nothing to fear from what the bride will say later.

## 597. A Legend about Family Values

It is hard to believe this ever could have happened. But there are those who say it is absolutely true. The legend goes like this:

In Medieval Bavaria, a castle filled with riches came under attack by a cruel enemy neighbor. The invading army was strong and soon claimed total victory. Surrounding the castle with hundreds of heavily-armed warriors, they demanded total surrender of the castle, all of its inhabitants and all of its treasures.

The men of the defeated castle accepted their defeat and were prepared to accept the enemy's terms. But the women protested and finally convinced the men that they be allowed to negotiate directly with the invaders on terms of the surrender.

They did so and, after much intense negotiation, the attacking force agreed that the women would be allowed to leave the castle safely with whatever possessions they could carry out on their backs.

The gates of the castle were opened and the woman walked out slowly, heads held high. But their backs were bent under the weight of the valuables they had selected. As the sight of these brave wives struggling with the weight on their backs, the enemy warriors were actually moved to tears.

For, as they watched in disbelief, the wives carried on their backs no gold, jewels, or other precious valuables. Instead they triumphantly carried on their backs their husbands.

## 598. A Reward for Bad Habits

On walking to his home in Hartford, Connecticut, one day, Mark Twain (Samuel Clemens) (1835-1910) was stopped by a down-and-out looking man who said, "Could you give a fellow the price of something to eat, sir?"

"You unfortunate man," said Twain, "Come on, I'll buy you a drink."

"I don't drink, sir," answered the man.

"Then, how about a cigar?" asked Twain.

"Look, sir," said the panhandler, "I'm hungry and besides never in my life have I smoked."

To this Twain said, "How would you like me to place a couple of dollars for you tomorrow on a sure-winner horse?"

"No," said the man, "maybe I have done some things wrong, but I have never gambled. Can't we cut out all this talk and you give me a nickle for a cup of coffee?"

With a burst of inspiration, Twain said, "I'll tell you what. I will stake you to a whole dinner if you will let me introduce you to Mrs. Clemens. I want to show her what becomes of a fellow who doesn't smoke, drink, or gamble!"

## 599. Mistletoe and Romance

Long ago, it was widely believed that mistletoe in the boughs of an oak tree held the juice of immortality, or Love. The plant was expected to reach full bloom on Midsummer Eve.

On that night a girl would spread a white cloth under the tree, collect the flower dust found there, and sprinkle it under her pillow so that she could see her future bridegroom in her dreams.

In the old days, lasting marriages, good luck, and long life were conjured for in many such ways. Girls in rural America spent their years of adolescence stitching quilts to the number eleven. On completion of the eleventh quilt, they would let it be known their readiness for a suitor. They then would set to work on the twelfth, the Wedding Quilt, which would be done in time for the bridal bed.

## 600. Wedding Customs

Jewish weddings include seven ritual blessings. In the Roman Catholic Church, marriage is one of the seven sacraments. And in the course of their wedding, a Hindu bride and groom take seven steps around a stone or fire on the altar representing the axis of the universe while they pray for seven blessings on their future lives.

"We have taken the seven steps," says the groom. "You are mine forever."

Why do we suppose this is. One reason is that the number seven appears in the liturgies of Judaism, Catholicism, and Hinduism. As with other details of marriage ritual, we have to seek the reason in the past where the roots of belief lie tangled with ancient suppositions about the nature of the world.

The number refers to the earth, sun, moon, and four planets visible to the naked eye, all apparently locked together in harmonious interrelationship governed by a single law.

To speak of "seven" then means to speak of a whole, a cosmic union.

## 601. Origin of Marriage Vows

Do you know the source of the marriage vows? Few do. The present wording of the marriage contract is not prescribed or specified by Holy Writ. It is nowhere to be found in the Bible.

The framework for the words dates back to the primitive Sarum, an English rite in 1078. That formula evolved out of centuries of trial and error. Its workability is based on the experience of many generations, on honesty, as much as on morality. We have learned that this code for human conduct is best.

## 602. An Ancient Law

A law was passed during the reign of Charles II (1630-1685) of England that read as follows:

"All women, at whatever age, whether virgins, maids, or widows, that shall impose upon and betray into matrimony any of His Majesty's male subjects by paints, cosmetics, washes, artificial teeth, false hair, Spanish wool, iron stay, hoops, high-heel shoes, or bolstered hips, shall incur the penalty of the law against witchcraft and the marriage upon conviction shall stand void and of no effect."

## 603. The Strong, Silent Type

Mark Twain (Samuel Clemens) was once criticized for not speaking at a dinner, and he replied that the host had talked incessantly.

Twain said it reminded him of the man who was reproached by a friend who accosted him and said: "I think it is a shame that you have not spoken to your wife for 15 years. How do you explain it? How do you justify it?"

And the man replied, "I didn't want to interrupt her."

## 604. The Wedding Ring

Upon dissecting human bodies it was found that a very fine nerve proceeded from the third finger of the left hand and made its way to the heart, and it therefore seemed reasonable that this finger should be honored with a ring, since it seems to be united in a special way with the heart.

## 605. Second Marriages

Samuel Johnson (1709-1784), the English lexicographer, writer, critic and conversationalist, was quoted by his friend and biographer James Boswell (1740-1795) concerning a gentleman who had been very unhappy in marriage and who had married immediately after his wife died.

Johnson said, "It was the triumph of hope over experience."

## 606. The Perfect Man

Abraham Lincoln liked to tell this story about a southern Illinois preacher who asserted in his Sunday sermon that the Saviour was the only perfect man to have ever appeared in this world.

His voice filled with emotion, the preacher said that, in addition, there was no record of that any perfect woman had lived on the earth. There was no record of this in the Bible, nothing.

At this one of the ladies in the congregation rose and interrupted the minister's sermon, saying "I know a perfect woman. I've heard about her every day for the last six years."

"And who might that be?" asked the minister, showing his annoyance at the interruption.

"My husband's first wife," the lady answered.

## 607. True Love

Winston Churchill, Britain prime minister and wartime leader, was asked who he would like to be if he could not be himself. His answer was:

"Lady Churchill's second husband."

## 608. Chinese in the White House

When Herbert Hoover (1874-1964), the 31st President of the United States, and his wife, Lou, didn't want the servants to know what they were talking about in the White House, they spoke to each other in Chinese.

The Hoovers' honeymoon trip had been a voyage to China, where 25-year-old Herbert was serving as chief mining engineer for the Chinese Imperial Bureau of Mines. During their time in China, the Hoovers picked up enough Chinese to communicate with each other.

## 609. Weird Wedding Lore

- Wednesday is considered the best day to marry, although Monday and Tuesday are the best for health.

- Ancient Romans studied pig entrails to determine the luckiest time to marry.

- Wedding rings are worn on the fourth finger because it was once thought that a vein in that finger led to the heart.

- A sapphire in a wedding ring means marital happiness. A pearl ring is said to be bad luck.

- Princess Mary (1516-1558), daughter of Henry VIII (1491-1547), was given an engagement ring at age two. Queen Victoria (1819-1901) started the white wedding dress trend in 1840. Her wedding cake weighed 300 pounds.

- Ancient Greeks and Romans thought the veil protected the bride from evil spirits.

- The custom of tiered cakes came from a game wherein the bride and groom attempted to kiss over an ever-higher cake without knocking it over.

- "Tying the knot" comes from Roman times. The bride wore a girdle tied in knots that the groom later untied.

- Stag parties were begun by Spartan soldiers to bid farewell to their bachelor days.

## 610. All about Wedding Dresses

Married in white, you have chosen all right.
Married in gray, you will go far away.
Married in black, you will wish yourself back.
Married in red, you will wish yourself dead.
Married in green, ashamed to be seen.
Married in blue, he will always be true.
Married in pearl, you will live in a whirl.
Married in yellow, ashamed of your fellow.
Married in brown, you will live out of town.
Married in pink, your fortune will sink.

## 611. History of the Wedding Ring

The idea of the wedding ring itself dates back to ancient times, when a caveman husband would wrap circles of braided grass around his bride's wrists and ankles, believing it would keep her spirit from leaving her body.

The bands evolved into leather, carved stone, metal, and later silver and gold. Luckily, you only have to wear them on your finger nowadays, and the groom usually reciprocates.

## 612. How the Wedding Shower Began

The custom of the bridal shower is believed to have started in Holland, where legend has it that a disapproving father would not provide his daughter with a dowry so that she might marry a less-than-wealthy suitor.

Her friends provided her with the then-essential dowry by "showering" her with gifts.

## 613. Crossing the Threshold

Have you ever wondered why the guy is supposed to carry his bride over the threshold?

Blame the Romans. They believed that good and evil sprits fought for control at a home's entrance. For good to prevail, Romans felt you must enter a room with your right foot first.

Romans concluded that a new bride in a highly emotional state might be careless and forget about the "right foot" stuff. To prevent possible tragedy, they decided it best for the groom to carry his bride.

## 614. History of the Wedding Cake

Wedding cakes originated in ancient Rome, where a loaf of wheat bread was broken over the bride's head to symbolize hope for a fertile and fulfilling life. The guests ate the crumbs, which were believed to be good luck.

The custom found its way to England in the Middle Ages. The guests would bring small cakes to a wedding. The cakes were put in a pile that the bride and groom later stood over while they kissed.

Apparently, someone came up with the idea of piling all the cakes together and frosting them, creating an early ancestor of the multi-tiered wedding cakes of today.

## 615. Too Big a Celebration

Although he stood less than five feet tall, Attila the Hun (406-453) was one of the most feared men in history. His army had conquered all of Asia by 450, from Mongolia to the edge of the Russian Empire, by destroying villages and pillaging the countryside.

He died in a weird way.

In 453, Attila married a young girl named Ildico. Despite his reputation for ferocity on the battlefield, he tended to eat and drink lightly during large banquets.

On his wedding night, however, he really cut loose, gorging himself on food and drink. Sometime during the night, he suffered a nosebleed, but was too drunk to notice.

He drowned in his own blood and was found dead the next morning.

## 616. Finding a Husband

June 21 in England, according to tradition, was a good date for a young lady to begin rituals designed to find a husband.

Sisters would place pieces of "dumb cake" under their pillows to determine their future spouse by dream selection. Called "Dreaming Bannocks," the recipe included the following: 1 cup flour, 1 cup salt, water to thicken (some people added a sprinkle of soot). Before pouring them onto the griddle, carve your initials in one sector. Everybody must take a turn flipping them while they cook, adding a sprinkle of salt with each inversion. These unpalatable treats are called "dumb cakes" not because of the recipe's sound, but because of an absolute rule that not a word is to be spoken during the entire process.

Visions to aid the lovelorn female can be enhanced if she will place her shoes in the form of a "T" next to her bed and reciting:

I place my shoes like a letter T,
in hopes my true love I shall see,
in his apparel and his array,
as he is now and every day.

As in many magical rites, repetition is vital: next you switch the positions of the shoes and repeat the lines, then reverse and repeat yet again. Say anything else during the process and you break the charm.

Once the potential groom is hooked, the next task is to ascertain his occupation. So break an egg into a bowl of water at high noon just at the spot where the sun's zenith image is reflected. The fantastic shapes of the flowing whites will indicate the profession of your destined paramour (a ship for a sailor; a desk for a school teacher: a book for a parson). With a bit more effort, you can do the same by pouring molten lead through the hole of a door key. But it is important that you wear the lead ball in your shoe the day before you smelt it.

## 617. Finding the Perfect Mate

A strange matchmaking game practiced during the 18th and 19th centuries in England and Ireland was called the "oracle of the nuts," and it went like this.

A couple who had been courting would each toss a nut into the fireplace. How the nuts behaved in the fire would predict the course of their courtship, and their suitability for each other.

A lasting and agreeable relationship could be expected if the nuts burned together quietly. However, if the two nuts thrown in the fire crackled and jumped apart, that was a very bad portent for future marital happiness.

Instructions for still another weird method connected with matchmaking went like the following: Peel an apple and throw the peel over your right shoulder. After it lands, examine its shape and you can determine the initial of your future loved one.

## 618. Sizing up a Newly-Married Couple

Many years ago in Austria they had a custom that helped villagers size up the future happiness of a newly-married couple.

After the marriage was completed in the local church, the village women would escort the bride and groom to a nearby forest and stand them before a large tree.

They would then hand the young couple a two-handled bucksaw and ask that they use it to cut the tree down. With the bride on one end of the saw, and the groom on the other, the village women watched as the young couple sawed through the tree.

The closer the cooperation between the man and wife, the shorter the time it took for the tree to come down. And the older villagers wisely reasoned that, the shorter the time, the happier the young couple would be — because they had learned that most valuable of marital lessons — teamwork!

## 619. Throwing Rice at Weddings

There are several theories about how the tradition of throwing rice at weddings got started. Some social historians believe the tradition of throwing rice at newly-weds originated in the belief that feeding any evil influences present would induce them to depart the scene.

But in other cases the practice seems to have developed as a systematic method of encouraging fertility.

Still other societies believed that throwing rice at weddings would be an inducement to the soul to stay. They believed that the bridegroom's soul is apt to fly away at marriage, and rice is therefore scattered over him to induce it to remain.

## 620. For the Marriage Minded

If you want to get married, stand on your head and chew a piece of gristle out of a beef neck and swallow it, and you will get anyone you want. — American folklore
If you can walk around the block with your mouth full of water you will be married within the year. — American folklore

Shed your clothes completely, and at the stroke of midnight beneath a cloudless moon, walk three times around a house. For each step you take, throw a handful of salt behind you. If no one has seen you by the time you have finished, the person you love will be mad for you. – Dutch folklore

## 621. Wedding Customs

The Assyrians, Hebrews and Egyptians gave a sandal as a token of good faith when transferring property or making a deal. In fact, it became customary to throw a sandal onto a piece of land to show that the new owner was taking possession. Eventually, it became a British tradition for a father to give his new son-in-law one of the bride's shoes, signifying a transfer of authority. Today, the bride's father ties old shoes to the bumper of the getaway car as a way of saying, "She's all yours now!"

Tradition says that June is a lucky month because of ties with Juno, Roman goddess of marriage and femininity. Also, many cultures have decided that June is the best month because it has the luckiest weather, a sign that the bride will be happy.

The age-old tradition of the father giving away his daughter in marriage has survived from the times when a bride was actually sold to the groom, and her father handed her over to her husband in return for compensation.

A Spanish groom gives his bride thirteen coins (the giving of "modedas" or "arras") to show his ability to support and care for her. (Thirteen represents Jesus Christ and his twelve apostles.) At the ceremony, the bride carries them in a purse, or a young girl holds them on a pillow or handkerchief.

Many cultural traditions place the bride and groom under a canopy. The Jewish couple stands under a "chuppah"; a Greek couple stands under a "thalamos" (a bridal bower); Spanish and Brahmin brides and grooms stand beneath a canopy; and in the villages of Scotland, newlyweds are escorted beneath a floral bower from the church to their new home.

In the Philippines, a silken cord or string of flowers, also called a nuptial tie, is wound around the necks of the bride and groom in the form of a figure eight, the sign of infinity.

When the bridal couple kneels during a German ceremony, the groom may "accidentally" kneel on the hem of his bride's gown to show that he'll keep her in order. Then, the bride may "accidentally" step on his foot when she rises, to reassert herself.

The kiss became part of the marriage ceremony as far back as early Roman times when it signified a legal bond that sealed contracts.

The tradition of flower girls began in the Middle Ages. They preceded the bride down the aisle carrying tiny stalks of wheat, symbols of a fruitful and happy marriage.

After a Chinese wedding ceremony, the groom's parents host a tea service where the bride and groom pay tribute to their families. First, they bow to heaven, then to heart, and then to their ancestors. Then, they bow to their grandparents and parents, serving each tea. In return, they receive jewelry and money.

An Australian tribesman kept it very simple: He became "engaged" by shooting a barbless arrow through the leg of a maiden. He then became "married" by removing the arrow before carrying her to his home.

## 622. About Toasts

In medieval times, a common way to kill an enemy was to offer him a poisoned drink. To prove to the guest that a drink was safe, the host would receive a small amount of the guest's drink in his own glass, and both would drink at the same time.

If the guest trusted the host, rather than pouring some of his drink into the host's glass, he would simply clink his glass against it. Although offering a poisoned drink is no longer a popular way to kill someone, the custom of clinking glasses still remains.

There is another reason why the custom has held so long. In medieval times, the sound of bells was thought to scare off the devil. The devil was thought to frequent festive occasions, so the bell-like sound of glasses clinking was often heard at such events.

The most extravagant toast ever recorded was that offered to Marc Antony (83 BC-30 BC) by Cleopatra (69 BC-30 BC) when she dropped two perfect pearls into her wine and drank them down. The extravagance of her toast outweighed the cost of all the other banquet expenses combined.

## 623. The Heart as Symbol of Romance

The symbol of the heart, simple and romantic, has been with us for centuries. The heart shape is used on valentines, sewn into quilts, and is celebrated in love songs and stories. For thousands of years, the heart shape has evolved into a powerful symbol of love and friendship.

We believe that cave men thousands of years ago painted heart pictures on the walls of their caves to represent their goal to capture the heart of a powerful foe, believing then that the enemy's power would become theirs. The ancient Greeks and Egyptians believed the soul resided in the heart, directing all their actions, both corporeal and spiritual.

It took until the Middle Ages until the symbol of the heart came to symbolize love and romance. When Christianity began to spread in Europe, pictures of hearts began to decorate illuminated religious manuscripts and paintings, symbolizing man's love for God. Later on, the heart came to represent an idealized kind of love between a man and a woman. Hearts were embroidered, sewn on, and woven into costumes worn at court and even armor.

Not long after this the heart was incorporated into the rituals of romantic life. An English tradition, which we believe began in the 17th century, was the gift of a pair of gloves to a lady that were embellished with a heart. Often the gift was accompanied by a verse that went like this: "If that from Glove you take the letter G/Then Glove is love and that I send to thee."

This heart-decorated love gift was often given as a marriage proposal. If the lady accepted, she wore the gloves to church Easter Sunday.

# MATHEMATICS

### 624. The Number Three

Like magic, the number three seems irresistible. Think about it. Note how frequently it appears in our culture. Remember the old saying, "All good things come in threes." The Greek philosopher and mathematician Pythagoras (between 580 BC and 572 BC-between 500 BC and 490 BC) regarded three as the perfect number.

The ancient Greeks, who believed the world was ruled by three gods, revered beauty, laughter, and love. The ancient Chinese worshiped gentleness, frugality, and humility. In Scandinavian mythology the "Mysterious Three" sat on three thrones above the rainbow. The Hindu Trimurti consists of three gods: Creator, Preserver, and Destroyer. Christians believe in the Trinity by which God exists in three persons. Faith, Hope, and Charity are the three Christian graces. Three wise men paid homage to the newborn Jesus and brought three gifts: gold, frankincense, and myrrh.

Three dimensions form the physical world — earth, sea, and air. Man himself has three dimensions: body, mind, and spirit. Nature is threefold: mineral, vegetable, and animal. Time has three aspects: past, present, and future. Government is divided into three levels: national, state, and local. To mark the boundary line of a state's territorial waters, the "three-mile limit" is prescribed.

### 625. An Ancient Mathematical Tale

The power of mathematics is mind boggling. An ancient Indian legend tells of a wise man who, upon doing his king a service, was offered any reward he wanted in return.

"Serving your Majesty is reward enough in itself," said the wise man, bowing low. "No, No," said the king, it must not be said that the King does not reward those who serve him." And the king insisted that the wise man request some kind of reward, no matter how small.

"Very well, sire," said the wise man, "I ask only this. I ask that you place on the first square of a chessboard one grain of rice on the first day; the next day, for the second square, two grains of rice; the next day after that, four grains of rice; then, the following day, eight grains for the next square of your chessboard, etc.

As your reward give me twice the number of grains placed on the square before it, and so on for each of the 64 squares on the chessboard."

On overhearing the wise man's response to the King, the Monarch's other advisers sneered in derision at such a ridiculous request. Even the King wondered why a man so wise would make such a stupid request when he could have named a princely sum.

However, the King agreed willingly and left for a trip. Imagine his amazement when, on returning a month later, the king discovered to his dismay that the one grain of rice (doubled daily for each of the 64 squares on a chessboard) had swelled to over 550 billion tons, completely bankrupting the Royal Granary.

If you would like to test this mathematics with, say a penny — try it and see what a tremendous fortune results. It makes winning a million dollar lottery seem like an ordinary thing.

## 626. Danger of Procrastination

This French riddle for children demonstrates the danger of not dealing promptly with signs of future trouble.

Suppose you own a pond on which a water lily is growing.

The lily plant doubles in size each day.

If the plant is allowed to grow unchecked, it will completely cover the pond in 30 days, choking off all other forms of life in the water.

For a long time the lily plant seems small, so you decide not to worry about it until it covers half the pond.

Question: On what day will that be?

Answer: On the twenty-ninth day.

Result: You have just one day to act to save your pond.

## 627. Einstein on Mathematics

"One reason why mathematics enjoys special esteem, above all other sciences, is that its laws are absolutely certain and indisputable, while those of all other sciences are to some extent debatable and in constant danger of being overthrown by newly discovered facts."

## 628. Galileo on Mathematics

Galileo Galilei (1564-1642), the brilliant Italian mathematician, astronomer and physicist, had this to say about the mathematical sciences:

"Philosophy is written in this grand book — I mean the universe — which stands continually open to our gaze, but it cannot be understood unless one first learns to comprehend the language and interpret the characters in which it is written. It is written in the language of mathematics, and its characters are triangles, circles, and other geometrical figures, without which it is humanly impossible to understand a single word of it; without these, one is wandering about in a dark labyrinth."

## 629. Bertrand Russell on Mathematics

"To me, pure mathematics is one of the highest forms of art; it has a sublimity quite special to itself, and an immense dignity derived from the fact that its world is exempt from change and time. I am quite serious in this. The only difficulty is that none but mathematicians can enter this enchanted region, and they hardly ever have a sense of beauty. And mathematics is the only thing we know of that is capable of perfection; in thinking about it we become gods."

## 630. Leonardo Da Vinci on Mathematics

Leonardo da Vinci (1452-1519), the Italian genius painter, sculptor, architect and engineer, said, "No knowledge can be certain if it is not based upon mathematics or upon some other knowledge which is itself based upon the mathematical sciences."

# MEDIA

## 631. Interview with Coolidge

It was a White House press conference and reporters were firing questions at President Calvin Coolidge (1872-1933).

"Have you anything to say about Prohibition?" said one.

"No," said the president.

"About the farm situation?"

"No," replied Coolidge.

"About the forthcoming senatorial campaign?"

"No."

The session ended and, as the reporters got up to leave, Coolidge called out to them, "And don't quote me."

## 632. Celebrity Interview

Jack Paar (1918-2004) was a national favorite as a late night talk host during the early days of television. One of his favorite stories was about Cornelius Vanderbilt, Jr. (1898-1974), recounting to a Hollywood interviewer some of his journalistic adventures during World War II.

"I was covering the fighting on the Russian front and one day I was captured by the Russians. I was thrown into an armored car and driven all night to an unknown destination. When I was dragged out of the car, I was stunned to see we were at the Kremlin. My captors hauled me into that forbidding bastion, down a long gloomy corridor, and finally hurled me to the floor. Looking up, I saw Stalin glowering down at me!"

At this cliffhanger, Vanderbilt paused for breath and dramatic effect.

"I see," said the interviewer. "Do you have any hobbies?"

## 633. Jefferson Disliked Newspapers

Thomas Jefferson (1743-1826) did not like newspapers. In writing to his friend John Norvell, June 14, 1807, he said, "to your request of my opinion of the manner in which a newspaper should be conducted so as to be most useful, I should answer by restraining it to true facts and sound principles only, yet I fear such a paper would find few subscribers."

He then went on to state:

"Perhaps an editor might begin a reformation in some such way as this: divide his paper into four chapters, heading the first, Truths, 2nd, Probabilities, 3rd, Possibilities, 4th, Lies.

"The first chapter would be very short, as it would contain little more than authentic papers and information from such sources as the editor would be willing to risk his own reputation for their truth.

"The second would contain what, from a mature consideration of all circumstances, his judgment should conclude to be probably true. This, however, should rather contain too little than too much.

"The third and fourth should be professedly for those readers who would rather have lies for their money than the blank paper they would occupy."

## 634. Journalism Lesson

In his first job as a journalist, Mark Twain (Samuel Clemens) was instructed by his editor never to report anything he couldn't personally verify as the truth.

Following this advice to the letter, Twain submitted the following item about a local society matron:

"A woman giving the name of Mrs. James Jones, who is reported to be one of the society leaders of this city, is said to give what is purported to be a party yesterday to a number of alleged ladies. The hostess claims to be the wife of a reputed attorney."

## 635. Lincoln and the Media

Abraham Lincoln was commenting on unjust and untruthful newspaper attacks.

"I'm like the traveler on the frontier who was lost in a wild country on a pitch-black night.

"A terrific storm was raging, yet though he was buffeted by wind and rain, the glare of the lightning alone showed him the way.

"Suddenly came a crashing bolt and the traveler dropped upon his knees. 'Oh, Lord,' he prayed, 'if it's all the same to You, give me a little more light and a good deal less noise.'"

# MEDICINE

## 636. Doctor-Patient Communications

An extensive study of more than 800 doctor-patient interactions found that less than five percent of doctors' communication with patients was either personal or friendly; but that the majority of doctors participating reported that they thought they were behaving in a friendly manner.

A second study found that patients described their complaints for an average of only 18 seconds before their physicians interrupted. Only 23 percent of patients studied reported they were able to tell their doctors everything they wanted.

Another study found that in 50 percent of all conversations, physicians used technical jargon. The AMA's 1989 survey of public perceptions of physicians found that less than half of those surveyed felt "doctors usually explain things well to their patients." This news is made even worse by the widely held view that communication skills deteriorate during medical school.

## 637. An Exercise to Change Your Life

We once read about a doctor, Dr. C. Ward Crampton, who always urged his patients to exercise. He specifically prescribed what he called his miracle exercise.

Dr. Crampton's miracle exercise does not require that people get into jogging suits and huff and puff around the neighborhood. You don't have to get down on the floor and go through a series of contortions that will leave you breathless. Nothing like that.

You can do this standing or sitting down. Do it in front of a mirror, or better still, with someone. Here's how:

- Raise the corners of your mouth an inch, take a deep breath and hold it for 10 seconds.

- You are smiling. If you have people watching you, they'll probably start smiling too.

- Now release your breath in short exhalations. You're now laughing. Unless those with you are curmudgeons, they'll undoubtedly start laughing too.

This simple muscular action of inhaling, raising the corners of the mouth, then exhaling in rhythmic, short bursts causes the diaphragm to bounce up and down, pats the liver on the back, and pleasantly vibrates the stomach. The heart, which rests above the diaphragm, begins to pump at a slightly faster rate, sending blood coursing throughout the body.

The effect, Dr. Crampton explains, is a general feeling of well-being. More important than this, however, is the effect on others who observe you going through this exercise. They feel better, too. This triggers happy emotions within you, and the stage is set for any number of pleasant personal and business relationships.

All this from one simple little exercise!

## 638. Hospital Visit

Dorothy Parker (1893-1967), the American writer and wit, was recuperating in the hospital and she sent for her secretary to help her get some work done.

When the secretary arrived, Parker pressed the "nurse call" button and said with confidence, "There, that should assure us of at least 45 minutes of undisturbed privacy."

## 639. Primitive Medical Precautions

When they moved their villages, African savages took with them to the new location some dirt from the floor of the old hut. They believed this helped them avoid the anger of their gods who might not wish them to move, fooling them by continuing to live on some of the same ground.

But the fact remains that by this process they brought to the new location the soil microorganisms that continued to give some degree of protection from certain ailments.

## 640. How Aspirin Was Invented

For thousands of years doctors told patients suffering from pain to chew on the bark of a willow tree. But it wasn't until the 1800s that scientists discovered what was in the willow tree that relieved pain and reduced fever.

We now know that the leaves and bark of the willow tree contain a substance called salicin, a naturally occurring compound similar to acetylsalicylic acid, the chemical name for aspirin.

IN 1897, a German chemist named Felix Hoffman (1868-1946) was searching for something to relieve his father's arthritis. He studied some experiments conducted in 1832 by a French chemist named Charles Gerhardt (1816-1856) and "rediscovered" acetylsalicylic acid — or aspirin, as we now know it.

Today more than 70 million pounds of this miracle drug are produced around the world each year.

## 641. Nurse Duties in 1887

In addition to caring for 50 patients each, every nurse will follow these regulations:

1.  Daily sweep and mop the floors of your ward, dust the patient's furniture and window sills.

2.  Maintain an even temperature in your ward by bringing in a scuttle of coal for the day's business.

3.  Light is important to observe the patient's condition. Therefore, each day fill kerosene lamps, clean chimneys, and trim wicks. Wash the windows once a week.

4.  The nurse's notes are important to aiding the physician's work. Make your pens carefully; you may whittle nibs to your individual taste.

5.  Each nurse on day duty will arrive every day at 7 a.m. and leave at 8 p.m.

6.  Graduate nurses in good standing with the director of nurses will be given an evening off each week for courting purposes or two evenings a week if you go regularly to church.

7.  Each nurse should lay aside from each payday a goodly sum of her earnings for her benefits during her declining years so that she will not become a burden. For example, if you earn $30 a month, you should set aside $15.

8.  Any nurse who smokes, uses liquor in any form, gets her hair done at a beauty shop or frequents dance halls will give the director of nurses good reason to suspect her worth, intentions, and integrity.

9.  The nurse who performs her labors and serves her patients and doctors faithfully and without fault for a period of five years will be given an increase by the hospital administration of five cents a day, providing there are no hospital debts that are outstanding.

## 642. Bathing

The Victorians seldom bathed. Glorification of the bathroom is a modern fetish. In 1882 only two percent of New York's homes had water connections, and these in all probability were leaky and, if attached to a stove, dangerous.

Bathing was considered harmful by some doctors, and one, C.E. Sargent, described it as "a needless waste of time."

## 643. Clara Barton

Clara Barton (1821-1912) was an American nurse who founded the American Red Cross in 1881 and was its president until 1904. A remarkable woman, she made it a rule never to hold resentment against anyone.

Once a friend reminded her of a cruel thing that had been done to Barton some years previously, but Clara seemed not to remember the incident.

"Don't you remember the wrong that was done to you?" the friend asked.

"No," Clara answered calmly. "I distinctly remember forgetting that."

## 644. Positive Thinking

"How are you feeling?" someone once asked famed actress Katherine Hepburn (1907-2003).

"Fine," she answered, "unless you want details."

## 645. Bad Habits

The author-humorist Mark Twain (Samuel Clemens) was a gifted lecturer who had audiences hanging on his every word, chuckling most of the time.

He once told a story about an elderly woman whose doctor, after a thorough examination, informed her she would have to quit smoking, drinking, and gorging herself on rich food.

"But doctor," she protested, "I have never done any of those things in my entire life!"

Twain looked out at the audience for a long pause, then shook his head sadly and delivered his grim prediction concerning the woman's health.

"There was nothing to be done for her," said Twain in mock sadness. "She had neglected her habits!"

## 646. That Symbol on Your Drug Prescription

The origin of the symbol, Rx, found in the upper left-hand corner of every prescription goes back 5,000 years.

The Egyptians used the magic eye of Horus as an amulet to guard them against disease and suffering. The eye has two tails hanging from the center, and centuries later it reappeared in a form resembling our numeral "4". Physicians scribbled it on their prescriptions to invoke the assistance of Jupiter. By slow transformation, the numeral changed into Rx.

## 647. Laughter and Health

There are some ailments that require a prescription for antibiotics and recommended rest in bed. But don't discount the healing power of frequent laughter. Doctors have long known that our minds have great influence on our health. For example, too much stress can overstimulate hormone production, leaving our bodies less able to cope.

On the other hand, happiness and laughter do just the opposite. Laughter triggers nerves in the brain that stimulate a chain of good-feeling reactions. When good humor is present, the body secretes natural painkillers and tranquilizers. Other substances aid digestion, and relaxed arteries improve blood flow. The overall effect leaves your mind and body better able to cope with whatever life's stresses sends your way.

## 648. Medical Education

A famous Austrian surgeon named Dr. Billroth used to tell his students that a doctor needed two abilities: freedom from nausea, and the power of observation. Then he'd dip his finger into a bitterly foul liquid — lick it off — and ask each student to do the same.

One by one, the students would taste the liquid, many of whom almost retched at the taste. Then with a grin Dr. Billroth would say, "You have passed the first test, but not the second. For none of you noticed that while I dipped my first finger into the liquid, I licked the second."

Note: this anecdote is sometimes credited to Dr. Joseph Bell (1837-1911), a British surgeon who some say was the model for Sir Arthur Conan Doyle's Sherlock Holmes character.

## 649. What Patients Expect from Doctors

Norman Cousins (1915-1990), was a highly-successful magazine publisher and writer who survived a critically-serious medical crisis with a treatment largely of his own invention. Believe it or not, his "treatment" included looking at all the funny movies he could find. He spent the final years of his life as a lecturer at the UCLA School of Medicine, working with medical students. The following is an excerpt from his book "Head First - the Biology of Hope:"

"There are qualities beyond our medical competence that patients need and look for in doctors. They want reassurance. They want to be looked after and not just looked over. They want to be listened to. They want to feel that it makes a difference to their physician, a very big difference, whether they live or die. They want to feel that they are in the doctor's thoughts. The physician holds the lifeline. The physician's words and not just his prescriptions are attached to that lifeline.

"This aspect of medicine has not changed in thousands of years. Not all the king's horses and all the king's men — not all the tomography and the thallium scanners and two-D echocardiograms and medicinal mood modifiers — can preempt the physician's primary role as the keeper of the keys to the body's own healing system.

"I pray that you will never allow your knowledge to get in the way of your relationship with your patients. I pray that all the technological marvels at your command will not prevent you from practicing medicine out of a little black bag. I pray that when you go into a patient's room you will recognize that the main distance is not from the door to the bed but from the patient's eyes to your own — and that the shortest distance between those two points is a horizontal straight line — the kind of straight line that works best when the physician bends low to the patient's loneliness and fear and pain and the overwhelming sense of mortality that comes flooding up out of the unknown, and when the physician's hand on the patient's shoulder or arm is a shelter against the darkness."

## 650. Medical Advances

The following remarks were made by Floyd D. Loop, M.D., to the City Club Forum in Cleveland, Ohio, when he was chairman of the Board of Governors and CEO of The Cleveland Clinic:

"Science and medicine have added 26 years to our life span in the 20th century alone.

"Do you remember Sir Samuel Luke Fildes' famous painting, "The Doctor," which showed a physician sitting at the bedside, a picture of devotion to the patient and very inspirational for physicians; but the fact of the matter is that when this was painted in 1891, physicians could do little else but sit at the bedside because there was no technology, no antibiotics, none of the intensity of care that we criticize today."

## 651. Medical Hygiene

Joseph Semmelweiss (1818-1865), the 19th century Hungarian physician, felt that doctors could reduce disease by washing their hands in chlorinated lime water before inspecting their patients.

His colleagues, because they thought that doctors were close to God, strongly resented his suggestion that they were "carrying death around on their hands," and denounced him. The later discovery of bacteria proved Semmelweiss correct.

## 652. The Art of Diagnosis

Speaking to a meeting of physicians, Mark Twain stated flatly that the art of diagnosis was what separated modern doctors from the old medicine man.

He announced he had himself joined the medical fraternity, opening his practice in a small town in Connecticut which had only four doctors.

"One day," he said, "a sailor walked into town, with a rolling gait and a distressed face. We asked him what was the matter. We always hold consultations on every case, as there isn't enough business for four. The patient said he didn't know, but that he was a sailor, and perhaps that might help us to give him a diagnosis.

"We treated him for that, and I never saw a man die more peacefully."

## 653. More about Norman Cousins

Norman Cousins (1912-1990) was a famous magazine editor and author when, at mid-life, he came down with what doctors believed was an incurable illness.

Undiscouraged, Cousins began an exhaustive study of the illness on his own and, in the process, proved to himself and others that laughter can be a major contributor to healing — because of the flow of endorphins from the adrenaline system every time you laugh or feel good.

To keep his flow of endorphins flowing, Cousins watched every Marx Brothers movie he could put his hands on. Anything to keep him in a positive frame of mind. It worked. Cured miraculously, Cousins spent the last part of his life as a lecturer at the UCLA School of Medicine, working with medical students.

He was fond of telling the students there that "the control center of your life is your attitude. Negative attitudes lead to illness, low self-esteem and depression. Positive attitudes lead to hope, love, caring, fun and endorphin flow from the adrenaline system."

Cousins proved that a big dose of positive thinking and laughter on a daily basis can do more for your continued health and well-being than a basket full of pills.

# MISTAKES

## 654. False Economy

Peter Marshall (1902-1949) was an eloquent religious leader and for a brief time (1947-48) served as the chaplain of the U.S. Senate. He used to love to tell the story of the "Keeper of the spring," a quiet forest dweller who lived high above an Austrian village along the eastern slope of the Alps.

The old gentleman had been hired many years earlier by a young town councilman to clear away the debris from the pools of water up in the mountain crevices that fed the lovely spring flowing through the town.

With faithful, silent regularity, he patrolled the hills, removed the leaves and branches, and carefully removed the silt that would otherwise have choked and contaminated the fresh flow of water.

The village soon became a popular attraction for vacationers. Graceful swans floated along the crystal clear spring, the mill wheels of various businesses located near the water turned day and night, farm lands were naturally irrigated, and the view from restaurants was picturesque beyond description.

Years passed. One evening the town council met for its semi-annual meeting. As they reviewed the budget, one councilman's eye caught the salary figure being paid the obscure keeper of the spring.

Said he, "Who is this old man? Why do we keep him on year after year? No one ever sees him. For all we know, this unseen stranger in the hills is doing us no good. He isn't necessary any longer." By a unanimous vote, the council dispensed with the old man's services.

For several weeks, nothing changed. But by early autumn, the trees began to shed their leaves. Small branches snapped off and fell into the pools, hindering the flow of spring water. One afternoon someone noticed a slight yellowish-brown tint in the spring. A few days later, the water was much darker. Within another week, a slimy film covered sections of the waters along the water's banks, and a foul odor was detected. The mill wheels moved more slowly, and some finally stopped altogether. Swans left, as did the tourists. Clammy fingers of disease and sickness reached deeply into the village.

Quickly, the embarrassed council called a special meeting. Realizing their gross error in judgment, they rehired the old keeper of the spring, and within a few weeks, the veritable river of life began to clear up. The mill wheels started to turn with renewed speed, and new life returned to the hamlet in the Alps.

## 655. Admittance of Mistakes

In 1961 President John Kennedy met with Soviet leader Nikita Khrushchev (1894-1971) in Vienna for foreign policy talks.

"Do you ever admit a mistake?" Kennedy asked Khrushchev.

"Certainly." the Russian leader replied. "In a speech before the Twentieth Party Congress, I admitted all of Stalin's mistakes."

## 656. Lincoln on Mistakes

When Abraham Lincoln was asked when he was going to emancipate the slaves, the President responded with this story.

"We've got to be very cautious on how we manage this matter," Lincoln said. "If we aren't, we shall be like the barber out in Illinois who was shaving a fellow who had a hatchet face and lantern jaw just like mine.

"The barber stuck his finger into his customer's mouth to make his cheek stick out so he could give him a real close shave. But while shaving away he cut through the fellow's cheek and cut off his own finger.

"If we are not very careful, we shall do as the barber did," Lincoln said.

## 657. Employee Mistake

Thomas Watson Sr., the founder of IBM, was once asked if he was going to fire an employee who had made a mistake that had cost the company $600,000.

"Certainly not," said Watson, "I just spent $600,000 training him. Why would I want anyone else to hire his experience?"

Note: Watson Sr. (1874-1956) was president of IBM from 1914 to 1949 and chairman from 1949 to 1956. He was succeeded by his son, Thomas Watson, Jr. (1914-1993). The son headed IBM from 1961 to 1971 and was the U.S. Ambassador to Russia from 1979 to 1981.

## 658. Human Mistakes

R. Buckminster Fuller (1895-1983), a famed American engineer and inventor, wrote this thoughtful essay about mistakes. Here is a lengthy excerpt:

"Humans have learned only through mistakes. The billions of humans in history have had to make quadrillions of mistakes to have arrived at the state where we now have 150,000 common words to identify that many unique and only metaphysically comprehensible nuances of experience.

"Chagrin and mortification caused by their progressively self-discovered quadrillions of errors would long ago have given humanity such an inferiority complex that it would have become too discouraged to continue with the life experience. To avoid such a proclivity, humans were designedly given pride, vanity and inventive memory, which, all together, can and usually do include us to self-deception.

"...So effective has been the non-thinking, group deceit of humanity that it now says, 'Nobody should make mistakes,' and punishes people for making mistakes.

"... the courage to adhere to the truth as we learn it involves them, the courage to force ourselves, with the clear admission of all the mistakes we have made — mistakes are sins only when not admitted."

## 659. God's Mistakes

Archie Bunker, the lead character in the enormously popular television program *All in the Family*, said, "God don't make no mistakes – that's how he got to be God."

## 660. Scientific Mistakes

Dr. Edward Teller (1908-2003), the Hungarian-born American physicist who played an important role in creation of the atom bomb, said, "If there ever was a misnomer, it is 'exact science.' Science has always been full of mistakes. The present day is no exception. And our mistakes are good mistakes; they require a genius to correct them. Of course, we do not see our own mistakes."

## 661. IBM Founder on Mistakes

Thomas J. Watson, Sr. (1874-1956), founder of IBM, said of mistakes, "Double your rate of failure...Failure is a teacher — a harsh one, perhaps, but the best...That's what I have to do when an idea backfires or a sales program fails. You've got to put failure to work for you... you can be discouraged by failure or you can learn from it. So go ahead and make mistakes. Make all you can. Because that's where you will find success. On the far side of failure."

# MONEY

## 662. Pinching Pennies

Vartan Gregorian (1934- ) was the distinguished head of the New York Public Library from 1981 to 1988, when he left to become President of Brown University in Providence, Rhode Island.

Soon after taking office at Brown, and after reviewing the University's financial situation, Gregorian convened a meeting of the university's board of trustees and said to them, "Brown has long been an institution that does more with less. Well, I'm here to tell you that we're out of less."

## 663. Compound Interest

Money at compound interest builds incredibly over time. If the American Indians had taken the $24 for which they sold Manhattan in 1626 and invested it at 8 percent daily compound interest, their $24 would today be worth $30 trillion.

## 664. Story on the Dollar Bill

There is much to be learned by taking a close look at the back of a U.S. dollar bill.

On the left side is a pyramid, with an eye at the top. Over the pyramid is the Latin inscription "annuit coeptis." It means: "Providence has Favored Our Undertakings."

The pyramid symbolizes the strength of the union of the states. The top of the pyramid is unfinished, meaning there is still work to be done to make our system even better. The eye stands for the all-seeing God, Supreme Builder of the Universe.

Benjamin Franklin chose this motto because he believed imagination was the singular characteristic of the people he helped to forge into a new nation.

## 665. The Wealth of George Washington

George Washington (1732-1799), the father of his country, was not only a very rich man. He was also a pragmatist.

Washington's family motto was "Exitus acta probat" (the end justifies the means).

When he died, Washington provided in his will for the emancipation of his slaves on the death of Martha (1731-1802), his wife. Washington was the only member of the Virginia dynasty to free all of his slaves. Aside from everything else, he could afford it.

Washington was one of the richest men in America. At his death his holdings were worth about half a million dollars and included: 33,000 acres of land in Virginia, Kentucky, Maryland, New York, Pennsylvania, Washington, D.C., and the Northwest Territory; $25,000 worth of stocks; 640 sheep; 329 cows; 42 mules; and 20 workhorses.

As commander-in-chief of the American forces, Washington refused a regular salary and worked for expenses only. He came out $400,000 better off than he otherwise would have. When offered the U.S. Presidency, he volunteered to work for expenses again, but this time Congress insisted he have a fixed salary.

## 666. Money and Einstein

Money meant little to the famous physicist Albert Einstein. When he first joined the Princeton Institute for Advanced Study, he requested a salary so low officials had to double it to preserve some semblance of institute standards.

He once used a $1,500 check from the Rockefeller Foundation as a bookmark, then lost the book. The foundation's records were out of kilter for months. When they finally sent a duplicate check, Einstein wrote back, "What's this for?"

## 667. How the Dollar Sign Was Born

The dollar sign was originally an abbreviation for pesos. Two hundred years ago, when we were still using Spanish money (believe it or not, we didn't get around to minting our own money until 1794, nearly 20 years after the Declaration of Independence), it was only natural to shorten 200 pesos to PS 200. As time went on, the P and S began to get smashed together.

Eventually people started writing the up-and-down stroke of the P on top of the S, and the dollar sign was born.

## 668. Rich Children

In an effort not to spoil his son, John D. Rockefeller (1839-1937) gave him one cent for finding each fence post that needed repairs on the family estate. One day the child made thirteen cents.

Later on, he paid his son fifteen cents an hour for repairing those fences. Junior also collected five cents from his mother for every hour he practiced the violin.

Such practices not to spoil offspring seems to have spread among the very rich. Gerald Bronfman (1914-1988), one of Sam Bronfman's (1889-1971) nephews, paid his daughters a weekly allowance of thirty-seven and a half cents. For some reason, he didn't overpay, he alternated between thirty-seven and thirty-eight cents each week.

## 669. Rattle Your Money

John Lennon (1940-1980) was a star among stars with the Beatles and he wrote many of their most popular songs. When the Beatles were appearing at the Royal Variety Performance in 1963, the audience was exceptionally well-heeled.

After completing a number, Lennon went to the microphone and announced, "Those in the cheaper seats clap. The rest of you rattle your jewelry."

## 670. Mark Twain on Money

The writer and humorist Mark Twain (Samuel Clemens) once complained to a friend that all people in the East seemed to talk about was money.

"In Hannibal, Missouri, where I was brought up," Twain said, "we never talked about money. There was not enough money in the place to furnish a topic of conversation."

## 671. Money Was No Joke to Him

Ever worry about having enough money when you are traveling far from home?

The actor-comic W.C. Fields (1880-1946) did and to make sure he would always have access to ready cash, he opened a bank account in every town he passed through.

He used such pseudonyms as Ludovic Fishpond, Colmonley Frampton-Blythe, Aristotle Hoop, Elmer Mergetroid-Haines and Figley E. Whitesides. His many accounts ranged from a few bucks to as much as $50,000.

However, Fields neglected to keep track of his many accounts and, before his death, was able to recall only 23 of them. He told friends he was sure he had opened at least 700 such accounts, and an estimated $1,300,000 was never recovered.

Fields would have been a great prospect for American Express's Travelers Checks division.

## 672. Creative Motivation

Paul McCartney (1942- ), the famous Beatle, denied to an interviewer that the Beatles were antimaterialistic.

"That's a huge myth," said McCartney, "John (Lennon) (1940-1980) and I literally used to sit down and say, 'Now, let's write a swimming pool.'"

# MUSIC

## 673. Don't Believe Everything You Hear

The man who wrote one of the world's most famous and romantic songs, "April in Paris," was named Vernon Duke (1903-1969).

A friend of Duke liked the song so much he decided to spend the month of April in Paris. But, when he returned home, he complained to Duke bitterly that the weather was terrible.

"Whatever made you go to Paris in April?" Duke asked. "Everybody knows the weather is bad then."

"I went because of your song," cried the frustrated friend.

"Ah," said the composer apologetically, "I really would have liked to have used May, but the rhythm required two syllables."

## 674. Musical Ethics

The great pianist Arthur Rubinstein (1887-1982) was once asked to judge a piano competition. The scorecards were to be marked on a scale of one to 20, the most gifted receiving the higher number. Rubinstein listened intently to the recitals and marked the cards.

But when the sponsors examined the scores, they were astonished. Most of the students had received zeros and a few received 20s; there were no intermediate scores.

Everyone demanded that Rubinstein explain himself. "It's simple," he replied. "Either they can play the piano or they cannot."

## 675. Beethoven's Working Habits

Washing himself continuously was often an obsession with the composer Beethoven while he was composing.

Frequently, in a fit of complete abstraction, he would go to his wash basin and pour several jugs of water on his hands, all the while humming and roaring, for sing he could not.

After dabbling in the water until his clothes were wet through, he would pace up and down the room, with a vacant expression and eyes frightfully distended. Often he had not shaved.

Then he would seat himself at his table and write; and afterwards get up again to splash in the wash basin, humming all the while. No one dared disturb him during these creative moments, despite the fact that residents of the floor below were frequently upset by water trickling down through the floor and into their living quarters.

## 676. No Shrinking Violet

John Francis McCormack (1884-1945) was an acclaimed Irish tenor who became an American citizen and was famous around the world for his golden voice. That is not to say he was all that modest.

The story goes that, after his death in 1945, McCormack was admitted readily to Heaven and immediately bustled about demanding that he be given some major artistic responsibilities. Somewhat annoyed at all the fuss, but finally giving in, the higher powers sent Saint Peter to offer McCormack a position suitable to his lofty musical achievements while on earth.

"I have good news for you, John," St. Peter began, "I have been authorized to tell you that you will be permitted to train a celestial choir to replace the old one. Some of us up here believe it has become a little over the hill."

"Wonderful," exclaimed McCormack. "First, I'll need 10,000 sopranos; also 10,000 contraltos; and finally, 10,000 baritones and bass singers. And hurry up, I want to have our first big concert by Easter."

"All right," agreed St. Peter, only slightly annoyed. "But won't you also be needing 10,000 tenors?"

McCormack fixed St. Peter with a scornful glare.

"I'll sing tenor!" he said.

## 677. No Baseball Fan

The greatest tenor in the world at the beginning of the 20th century was the Italian tenor Enrico Caruso (1873-1921). He was easily as admired as the tenor Luciano Pavarotti (1935-2007), who enthralled audiences many years later.

In a visit to New York, a group of reporters asked Caruso what he thought of Babe Ruth, the Yankees renowned home-run hitter.

Always polite and amiable, Caruso replied that he didn't know because unfortunately, he had "never heard her sing."

## 678. When the President Appears

Have you ever wondered why "Hail to the Chief" is played every time the President of the United States enters a function?

It is because President James K. Polk (1795-1849), the eleventh President of the United States, was a physically unimpressive person and sometimes went unnoticed when he entered a reception.

His wife, Sarah, decided to arrange for the Marine band to play "Hail to the Chief," an old Scottish anthem, to announce the President's arrival. The tradition has lasted to this day.

### 679. Music and Einstein

Albert Einstein (1879-1955), who fancied himself as a fairly talented violinist, was rehearsing a Haydn composition with a string quartet.

When Einstein failed for the fourth time to get his entry in the second movement, the group's cellist looked up somewhat annoyed and said, "The problem with you, Albert, is that you simply can't count."

### 680. Oscar Wilde out West

The famous English writer and wit Oscar Wilde (1854-1900) was touring the Old West when he observed a notice posted above the saloon piano in the rowdy mining town of Leadville, Colorado. It read:

"Please don't shoot the piano player. He is doing the best he can."

This message can teach us a lot about patience and understanding in dealing with our fellow human beings.

### 681. Beethoven's Funeral

Beethoven's (1770-1827) funeral was that of a great man. Some 30,000 persons surged through the streets of Vienna where the funeral procession was scheduled to pass.

Struck by the size and emotions of the crowd, a passing stranger asked of a woman caretaker, "Whose funeral is this?"

"Well, don't you know," answered the old caretaker, "the general of the musicians has died..."

### 682. Such Is Fame

At a New York party, famed violinist Isaac Stern (1920-2001) was introduced to world champion boxer Muhammad Ali (1942- )

Shaking hands with Ali, Stern said, "You might say we're in the same business. We both earn a living with our hands."

"You must be pretty good," replied Ali. "There isn't a mark on you."

Note: Ali was world heavyweight champion 1964-1971 and 1974-1978. He changed his name from Cassius Marcellus Clay when he became a Muslim.

## 683. Importance of Being Number Two

Leonard Bernstein (1918-1990) was one of America's greatest composers and conductors, directing and conducting the New York Philharmonic from 1958 to 1969. His Broadway musical "West Side Story" brought him wide acclaim.

An admirer once asked Bernstein what was the hardest instrument to play. He replied without hesitation:

"Second Fiddle. I can always get plenty of first violinists but to find one who plays second violin with as much enthusiasm, or second French horn, or second flute, now that's a problem. And yet, if no one plays second, we have no harmony."

## 684. Lincoln the Music Lover

Abraham Lincoln once told singer Lillie de Hegerman-Lindencrone that, if he heard her sing often, he might have to become a musician himself.

"But," he added, "so far I only know two tunes."

"You know the song 'Hail Columbia' certainly," she said.

"Oh, yes," replied Lincoln, "I know that for I have to stand up and take off my hat."

"And the other song?" she asked.

"The other one?" said Lincoln. "Oh, that is the one when I don't stand up."

## 685. Money and the Opera Star

Soprano Maria Callas (1923-1977) was one of the world's most acclaimed, glamorous, and well-paid opera stars in her day.

The famed diva was once asked by a reporter, "Madame Callas, you were born in the United States, raised in Greece, and you live in Italy, which language do you think in?"

Callas replied, "I count in English."

## 686. Positive Thinking

The talented Broadway musical star Mary Martin (1913-1990) was beloved by all who knew her. No matter what the circumstances, she was always sunny and cheerful.

When she died, a good friend, the noted actress Helen Hayes (1900-1993), recalled during the memorial service a trip she had taken to Paris with Mary Martin.

"Mary took along beautiful, expensive clothes," Helen Hayes remembered. "We were walking through one of the many beautiful parks in Paris and suddenly there was a swoosh of birds overhead — one of whom took perfect aim on the beautiful suit Mary was wearing."

Miss Hayes said Mary looked at her with half a smile and said, "For some people, they sing."

## 687. Sharing the Credit

The famous conductor and composer Leonard Bernstein (1918-1990) asked Stephen Sondheim (1930- ) to co-write the lyrics for *West Side Story* (1957), giving Sondheim his biggest break in show business. Sondheim almost lost the chance, however, when he attempted to excuse himself from the assignment because he didn't know any poor people, let alone any Puerto Ricans.

After two years of preparation, the show opened to outstanding reviews. However, at the premiere, Bernstein saw Sondheim looking rather dejected and realized that the young man felt he had been slighted in not receiving proper credit for his contribution.

Bernstein knew the amount of effort Sondheim had put into the hit show. So he called his agent and his music publisher and asked that the score be reprinted with only Sondheim's name appearing as lyricist.

Stephen Sondheim's longtime agent, Flora Roberts, was amazed. "I think, quite frankly," she said, "what Lenny did is fairly unheard of in the theater. Too many people get credit for things they don't do, much less remove their names."

## 688. Instant Fame Wanted

The famous composer Wolfgang Mozart (1756-1791) was once approached by a young composer on how to develop creatively.

"Begin writing simple things first," Mozart counseled, "songs, for example."

"But you composed symphonies when you were only a child," the young man exclaimed.

"Ah," said Mozart, "but I didn't go to anybody to find out how to become a composer."

## 689. Practice Makes Perfect

Ignace Jan Paderewski (1860-1941), the renowned Polish concert pianist, told some reporters in 1936, "If I miss one day's practice, I notice it. If I miss two days, the critics notice it. If I miss three days, the audience notices it."

## 690. Send Me the Money

This is a story told about Birgit Marta Nilsson (1918-2005), the Swedish soprano celebrated for her Wagnerian interpretations.

As tickets for a New York concert by Nilsson were sold out many weeks in advance, the organizers cabled Nilsson to ask if she would object to their selling some extra seats on the podium.

She replied by return cable: "Sell everything, and please don't forget the space on the piano lid."

## 691. The Importance of Self-Confidence

One of the greatest violinists of all time was named Niccolo Paganini. Born in 1782, he had a long illustrious career before his death in 1840.

One day as Paganini was about to perform before a packed opera house, he suddenly realized that he had walked out on the stage with a strange violin in his hands, not his own treasured instrument made by the master violin maker Guarneri.

Panic-stricken, but realizing that he had no other choice, he began to play with all the skill he possessed. Everyone agreed afterward that he gave the performance of his life. When he was finished, the audience gave him a standing ovation.

In his dressing room after the concert, when he was praised for his superlative performance, Pagannini replied, "Today, I learned the most important lesson of my entire career. Before today I thought the music was in the violin, today I learned that the music is in me."

## 692. Playing the Cymbals

The famous British orchestra conductor Sir Malcolm Sargent (1895-1967) was once asked:

"What do you have to know to play the cymbals?"

"Nothing," he replied. "Just when."

## 693. Some Valuable Advice

From the perspective of jazz great Ray Charles (1930-2004), "you either cut the mustard or have mustard smeared all over your sorry face."

When he was preparing to star as Ray Charles in the movie *Ray*, actor Jamie Foxx (1967- ) met several times with the famous musician. A talented African-American actor-comedian, Foxx wanted to learn how to portray Charles as accurately as possible in the film.

On their first meeting, Charles invited Foxx to sit down and play some blues. Foxx sang and played on one piano as Charles led the jam session on another.

Without warning, Charles began playing the works of another jazz great, Thelonious Monk (1917-1982). Foxx didn't expect such a challenge and he found it difficult to keep up. In doing so, he hit several wrong notes.

Charles abruptly stopped playing and asked Foxx, "Why did you do that?"

Foxx had no answer.

"Look," said Charles, "The notes are right underneath our fingers. All you have to do is to take the time to hit the right ones."

Foxx's movie performance won him an Academy Award in 2004. He also came away from the encounter with an insight into the reason for Charles' greatness. Charles's words are also good advice for anyone facing a new challenge.

## 694. Loss of Perspective

We all know that experts frequently get carried away with their expertise and lose their perspective.

The story is told that, in 1909, during rehearsals for his opera *Elektra*, Austrian composer Richard Strauss (1864-1949) shouted at the orchestra's conductor, "Louder, louder! I can still hear the singers."

## 695. Showing Not Telling

This is a story about Arturo Toscanini (1867-1957), the famous Italian conductor.

During a rehearsal of Debussy's *La Mer*, Toscanini found himself unable to describe the effect he hoped to achieve from a particular passage.

After a moment's thought, he took a silk handkerchief from his pocket and tossed it high into the air. The orchestra, mesmerized, watched the slow, graceful descent of the silken square.

Toscanini smiled with satisfaction as it finally settled on the floor. "There," he said, "play it like that."

## 696. Edison and Music

One of Thomas Edison's (1847-1931) most popular inventions was the phonograph. He called it the "talking machine" and he thought it had ten possible uses, only one of which was the reproduction of music.

Soon after the phonograph was invented, a list of new records was often handed to Edison for his approval.

"After hearing them," Edison said, "I would mark 'good', 'fair' or 'rotten' to classify them for the trade."

Edison used to joke that the records he labeled "rotten" always became a hit with the public and the factory had to work overtime to meet the demand.

## 697. Whoops!

The world-renowned violinist Mischa Elman (1891-1967) gained early fame in Berlin at the age of 13. Actually, the Russian-born youngster had been playing concerts since he was a small boy.

"I was an urchin of seven," said Elman, "and I flattered myself that I rattled off Beethoven's 'Kreutzer Sonata' very well.

"The sonata has in it several long, impressive rests. During one of these rests, an elderly lady leaned forward, patted me on the shoulder, and said, 'Why don't you play something you know, dear.'"

## 698. The Music Lover

Ulysses S. Grant (1822-1885), who led Union armies to victory in the Civil War, later became the 18th President of the United States. Having no appreciation of music, he found it hard when he was obliged as President to attend concerts.

After one such occasion, someone asked him if he had enjoyed the evening. "How could I?" he is reported to have replied. "I know only two tunes. One of them is 'Yankee Doodle,' and the other isn't."

## 699. Paganini's Violin

The great Italian violinist Niccolo Paganini (1782-1840) on his death, bequeathed his beloved violin (named "Cannone") to Genoa, the city of his birth. But he made one condition — the violin was never to be played again. This proviso of his will proved to be most unfortunate.

It is a peculiarity of wood that, if it is used regularly and cared for properly, it will last indefinitely. Unused, it soon begins to decay. And that is what was happening to Paganini's beloved instrument over many years.

So after many discussions and different opinions, it was decided to not respect the condition of Paganini's will that his famous, golden-toned instrument not be played again.

Instead the violin is played periodically in the same room of Palazzo Tursi in Genoa where it is displayed. A special violinist appointed by the city administration is responsible for the task of "keeping the violin alive."

In addition, every year, on October 12 (celebration day for Genoa and Columbus) the instrument is played by the winner of the International Competition for violin dedicated to Niccolo Paganini.

This story has a profound moral for all of us. No matter what we have previously accomplished, staying at our best requires that we remain active and involved with everything that goes into making our life worthwhile.

## 700. The Story of "Taps"

"Taps," the bugle call played as "lights out" at military encampments and as "farewell" at military funerals, was originally played on a drum, hence its name.

The musical form of "Taps" was written toward the beginning of July, 1862, in a Union Army camp by General Daniel Butterfield (1831-1901). General Butterfield wrote the music on the back of a torn envelope and whistled the tune to Oliver Willcox Norton, bugler and aide-de-camp of General Strong Vincent, commander of the 83rd Regiment Pennsylvania Volunteers of the Army of the Potomac.

# NEGATIVE THINKING

## 701. Personal Monsters

Hercules, according to legend, grew increasingly irritated by a strange, menacing animal that kept blocking his path. In a fit of anger, he struck the animal with his club, killing it.

As he continued his path, he kept encountering the same animal, each time larger and more menacing than before. At last a wise messenger appeared and warned Hercules to stop his furious assaults.

"The Monster is Strife, and you are stirring it up," said the messenger. "Just let it alone and it will shrivel and cease to trouble you."

## 702. Negative Thinking Can Be Fatal

Most experts agree that the greatest tightrope walker who ever lived was Karl Wallenda (1905-1978). He walked tightropes over great distances, high in the air, and he did so without a safety net.

As he grew older, Wallenda kept on doing he death-defying walks. He performed the same breathtaking stunts in his seventies that he had done as a young man in his twenties.

Then in 1978, he fell to his death while walking a tightrope strung between two buildings in San Juan, Puerto Rico.

His wife was interviewed on television several weeks later and questioned about Wallenda's fall.

"It was very strange," she said. "For months prior to his performance, he thought about nothing else. But for the first time, he didn't see himself succeeding. He saw himself falling."

Mrs. Wallenda went on to say that he even went so far as to personally check the installation and construction of the wire itself. "This," she said, "was something Karl had never done previously." There seems little doubt that Karl Wallenda's negative mental imagery and fears contributed to his falling.

## 703. Small Thinker

Once upon a time there was a tiny man no more than three feet tall. He longed to be tall — "tall and sizable" as he put it — so he decided to ask his animal friends how he might grow.

"Horse" was eager to help. "Eat lots of oats and corn," he said, "do lots of running, and you will soon grow tall."

So the little man did just that, eating so much oatmeal that sometimes he felt quite sick to his stomach. But he did not grow.

His next approach was to a huge bull who lived in the pasture nearby.

"Eat lots of grass," said Bull, "and charge fiercely at anyone who comes near you, snorting out loud in a threatening way. That is bound to make you grow. It worked for me."

So the little man tried that too but he found that all that grass didn't agree with him either and the people he charged at just laughed and ignored him.

Discouraged, the tiny man went to see a wise old Owl of his acquaintance. After listening solemnly to the little man's complaint, Owl asked, "Why do you want to grow tall?"

"So that I won't be beaten when I get into a fight!" he answered quickly.

"Have you ever been in a fight?" asked the Owl calmly.

"No-o-o," said the tiny man, slightly flustered, "but who knows when I might."

"Well, then," said the Owl, "it doesn't seem to me that you have a very good reason to want to be big." And with this the old bird gave a few hoots and closed his eyes sleepily.

"Wait," cried the little man, "I need to be tall so I can see far into the distance."

"Have you never climbed a tree to get a long-distance look?" said the Owl, beginning to be a bit bored with the conversation.

"Well, y-e-e-s," said the tiny man in an embarrassed voice and he began to think of some more reasons to convince the Owl that he needed to be tall.

At this the old bird opened his big eyes and looked down at the little man with just a trace of impatience.

"There ain't nothing wrong with your body size, my friend," said the Owl. "What needs growing is your brain."

## 704. Negative Thought

Dorothy L. Sayers (1893-1997), a well-known English writer said this about negative thinking, "Tolerance, Apathy, Inaction... the sin that believes in nothing, cares for nothing, seeks to know nothing, interferes with nothing, enjoys nothing, hates nothing, finds purpose in nothing and remains alive because there is nothing for which it will die."

## 705. The Pessimist

The following was written by Benjamin Franklin King (1857-1899), an American poet:

"Nothing to do but work,
Nothing to eat but food,
Nothing to wear but clothes
To keep one from going nude.

Nothing to breathe but air,
Quick as a flash it's gone;
Nowhere to fall but off,
Nowhere to stand but on.

Nothing to comb but hair,
Nowhere to sleep but in bed,
Nothing to weep but tears,
Nothing to bury but dead.

Nothing to sing but songs,
Ah, well, alas! alack!
Nowhere to go but out,
Nowhere to come but back.

Nothing to see but sights,
Nothing to quench but thirst,
Nothing to have but what we've got;
Thus thro' life we are cursed.

Nothing to strike but a gait;
Everything moves that goes,
Nothing at all but common sense
Can ever withstand these woes.

## 706. Your Mind

Ralph Waldo Emerson (1803-1882), eminent American essayist, poet and philosopher, said this about negative thoughts, "Your own mind is a sacred enclosure into which nothing harmful can enter except by your permission."

## 707. A Ship That Lost Its Nails

This is a story about an 18th-century trading schooner named *The Dolphin* which sailed the South Pacific more than 200 years ago, and how it perished because it gave up something it depended upon for its existence.

The story begins when *The Dolphin* dropped anchor in the harbor of a little South Sea island late one summer. It was a beautiful island and the crew fell in love with the place. They fell in love with the natives' way of life, with the exotic fruit and flowers, the friendliness of the people, not to mention the beautiful native women. Even the captain seemed to be in no hurry to move on.

After a while, the crew discovered the natives would give anything they had for something the crew thought had little value — iron nails. Though they were almost invisible, it was iron nails that held the wooden ship together. It was nails that kept the decks secure, the hull sturdy, and the keel true. To the natives, who had to tie things together with crude ropes, iron nails were a form of powerful magic and no price was too high to acquire them.

One morning the captain of *The Dolphin* noticed that the decking on the ship was coming up and that the hull was taking on water. He discovered the disintegration was due to nails being missing — so he posted a 24-hour watch against nail thieves.

But it was too late. The ship's own crew had stripped their vessel of nails to trade with the natives — often for romantic favors from the women on the island.

It was not long before *The Dolphin* went down, a broken ship, robbed of its integrity and purpose.

One can draw many lessons from such a story. But it is not stretching a point too far to say that what happened to *The Dolphin* can happen to any organization or person when they let slip away the basic strengths that made them successful in the past, and fail to think of the future.

## 708. Neglect of Daughters

Abigail Adams (1744-1818), wife of an American president, John Adams (1735-1826), and mother of a second president, John Quincy Adams (1767-1848), wrote the following to her husband on August 14, 1776, "If you complain of neglect of education in sons, what shall I say with regard to daughters, who every day experience the want of it? With regard to the education of my own children, I find myself soon out of my depth, destitute and deficient in every part of education. I most sincerely wish...that our new Constitution may be distinguished for encouraging learning and virtue. If we mean to have heroes, statesmen, and philosophers, we should have learned women."

## 709. Art before All

George Bernard Shaw (1856-1950), Irish-born British playwright and critic, once said of true artists, "The true artist will let his wife starve, his children go barefoot, his mother drudge for his living at seventy, sooner than work at anything but his art."

## 710. Lack of Praise

Frederick Winslow Taylor (1856-1915), pioneer management teacher, remarked in a 1912 Harvard Business School lecture that "Men would far rather even be blamed by their bosses...than be passed by day by day with no more notice than if they were a part of the machinery."

# NEGOTIATION

## 711. Franklin the Persuader

At the end of the Revolutionary War, Benjamin Franklin was appointed to head the diplomatic team that went to Paris to work out a treaty with the British. The negotiations ended at Lansdowne House in London.

The negotiations were difficult from the beginning. The Americans wanted all the British territory from the Atlantic to the Mississippi, fishing rights off New England and Canada, and non-harassment of American commercial ships on the high seas. On the other hand, the British had little to gain by formally recognizing the new American government.

Despite the obstacles, Franklin succeeded in hammering out an agreement with the British. But when the time came for putting pen to treaty, Lord Shelburne, who represented the British, balked and began to walk out of the Round Room at Lansdowne House.

"Just a minute," said Franklin. "First you had better settle your bill." And Franklin dug into his traveling case and pulled out, one by one, hundreds of itemized records — of American houses requisitioned by the British during the war, warehouses taken over, barns burned, wagons appropriated, and horses seized.

Lord Shelburne looked at them, sighed, and then signed the treaty, saying "you're a hard man, Franklin."

## 712. A Negotiation Secret

President Kennedy once praised his then Secretary of Labor Arthur Goldberg (1908-1990) for his uncanny ability to prevent strikes by organized labor.

"How do you do it, Arthur?" asked the President admiringly.

"The trick is," replied Goldberg, "be there when it's settled."

## 713. How to Negotiate

In the course of negotiations, do you position yourself to come out on top? If not, take a tip from this bit of history from the Rockefeller family.

J.P. Morgan (1837-1913) was once interested in buying a mining tract owned by John D. Rockefeller, Sr. (1839-1937). Rockefeller responded to the request by sending around his son, John D., Jr. (1874-1960).

Morgan led the conversation by asking, "Well, what's your price?" Replied John D., Jr., "Mr. Morgan, I think there must be some mistake. I did not come here to sell. I understood you wished to buy."

## 714. Lincoln on Negotiations

During the Civil War, President Lincoln was urged by a friend to give up Forts Sumter and Pickens and all government property in the Southern states. In reply, Lincoln said:

"Do you remember the fable of the lion and the woodman's daughter?

The friend said he did not.

"Aesop," said Lincoln, "writes that a lion was very much in love with a woodman's daughter. The fair maid referred him to her father. And the lion went to the father and asked for her hand.

"The father replied: 'Your teeth are too long.'

"The lion went to a dentist and had them extracted. Returning, he asked again for his bride.

"'No,' said the woodman. 'Your claws are too long.'

"Going back to the dentist, he had the claws removed. Then he returned to claim his bride, and the woodman, seeing that he was unarmed, beat out his brains.

"May it not be so with me," concluded Lincoln, "if I give up all that is asked?"

## 715. A Bad Bargain

The story goes that a destitute young man approaches the Circus Master in Krakow, Poland, and tells the Circus Master that for five dollars each time, he will jump off a tower 100 feet in the air during circus performances.

"I will use no net," he says. "No parachute. No bungee cords. Straight off the platform to the ground. Five bucks a shot."

The Circus Master is interested. This could be a big attraction. But he tells the young man he'll have to see the performance once before he hires him. So the young man climbs to the top of the 100 foot tower, jumps off, and — SPLAT! — slams to the ground.

The young man picks himself up slowly and painfully. Limping over to the Circus Master, he says, "The price went up. Now it's 10 dollars a jump."

The Circus Master asks him, "How come? You said five dollars."

The young man says, "That was before I knew how much it was going to hurt."

# NOBEL PRIZE

## 716. How the Nobel Prizes Came to Be

Alfred Bernhard Nobel (1833-1896), the inventor of dynamite, was born in Stockholm, Sweden, on October 21, 1833. He was a gifted student who took a special interest in chemistry and foreign languages. He did most of his studying on his own and never did take any college or university examinations.

Applying the Italian Sobrero's methods, Nobel succeeded in developing a type of explosive nitroglycerin that he named "dynamite." It soon became widely used in building and construction in many countries. Income from his many enterprises soon made Nobel one of the wealthiest men in Europe.

Nobel, who never married, was a lonely man, often in poor health, and who appeared shy to other people. He devoutly believed that his invention of dynamite would end all wars because of its power to destroy. You can then imagine his horror and surprise when, in 1888, a French newspaper mistakenly ran an obituary labeling him, the "merchant of death."

Not wanting to go down in history with such an epitaph, Nobel changed his will to create the famous Nobel Prizes for peace, physics, chemistry, physiology or medicine, and literature. His relatives, who were included in his previous wills, were shocked and many of them wanted to contest the will.

On the fifth anniversary of Alfred Nobel's death, December 10, 1901, the first set of Nobel Prizes were awarded and it has become an annual event ever since. The shy "Merchant of Death" scientist, Alfred Nobel, had created awards that are given each year to honor the contributions of men and women whose efforts help make this a better world.

# OLD AGE

## 717. Philosophy At 80

The German statesman Bismarck (1815-1898), who became the first chancellor of the German Empire, was congratulated by friends on his eightieth birthday. Bismarck thanked them and added, "You know, the first eighty years of a man's life are always the happiest."

## 718. Julie Andrews on Old Age

To commemorate her 69th birthday on October 1, 2004, the actor/singer Julie Andrews (1935- ) made a special appearance at New York City's Radio City Music Hall for the benefit of AARP.

One of the musical numbers she performed was "My Favorite Things" from the legendary movie *Sound of Music*, in which she starred. However, the lyrics of the song were deliberately changed to reflect the audience's advanced age. Here are the lyrics as she sang them:

Maalox and nose drops and needles for knitting,
Walkers and handrails and new dental fittings,
Bundles of magazines tied up in string,
These are a few of my favorite things.

Cadillacs and cataracts and hearing aids and glasses,
Polident and Fixodent and false teeth in glasses,
Pacemakers, golf carts and porches with swings,
These are a few of my favorite things.

When the pipes leak,
When the bones creak,
When the knees go bad,

I simply remember my favorite things,
and then I don't feel so bad.

Hot tea and crumpets, and corn pads for bunions,
No spicy hot food or food cooked with onions,
Bathrobes and heat pads and hot meals they bring,
These are a few of my favorite things.

Back pains, confused brains, and no fear of sinnin',
Thin bones and fractures and hair that is thinnin',
And we won't mention our short shrunken frames,
When we remember our favorite things.

When the joints ache,
When the hips break,
When the eyes go dim,

Then I remember the great life I've had,
And then I don't feel so bad.

Note: Ms. Andrews received a standing ovation from the crowd that lasted over four minutes, and included repeated encores.

## 719. Life's Timetable

Which sounds longer to you, 569,400 hours or 65 years? They are exactly the same in length of time.

The average man spends his first eighteen years — 157,000 hours – getting an education. That leaves him 412,000 hours from age 18 to 65. Eight hours of every day are spent in sleeping; eight hours in eating and recreation. So there is left eight hours to work in each day.

One third of 412,000 hours is 134,000 hours — the number of hours a man has in which to work between the age of 18 and 65. Expressed in hours it doesn't seem a very long time, does it? It is not recommended that you tick off the hours that you worked, 134,000, 138,999, 133,990, etc., but good advice would suggest that, whatever you do, you do it with all that you have in you.

If you are sleeping, sleep well. If you are playing, play well. If you are working, give the best that is in you, remembering that in the last analysis the real satisfactions in life come not from money and things, but from the realization of a job well done.

## 720. Mark Twain on Reaching 70

Reaching 70 isn't considered old age today but in Mark Twain's (Samuel Clemens) (1835-1910) day it was so considered. On reaching his 70th birthday in 1905, Twain made a speech that perfectly captures his life style and sense of humor. The speech has become quite famous. Here is a long excerpt.

"The seventieth birthday! It is the time of life when you arrive at a new and awful dignity; when you may throw aside the decent reserves which have oppressed you for a generation and stand unafraid and unabashed upon your seven-terraced summit and look down and teach — unrebuked. You can tell the world how you got there. It is what they all do. You shall never get tired of telling by what delicate arts and deep moralities you climbed up to that great place. You will explain the process and dwell on the particulars with senile rapture. I have been anxious to explain my own system this long time, and now at least I have the right.

"I have achieved my seventy years in the usual way by sticking strictly to a scheme of life which would kill anybody else. It sounds like an exaggeration, but that is really the common rule for attaining to old age. When we examine the program of any of these garrulous old people we always find that the habits which have preserved them would have decayed us; that the way of life which enabled them to live upon the property of their heirs so long, as Mr. Choate says, would have put us out of commission ahead of time. I will offer here, as a sound maxim, this: That we can't reach old age by another man's road.

"I will now teach, offering my way of life to whomsoever desires to commit suicide by the scheme which has enabled me to beat the doctor and the hangman for seventy years. Some of the details may sound untrue, but they are not. I am not here to deceive; I am here to teach.

"We have no permanent habits until we are forty. Then they begin to harden, presently they petrify, then business begins. Since forty I have been regular about going to bed and getting up — and that is one of the main things. I have made it a rule to go to bed when there wasn't anybody left to sit up with, and I have made it a rule to get up when I had to. This has resulted in an unswerving regularity of irregularity. It has saved me sound, but it would injure another person.

"In the matter of diet — which is another main thing — I have been persistently strict in sticking to the things which didn't agree with me until one or the other of us got the best of it. Until lately I got the best of it myself. But last spring I stopped frolicking with mince-pie after midnight; up to then I had always believed it wasn't loaded. For thirty years I have taken coffee and bread at eight in the morning, and no bite nor sup until seven-thirty in the evening. Eleven hours. That is all right for me, and is wholesome, because I have never had a headache in my life, but headachy people would not reach seventy comfortably by that road, and they would be foolish to try it. And I wish to urge upon you this — which I think is wisdom — that if you find you can't make seventy by any but an uncomfortable road, don't you go. When they take off the Pullman and retire you to the rancid smoker, put on your things, count your checks, and get out at the first way station where there's a cemetery.

"I have made it a rule never to smoke more than one cigar at a time. I have no other restriction as regards smoking. I do not know just when I began to smoke. I only know that it was in my father's lifetime, and that I was discreet. He passed from this life early in 1847, when I was a shade past eleven; ever since then I have smoked publicly. As an example to others, and not that I care for moderation myself, it has always been my rule never to smoke when asleep, and never to refrain when awake. It is a good rule, I mean, for me, but some of you know quite well that it wouldn't answer to everybody that's trying to get to be seventy.

"I smoke in bed until I have to go to sleep; I wake up in the night, sometimes once, sometimes twice, sometimes three times, and I never waste any of these opportunities to smoke. This habit is so old and dear and precious to me that if I should break it I should feel as you, sir, would feel if you should lose the only moral you've got — meaning the chairman — if you've got one: I am making no charges. I will grant, here, that I have stopped smoking now and then, for a few months at a time, but it was not on principle, it was only to show off; it was to pulverize those critics who said I was a slave to my habits and couldn't break my bonds.

"Today it is all of sixty years since I began to smoke the limit. I have never bought cigars with life-belts around them. I early found that those were too expensive for me. I have always bought cheap cigars — reasonably cheap, at any rate. Sixty years ago they cost me four dollars a barrel, but my taste has improved, latterly, and I pay seven now. Six or seven. Seven, I think. Yes, it's seven. But that includes the barrel. I often have smoking parties at my house; but the people that come have always just taken the pledge. I wonder why that is?

"As for drinking, I have no rule about that. When the others drink I like to help; otherwise I remain dry, by habit and preference. This dryness does not hurt me, but it could easily hurt you, because you are different. You let it alone.

"Since I was seven years old, I have seldom taken a dose of medicine, and have still seldomer (sic) needed one. But up to seven I lived exclusively on allopathic medicines. Not that I needed them, for I don't think I did; it was for economy; my father took a drug-store for a debt, and it made cod-liver oil cheaper than the other breakfast foods. We had nine barrels of it, and it lasted me seven years. Then I was weaned. The rest of the family had to get along with rhubarb and ipecac and such things, because I was the pet. I was the first Standard Oil Trust. I had it all. By the time the drug-store was exhausted my health was established, and there has never been much the matter with me since. But you know very well it would be foolish for the average child to start for seventy on that basis. It happened to be just the thing for me, but that was merely an accident; it couldn't happen again in a century.

"I have never taken any exercise, except sleeping and resting, and I never intend to take any. Exercise is loathsome. And it cannot be any benefit when you are tired, and I was always tired. But let another person try my way, and see where he will come out.

"I desire now to repeat and emphasize that maxim: We can't reach old age by another man's road. My habits protect my life, but they would assassinate you."

## 721. Lengthening Life Spans

The life span of a caveman averaged only about 18 years. The ancient Romans lived to be about 22 years old. The Egyptians did a little better, with an average life span of 29 years.

Several thousand years later in 1850, the average life span in the civilized world was still only about 37 years. Today the average life span is over 70 years in most industrialized nations.

## 722. No End to Learning

Michelangelo was seventy-two years old when he was appointed chief architect of St. Peter's and commissioned to embellish this great temple with his paintings and statues.

For eighteen years he continued this work, which made his fame as imperishable as the church itself. Toward the end, when his eyesight failed and he had become feeble, he had his servants carry him into the great halls and galleries and chapels, where he had labored with such vim and enthusiasm.

He would run his hands over the statues and carvings, feeling out with his dexterous fingers the details that his eyes could no longer see, and he often exclaimed, "I still learn."

## 723. At a Loss for Words

When the English novelist Somerset Maugham (1874-1965) reached the age of 80, he was invited to speak before one of England's most exclusive groups at the Garrick Club in London.

It was a gala occasion and every guest was eager to hear what wisdom the distinguished author was about to share with them.

Maugham, who had always been bothered by a hesitation or stutter in his speech, was introduced with a great flourish by the dinner's chairman.

Taking a sip from his glass of water, Maugham rose and began to speak. "Old age," he said, "has many benefits."

Then followed a long pause while Maugham seemingly looked about him for help. He took another sip of water, shuffled his notes, and seemed unable to continue.

Finally, when the tension in the audience has reached an almost unbearable level, Maugham with a sly look on his face continued in this manner, "....and I have been trying to think of what they are."

## 724. How Today's Retirement Age Was Born

For many nations, the retirement age of 65 was established back in the 1870s. The age of 65 was selected arbitrarily by German chancellor Otto von Bismarck (1815-1898) as the age at which German civil servants could retire and receive pensions.

The decision made good fiscal sense at that time because the average life expectancy then was considerably less than that. The problem for pension planners today is that life expectancy is currently much longer than 65 years. Despite this, the age of 65 is still widely maintained even though prudent fiscal judgment might dictate otherwise.

## 725. Old Age Needn't Slow You Up

Here is a list of famous people who kept on creating and contributing long after their 70's and 80's:

- Grandma Moses (1860-1961) took up painting at the age of 80 and continued to do her quaint and appealing work to the end of her life at 99. She completed more than 1,500 paintings during her life.

- Mahatma Gandhi (1869-1948) served as the moving force behind the drive for freedom in India until he was cut down by an assassin at 78.

- Spanish-born Pablo Casals (1876-1973) is considered by many to be the greatest cellist of all time. Casals continued to play, conduct, and teach up to the time of his death at 97.

- Titian (1477-1576), the celebrated painter, lived to be 99, painting until he died.

- Goethe (1749-1832), the German poet, died at 83, and finished his famous *Faust* only a few years earlier.

- Robert Frost (1874-1963), nearly 87, read his poem, "The Gift Outright" at the inauguration of President John F. Kennedy in 1962.

- Actor and comedian George Burns (1896-1996) won his first Oscar at age 80.

- Golda Meir (1898-1978) was 71 when she became prime minister of Israel.

- Benjamin Franklin (1706-1790) participated in helping frame the U.S. Constitution when he was 82.

- Physician and humanitarian Albert Schweitzer (1875-1965) was still performing operations in his African hospital at 89.

- Astronaut John Glenn (1921- ) returned to space flight at 75.

- Verdi (1813-1901) wrote operas into his eighties.

- Admiral Rickover (1900-1986), the designer of the first nuclear submarine, was still a consultant to the Navy at the age of 82.

- Pablo Picasso (1881-1973) was still turning out paintings and sculptures when he was 90. Picasso painted over 20,000 pictures, and is considered by many to be the greatest artist of the 20th century.

- Marc Chagall (1887-1985), who was born in Russia, was designing stained glass windows for churches in many parts of the world at the age of 90. Both Picasso and Chagall lived to the ripe old age of 97.

- George Bernard Shaw (1856-1950), the Irish playwright, was still working on a play at the age of 93.

- Arthur Rubinstein (1887-1982) gave a concert at Carnegie Hall at the age of 90. He was almost blind and unable to read the notes. Nevertheless, he played with his usual perfection.

## 726. Old Folks Prayer

For twenty years after he retired, the Hollywood movie star Cary Grant (1904-1986) made appearances across the country. He called it, "A Conversation with Cary Grant."

It took just a small newspaper ad and the house was sold out. He had no routine. He sat on a stool for 90 minutes, told stories and answered questions. The people loved it, and so did he. He closed with what he called, "A Meditation." He said he didn't know who wrote it but it expressed his own feelings about growing older. Here it is:

"Lord, you've known me a long time. You know me better than I know myself. You know that each day I am growing older, and someday I may even be very old. So, please keep me from thinking I must say something on every subject and on every occasion.

"Release me from trying to straighten out everyone's affairs. Make me thoughtful, but not moody, helpful but not overbearing. I have a certain amount of knowledge to share; still, it would be nice at the end to have a few friends who recognized and forgave the knowledge I lacked.

"Keep my tongue free from the recital of endless details. Seal my lips on my aches and pains: They increase daily and the need to speak of them can become a compulsion. Give me grace instead to listen to the retelling of others' afflictions, and be helped to endure them with patience.

"I would like to have improved memory, but I'll settle for growing humility and an ability to capitulate when my memory clashes with the memory of others.

"Teach me the glorious lesson that on some occasions I may be mistaken. Keep me reasonably kind. I've never aspired to be a saint. Saints can be rather difficult to live with; yet — on the other hand — an embittered old person is a constant burden. Please give me the ability to see good in unlikely places and talents in unexpected people. And give me the grace to tell them so, dear Lord. Amen."

### 727. Chinese on Age

To the Chinese, the sixtieth birthday is quite a big deal — the most revered of all birthdays. This has to do with the Chinese astrological system of twelve animals (Rat, Ox, Tiger, Rabbit, Dragon, Snake, Horse, Ram, Monkey, Rooster, Dog, and Pig) and five elements (Wood, Fire, Earth, Metal, and Water).

Every year is assigned an element and an animal; for example, you could have been born under the sign of the Dragon in a Fire year or under the sign of the Monkey in a Wood year.

The exact combination of animal and element repeats itself only once every sixty years, which is why the Chinese consider the age of sixty to be such a special year (assuming that practically no one lives to age 120).

# OPPORTUNITY

### 728. Mindless Habit

In the days of ancient Egypt, the greatest library in the world was located in Alexandria. But one awful day it burned down and, as the legend goes, only one book was saved.

It was not a particularly valuable book but between its pages was something that held out the promise of great riches. It was a thin strip of vellum on which was written the "Secret of the Touchstone."

The Touchstone was a common pebble that had the power to turn any common metal into pure gold. The magic pebble, said the writing on the vellum, was lying among thousands and thousands of other pebbles that looked exactly like it. The secret, said the vellum, was that the real stone would feel warm, while ordinary pebbles would feel cold.

The man who got possession of the book, and who found the piece of vellum within its pages, said nothing to anyone about the secret he had found. He sold all his belongings, bought some supplies, and, with dreams of wealth dancing through his head, camped out on the seashore to begin testing pebbles.

Each time he picked up a pebble, and if it was cold, he would fling it into the sea, and quickly pick up the next one. He kept doing this from dawn to dark for days on end, then weeks and months and years. As time went by, the man was dazed from fatigue but convinced that at any moment he would find the magic pebble.

One day, soon after his midday meal, the man picked up a pebble that felt warm. But before he knew what he was doing, he threw it into the sea. He had built up such a habit of throwing each pebble into the sea that he unthinkingly threw away the warm pebble that would have brought him endless fortune. Mindless habit had been his undoing.

So it is with opportunities in our daily lives. Unless we are vigilant and open-minded about our activities, we can let priceless opportunities slip through our fingers. Keeping an open mind about how we pursue our objectives can be the Touchstone to success beyond our wildest dreams.

## 729. The Ninth Wave

There is an ancient superstition of the sea that periodically a wave comes along that is greater than any that has preceded it.

It is called the Ninth Wave, a powerful culmination of sea and wind. There is no greater force.

To catch the Ninth Wave at the critical moment requires a special skill and daring. You must mount the wave precisely at its peak, and it will carry you a great distance to where you want to go.

There is a great lesson here for grasping opportunities in our daily lives.

## 730. Source of the Word "Opportunity"

In the days of sailing ships, a vessel had to wait for the flood tide before it could sail into port. The Latin term for this situation was "ob portu"; that is, a ship standing over against a port waiting for the right moment when it could ride into harbor.

This is the source from which the English word "opportunity" is derived.

# PARENTING

## 731. Some Wise Advice

At the christening of her baby, a mother asked the great general, Robert E. Lee, for some wisdom that would help her guide her son along the road to manhood.

The general's immediate answer was: "Teach him to deny himself."

## 732. Motivation

Once upon a time, there were two tribes at war with one another. One of the tribes lived in the lowlands and the other lived high in the mountains.

One day the mountain people conducted a raid on the lowlanders and plundered a village. During the raid, they kidnapped a baby of one of the lowlander families and took the infant with them back up into the mountains.

Enraged at the loss, the lowlanders resolved to recover the kidnapped baby no matter what the cost. But they didn't know how to climb the mountain. They didn't know any of the trails that the mountain people used, and they didn't know where to find the mountain people or how to track them in the steep terrain. Even so, the lowlanders sent out a rescue party of their best fighting men to climb the mountain and bring the baby home.

The men tried first one method of climbing and then another, all to no avail. After several days of effort, they had succeeded in climbing only several hundred feet up the mountain. Thoroughly discouraged, the lowlander men decided that the cause was lost, and they reluctantly prepared to return to their village below empty-handed

But, as they were packing their gear for the descent, they suddenly saw the baby's mother walking toward them. They stood staring at her in amazement that she was coming down the mountain they had totally failed to climb.

Then they saw that she had the kidnapped baby strapped to her back. They shook their heads and gasped in astonishment. How was that possible?

The first man to greet her said, "We couldn't climb this mountain. How did you do so when we, the strongest and most able men in the village, couldn't do it?"

She shrugged her shoulders and replied, "It wasn't your baby."

## 733. Legacy of Kindness

There is an old story about a king who had a beautiful ring and three sons. Each son wanted the ring.

When the king died, he left three rings for his sons and a note that said, "My dear sons, one of these rings is real and two are fake. The way you will know who has the real ring is that the son with the real ring will be kind and generous to all people."

Each of the three sons spent the rest of his life being good to others to prove that he had the real ring.

## 734. What Is a Grandmother?

An 8-year-old wrote, "A grandmother is a lady who has no children of her own, so she likes other people's boy and girls.

"Grandmas don't have anything to do except be there. If they take us for walks, they slow down past pretty leaves and caterpillars. They never say, 'Hurry up.'

"Usually they are fat but not too fat to tie shoes. They wear glasses, and sometimes they can take their teeth out. They can answer questions like why dogs hate cats and why God isn't married. They don't talk like visitors do which is hard to understand.

"When they read to us, they don't skip words or mind if it is the same story again. Everybody should try to have a grandma, especially if you don't have television, because grandmas are the only grownups who always have time."

## 735. Born to the Job

Britain's Manchester Guardian reported that Mikhail Gorbachev (1931- ), when he was head of the Soviet Union, took his new grandson to the Kremlin for his staff to admire.

"He'll be a general," said the Defense Minister, "See how he stamps his feet to get his way!"

"No, he'll be a banker," said the Finance Minister, "Observe how he grabs everything with both hands."

"No," said Gorbachev, "He will be President! Notice how he can soil his diapers and keep right on smiling!"

## 736. How Mothers Were Created

When God was creating mothers He was into His sixth day of overtime when an angel appeared and said, "You're doing a lot of fiddling around on this one."

And the Lord said, "Have you read the specs on this order? She has to be completely washable, but not plastic; have 180 movable parts, all replaceable; run on black coffee and leftovers; have a lap that disappears when she stands up; a kiss that can cure anything from a broken leg to a disappointed love affair; and six pairs of hands."

The angel shook its head slowly and said, "Six pairs of hands...no way!"

"It's not the hands that are causing me problems," said the Lord. "It's the three pairs of eyes that mothers have to have."

## 737. Like Father Like Son

Child psychiatrists have found that children pay very close attention to how their parents treat their grandparents. This story demonstrates that fact:

A frail old man went to live with his son, daughter-in-law, and 4-year-old grandson. The old man's hands trembled, his eyesight was blurred, and his step faltered. The family ate together at the table.

But the grandfather's shaky hands and failing eyesight made eating difficult. For example, peas frequently rolled off his spoon on to the floor. When he grasped a glass, milk often spilled on the tablecloth.

The son and daughter-in-law became irritated with the mess. "We must do something about father," said the son. "We can't live with his spilled milk, noisy eating, and food on the floor."

So the husband and wife set a small table in the corner. There the grandfather ate alone while the rest of the family enjoyed dinner. Since grandfather had broken a dish or two, his food was served in a wooden bowl.

When the family glanced in grandfather's direction, sometimes he had a tear in his eye as he sat alone. Still, the only words the couple had for him were admonitions when he dropped a fork or spilled food.

The 4-year-old watched it all in silence. One evening before supper, the father noticed his son playing with wood scraps on the floor. He asked the child, "What are you making?"

The boy responded, "Oh, I am making a little bowl for you and Mama to eat your food in when I grow up."

Though no words were spoken, both parents knew what must be done. That evening, the husband took the grandfather's hand and gently led him back to the family table. For the remainder of his days, he ate every meal with the family. And neither husband nor wife seemed to care when a fork or spoon was dropped, milk spilled, or the tablecloth soiled.

## 738. A Parent's Love

Following the couple's divorce, their teenage daughter became increasingly rebellious. It culminated late one night when the police called to tell the mother that she had to come to the police station to pick up her daughter, who had been arrested for drunk driving.

The mother and daughter did not speak until the next afternoon. Mom broke the tension by giving her daughter a small gift-wrapped box. The daughter reluctantly opened it and found a small piece of rock. She rolled her eyes and said, "Cute, Mom, what's this for?"

"Here's the card," Mom said.

Her daughter took the card out of the envelope and read it. Tears started to trickle down her cheeks. She got up and gave her mom a big hug as the card fell to the floor.

On the card were these words: "This rock is more than 200 million years old. That's how long it will take before I give up on you."

# PATRIOTISM

## 739. The Man Who Designed Washington, D.C.

Pierre Charles L'Enfant (1754-1825) was a French engineer and architect who came to America at the age of 23 to fight in the Revolution. He designed Federal Hall in New York City, originally the U.S. Capitol. George Washington, who was sworn in as the first president on its balcony, liked L'Enfant's work so much he asked L'Enfant to do the planning for the nation's new capital city in the District of Columbia.

The designs L'Enfant's came up with rejected the usual rectangular layout as lacking "a sense of the real grand and truly beautiful." Instead, he envisioned a city of wide radiating streets, circles, malls and parks.

Unfortunately, the young architect's vision was not matched by practicality or discretion. He overspent prodigiously, antagonized the city commissioners and members of Congress, and, finally, irritated George Washington enough so that he fired him.

The fee for L'Enfant's work had not been agreed upon in advance, and President Washington thought $2,500 to $3,000 would be generous. Instead, L'Enfant's bill was a whopping $95,500 and he refused to discuss any compromise offers. In 1890, Congress voted him $1,394.20, which his creditors seized before he could turn it down.

Over time, poverty engulfed L'Enfant. When he died on June 14, 1825, his estate was a few maps, books, and surveying instruments valued at $45.

The architect of Washington, D.C. was buried in an unmarked grave and forgotten. His plan for the capital was largely ignored until 1901, when its importance was belatedly recognized. Since then, L'Enfant's spirit has governed the design of the city. In 1909, his remains were disinterred and carried to the Capitol to lie in state, then reburied in Arlington National Cemetery on a hill overlooking the great city which was his brainchild.

## 740. America's New Day

During the Constitutional Convention, the chair from which George Washington was presiding was decorated with a design of a sun poised low on the horizon. . Looking at the design during the long, and sometimes discouraging sessions, some of the delegates had wondered aloud whether the sun was a rising or a setting sun.

At the close of the history making convention, Benjamin Franklin said, "We know now that is it a rising sun and the beginning of a great new day!"

## 741. A Perilous Journey

One of America's most revered documents is the "Declaration of Independence" which was signed on July 4, 1776.

Today it rests in a bullet-proof, helium-filled display case in the National Archives. A push of a button can send the whole display down 22 feet through the floor into a 55-ton vault built of steel and reinforced concrete. But it was not always so safe. Consider the following:

1776 to 1790: When the British invaded Philadelphia, the Declaration was packed into a trunk and taken to such places as Lancaster and York, Pennsylvania; Annapolis, Maryland, and Trenton, New Jersey.

1790 to 1814: The Declaration was moved by ship from New York to Philadelphia, and then to Washington, D.C., America's new capital. During the War of 1812, the Declaration and other important papers were packed into linen sacks, loaded onto wagons, and sent to Virginia. While the British burned Washington in 1814, the Declaration was hidden in a clergyman's home in Leesburg, Virginia.

1814-1875: After the war, the Declaration was returned to the ravaged capital and stored in various buildings until 1820, when it was moved to the headquarters of the Department of State. There it was kept rolled up like a scroll. In 1841, it was unrolled, mounted, and framed for public view. It hung opposite a window in the new Patent Office, yellowing and fading for 35 years.

1876 to 1877: The Declaration was shipped to Philadelphia for the Centennial Exposition. The years of rolling and unrolling, as well as fading, had taken their toll. Many of the signatures were now so dim as to be unrecognizable.

1877: The Declaration was moved from the Patent Office to the library of the Department of State, where it was displayed for another 17 years. It was a good thing because the Patent Office burned down a few months later.

1894-1921: The Declaration's deterioration caused so much concern that it was sealed between two plates of glass and locked away in a steel safe in the State, War and Navy Building. It was exhibited only on rare occasions.

1921: The Declaration was moved to the Library of Congress which was thought to be a more appropriate home than the State Department. There it was given special care and lighting and put back on display.

1941-1944: On December 26, 1951, a few days after Pearl Harbor, the Declaration was packed in a bronze container of special design. Escorted by a Secret Service guard, it traveled in a Pullman compartment to Fort Knox, Kentucky, where it was stored in an underground vault at the Bullion Depository.

1944 to 1952; On October 1, 1944, it was considered safe enough to return the Declaration to the Library of Congress. It was sealed in insulating glass with the air expelled. Cellulose paper was put behind the aging parchment to absorb moisture and to offset changes in temperature. New lighting was installed and it was put back on display.

1952 to Present: On December 13, 1952, the Declaration was transported in an army armored personnel carrier and escorted by tanks, an army band, and troops armed with machine guns to the new Archives Building, where it is housed today. Thanks to modern sophisticated techniques, the Declaration has been restored and, along with the Constitution and the Bill of Rights, is displayed in its present totally-protected case.

At long last, Thomas Jefferson's famous document, and the nation's, has found a permanent, and totally safe, home.

## 742. Who Designed the First American Flag

The popular legend is that Betsy Ross, a Philadelphia seamstress, designed and sewed the first U.S. flag. We know that George Washington knew her and that she used to embroider the ruffles on his shirts.

The Betsy Ross legend became so firmly established that President Woodrow Wilson, when asked about its authenticity, said, "Would that it were true!"

However, it has been quite firmly established that the first U.S. flag was designed by Francis Hopkinson (1737-1791), a lawyer, a Congressman from New Jersey, and a signer of the Declaration of Independence. He was also a poet and artist.

Hopkinson was appointed to the Continental Navy Board on November 7, 1776, and it was while serving there that he turned his attention to designing the flag of the United States. In a letter to the Board of Admiralty in 1780, Hopkinson asserted that he had designed "the flag of the United States of America" and asked whether a "Quarter Cask of the public wine" would not be a reasonable and proper reward for his labors.

Though Hopkinson's political adversaries blocked all attempts to have him paid for his services, they never denied that he made the design. The journals of the Continental Congress clearly show that he designed the flag.

## 743. Patriotic Bravery

Most Americans know the story of the Declaration of Independence and how it came to be, but few know the story behind the story.

During a time when women were openly deemed inferior to men legally, politically and socially, the founding fathers turned to a woman to print the first signed copy of the Declaration of Independence.

In January 1777, the Continental Congress was in hiding from the British and apparently male printers were also in hiding. The Congress engaged Baltimore's Mary Katherine Goddard (1738-1816) to publish the official signed copy. She risked arrest by the British but her courage under fire was demonstrated by five words at the bottom of the Declaration of Independence: "Printed by Mary Katherine Goddard."

Even though no other female name appears on this historical document, Mary Katherine's patriotism was so strong that she even paid the post riders to deliver the sacred document throughout the colonies.

## 744. Knowledge of George Washington

According to a study conducted by the American Council of Trustees and Alumni for Mount Vernon, and published in the New York Times in 2002, only 42 percent of students questioned at 55 top universities could name George Washington as the man who was called "first in war, first in peace, and first in the hearts of his countrymen."

By contrast, 99 percent of the students could identify the cartoon characters Beavis and Butthead and 96 percent knew the rapper Snoop Doggy Dogg.

Some years back, Washington's portrait hung in countless classrooms, his birthday was a separate national holiday, and his exploits and achievements were taught in almost every elementary and secondary school. Today the portraits are gone and the birthday (along with Lincoln's) has morphed into President's Day.

By comparing textbooks used in the 1960's with those of today, researchers at Mount Vernon [Washington's home in Virginia] concluded that Washington is now accorded just 10 percent of the space he had then.

More than three-quarters of the universities where the study was done did not require a single course in American history.

## 745. How "God Bless America" Was Born

The song, "God Bless America" started off as one of composer Irving Berlin's (1888-1989) failures. In 1918, Berlin put together a traveling revue to build up patriotism after the United States entered World War I. The now celebrated song didn't satisfy him at the time so it was dropped from the revue.

Twenty years later, he stumbled across a manuscript for the song that he had all but forgotten. He did a little editing and ended up with a revised version that sought to express his great love for the country to which he believed he owed everything.

As part of the 20th anniversary celebration for Armistice Day, singing star Kate Smith (1907-1986) sang "God Bless America" on radio for the first time on November 11, 1938. It quickly gained popularity and became a popular standard during World War II.

Berlin heavily guarded all his copyrights except one. He knew "God Bless America" was special so he gave all of his royalties to the Boy Scouts and Girl Scouts of America. The song has made more than $6 million for the two organizations.

## 746. Why Is July 4 the United States Birthday?

Why exactly was July 4, 1776, chosen as the date to mark the nation's founding? The reason is that the Declaration of Independence was approved on that day by the Continental Congress meeting in Philadelphia. It is an amazing document and, in eloquent language, it announced the Colonies' determination to free themselves of British rule.

The only person to sign the Declaration on July 4 was John Hancock (1737-1793) of Massachusetts, an extremely wealthy man who risked his life and his fortune on the success of the Revolution. He was president of the Continental Congress. When the Continental Congress adjourned on July 4 after debating the Declaration for three days and having voted to adopt the document with some revisions, Hancock was charged with authenticating the revised document, signing it, and sending copies to the colonial legislatures for approval. When Hancock affixed his boldly-written signature to the Declaration, he did so in an empty chamber.

The only other person present was Charles Thomson, a Pennsylvanian serving as secretary of Congress. Thomson was never a signatory. His name appeared on printed copies of the document due to his position as secretary of Congress.

Thus, it is apocryphal that, on signing the Declaration with a flourish and in big letters, that Hancock declared, "There, I guess King George will be able to read that without his spectacles." Like many great historical legends, it apparently never happened.

Most of the other delegates signed the Declaration on August 2, 1776, and the last of 56 signatures would not be added until five years later.

## 747. How Early Painted Portraits Were Priced

In George Washington's days there were no cameras. One's image was either sculpted or painted. Some paintings of George Washington showed him standing behind a desk with one arm behind his back while others showed both legs and both arms.

Prices charged by painters were not based on how many people were to be painted, but by how many limbs were to be painted. Arms and legs are "limbs," therefore painting them would cost the buyer more.

Hence the expression, "Okay, but it'll cost you an arm and a leg."

## 748. The Emancipation Proclamation

Three hours of handshaking could leave President Abraham Lincoln's hand, as he said, "swollen like a poisoned pup."

So on New Year's Day in 1863, Lincoln knew he would have a problem. Not only did he have to face the traditional handshaking ceremonies with the public at the White House open house, but January 1 was the day he had promised to issue his famous Emancipation Proclamation.

If his signature was shaky when he signed the document, people might think he had hesitated. Just before the historic moment, he said, "I have been shaking hands since nine o'clock this morning and my right arm is almost paralyzed."

However, with a conscious effort, Lincoln managed to sign the Proclamation with a firm hand.

## 749. Financier of the Revolution

Robert Morris (1734-1806), signer of the Declaration of Independence and whose contributions earned him the title of "Financier of the Revolution," died in poverty and obscurity.

Following the Revolutionary War, Morris lost his fortune in land speculation. His debts amounted to almost $3 million when he was sent to debtor's prison on February 15, 1798.

In prison, Morris had a spacious room with a writing desk, bedstead, settee, chairs, and mirrors. Although he was penniless, the prison charged him rent. He had many visitors, including Alexander Hamilton and George Washington.

Morris spent three and a half years in what he calls his "hotel with the grated door" before a settlement was reached with his creditors.

## 750. What Cracked the Liberty Bell?

There used to be "legend" that the Liberty Bell cracked when it was rung to celebrate American independence in 1776. The facts are a little less dramatic. This is the famous bell's history

In 1751, Pennsylvania celebrated its 50th birthday as a British province by ordering a bell from London. It was inscribed with a verse from the Bible: "Proclaim liberty throughout the land unto all the inhabitants thereof," a phrase later associated with the Revolutionary War.

The bell was first rung hanging from a temporary stand in front of the unfinished State House. It cracked immediately. John Pass and Charles Stow were hired to melt it down and recast it. This second bell had such a harsh tone it was compared to striking two coal scuttles, so it was melted down again. Finally, on the third try, a melodious bell was hung in the State House tower.

The bell was rung to celebrate good King George II's (1683-1760) accession to the throne in 1761. And it did call the people out to hear the reading of the Declaration of Independence on July 8, 1776. But it didn't crack then.

When the British occupied Philadelphia during the Revolution, the bell was carried on a wagon and hidden in the basement of a church in Allentown, Pennsylvania. However, it was returned in time to toll when the British surrendered at the end of the war.

It was rung again when the Constitution was adopted in 1788 and on many important occasions until July 8, 1835, when it cracked while tolling for the funeral of Chief Justice John Marshall (1755-1835).

Since then the bell has traveled to many patriotic celebrations, including one in 1915 to San Francisco. On the return trip it cracked further, so an embargo was put on future travel. The Liberty Bell is now encased in a pavillion in front of Independence Hall in Philadelphia.

## 751. Flag Raising Speech

"Die when I may, I want it said of me by those who know me best that I always plucked a thistle and planted a flower where I thought a flower would grow."

The above is probably the briefest speech ever given by President Abraham Lincoln on a public occasion.

Participating in a flag raising ceremony before the Treasury Building in Washington, Lincoln added, "The part assigned to me is to raise the flag, which, if there be no fault in the machinery, I will do; and when up, it will be for the people to keep it up."

## 752. How the Term "Uncle Sam" Came to Be

The "original" Uncle Sam was named Samuel Wilson (1766-1854). He was born in Arlington, Massachusetts, on September 13, 1766. At the age of 14, he joined the army and fought in the American Revolution.

Sam moved in 1789 to Troy, New York, and opened a meat-packing company. Because of his jovial manner and fair business practices, he was affectionately known as "Uncle Sam."

During the War of 1812, government troops were quartered near Troy. Sam Wilson's fair-dealing reputation won him a military contract to provide beef and pork to soldiers. To indicate that certain crates of meat produced at his warehouse were destined for military use, Sam stamped them with a large "U.S." — for "United States," although the abbreviation was not yet in the vernacular.

On October 1, 1812, government inspectors made a routine tour of the plant. They asked a meat packer what the ubiquitously stamped "U.S." stood for. Himself uncertain, the worker joked that the letters must represent the initials of his employer, "Uncle Sam."

The error was perpetuated. Soon soldiers began referring to all military rations as bounty from Uncle Sam. Before long, they were calling all government-issued supplies the property of Uncle Sam.

Sam Wilson's role as the origin of the term "Uncle Sam" was officially acknowledged during the administration of President John F. Kennedy. An act of the 87th Congress stated that "the Congress salutes 'Uncle Sam' Wilson of Troy, New York, as the progenitor of America's National symbol."

## 753. Uncle Sam's Wardrobe

The familiar and picturesque image of Uncle Sam is instantly familiar to all Americans. How did the image of this fictional character get to be what it is today? The facts are its basic elements evolved piecemeal, almost one item at a time, each the contribution of an illustrator.

New England newspapers ran the first Uncle Sam illustrations in 1820.

During Andrew Jackson's (1767-1845) presidency, solid red pants were added.

During the term of Abraham Lincoln, the beard first appeared, inspired by the President's own beard, which set a trend at the time.

Uncle Sam was such a popular national figure by the late nineteenth century that cartoonists decided his attire should be more patriotic. They embellished his red pants with white stripes and his top hat with both stars and stripes, making his costume an embodiment of the nation's flag.

Thomas Nast (1840-1902), the famous cartoonist of the Civil War and Reconstruction period, made Uncle Sam tall, thin, and hollow-cheeked. Coincidentally, Nast's Uncle Sam strongly resembles drawings of the real-life Sam Wilson (about whom the name "Uncle Sam" was born). But students of the subject say Nast's model was actually Abraham Lincoln.

The portrayal of Uncle Sam most frequently reproduced and widely recognized today was painted by American artist James Montgomery Flagg (1877-1960). The stern-faced, stiff-armed, finger-pointing figure appeared on World War I posters captioned: "I Want You For the U.S. Army." However, we are told Flagg's Uncle Sam is not an Abe Lincoln likeness, it was a self-portrait.

## 754. American Flag History

The American flag has not always had thirteen stripes. When Vermont and Kentucky came into the Union in the 1790s, Congress adopted a flag of fifteen stars and fifteen stripes. In 1818 Congress, not wanting to crowd the flag, voted to indicate the admission of new states by the addition of stars only. On May 1, 1795, the Congress also voted to revert to a flag of thirteen stripes.

## 755. History of a Famous Flag

Oh, say, can you name the woman who sewed the Star-Spangled Banner, the flag that inspired Francis Scott Key to write the national anthem?

No, it was not Betsy Ross. It was Mary Young Pickersgill (1776-1857), a professional flag maker who was hired by the United States Army to create a 30 by 42 foot flag in 1813. A year later, it flew over Fort McHenry during the Battle of Baltimore, inspiring Key to write the poem that became the anthem.

The Pickersgill flag (now 30 by 34 feet) originally had 15 broad stripes and 15 bright stars (one of the stars is missing), and is the property of the Smithsonian Institution in Washington, D.C., which is restoring it. The Smithsonian, however, has a difficult problem — how to keep the flag from deteriorating further and still allow the public to view it. The flag has drawn millions of viewers to the museum to see the famous flag.

## 756. Courage of America's Founders

Have you ever wondered what happened to those fifty-six men who signed the Declaration of Independence?

Five signers were captured by the British as traitors and tortured before they died. Twelve had their homes ransacked and burned. Two lost their sons in the Revolutionary Army, another had two sons captured. Nine fought and died from wounds or the hardships of the Revolutionary War.

What kind of men were they? Twenty-four were lawyers and jurists. Eleven were merchants, nine were farmers and large plantation owners, men of means, well educated. But they signed the Declaration of Independence knowing full well that the penalty would be death if they were captured.

They signed and they pledged their lives, their fortunes and their sacred honor.

Carter Braxton (1736-1797) of Virginia, a wealthy planter and trader, saw his ships swept from the seas by the British navy. He sold his home and properties to pay his debts and died in rags.

Thomas McKean was so hounded by the British that he was forced to move his family almost constantly. He served in the Congress without pay, and his family was kept in hiding. His possessions were taken from him, and poverty was his reward.

Vandals or soldiers or both looted the properties of Ellery, Clymer, Hall, Walton, Gwinnett, Heyward, Rutledge, and Middleton.

At the Battle of Yorktown, Thomas Nelson, Jr. (1738-1789), noted that the British General Cornwallis had taken over the Nelson home for his headquarters. The owner quietly urged General George Washington to open fire, which was done. The home was destroyed and Nelson died bankrupt.

Francis Lewis (1713-1803) had his home and properties destroyed. The enemy jailed his wife and she died within a few months.

John Hart (1711-1779) was driven from his wife's bedside as she was dying. Their thirteen children fled for their lives. His fields and gristmill were laid waste. For more than a year he lived in forests and caves, returning home after the war to find his wife dead, his children vanished. A few weeks later he died from exhaustion and a broken heart.

Norris and Livingston suffered similar fates.

Such were the stories and sacrifices of the American Revolution. These were not wild-eyed, rabble-rousing ruffians. These were soft-spoken men of means and education. They had security, but they valued liberty more.

Standing tall, straight and unwavering, they pledged: "For the support of this declaration, with a firm reliance on the protection of the Divine Providence, we mutually pledge to each other, our lives, our fortunes, and our sacred honor."

# PERSISTENCE, PERSEVERANCE

### 757. That Little Bit Extra

Richard L. Weaver II, a university professor known for his excellent motivational speeches, made these remarks at a meeting of Bowling Green State University:

"A prominent salesman friend of mine summed up his success in three simple words: 'and then some.'

"He discovered at an early age, that most of the difference between average people and top people could be explained in these simple three words.

"The top people did what was expected of them — 'and then some.'

"They were thoughtful of others; they were considerate and kind — 'and then some.'"

"They met their obligations and responsibilities fairly and squarely — 'and then some.'"

"They were good friends to their friends — 'and then some.'"

"They could be counted on in an emergency — 'and then some.'"

"These three little words," said Professor Weaver, "could transform our society as well as your academic and personal life. It could become a philosophy of life — a way of living."

## 758. Don't Give Up

The following was taken from Chapter 14 of *Up Ffrom Slavery* by Booker T. Washington:

A ship lost at sea for many days suddenly sighted a friendly vessel. From the mast of the unfortunate vessel was seen a signal with this message, "Water, water; we die of thirst!"

The answer from the friendly vessel at once came back, "Cast down your bucket where you are."

A second time the distressed ship sent up the signal, "Water, water; send us water!"

And the friendly vessel responded again, "Cast down your bucket where you are."

The captain of the distressed vessel signaled a third and fourth time of his desperate need for water, and each time the other vessel responded with the same message, "Cast down your bucket where you are."

Finally, the captain of the distressed vessel cast down his bucket and it came up full of fresh, sparkling water from the mouth of the Amazon River.

## 759. A Costly Lack of Perseverance

This is a story about a dreamer whose name was Henry Comstock (1820-1870). Henry was a miner of precious metals whose story took place in the American West in the mid-1800's.

Henry found a mine, staked his claim, and dug until he found his treasure. He unearthed a little bit of ore; but he knew there was more to be found in that mine. So he picked and scratched, always convinced that somewhere there had to be the mother lode. He was determined to find it. He was really going to make it big.

The days turned to weeks, the weeks to months, the months to years and finally he gave up in 1859 when someone offered him $11,000 for his claim. In those days, that was a lot of money.

Henry Comstock looked at the buyer and said, "You've made yourself a deal. You've got yourself a mine."

And the person who bought it dug a little deeper — just a few feet deeper - and the mother lode was found. Within a short period of time, the Comstock mine produced $340,000,000! Dreams take work, they take practice, they take patience, and sometimes they require you to dig deeper.

## 760. Persistence

Here are some examples of famous people who accomplished their dreams and goals by unwavering persistence, despite long odds and discouragement by others:

- No one had a more difficult time in getting his invention, the telephone, accepted than Alexander Graham Bell (1847-1922). Even President Rutherford Hayes said of it in 1876, "that's an amazing invention, but who would ever want to use one of them?

- Chester Carlson (1906-1968), another young inventor, took his idea to 20 big corporations in the 1940s. After seven years of rejections, he was able to persuade Haloid, a small Rochester, New York, company, to purchase the rights to his electrostatic paper- copying process. Haloid became the Xerox Corporation.

- Jonas Salk (1914-1995) failed 200 times before he found the right vaccine for polio.

- All kinds of experts told Orville (1871-1948) and Wilbur Wright (1867-1912) that their dream of building a flying machine was pure lunacy. Even their father insisted that man was not meant to fly. "Sorry," said the Wright brothers, "we have a dream and we can make it happen." As a result, a place called Kitty Hawk, North Carolina, became the setting for the launching of their "ridiculous" idea.

- Thomas Edison (1847-1931) tried over 2,000 experiments before he was able to get his light bulb to work. Upon being asked how he felt about failing so many times, he replied, "I never failed once. I invented the light bulb. It just happened to be a 2,000-step process."

- Franklin Delano Roosevelt (1882-1945), elected President of the United States for four terms, had been stricken with polio at the age of 39.

- Persistence paid off for General Douglas MacArthur (1880-1964). After applying for admission to West Point twice, he applied a third time and was accepted. The rest is history.

- In 1927 the head instructor of the John Murray Anderson Drama School, instructed student Lucille Ball (1911-1989), to "Try any other profession. Any other."

- Buddy Holly (1936-1959) was fired from the Decca record label in 1956 by Paul Cohen, Nashville "Artists and Repertoire Man". Cohen called Holly "the biggest no-talent I ever worked with."

- Academy Award-winning writer, producer and director Woody Allen (1935- ) failed motion picture production at New York University and City College of New York. He also flunked English at NYU.

- Chuck Yeager (1923- ), the famous test pilot, on his first flight as a passenger, threw up all over the back seat. He vowed never to go back up again, yet later he became the first man to break the sound barrier.

- During its first year, the Coca Cola Company sold only 400 cokes.

- During his first three years in the automobile business, Henry Ford (1863-1947) went bankrupt twice.

- Then there was a little girl from Tennessee who was born to face poverty, obesity, a broken home, and physical abuse. Today, she is a billionaire and one of the most admired celebrities in the world. That's right. Her name is Oprah Winfrey (1954- ).

## 761. A Miracle

Wilma Rudolph (1940-1994) was 20th in a family of 22 children. Born prematurely, her survival was doubtful. At four years of age she contracted scarlet fever and double pneumonia, leaving her with a paralyzed leg.

By age 9, the metal leg brace, upon which she had become dependent, was removed and she began to walk without it. The doctors were amazed when, at age 13, she developed a rhythmic walk. Having been told she would never walk again, this little girl went on to win three Olympic gold medals.

"My mother taught me very early to believe I could achieve any accomplishment I wanted to," Rudolph said. "The first was to walk without braces."

## 762. He Spoke to Children

Theodore Geisel (1904-1991) died in 1991 at the age of 87. Before he died, he wrote 47 books that sold more than 100 million copies in 18 languages. Some of Dr. Seuss's more famous books you may recognize: *The Cat in the Hat*, and *Green Eggs and Ham*.

What you may not know about him is that when he was 33 he wrote his first book, *And to Think I Saw It On Mulberry Street*, but it was rejected by 28 publishers before Vanguard Press picked it up.

Did Dr. Geisel give up? Not at all. With every rejection he kept going on.

## 763. Electioneering

Lyndon Johnson (1908-1973) was visiting a high school during his 1948 campaign for the Senate and announced that, before leaving, he was going to shake hands with every student in the school.

"We don't have time, sir," objected a young aide, showing Johnson a list of stops he had promised to make during the rest of the day."

Johnson glared at the aide and said in a low, threatening tone that his aides feared more than any other, "Are we gonna join the "Can't Do It Club" right here on the steps of Robstown High School?"

He went on to shake the hand of every student in the Texas school.

## 764. Talk about Heartbreak

When you lose something you consider irreplaceable, it may help some to think of this story about what happened to the English author Thomas Carlyle (1795-1881).

When Carlyle finished the first volume of his book, *The French Revolution*, he handed the finished manuscript to his friend, John Stuart Mill (1806-1873), asking him to read it and to give him his comments.

As Mill read the manuscript at his home, he realized it was truly a great masterpiece. Reading the manuscript in his den, Mill finished it late one night and, before retiring, laid the manuscript on a table by his easy chair.

Mill's maid the next morning came in to clean the den and, seeing the manuscript on the chair, thought it was a stack of papers meant to be discarded. Without saying anything to anyone, she threw the pages into the fireplace, where they were totally destroyed.

On March 6, 1835 — Mill never forgot the exact day — he called on Carlyle and in deep personal agony told him that the masterwork he had entrusted to him had been destroyed by fire.

Who knows how he must have felt inside, but Carlyle replied, "It's all right, John. I am sure I can start over in the morning and do it again." With abject apologies, John Mill left and started back home. Watching his friend walking away in deep sadness, Carlyle said to his wife, "Poor Mill. I feel so sorry for him. I did not want him to see how crushed I really am."

Then, heaving a deep sigh, he said, "Well, the manuscript is gone, so I had better start writing again."

It was a long, hard, excruciating process, especially since Carlyle's original inspiration was gone. But he did rewrite the manuscript and it became the classic literary work we know today. What a testament to one man's forgiveness of a friend and his personal courage and commitment to redo and finish a difficult creative task.

## 765. A Classic Aesop Fable

A Hare insulted a Tortoise because of its slowness, and vainly boasted of its own speed in running.

"Let us make a match." replied the Tortoise. "I will run with you five miles for five pounds, and the fox yonder shall be the umpire of the race." The Hare agreed, and they both started the contest together. But the Hare, because of its swiftness, outdistanced the Tortoise to such a degree that it made a jest of the matter.

Finding itself a little tired, the Hare lay down on a tuft of ferns that grew by the way, and took a nap. It reasoned that, if the Tortoise went by, it would know it and could with ease catch up and pass the Tortoise to win the race.

However, when the Tortoise came jogging on with slow but continued motion, the Hare, out of a too great sense of security and confidence of certain victory, overslept and did not wake up, allowing the Tortoise to arrive at the end of the race first, thus winning the contest.

## 766. Persistence Pays Off

In 1935, Charles Darrow (1879-1967) brought his invention of Monopoly to Parker Brothers. The experts at Parker Brothers rejected the game for "containing fifty-two fundamental errors."

Ironically, in 1936, Mr. Darrow was well-received by the embarrassed Parker Brothers. The persistent Charles Darrow had spent the year after his rejection demonstrating the potential success of the game by selling numerous editions of the board game himself.

Parker Brothers helped make the unemployed heating engineer from Germantown, Pennsylvania, a multi-millionaire. Since that time, over 100 million copies of Monopoly have been sold in 31 countries.

Each year Parker Brother prints more than $40 billion worth of Monopoly money — more than twice the amount printed annually by the U.S. Mint. Monopoly's success has produced 3.2 billion of those little green houses, enough to circle the globe.

Persistence does have its benefits!

## 767. Lack of Faith

There was a man who left home in search of a gold mine. He went into the hills and discovered a very rich vein of ore.

The gold began to flow as easily as water and soon the man had recouped approximately half of what he had spent on mining equipment. Then, without warning, the vein ended.

The man worked furiously, but he could not recapture the vein. Finally he gave up, sold the mine and his equipment to a junk dealer for scrap, and returned home, broke.

Before scrapping the equipment, the junk dealer decided to hire a mining expert to study the mine. The expert, upon a detailed survey of the land, revealed that the vein had not dried up but rather shifted three feet to the left due to a fault in the earth. He advised that if the junk dealer were to continue digging in the new direction, he would soon recapture the vein and become fabulously wealthy. The junk dealer went on to retap the vein and quickly became rich.

The original miner had to live the rest of his life knowing that he had stopped just three feet short.

### 768. A Scottish Legend

According to legend, the 14th century Scottish king, Robert the Bruce (1274-1329), was once hiding out from English pursuers on a remote island.

Defeated and without hope, he noticed a spider trying painfully to fix its web onto a wooden beam. The spider tried again and again, only to fail each time. But it wouldn't quit. And, after many, many tries, it succeeded.

Inspired by this example of persistence, Robert the Bruce organized a new band of followers and, against great odds, drove the English out of Scotland.

# PERSONAL GROWTH

### 769. How a Shock Can Bring New Life

This is a story about almost magical renewal recounted by the famous author James Michener (1907-1994) who authored more than 40 books, including such memorable best-sellers as *Tales of the South Pacific*, *Hawaii* and *Texas*.

Michener remembers as a boy walking down a country road in Pennsylvania where he grew up, and happening upon a fabulous apple tree laden with fruit.

As he drew closer, Michener saw a farmer standing next to the tree. Seeing the boy admiring the tree, the farmer said, "Let me tell you about this tree. This is a very old tree and several years ago it stopped bearing fruit."

"What did you do?" asked Michener.

"Well," said the farmer, "I took a nail about a foot long and drove it into the tree's trunk. Next year it started bearing all over again. In fact, better than ever."

There is a valuable moral to this unusual story. Despite our troubles, and no matter how severe, we should force ourselves to seek out new experiences that will move us profoundly — even shock us into looking at life differently.

## 770. Secrets of a Successful Life

A philosophy professor called his class into session and proceeded to fill a large mayonnaise jar with rocks about two inches in diameter.

After doing this, he asked the students if the jar was full. The class quickly agreed that it was. The professor then picked up a box of small pebbles and poured them into the jar. He shook the jar gently so that the pebbles filled in the spaces between the rocks.

"Now, is the jar full?" asked the professor, and the class agreed that it was. At this point, the professor picked up a box of sand and poured it into the jar. Of course, the sand filled in the tiniest spaces left between the rocks and pebbles.

"Is the jar really full now?" asked the professor, and the class responded with a unanimous "Yes!"

"Now," said the professor to the class, "I want you to recognize that this jar represents your life. The rocks are the important things — your family, your partner, your health, your children. The pebbles are the other things that matter in your life like your job, your house, your car. The sand is everything else. The small stuff."

"If you put the sand into the jar first," continued the professor, "there is no room for either the pebbles or the rocks. The same goes for your life. If you spend all your time and energy on the small stuff, you will never have room for the things that are important to you, the things essential to your happiness.

"Take care of the rocks first," he added, "the things that really matter. Set your priorities. The rest is just sand."

## 771. Lesson in a Hen House

Abraham Lincoln once told a group of government employees the following story:

"You people remind me of the boy who set a hen on 43 eggs and expected them to hatch. Then he rushed to tell his mother what he had done.

"But a hen can't set on 43 eggs," replied his mother.

"No," replied the boy, "I guess she can't. But I just wanted to see her spread herself."

"That is what I would like to see you people do," concluded President Lincoln.

## 772. Discovering Who We Are

Wystan Hugh Auden (1907-1973), English-born American poet, said of personal growth, "Between the ages of twenty and forty we are engaged in the process of discovering who we are, which involves learning the difference between accidental limitations which it is our duty to outgrow and the necessary limitations of our nature beyond which we cannot trespass with impunity."

## 773. Learning Life's Lessons

Maya Angelou (1928- ) is one of America's greatest poets and her poems capture the finest things that occur in life.  In April of 2003 she read this poem on the Oprah Winfrey television program to millions of viewers.

"When I was in my younger days, I weighed a few pounds less,
I needn't hold my tummy in to wear a belted dress.
But now that I am older, I've set my body free;
There's the comfort of elastic where once my waist would be.

Inventor of those high-heeled shoes, my feet have not forgiven;
I have to wear a nine now, but used to wear a seven.

And how about those pantyhose — they're sized by weight, you see,
So how come when I put them on, the crotch is at my knee?

I need to wear these glasses, as the print's been getting smaller;
And it wasn't very long ago I know that I was taller.
Though my hair has turned to gray and my skin no longer fits,
On the inside, I'm the same old one, it's the outside's changed a bit.

But on a positive note...

I've learned that, no matter what happens, or how bad it seems today, life does go on, and it will be better tomorrow.

I've learned that you can tell a lot about a person by the way he/she handles these three things: a rainy day, lost luggage, and tangled Christmas tree lights.

I've learned that regardless of your relationship with your parents, you'll miss them when they're gone from your life.

I've learned that making a 'living' is not the same thing as making a 'life.'

I've learned that life sometimes gives you a second chance.

I've learned that you shouldn't go through life with a catcher's mitt on both hands. You need to be able to throw something back.

I've learned that whenever I decide something with an open heart, I usually make the right decision.

I've learned that, even when I have pains, I don't have to be one.

I've learned that every day you should reach out and touch someone. People love a warm hug, or just a friendly pat on the back.

I've learned that I still have a lot to learn.

I've learned that people will forget what you said, people will forget what you did, but people will never forget how you made them feel."

## 774. Filling Our Blank Canvas

We don't know the author but the following is a profound statement about the need for personal growth:

"We are born into the world like a blank canvas, and each person who crosses our path takes up the brush and makes his mark upon our surface. So it is that we develop. But we must realize that there comes a day when we must take up the brush and finish the work. For only we can decide if we are to be just another painting or a masterpiece."

# PERSONAL HEALTH

### 775. Washington's False Teeth

There are many myths about George Washington's dentures. One says that he had a set of wooden teeth. He did not. But he did have teeth made of teeth and tusks from elephants, hippopotami, walruses, cattle, and humans. He was ashamed of his false teeth, and once paid his dentist to conceal his dental bills.

### 776. Lincoln's Physical Strength

Few people in his day were aware of Abraham Lincoln's amazing physical strength. In muscular endurance, he was one in a thousand.

Once, while sitting on the deck of a revenue cutter, Lincoln saw an ax that was placed in a socket on the bulwarks. Taking it up, he held it at arm's length at the extremity of the handle with his thumb and forefinger, and continued to hold it there for a several minutes.

The strongest sailors on board tried in vain to match his feat. Lincoln told them he could do this when he was eighteen and had never seen a day since that time when he could not.

### 777. Lincoln on Anatomy

Abraham Lincoln (1809-1865) once was asked to mediate an argument concerning how long a man's legs should be in proportion to the size of his body.

After listening intently to the arguments of both sides, he announced with great gravity that, "It is my opinion that a man's lower limbs, in order to preserve harmony of proportion, should be at least long enough to reach from his body to the ground."

### 778. Thoreau on Health

Henry David Thoreau (1817-1862), an American naturalist, writer and philosopher, had a unique ability to write about nature and man's connection to it. Of personal health, he wrote:

"Let Nature do your bottling and your pickling and preserving. For all Nature is doing her best each moment to make us well.

"She exists for no other end. Do not resist her. With the least inclination to be well, we should not be sick.

"Men have discovered— or think they have discovered — the salutariness of a few wild things only, and not of all nature. Why, 'nature' is but another name for health, and the seasons are but different states of health.

"Some men think that they are not well in spring, or summer, or autumn, or winter; it is only because they are not well in them."

# PERSPECTIVE

## 779. Blind Men and the Elephant

There is no better example of how differently people view the same subject or object than this ancient fable. As you will remember, four blind men were asked to examine an elephant and to describe its appearance.

The first blind man felt the elephant's leg and declared that the creature was like a tree.

The second blind man felt the elephant's enormous side and said that it was like a wall.

The third man felt the tail and was positive that the elephant was like a rope.

The fourth felt the tusk and likened it to a spear.

Each man's notion of reality was limited by the number and kind of attributes he had been able to perceive.

## 780. Personal Evaluation

Thomas Watson, Jr. (1914-1993), chairman of IBM, was fond of telling anecdotes about his father, Thomas Watson, Sr. (1874-1956), founder of the company. One of them went like this:

"Father was fond of saying that everybody, from time to time, should take a step back and watch himself go by."

This was the elder Watson's way of saying that everybody needs to step back once in a while and get himself or herself in perspective. Good advice for anyone.

## 781. Shaw on Perspective

George Bernard Shaw (1856-1950), the Irish-born playwright and critic, was a popular worldwide seer in his time. Here are some of his views of the necessity for man to have perspective on his life:

"If a man sees with only one eye, the world appears flat to him, objects and people become mere two-dimensional images. And he cannot discern any meaning in life beyond the crassness of superficial existence.

"If he uses both eyes, he gains perspective and can perceive a third dimension of depth, ideas and activities assume relative importance and value and he understands that there is no more than one way of living.

"How deep his understanding and how acute his perception, then, if he sees through four or six or seven different eyes, each distinct and yet each focused on the same situation and the same conflict."

## 782. Will Rogers on Perspective

Will Rogers (1879-1935) was a uniquely American humorist and actor who was one of the nation's most revered personalities in his day. He was an advisor to presidents, was a famous movie star, wrote a daily humor column, a much sought-after speaker, and was Mayor of Beverly Hills. He was famous for saying "I never met a man I didn't like." On keeping one's perspective about other people, he once wrote:

"You must never disagree with a man while you are facing him. Go around behind him and look the same way he is looking and you will see that things look different from what they do when you're facing him. Look over his shoulder and get his viewpoint, then go back and face him and you will have a different idea."

## 783. A Different View of Work

Bertrand Russell (1872-1970), English mathematician and philosopher, wrote in his autobiography, "One of the symptoms of approaching nervous breakdown is the belief that one's work is terribly important. If I were a medical man, I should prescribe a holiday to any patient who considered his work important."

## 784. Einstein on Perspective

Asked by the press for an explanation of his theory of relativity which would be meaningful to lay people, Albert Einstein (1879-1955) gave to his secretary this statement, "An hour sitting with a pretty girl on a park bench passes like a minute, but a minute sitting on a hot stove seems like an hour."

## 785. Proust on Perspective

Marcel Proust (1871-1922), the French novelist, said of perspective, "The only real voyage of discovery, the only Fountain of Youth, consists not in seeking new landscapes, but in having new eyes, in seeing the universe with the eyes of another, of a hundred others, in seeing the hundred universes that each of them sees."

# PERSUASION

## 786. Ben Franklin on Persuasion

Benjamin Franklin's methods of persuading others to his point of view took patience and endurance. It assumed that people are won over slowly, often indirectly. If you don't win the bargain today, Franklin would say, go after it again tomorrow — and the next day.

Here are some of Franklin's bargaining tips:

1. Be clear, in your own mind, about exactly what you're after.
2. Do your homework, so that you are fully prepared to discuss every aspect and respond to every question and comment.
3. Be persistent. Don't expect to "win" the first time. Your first job is just to start the other person thinking.

4.  Make friends with the person with whom you are bargaining. Put your bargain in terms of his or her needs, advantages, and benefits.

5.  Keep your sense of humor.

## 787. A Fable about Persuasion

Once upon a time, Truth went about the streets as naked as the day he was born. As a result, no one would let him into their homes. Whenever people caught sight of him, they turned away and fled.

One day when Truth was sadly wandering about, he came upon Parable. Parable was dressed in splendid clothes of beautiful colors. And Parable, seeing Truth, said, "Tell me, neighbor, what makes you look so sad?"

Truth replied bitterly, "Ah, brother, things are bad. Very bad. I'm old, very old, and no one wants to acknowledge me. No one wants anything to do with me."

Hearing that, Parable said, "People don't run away from you because you're old. I too am old. Very old. But the older I get, the better people like me. I'll tell you a secret: Everyone likes things disguised and prettied up a bit. Let me lend you some splendid clothes like mine, and you'll see that the very people who pushed you aside will invite you into their homes and be glad of your company."

Truth took Parable's advice and put on the borrowed clothes. And from that time on, Truth and Parable have gone hand in hand together. Everyone loves them. They make a happy pair.

## 788. Lincoln's Art of Persuasion

One of Abraham Lincoln's most valuable skills was his ability to persuade others to his point of view, no matter how entrenched their position. Lincoln described the art of persuasion in this speech to the Springfield Washington Temperance Society in 1842, long before he began his political career. It goes like this:

"When the conduct of men is designed to be influenced, persuasion, kind, unassuming persuasion, should ever be adopted. It is an old and true maxim that a 'drop of honey catches more flies than a gallon of gall.' So with men. If you would win a man to your cause, first convince him that you are his sincere friend. Therein a drop of honey that catches his heart, which, say what he will, is the great high road to his reason, and which, when once granted, you will find but little trouble in convincing his judgment of the justice of your cause, if indeed that cause really be a just one.

"On the contrary, assume to dictate to his judgment, or to command his action, or to mark him as one to be shunned and despised, and he will retreat within himself, close all the avenues to his head and his heart; and tho' your cause be naked truth itself....you shall no more be able to [reach] him, than to penetrate the hard shell of a tortoise with a rye straw.

"Such is man, and so must he be understood by those who would lead him, even to his own best interest."

## 789. Demosthenes

Aeschines (c. 389 BC-314 BC) was an Athenian orator who advocated peace with Philip II (382 BC-336 BC) of Macedonia and was a bitter political opponent of another famed Athenian orator named Demosthenes (384 BC-322 BC). A story handed down through the years says that, when Aeschines finished speaking, the people said, "How well he spoke!" But when Demosthenes finished speaking, the people said, "Let us march against Philip."

## 790. Humor and Persuasion

John M. Cleese (1939- ), an English actor and comedian known for his expertise in business communications, said of humor in speeches, "If I can get you to laugh with me, you like me better, which makes you more open to my ideas. And if I can persuade you to laugh at the particular point I make, by laughing at it, you acknowledge the truth."

## 791. Churchill on Persuasion

Winston Churchill (1874-1965) said of persuading others, "If you have an important point to make, don't try to be subtle or clever. Use a pile driver. Hit the point once. Then come back and hit it again. Then hit it a third time – a tremendous whack."

## 792. Ben Franklin on Persuasion

Benjamin Franklin (1606-1790), a master of persuasion in America's early history, advised, "If you state an opinion to me in a dogmatic manner, which is in direct opposition to my thought, and you imply no room to negotiate, then I must conclude, in order to protect my own self-esteem, that you are wrong and will immediately undertake to prove you wrong.

"On the other hand, if you state your opinion as a hypothesis, with evidence of a willingness to discuss and explore, I will most likely undertake to prove you correct."

## 793. Good Advice

Samuel Butler (1612-1680), an English poet, made a good point about browbeating people into "agreeing" with you. Here it is:

"He that complies against his will,
Is of his own opinion still.
Which he may adhere to, yet disown,
For reasons to himself best known."

## 794. Changing Opinions

Robert A. Heinlein (1907-1988), American science fiction writer, said about persuasion, "The hardest part about gaining any new idea is sweeping out the false idea occupying that niche. As long as that niche is occupied, evidence and proof and logical demonstration get nowhere. But once the niche is emptied of the wrong idea that has been filling it — once you can honestly say, 'I don't know,' then it becomes possible to get at the truth."

# PHILANTHROPY

## 795. How the Smithsonian Was Founded

The Smithsonian Institution in Washington, D.C. was founded with a gift from a man who had never even set foot in America.

James Smithson (1765-1829), an English scientist, in 1820 bequeathed his entire estate of over $500,000 to the United States to found the Smithsonian Institution. Adjusted for inflation, that would have been millions of dollars today.

Eighty years after his death, Smithson was to visit both America and the famous institution he founded, and thereby hangs a wonderful story.

On Smithson's death in Genoa, Italy, he was buried in the English cemetery on a hill overlooking the harbor. As the years went by, the Italians began quarrying the hill on which the cemetery was located to fill in the harbor. As the quarrying continued, the cemetery was in danger of caving in. However, the English owners couldn't do anything about it because they only owned the surface of the hill, not the ground underneath.

Finally, on December 31, 1903, Smithson's grave was opened and his skeleton, "in perfect condition," was placed in a metal casket and shipped to Washington, D.C. Early in the next year, a troop of cavalry and a marine band escorted the body to a new sarcophagus in the Smithsonian, and protected by an iron railing. There he lies in an honored place today in the institution his generosity made possible.

## 796. Charities Need a "Tall Tree"

Carole Howard, former vice-president of the Reader's Digest Association, tells this story about when she was also head of the Digest's charitable foundation.

A member of the board was Laurance Rockefeller (1910-2004), one of the world's most famous and experienced philanthropists. "Laurence was not a big talker," Howard remembers, "but when he made a suggestion, you knew you were getting valuable advice."

As Howard talked about her foundation's charitable programs, she suddenly realized that its contributions were a lengthy laundry list with no coherent theme.

Halfway through her presentation, Rockefeller interrupted to say, "What you really need is a Tall Tree project."

He explained that the best charitable grants stand out like a tall tree towering over the other trees in the forest. He said tall trees change the landscape by making a unique and lasting difference in the community or the world. He added that the Digest foundation would do more good with one significant Tall Tree project than with dozens of small grants.

Rockefeller's insight energized the foundation staff and, within a few months, the Digest announced a library-school literacy partnership in New York that became a model for the nation.

## 797. Andrew Carnegie

Andrew Carnegie (1835-1919) was a Scotch-American industrialist who became famous for his philanthropy, one form of which was funding public libraries. He once said, "The day is not far distant when the man who dies leaving behind him millions of available wealth, which was free to him to administer during life, will pass away 'unwept, unhonored, and unsung,' no matter to what uses he leaves the dross which he cannot take with him. Of such as these the public verdict will then be: "The man who dies thus rich dies disgraced.""

## 798. David Rockefeller on Wealth

David Rockefeller (1915 - ), a member of the fabulously rich Rockefeller family, once said about philanthropy, "You'll never see a hearse with a luggage rack."

## 799. Eight Grades of Charity

The Jewish sage Moses Maimonides (1135-1204), in the 12th century, outlined what, for him, were the eight grades of charity. They were:

- the first is to give reluctantly;

- the second is to give cheerfully but not sufficiently;

- the third is to give cheerfully and sufficiently, but only after being asked;

- the fourth is to give cheerfully and sufficiently without being asked, but to put it in the recipient's hand in such a way as to make him feel shamed;

- the fifth is to let the recipient know who the donor is but not let the donor know the identity of those receiving the charity;

- the sixth is to know who is getting your charity but to be unknown to them.

- the seventh is to have neither the donor nor the recipient aware of the other's identity;

- and the eighth is to forestall it by enabling your fellow humans to have the right to earn a livelihood.

### 800. Definition of Philanthropy

The word "philanthropy" has its roots in the Greek language meaning "love for mankind." It was never meant to apply only to donors of thousands or millions of dollars.

# POLITICS

### 801. Media Image

Senator Paul Simon (1928-2003), of Illinois, who ran for the democratic nomination for president in 1988, was described by the press as having "a great face for radio."

### 802. Political Platform

William Jennings Bryan (1860-1925) was one of the nation's most popular politicians in his day, representing Nebraska in the U.S. House of Representatives. His famous "Cross of Gold" speech at the Democratic convention in Chicago in 1896 won him the nomination for the Presidency.

Once when Bryan was campaigning in farm country, he was asked to address a gathering in an open field. Climbing up on top a manure spreader, he said to his audience, "This is the first time I have ever spoken from a Republican platform."

## 803. Electoral Mandate

The next time you hear people arguing about whether or not a President of the United States has a mandate from the people, consider this:

When Abraham Lincoln was elected on the Republican ticket for the first time in 1860, he received 1,866,452 votes. However, this was a million votes less than received by his Democratic opponents.

Out of the 4,700,000 votes cast, Lincoln polled little more than a third. Fifteen states gave him no electoral votes at all, and in 10 states not a single ballot was cast for him.

## 804. Campaigning

President Calvin Coolidge's (1872-1933) reputation for being stingy with words has never been equaled.

When he was running for office, the common method of reaching the people was the campaign train, stopping at every little town where a crowd could be assembled.

At one such stop, Coolidge stepped to the rear of the observation car, took one look at the crowd assembled there, and stepped back inside.

"What's the matter," asked his campaign manager?

"This crowd," said Coolidge, "is too big for an anecdote and too small for an oration."

## 805. Democrats and Bibles

Feelings ran high in presidential campaigns even in Thomas Jefferson's day.

A lady belonging to the Federalist Party was so afraid of what would happen to the family Bible if Jefferson was elected president that she took it to the only Jefferson follower she knew and asked him to keep it for her.

The Jeffersonian Democrat tried to convince her that her fears were groundless but she remained unconvinced.

"My good woman," he assured her, "even if all Bibles were to be destroyed, and of course they are not, what good would it do to bring yours to me?"

"I know it will be perfectly safe with you," the woman responded, "since they will never think of looking in the house of a Democrat for a Bible."

## 806. The Importance of One Vote

- In 1645, one vote gave Oliver Cromwell (1599-1668) control of England.

- In 1649, one vote caused Charles I of England (1600-1649) to be executed.

- In 1845, one vote brought Texas into the Union.

- In 1868, one vote saved President Andrew Johnson (1767-1845) from impeachment.

- In 1875, one vote changed France from a monarchy to a republic.

- In 1876, one vote gave Rutherford B. Hayes (1822-1893) the Presidency of the United States.

- In 1923, one vote gave Adolph Hitler (1889-1945) leadership of the Nazi Party.

- In 1941, one vote saved Selective Service, just weeks before Pearl Harbor was attacked.

- In 1960, one vote change in each precinct in Illinois would have denied John F. Kennedy the Presidency.

## 807. Campaign Spending

The nomination of Lincoln in 1860 cost his friends less than $700.

Judge David Davis, one of Lincoln's intimates, told Senator John J. Ingalls of Kansas that this covered everything "including headquarters, telegraphing, music, fare of delegates, incidentals."

Things are a bit different today.

## 808. Voter Loyalty

In Boston they still talk about the legendary Mayor James Michael Curley (1874-1958) who ran for office even when he was in jail.

One of Curley's assistants was asked about the number of deceased people whose names appeared on Curley's voter rolls.

The loyal aide replied, "The Mayor is so beloved, that people come out of their graves to vote for him."

## 809. A Little Girl's Suggestion

The letter quoted below was written to Abraham Lincoln while he campaigned for president in 1860. Written by an 11-year-old girl, the letter inspired Lincoln to grow a beard.

Westfield, Chautauqua Co., N.Y.
October 15, 1860

Dear Sir:

I am a little girl 11 years old, but want you should be President of the United States very much so I hope you won't think me very bold to write to such a great man as you are. Have you any little girls about as large as I am, if so give them my love and tell her to write me if you cannot answer this letter.
I have got four brothers and part of them will vote for you any way and if you will let your whiskers grow, I will try to get the rest of them to vote for you. You would look a great deal better, for your face is so thin. All the ladies like whiskers and they would tease their husbands to vote for you and then you would be President.

(signed) Grace Bedell

Note: the original letter belongs to the Detroit, Michigan, public library

## 810. Partisan Politics

Partisan politics is nothing new.

Proof of that is a story Mark Twain (Samuel Clemens) liked to tell about his days as a river boat pilot on the Mississippi before the Civil War. In his story, Twain recalled an extreme method used to prevent "Democrats" from voting. (Note: Democrats then were not necessarily the same as the Democratic Party today.):

During a Yellow Fever attack, Twain said, passengers on the steamer, "Aleck Scott," kept dying right and left, "eight or nine a day for the first six or eight hundred miles" going north from New Orleans.

The steamer's carpenter, Robert Roach, was given the job of "planting" the fever victims every time the boat landed. "Plant" was the carpenter's word, explained Twain. And when the deceased was a Democrat, Roach planted him in the ground head first.

The ship's captain approached Roach as he was burying the victims he knew were Democrats and said, "God bless my soul, Roach, what do you mean by shoving a corpse into a hole in the hillside in this barbarous way, face down and its feet sticking out?"

"I always plant them Democrats in that manner," said Roach, "because, damn their souls, if you plant 'em any other way they'll dig out and vote the first time there's an election."

Note: this story appeared in the *San Francisco Examiner* on November 30, 1865.

## 811. Making Friends

After he was elected President, a woman chided Abraham Lincoln, saying he should destroy the rebels, not speak kindly of them.

He answered, "What, madam, do I not destroy my enemies when I make them my friends?"

## 812. Political Appointments

Abraham Lincoln liked to tell this story about a king who wanted the weather forecast to be more accurate. After some searching, he finally found a stable boy who could do it with amazing accuracy.

Every day, on the king's request, the boy would leave the palace for a time and then come back with the correct prognostication. Curious at the accuracy of the boy's forecasts, the king decided to have the boy followed. His agents did so and discovered that the boy went to a nearby stable and asked a donkey if the next day's weather was to be fair. If it was, the donkey's ears would go forward. If not, they would point backward.

Overjoyed at discovering the boy's secret, the king appointed the donkey Court Astrologer.

Lincoln said that the King afterward realized it was the biggest mistake of his life, because every jackass in the country wanted a political office.

## 813. Political Spoils

Mark Twain recalled an ancient Aesop fable that he said was reminiscent of partisan party politics.

"Political parties who accuse the one in power of gobbling the spoils," said Twain, "are like the wolf who looked in at the door and saw the shepherds eating mutton."

The wolf said, "Oh, certainly. It's all right as long as it's you, but there'd be hell to pay if I was to do that!"

## 814. Making Changes

Speaking to a delegation of the National Union League on his nomination as President on June 9, 1864, Abraham Lincoln said:

"I do not allow myself to suppose that either the convention or the League have concluded to decide that I am either the greatest or the best man in America, but rather they have concluded that it is not best to swap horses while crossing the river, and have further concluded that I am not so poor a horse that they might not make a botch of it in trying to swap."

## 815. Learning How to Network

At the 63rd Annual Dinner of the Washington Press Club in 2007, Senator Ted Kennedy (1932- ), at the age of 75, told this story on himself:

After being elected to the U.S. Senate as a young man, Kennedy was told that the Senate is all about networking. On entering the Senate Dining Room on his first day at the Capital, his advisor said, "See that old southern senator lunching with his wife? He's one of the most important men in town. Go and introduce yourself."

Kennedy walked over to the Senator's table, smiled and said, "Good afternoon, Senator, I'm Ted."

The Senator smiled back and said, "Good morning, Ted. My wife wants the peach cobbler and I'll have another bourbon and branch water."

## 816. Disappointment

Asked how he felt about the Democrats winning the New York State elections in 1862, Abraham Lincoln said:

"I feel somewhat like the boy in Kentucky who stubbed his toe while running to see his sweetheart. The boy said he was too big to cry, and far too badly hurt to laugh."

Note: Adlai Stevenson (1900-1965), the Democratic candidate for President in 1952, used the same Lincoln anecdote to describe his feelings after being defeated in the presidential election of that year.

## 817. Rolling with the Punch

When Bessie Braddock, a political rival to Winston Churchill, accused him of being drunk, Churchill replied, "Yes, and you are ugly. But tomorrow I shall be sober."

## 818. Lincoln and the Flu Bug

Like all of us, Abraham Lincoln came down with an occasional bout of the flu. But unlike most of us, he had thousands of people approaching him constantly who wanted something from him.

"Well," said Lincoln philosophically when he felt himself coming down with a contagious bout of influenza, "at least now I will have something that I can give to everybody."

## 819. Farewell to Office

When Stanley Baldwin (1867-1947), a prime minister of Great Britain, stepped down from his post in May of 1937, he made this statement to his cabinet, and later released it to the press:

"Once I leave, I leave. I am not going to speak to the man on the bridge, and I am not going to spit on the deck."

This was Baldwin's way of saying he was promising not to give his successor any unwanted advice or criticism.

"A good sailor," said Baldwin, "does not spit on the deck, causing unnecessary work for someone else, nor does he speak to the man at the wheel, but leaves him free to devote his full attention to steering the ship."

## 820. Lincoln on Being President

Asked what it felt like to be President of the United States, Abraham Lincoln replied:

"I feel like the man who was tarred and feathered and ridden out of town on a rail. When a man asked him how he liked it, he said, 'If it wasn't for the honor of the thing, I'd rather walk.'"

## 821. A Big U.S. President

There has been only one man in American history who served as President of the United States and later as Chief Justice of the Supreme Court.

His name was William Howard Taft (1857-1930) and he was also the only President who couldn't fit in the White House bath tub. So he had a specially-made tub to accommodate his 325 pounds.

Before he became President, he once put his considerable heft to advantage. Stranded at a whistle stop train station, Taft was told the express train would stop only if there were a number of passengers ready to board.

Undaunted, the future President of the United States wired the conductor, "Stop at Hicksville. Large party waiting to catch the train."

When the train stopped, Taft climbed aboard. "You can go ahead now," he told the conductor, "I am the large party."

## 822. Appointing Judges

After Abraham Lincoln was elected to the presidency, he was besieged by people seeking political appointments.

One man seeking a judgeship was told by Lincoln that he could not be appointed because there were no vacancies.

After leaving the White House, and walking along the Potomac River, the rejected job-seeker saw a man drowning and plunged in to save him. Regrettably, however, he was too late to save the man, whose identification showed that he was a federal judge.

Armed with this information, the disappointed job-seeker rushed back to Lincoln and said, "I have just pulled a dead man out of the Potomac who was a federal judge, so now I know there is an opening.

Lincoln replied, "I am sorry but you are too late. I just appointed a man who SAW the deceased fall into the river."

## 823. Campaign Financing

Campaign spending is as old as the republic. When George Washington ran for the Virginia House of Burgesses in 1757, his total campaign expenditures, in the form of "good cheer," came to "28 gallons of rum, 50 gallons of rum punch, 34 gallons of wine, 36 gallons of beer, and 2 gallons of cider."

## 824. Doing One's Best

Few American Presidents have had to endure as much vicious criticism as did Abraham Lincoln, the nation's Sixteenth President. Regarding the nature and bitterness of the criticism, he once said the following:

"If I were to try to read, much less answer, all the attacks made on me, this shop might as well be closed for any other business. I do the very best I know how, the very best I can; and I mean to keep doing so until the end. If the end brings me out all right, what is said against me won't amount to anything. If the end brings me out wrong, ten angels swearing I was right would make no difference.

Note: Winston Churchill had this Lincoln quotation (beginning with the words, "I do the very best I can, etc.") framed on the wall of his office.

## 825. A Verbal Slip

Vice President George H.W. Bush (1924- ) was describing the closeness of his relationship with President Ronald Reagan (1911-2004) when he got a bit carried away. Emphasizing the seven and a half years they had worked side by side, Bush said, "We have had triumphs, we have made mistakes, we have had sex."

(Note: there was a stunned silence in the audience).

Vice President Bush quickly corrected his last line to: "We have had setbacks", and drew hearty laughter from the audience. Then came a perfect adlib from the Vice-President: "I feel like a javelin thrower who won the coin toss and elected to receive."

## 826. The Civil War

No American President has ever been under greater pressure than Abraham Lincoln (1809-1865) when he was faced with the threat of secession by the southern states.

A foreign visitor at the time asked Lincoln what was his policy.

"I have none," Lincoln replied. "I pass my life in preventing the storm from blowing down the tent, and I drive in the pegs as fast as they are pulled."

## 827. The Age of Candidates

Ronald Reagan (1911-2004) was 69 when he ran successfully for the Presidency in 1980. America had never had a presidential candidate that old before.

Four years later, during a televised debate with the 56-year-old Democratic challenger, Walter Mondale (1928- ), in the 1984 presidential campaign, the then 73-year-old Reagan was asked whether he was too old to serve another term.

Reagan replied: "I'm not going to inject the issue of age into this campaign. I am not going to exploit for political gain my opponent's youth and inexperience."

There was instant audience laughter and Mondale later said that, at that moment, he knew he was going to lose the election, which he did in a landslide vote for Reagan.

## 828. Political Strife

Senator Benjamin Wade (1800-1878) of Ohio was hot-tempered and usually "on the outs" with President Abraham Lincoln.

One day he stormed into the President's office on the second floor of the White House and accosted Lincoln saying, "Mr. President this Administration is on the way to hell. On the way to hell, sir – it's only a mile away from it!"

"Why, Wade," replied Lincoln with a patient smile, "that's the exact distance from here to the Capitol."

## 829. Politics of Social Security

Longtime House Speaker Tip O'Neill (1912-1994) (a Democrat), in an analogy to a city subway system, used to refer to Social Security as "the third rail of American politics."

"Touch it," he warned his fellow Congressmen, "and you die!"

## 830. An Early Lincoln Political Speech

"Fellow citizens, I presume you all know who I am, I am humble Abraham Lincoln. I have been solicited by many friends to become a candidate for the legislature.

"My politics are short and sweet, like the old woman's dance. I am in favor of a national bank. I am in favor of the internal improvement system, and a high protective tariff. These are my sentiments and political principles. If elected, I shall be thankful; if not it will be all the same."

## 831. Talk Net

When Calvin Coolidge (1872-1933) was Vice President, Channing Cox, his successor as Governor of Massachusetts, paid him a visit.

Cox asked how Coolidge as Governor had managed to meet with so many visitors every day and still leave the office at 5 p.m. Cox himself found he often left the office as late as 9 p.m.

Coolidge replied, "You talk back."

## 832. Lincoln's Jokes

During the darkest days of the Civil War, even Abraham Lincoln's cabinet members were critical of his penchant for telling jokes during serious meetings. "How can you tell jokes while this awful war is continuing?" asked one of the cabinet members? Lincoln's reply was:

"Were it not for my little jokes, I could not bear the burdens of this office."

## 833. Women in Elective Office

In a Federal Women's Award Ceremony in the White House in 1965, President Lyndon Johnson (1908-1973) said the following:

"America has come a long way since the first woman government employee was appointed Postmaster at Baltimore in 1773. Her name was Mary Goddard.

"But Miss Goddard faced formidable opposition. None other than Thomas Jefferson questioned the appointment, saying: "'The appointment of a woman to office is an innovation for which the public is not prepared.'"

## 834. Fooling the Public

Abraham Lincoln (1809-1865) is credited with the maxim: "You can fool some of the people all of the time, all the people some of the time, but you cannot fool all the people all the time."

The saying has not been found in any of Lincoln's works, and the only source is "Abe" Lincoln's Yarns and Stories (1904), by Alexander K. McClure, who claimed the President addressed the comment to a White House guest.

## 835. Lincoln Thought He Was Ugly

Abraham Lincoln believed himself to be the ugliest person in the world, and he once told this story on himself.

"One day, I got into a fit of musing in my room. Looking into the glass, it struck me what an ugly man I was, and I made up my mind that I must be the ugliest man in the world. It so maddened me that I resolved, should I ever see an uglier, I would shoot him on sight.

"Not long after this, Andy (naming a lawyer who was present) came to town, and the first time I saw him I said to myself, 'There's the man.'

"I went home, took down my gun and prowled around the streets waiting for him. He soon came along.

"Halt, Andy," said I, pointing the gun at him. "Say your prayers for I am going to shoot you."

"'Why, Mr. Lincoln, what's the matter?' said the lawyer.

"Well," said Lincoln, "I made an oath that if I ever saw an uglier man than I am, I'd shoot him on the spot. You are uglier, surely; so make ready to die!"

"'Mr. Lincoln,' said Andy, 'do you really think that I am uglier than you?'

"Yes," replied Lincoln.

"'Well, Mr. Lincoln,' said Andy deliberately, and looking at Lincoln square in the face, 'if I am any uglier, fire away.'"

## 836. Inauguration Day

At his presidential inauguration, Abraham Lincoln arrived at the rostrum holding, in addition to a copy of his speech, his trademark black stovepipe hat and cane.

After laying down the cane, he was dismayed to find no room for his hat. Senator Stephen Douglas (1813-1861), Lincoln's chief electoral opponent, gracefully came forward and took it from him.

"If I can't be President," said Douglas, "the least I can do is hold his hat."

## 837. Prayer Meeting

There is a story about Preacher Cartright, the evangelical minister who supported Abraham Lincoln in a Congressional race.

At a prayer meeting Cartright spied Lincoln and said, "All those who want to go to Heaven rise."

Everybody but Lincoln rose, then again he said, "All who do not want to go to Hell rise."

Again everybody but Lincoln got up. Cartright then challenged Lincoln. "Where, Mr. Lincoln, do you want to go?"

Lincoln replied, "I want to go to Congress."

# POSITIVE THINKING

### 838. Definition of Work

Christopher Wren (1632-1723), one of the greatest of English architects was walking around the construction site of St. Paul's cathedral in London which he had designed. No one recognized him and he stopped to ask a question of one of the workmen there.

"What are you doing?" he asked of the workmen, and the man replied, "I am cutting a piece of stone."

Moving on, he put the same question to another man, and the man replied, "I am earning five shillings two pence a day."

A third man to whom he addressed the same question, looked up and said proudly, "I am helping Sir Christopher Wren build a beautiful cathedral."

### 839. A Message of Hope

"We found that anything is possible."

The above was the text of a framed message hanging on the wall of Christopher Reeve's (1952-2004) room at the rehabilitation hospital where the actor was recovering from a horseback riding accident which left him paralyzed from the neck down. The message was signed by all of the current astronauts in the NASA space program.

Note: Reeve referred to the message in a 1995 television interview with Barbara Walters. Reeve was born in 1952 and died of a heart attack in 2004. Although he never recovered from the paralysis, he did make great strides and even directed a television production from his wheelchair.

## 840. The Flying Horse

The noted financier and adviser to Presidents, Bernard Baruch (1870-1965), liked to tell this story.

In ancient times, a king had sentenced a man to death who had been caught stealing one of the royal horses.

The man begged for mercy, saying, "If you will not kill me, I will promise to teach this horse to fly by the end of a year. If am not successful you can kill me any way you want to."

Although the King was skeptical, he spared the man's life but warned him that, if the horse could not fly by year's end, he would be put to a slow and painful death for his crime.

"Why would you make such a ridiculous promise?" said the man's best friend. "You know you can't make a horse fly."

With a smile, the thief replied, "Who knows? Within a year, the King may die, or I may die, or the horse may die. Furthermore, in a year, who knows? Maybe the horse will learn to fly."

## 841. Advice on Life from Mel Brooks

Let's have a merry journey
And shout about how light is good and dark is not.
What we should do is not "future" ourselves so much.
We should "now" ourselves more.
"Now thyself" is more important than "know thyself."
Reason is what tells us to ignore the present and live in the future.
So all we do is make plans.
We think that somewhere there are going to be green pastures.
It's crazy.
Heaven is nothing but a grand, monumental instance of future.
Listen, now is good. Now is wonderful!

Mel Brooks (Melvin Kaminsky) (1928- )
American writer and comedian

## 842. The Optimist vs. the Pessimist

The following poem by William Arthur Ward (1921-1994) says a lot about positive and negative thinking:

The optimist turns the impossible into the possible;
the pessimist turns the possible into the impossible.
The optimist pleasantly ponders how high the kite will fly;
the pessimist woefully wonders how soon the kite will fall.
The optimist sees a green near every sand trap;
the pessimist sees a sand trap near every green.
The optimist looks at the horizon and sees an opportunity;
the pessimist peers into the distance and fears a problem.
To the optimist all doors have handles and hinges;
to the pessimist all doors have locks and latches.
The optimist promotes progress, prosperity and plenty;
the pessimist preaches limitations, liabilities and losses.
The optimist accentuates assets, abundance, and advantages;
the pessimist majors in mistakes, misfortunes and misery.
The optimist goes out and finds the bell;
the pessimist gives up and wrings his or her hands.

## 843. Reagan's Positive Thinking

One of the hallmarks of truly successful leaders is their irrepressible optimism. An outstanding example was President Ronald Reagan (1911-2004).

Richard Wirthlin (1931- ) was for years President Reagan's pollster and he would visit him at the White House every other week.

Following an assassination attempt on President Reagan's life, his approval ratings by the public were about 90 percent, virtually the highest on record. But a year later, when the country was struggling out of a recession, Reagan's poll ratings plummeted to about 30 percent. When the news was good, there was usually a lineup of White House assistants waiting to get into the Oval Office with the good news. But when Wirthlin came in with the 30 percent figure, they practically shoved him into the Oval Office all by himself.

"You tell him, Dick," they said.

So Wirthlin went in and Reagan said, "Well, how am I doing? What do the figures look like?"

"Well," said Wirthlin, "they are pretty bad, Mr. President."

"Well, how bad are they?" said Reagan.

"Well, they are as low as they can get." said Wirthlin apologetically.

"So what do you mean?" asked the President.

Bracing himself for an unfavorable reaction, Wirthlin said, "Well, they're about 32 percent."

"Anything lower than that in the second year of the presidency?" Reagan asked.

"I think that's the lowest," Wirthlin replied, and he braced himself for some kind of Presidential explosion.

At this, Reagan's face broke into a broad smile and he said to his apologetic pollster, "Dick, don't worry. I'll just go out there and try to get shot again."

## 844. A Valuable Lesson

Three men set out on a journey. Each carried two sacks around his neck — one in front and one in back. The first man was asked what was in his sacks.

"In this one on my back," he said, "I carry all the kind deeds of my friends. In that way, they are out of sight and out of mind and I don't have to do anything about them. They're soon forgotten. This sack in front carries all the unkind things people do to me. I pause in my journey every day and take these out to study. It slows me down, but nobody gets away with anything."

The second man said he kept his own good deeds in his front sack. "I constantly keep them before me," he said. "It gives me pleasure to take them out and air them."

"The sack on your back seems heavy," someone remarked to the second traveler. "What is in it?"

"That's where I carry my mistakes," said the second man. "I always keep them on my back."

The third man was asked what he kept in his sacks. "I carry my friends' kind deeds in this front sack," he said.

Said an observer, "It looks full. It must be heavy."

"No," said the third man, "it is big, but not heavy. Far from being a burden, it is like the sails of a ship. It helps me move ahead."

Added the observer, "I notice that the sack behind you has a hole in the bottom. It seems empty and of very little use."

To which the third man replied, "That's were I put all the evil I hear from others. It just falls out and is lost, so I have no weight to impede me."

Guess which of the three travelers finished first in their journey through life?

## 845. The Eye of the Beholder

The famous American poet Edwin Markham (1852-1940) once wrote a poem about a traveler who came upon a city located in the plains. The traveler paused at the outskirts of the town and asked an old man napping beneath a tree what kind of people lived there.

"What sort of people were there from where you came?" asked the old man.

"What sort?" the traveler growled, "why, knaves and fools, of course."

"You'll find the people here the same," said the old man and he closed his eyes to continue his nap.

Soon another traveler approaching the city stopped where the old man was sitting and asked the same question: "What sort of people live here?"

"What kind of people were there where you came from?" asked the old man, stifling a yawn.

"What sort?" said the second traveler. "Why good, true and wise, of course."

"You'll find the people here the same," said the wise old townsman and went back to his catnap.

## 846. Acceptance

There was an old farmer who had suffered through a lifetime of troubles and afflictions that would have leveled an ordinary mortal. But through it all he never lost his sense of humor.

"How have you managed to keep so happy and serene?" asked a friend.

"It ain't hard," said the old fellow with a twinkle in his eye, "I've just learned to cooperate with the inevitable."

An Asian saying advises, "When fate throws a dagger at you, there are only two ways to catch it, either by the blade or by the handle."

"Cooperating with the inevitable" requires us to catch adversity by the handle and use it as the tool for which it was intended.

## 847. We Are What We Do and Think

A son and his father were walking in the mountains. Suddenly, his son falls, hurts himself and screams, "AAAhhhhhhhhh!!!"

To the son's surprise, he hears his voice repeating, somewhere in the mountains, "AAAhhhhhhhhh!!!"

Curious, he yells, "Who are you?" He receives the same answer, "Who are you?"

Angered at the response, he screams, "Coward!" He receives the answer, "Coward!"

He looks to his father and asks, "What's going on?"

The father smiles and says, "My son, pay attention." And he screams to the mountain, "I admire you!" The voice answers, "I admire you!"

Again the man screams, "You are a champion!" The voice answers, "You are a champion!"

The boy is surprised but does not understand.

Then the father explains: "People call this ECHO, but really this is LIFE. It gives you back everything you say and do. Our life is simply a reflection of our actions. If you want more love in the world, create more love in your heart. If you want competence in your team, improve your competence. This relationship applies to everything; in all aspects of life; LIFE WILL GIVE YOU BACK EVERYTHING YOU HAVE GIVEN IT."

## 848. Mind over Body

There once lived a wealthy king who had a son he greatly loved. The boy was both handsome and intelligent. He had only one flaw. His back was hunched and not straight.

The distraught king proclaimed that a rich reward would be given to anyone who could find a way to straighten the young prince's back. Many months passed without anyone coming forward with a solution. Wise subjects with good ideas came to the palace from all over the kingdom. But no one could find a cure that worked.

However, one day a strange-looking woman arrived in the kingdom and heard about the problem.

"I don't want your reward," said the old woman who was herself all bent over with age and whose skin was yellowed and wrinkled. "But," she added, "I do have your answer for you."

She told the king: "In the center of your courtyard, you must create a sculpture — an exact replica of your dear son, with one exception. His back must be straight and lovely in appearance. That's all. Trust God to do the healing."

With that, the old woman disappeared and the king's sculptors went to work. In a week or two, a beautiful marble sculpture stood at a prominent place in the palace courtyard.

As the little boy played in the courtyard every day, he looked at the sculptured figure admiringly. And slowly he started to feel, "Why that's me! That looks exactly like me!"

Every day, the young prince gazed fondly at the sculpture until he identified with it completely. And bit by bit, the boy's back straightened.

A year or so later, the king was watching his son frolicking in the palace gardens when he suddenly noticed the prince's back was totally straight. The young boy's identification with the marble sculpture had been so intense that the boy came to believe the sculpture represented him — straight back and all. His little body had obeyed belief.

## 849. Balm for Sensitive Feelings

Red Skelton was a much beloved comedian devoted to prat falls and other tricks he learned in vaudeville where he learned his trade. He was also a very sensitive human being.

"When anyone hurts us, my wife and I sit in our Japanese sand garden and drink iced tea," Skelton told the *New York Times* in 1977. "There are five stories in the garden — for sky, wind, fire, water and earth. We sit and think of five of the nicest things we can about the person who hurt us.

"If he hurts us a second time, we do the same thing."

"The third time, we light a candle, and he is, for us, dead."

In today's complex world, where others often don't seem to have our best interests at heart, this is a technique some of us might find helpful.

Note: Richard Bernard Skelton (1913-1997) was born in Vincennes, Indiana. He had a long career as a television comedian.

## 850. No Place like Home

A great many years ago a caravan of men were crossing a barren desert on camels. Finally they reached a place where they expected to find much-needed water. Instead, all they found was a deep round hole going deep into the earth. Expectantly, they lowered bucket after bucket down the hole, but each time the bucket came back empty.

Parched with thirst, they decided to lower men into the hole in the hope of finding precious water. But the men, too, disappeared and the lowered rope came up attached only to an empty bucket. Finally, the leader of the party volunteered to go down into the hole to see if he could solve the mystery.

When the leader, who was also very wise, reached the bottom of the hole, he found himself face to face with a horrible monster. Quickly, he thought to himself, "I can't hope to escape from this place, but I can at least keenly observe everything I am experiencing."

"I will let you go," said the fearsome monster with a growl, "but only if you will answer one question."

The wise leader answered, "Ask your question."

The monster said, "Where is the best place to be?"

The trapped man thought to himself, "I don't want to hurt his feelings. If I name some beautiful city, he may think I'm disparaging some place he loves. Or maybe this hole is the place he thinks is best."

So to the monster he said, "The best place to be is wherever you feel at home, even if it's a hole in the ground."

With a trace of a smile on his frightening face, the monster said, "You are so wise that I will not only let you go, but I will also free the foolish men who came down before you. And I will release the water in this well."

Note: There have been several language scholars who have said that "home" is the most beautiful word in the English language.

# PROBLEM SOLVING

## 851. A Consultant's Bill

Charles Steinmetz (1865-1923) was a German-born electrical engineer whose genius and inventions played a major role in making General Electric the industrial power it is today.

Once, after he had retired, GE called him in to help in locating a malfunction in a system of complex machinery. All of GE's experts were at a loss to find the problem.

After walking around and testing different components of the machinery, Steinmetz took a piece of chalk and marked an "X" at a specific location on one of the machines.

The machine was quickly disassembled and the GE experts somewhat sheepishly found a defect exactly where Steinmetz had made his chalk mark. Everyone was much relieved.

However, when GE later received a bill from Steinmetz for $10,000, company officials questioned the amount and asked for an itemized bill.

Steinmetz readily sent an itemized bill which read as follows:

"Making one chalk mark....$1

"Knowing where to place it....$9,999."

## 852. Analyze the Problem

For a lesson in solving many complex problems, one good approach is to do what loggers do when clearing a log jam.

The pro climbs a tree and locates the key log, blows it up with an explosive, and lets the stream do the rest.

An amateur would start at the edge of the jam and move all the logs, eventually moving the key log. Both approaches work, but the "essence" concept saves time and effort.

Almost all problems have a "key" log if we learn how to find it.

## 853. When All Else Fails

There once lived a king, a very benevolent fellow, loved by his community. He ruled a little kingdom tucked away in a pleasant corner of one of those European regions that used to have little kingdoms tucked away in their corners.

One day a neighboring army came and overran the castle, making off with half the king's treasury. After much deliberation, the king decided to tell the people he must increase taxes to make up for the loss. He called in one of the court's wise men for advice on how to do it.

"How can I break the news without inciting a revolt?" he asked. The wise man pondered and came up with a gentle way of explaining the theft as a tragedy for the entire kingdom, and asking the people for their patriotic support. The king's appeal to his subjects went over very well.

Time passed, and once again the neighboring army raided the castle, this time carting away much of the food stored for the winter. And once again, the king called upon his wise man, (by this time, his title was Director of Wisdom) and laid bare the facts.

"What can I tell my subjects this time?" the king asked. "They will lose confidence in me if I can't defend the kingdom's food and money."

Again, the wise man pondered. He advised the king to be frank about the loss, but to say only that it had gone to a neighboring kingdom that seemed to need it desperately. And the king implored the people to work even harder on the year's harvest to make up for the loss. They did, and all was well.

By this time, the neighboring army was getting rather good at raids. Once again they struck, hauling away horses, hay and other foodstuffs. and most of the royal jewels. Once again, the king summoned his trusted advisor (now titled V.P. of Wisdom and Sage Advice). This time, the king was despondent.

"They raid the treasury. They take our food. They steal our livestock," the king wailed. "And the queen's going to kill me about those jewels. You are my most trusted advisor. What shall I do?"

The wise man hesitated. "I think," he said, "I think the time has come for your highness to put the water back in the moat."

## 854. A Blue Ribbon Formula

The farmer had won a blue ribbon at the county fair. His prize entry? A huge radish the exact shape and size of a quart milk bottle.

Asked how he got the radish to look just like a quart milk bottle, the farmer replied:

"It was easy, I got the seed growing and then put it into the milk bottle. It had nowhere else to go."

In a similar way, our lives are shaped by the kind of surroundings we place ourselves in and the challenges we give ourselves.

## 855. Wise Advice

Twenty-five hundred years ago a new Chinese emperor took the throne of the Middle Kingdom. Because he was only 18, he called to him the court's wisest adviser.

"O learned sage. O venerable counselor," said the young emperor, "you advised my grandfather the emperor for many years. What is the single most important advice you can give me now for ruling my kingdom?"

And the adviser, who was the famous Chinese philosopher named Confucius (551 BC-479 BC), replied, "First, you must define the problem."

## 856. Sisyphus Needed Help

Some will argue that a life of continuous problem-solving bears a depressing resemblance to the life of Sisyphus.

In the legend, Sisyphus was condemned to push a great stone to the top of the mountain, and just as he reached the top it would slip from his grasp and roll to the bottom and he would have to push it up again — and so on for all eternity.

But some have pointed out that it was the monotony, not the futility, of the task what made it punishment. If Sisyphus could have rolled a different stone each time, or the same stone up different mountains, or if he could have experimented with improved ways of rolling it, it might not have been so bad. Certainly it would have been better than just loafing around Hades.

## 857. Ice Cream and Car Failure

Some years ago the following complaint letter was received by the Buick division of General Motors. The letter went like this:

"This is the second time I have written you, and I don't blame you for not answering me, because I kind of sounded crazy, but it is a fact that we have a tradition in our family of ice cream for dessert after dinner each night. But the kind of ice cream varies. So, every night, after we've eaten, the whole family votes on which kind of ice cream we should have and I drive down to the store to get it.

"It's also a fact that I recently purchased a new Buick, and since then my trips to the store have created a problem. You see, every time I buy vanilla ice cream, when I start back from the store my car won't start. If I get any other kind of ice cream, the car starts just fine.

"I want you to know I'm serious about this question, no matter how silly it sounds. What is there about a Buick that makes it not start when I get vanilla ice cream, and easy to start whenever I get any other kind?"

The Buick president was understandably skeptical about the letter, but sent an engineer to check it out anyway. The engineer was surprised to be greeted by a successful, obviously well-educated man in a fine neighborhood.

The engineer had arranged to meet the man just after dinner time, so the two hopped into the car and drove to the ice cream store. It was vanilla ice cream that night and, sure enough, after they came back to the car, it wouldn't start.

The engineer returned for three more nights. The first night, the man got chocolate. The car started. The second night, he got strawberry. The car started. The third night he ordered vanilla. The car failed to start.

Being a logical man, the engineer refused to believe that this man's car was allergic to vanilla ice cream. He arranged, therefore, to continue his visits for as long as it took to solve the problem. And toward this end he began to take notes. He jotted down all sorts of data, time of day, type of gas used, time to drive back and forth, etc.

In a short time, he had a clue. The man took less time to buy vanilla than any other flavor. Why? The answer was in the layout of the store.

Vanilla, being the most popular flavor, was in a separate case at the front of the store for quick pick-up. All the other flavors were kept in the back of the store at a different counter where it took considerably longer to find the flavor and get checked out.

Now the question for the engineer was why the car wouldn't start when it took less time. Once time became the problem — not the vanilla ice cream — the engineer quickly came up with the answer: vapor lock. It was happening every night, but the extra time taken to get the other flavors allowed the engine to cool down sufficiently to start. When the man got vanilla, the engine was still too hot for the vapor lock to dissipate.

Moral of the story: even insane-looking problems are solvable if you do your homework and take the right approach.

## 858. Value of Thinking

An efficiency expert hired by Henry Ford (1863-1947) was giving the pioneer auto magnate a rundown on what he had observed during an analysis of the fledgling Ford Motor Company.

"I am quite impressed with what I saw," said the consultant, "except that I am very bothered by one of your employees who has an office just down the corridor. "Every time I go by his office, he's just sitting there with his feet on his desk. He's wasting your money."

"That man," replied Ford, "once had an idea that saved us millions of dollars. At the time, I believe his feet were planted right where they are now."

## 859. Common Sense Wins

Once upon a time there was a king who wanted to pick the wisest person among his subjects to be prime minister. After an exhaustive search of his kingdom, the choice was finally narrowed down to three men. Before making his decision, the king decided to put them to an unusual test.

He placed the three candidates together in a room of his palace, the door of which was equipped with the most complicated lock ever designed by the Royal Locksmith.

"Whoever is able to open the door first," said the king, "will be appointed Royal Prime Minister."

The three men immediately set themselves to the task. One of them began at once to work out complicated mathematical formulas to discover the secret lock combination. Another began consulting thick textbooks on how locks are constructed. The third man just sat by a window, totally calm and apparently lost in thought.

Finally, as the first two men worked feverishly at the puzzle given them by the king, the third man walked over to the door and turned the handle. With absolutely no pressure, the door swung upon to his touch. It had been unlocked all the time!

For his common sense and activist approach, the third man had won the most powerful post in the kingdom. Something to think about!

## 860. The Gordian Knot

In the winter of 333 BC, the famous Macedonian general Alexander (366 BC-323 BC) and his army arrived in the Asian city of Gordium to spend the winter.

While there, Alexander is told the legend which surrounds the town's famous knot, the "Gordian Knot." According to the legend, whoever can untie this exceptionally complex knot will become the King of Asia. He is told that, although many have struggled mightily to untie the knot, no one has ever succeeded.

Fascinated, Alexander asks to be shown the knot so he can attempt to untie it. He studies its intricacies intently and makes several unsuccessful attempts to untie the knot.

Finally, in a burst of inspiration (or was it frustration), Alexander pulls out his sword and slices the knot in half — becoming part of the legend himself. He and his armies went on to capture and rule more territories in the ancient world than anyone who had gone before him. This included Asia, although in Alexander's day that extended only as far as India.

Sometimes, the best way to solve a difficult problem is to slice away some of the complexities with a single stroke, despite opposition and advice to do otherwise.

## 861. One Way to Solve a Problem

Mark Twain (Samuel Clemens) (1835-1910) once proudly recalled how he had deftly answered a question thrown at him about how to solve a difficult problem. "I was gratified to be able to answer promptly," he said. "I said I didn't know."

## 862. Lincoln on Unsolvable Problems

President Abraham Lincoln (1809-1865) was once approached by a Civil War general on how to best handle a particularly difficult problem. Lincoln told him to use his own best judgment and then related this story of an old farmer who had the task of ploughing a large field covered with many tree stumps.

"'He wasn't able to get all the stumps removed," said Lincoln, "but he succeeded in planting a patch of corn, a few hills of beans, etc."

One day a stranger stopped to look at the farmer's place and he asked the farmer how he managed to grow crops in such difficult terrain.

"Well," said the farmer, "I can generally root out or burn out most of the stumps, but now and then there is one so large that I just have to plough around it."

That is what Lincoln thought the General should do if he wasn't able to solve his problem.

## 863. Traffic Control

The storied showman P.T. Barnum (1810-1891) once had a New York Museum which was so popular he could not get customers to pass through it fast enough, causing great crowding inside.

Barnum solved the problem by placing a sign over one of the doorways which read TO THE EGRESS. Once through the door, visitors found themselves outside with a return impossible.

## 864. A Wise Answer

This story concerns a wise old Egyptian Pharaoh and an ambitious young political rival. Impatient to assume the leadership role of the kingdom, the young rival challenged the old Pharaoh to a test. If the Pharaoh failed the test, the young rival would assume the role as leader. The young rival confronted the Pharaoh holding a small bird cupped in his hands.

"Is the bird dead or alive?" he asked.

If the Pharaoh said the bird was dead, the rival would simply open his hands and allow the bird to fly away. If the Pharaoh said the bird was alive, the rival would squeeze the bird between his fingers, open his hand and the bird would be dead.

Either way the old Pharaoh would be seen as a fool and fail the test. Upon being confronted, the wise old Pharaoh said, "It is as you will it. The answer is in your hands."

## 865. Boiling down the World's Knowledge

Many years ago, the ruler of a Middle Eastern kingdom called a meeting of the wise men in his realm, and said, "Your assignment is to gather all the world's knowledge together in such a manner that my sons can read it and learn."

After a year, the wise men came back with 25 volumes of knowledge. The potentate shook his head and said, "No. It's too long."

So the wise men went away for another year and they came back to the king with a single volume. The king looked at it disapprovingly and said, "No. It is still too long."

Somewhat discouraged, the wise men went away to work and ponder for another year. When they came back, they gave the potentate a piece of paper with one sentence written on it.

It read: "This too shall pass."

The king was satisfied and thanked them for their wisdom.

## 866. Considering All Alternatives

To solve most problems, it is necessary to first consider all the alternatives. In a scene from the classic movie, "Butch Cassidy and the Sundance Kid." Butch and Sundance are trapped on the side of a cliff. Above them, in goodly numbers, is the armed posse that's been chasing them.

Butch sums up the situation to Sundance by saying, "They could go for position, pick us off. Or they could rush us, overwhelm us. Maybe they'll just wait, starve us out, or maybe they'll get a rockslide going, get us that way."

Butch asks Sundance, "What else could they do?"

And Sundance responds, "Well, they could surrender to us, but I wouldn't count on it."

## 867. Few Ideas Are New

The famous inventor Charles Kettering (1876-1958) had an unusual technique for solving difficult problems. He would break down each problem into its smallest components.

Then he did research to find out which of the subset problems had already been solved by someone else. He often found that what looked like a huge mystery had previously been 98 percent solved by others. Then he went to work on the remainder.

## 868. The Augean Stables

This story about how an unsolvable problem was solved by one master stroke comes from Greek mythology. The act also added a new phrase to the English language.

Hercules was a Greek hero of superhuman physical strength. Unfortunately for him, he had, in a fit of madness inflicted on him by the god Juno, slew his wife and children.

For punishment, Hercules was ordered by the god Apollo to serve the Argive king, Eurystheus, for 12 years. The penalty Eurystheus came up with was to impose upon Hercules 12 tasks of enormous difficulty and danger.

One of the worst problems he was asked to solve was to cleanse the Augean stables, which housed a herd of 3,000 oxen owned by the mythological Greek King of Elis. The stables had not been cleaned for years and were an impossible mess.

Not to be stumped by such a momentous task, Hercules got the stables clean in a single day by diverting the rivers Alpheus and Peneus to wash away all the terrible residue.

Ever since then in the western world, the phrase, "to cleanse the Augean stables" means to clear away any accumulated mass of rubbish or corruption, physical, moral, religious or legal.

## 869. Solving Problems in Wonderland

One of the first things Alice discovered when she found herself in Lewis Carroll's (1832-1898) *Alice in Wonderland* was some of their curious ways for solving problems. This can be illustrated by this conversation between Alice and the Mad Hatter:

Alice: Where I come from, people study what they are not good at in order to be able to do what they are good at.

Mad Hatter: "We only go around in circles in Wonderland, but we always end up where we started. Would you mind explaining yourself?"

Alice: "Well, grown-ups tell us to find out what we did wrong, and never do it again."

Mad Hatter: "That's odd! It seems to me that in order to find out about something, you have to study it. And when you study it, you should become better at it. Why should you want to become better at something and then never do it again? But please continue."

Alice: "Nobody ever tells us to study the right things we do. We're only supposed to learn from the wrong things. But we are permitted to study the right things other people do. And sometimes we're even told to copy them."

Mad Hatter: "That's cheating!"

Alice: "You're quite right, Mr. Hatter. I do live in a topsy-turvy world. It seems like I have to do something wrong first, in order to learn what not to do. And then, by not doing what I'm not supposed to do, perhaps I'll be right. But I'd rather be right the first time, wouldn't you?"

## 870. Problem Analysis

One of New York's leading museums was in the process of deciding to commission an expensive study to find out which of its many exhibits was most popular with visitors.

However, just before the study contract was signed, a committee member suggested asking the janitors where they had to mop the floors most frequently.

The study was dropped.

# PRODUCTIVITY

## 871. A Benjamin Franklin Story

Nothing exasperated Benjamin Franklin more than to see ineffectual work activity. Franklin said it reminded him of a ship where two lazy sailors sneaked up from the deck to the helm and hid out from a work detail.

A boatswain spotted them from the quarterdeck and shouted up to them, "Tom, what are you doing there?"

The sheepish seaman replied, "Nothing."

"And what are you doing, Jack?" the boatswain said to the second sailor.

"Helping him," was the reply.

## 872. Inefficient Labor

An older man was walking through a forest near his home when he came upon a man busily sawing a giant tree. He watched the man for a while and noticed that he was getting nowhere. He noticed also that the saw looked rusty. However, he decided this was none of his business and decided to continue on his errand to a nearby village.

On his return trip, the older man again passed the man still sawing away at the same tree, but with very little progress.

Pausing again to watch, he finally shouted, "Hello, sir, I notice you aren't getting anywhere. You need to stop and sharpen the saw."

The man looked up, sweat pouring from his cheeks, and yelled back, "Thank you, old-timer, but I AIN'T GOT TIME, AIN'T GOT TIME!"

Moral: sometimes we let ourselves get so busy we neglect the important things needed to get things done — like sharpening the saw.

## 873. Management by Walking around

The auto pioneer Henry Ford was once asked why he made a habit of visiting his executives when problems arose rather than inviting them to his own office.

"I go to them to save time," Ford explained, "and besides I've found I can leave their office a lot quicker than I can get them to leave mine."

## 874. Clock Watchers

Soon after he opened his first plant, the inventor Thomas Edison noticed that his employees spent a lot of their time watching the lone factory clock.

To Edison, who was an indefatigable worker, this was absolutely unacceptable. He said nothing to his employees. Instead he had dozens of clocks placed around the plant, no two of them keeping the same time.

From then on, clock watching led to so much confusion that nobody cared what time it was.

## 875. Productivity Growth

Carver A. Mead (1934- ), a noted microchip designer from the California Institute of Technology, said in a lecture in 1988, "The entire Industrial Revolution increased productivity by a factor of about 100. The micro-electronic revolution has already enhanced productivity by a factor of more than a million, and the end isn't in sight yet."

## 876. Motivation for Productivity

Will and Ariel Durant (1885-1981, 1898-1981), two American historians known worldwide for their writings, said "The experience of the past leaves little doubt that every economic system must sooner or later rely upon some form of the profit motive to stir individuals and groups to productivity. Substitutes like slavery, police supervision, or ideological enthusiasm prove too unproductive, too expensive, or too transient."

## 877. Peter Drucker on Productivity

Peter F. Drucker (1909-2005), Austrian-born American management consultant and author, wrote this about Frederick Winslow Taylor (1866-1915), who inspired Henry Ford's mass-production revolution: "Thanks to him, we have increased the productivity of manual work three percent to four percent compounded – which is 50-fold – and on that achievement rests all the prosperity of the modern world."

Note: In was in 1881 that Taylor first applied knowledge to the study of work, the analysis of work, and the engineering of work. This led to the productivity revolution to which Drucker was referring.

# PROFANITY

## 878. Campaign Profanity

When John F. Kennedy was campaigning for President against Richard Nixon in 1960, he poked some good-natured fun at Nixon for criticizing in their last debate political candidates who use profanity when they are on the stump.

"I know after fourteen years in the Congress with the Vice President Nixon), that he was very sincere in his views about the use of profanity," Kennedy said. "But I am told that a prominent Republican said to him yesterday in Jacksonville, Florida, 'Mr. Vice resident, that was a damn fine speech.' And the Vice President said, '"I appreciate the compliment but not the language.'

"And the Republican went on, 'Yes, sir, I liked it so much that I contributed a thousand dollars to your campaign.' And Mr. Nixon replied, 'The hell you say.'"

Note: Kennedy (1917-1963), the Thirty-fifth President of the United States made the above remarks at the Alfred Smith Memorial Dinner, Waldorf Astoria Hotel, New York City, 1960

## 879. Mark Twain and Profanity

Mark Twain's forceful and imaginative swearing bothered his wife, Livy, a lot and she tried religiously to cure him of the habit. One day the author and wit cut himself while shaving and recited with great fervor his entire litany of curses.

Livy, who was in the next room, was shocked and, when he was finished, repeated to him what he had said word for word.

"I wanted you to hear just how it sounded," she said reproachfully.

Mark Twain grimaced and said, "It would pain me to think that when I swear it sounds like that, Livy. However, you got the words right, but you just don't know the tune."

## 880. History of Profanity

H.L. Mencken (1880-1956), a salty talking American journalist and writer, wrote in defense of profanity, the following, "A large vocabulary of profanity is the inevitable possession of every cultured nation. It represents the accumulated ingenuity of countless talented and resourceful men, working in series for ages. Its extent and plasticity, indeed, are fair measures of the civilization of the race that claims it. The savage, for all his savagery, is utterly incapable of effective swearing.

## 881. A Harsh Letter

The following is the text of a letter received by President Abraham Lincoln (1809-1865) on November 25, 1860: "God damn your god damned old hellfired god damned soul to hell god damn you and goddam your god damned family's god damned hellfired god damned soul to hell and god damnation god damn them and god damn your god damn friends to hell."

# PRUDENCE

## 882. Don't Do Everything You Are Told

Sometimes we can react too quickly by instructions from authority figures. This story aptly illustrates that fact.

Two big turtles and a little turtle were crawling down the street when they decided to stop in at a local bar and have some sarsaparilla. They had just arrived inside and ordered their drinks when one of the big turtles glanced out the window.

"I think it's going to rain," said the first big turtle. "Someone will have to go back and get an umbrella." And with that, both of the big turtles looked straight at the little turtle.

"Oh no," said the little turtle. "I'm not going to go get an umbrella because then you will drink my sarsaparilla."

"No, we won't," said one of the big turtles. "Just go and get it."

Two weeks went by and one of the big turtles said, "I don't think that little guy is coming back," and the other turtle replied, "I don't think so either. Do you know what I was thinking?" "Yeah," said the other big turtle. "Let's drink his sarsaparilla."

Just then, a little voice came from the end of the bar. "If you do," said the little turtle, I won't go."

## 883. A Fable about Life's Decisions

There once was an old man who lived in a small village. He was the poorest man in the village, but he owned the most beautiful white stallion. And the king had offered him a small fortune for it.

After a terribly harsh winter, during which the old man and his family nearly starved, the townspeople came to visit.

"Old man," they said, "you can hardly afford to feed your family. Sell the stallion and you will be rich. If you do not, you are a fool."

"It's too early to tell," replied the old man. A few months later, the old man woke up to find that the white stallion had run away.

Once again the townspeople came, and they said to the old man, "See. If you had sold the king your horse, you would be rich. Now you have nothing! You are a fool!"

"It's too early to tell," replied the old man.

Two weeks later, the white stallion returned, and along with it came three other white stallions.

"Old man," the townspeople said, "We are the fools! Now you can sell the stallion to the king and you will still have three stallions left. You are smart."

"It's too early to tell," said the old man.

The following week, the old man's son, his only son, was breaking in one of the stallions and was thrown, crushing both his legs.

The townspeople paid a visit to the old man and they said, "Old man, if you had just sold the stallion to the king, you'd be rich, and your son would not be crippled. You are a fool."

"It is too early to tell," said the old man.

Well, the next month, war broke out with the neighboring village. All of the young men in the village were sent into the battle, and all were killed.

The townspeople came and they cried to the old man, "We have lost our sons. You are the only one who has not. If you had sold your stallion to the king, your son, too, would be dead. You are so smart!"

"It is too early to tell," said the old man.

Moral: The old man was smart. He was smart because he knew that life is a journey. He did not know where that journey was leading him. He only knew that that, if he listened to his heart, his inner voice, and not to the voices of others who may call him a fool, he would be making the right decisions for his journey.

# QUALITY

## 884. Definition of Quality

What is the source of quality that one finds, let us say, in a Puma Indian basket so tightly woven that it was used to hold boiling water and never leaked a drop? Or in an Eskimo skin boat with its matchless combination of lightness, strength and seaworthiness?

Throughout history it was the fact that producers and consumer were either one and the same individuals or close kin, guaranteeing the highest degree of reliability and durability in manufactured items.

A man was not likely to fashion a spear for himself where the point might fall off in mid-fight. Similarly, if one is sewing a parka for a husband who is about to go hunting for the family with the temperature at 60 below, all stitches will be perfect. And when the men who made boats are the uncles and fathers of those who sail them, they will be as seaworthy as the state of art permits.

In contrast, it is very hard for people to care about strangers or about products to be used by strangers. In our era of industrial mass products and mass marketing, quality is a constant concern because the personal bonds which once made us responsible to each other have withered.

Not only are the producers and consumers strangers, but the women and men involved in various stages of production and distribution can be strangers. And since each new employee contributes a diminishing share to the overall production process, distance from the products is likely to increase even more. How to solve the problem of consistent quality must be faced by all of us.

## 885. The Long View

The American Society for Quality Control has published a booklet called *The Hare and the Tortoise Revisited: The Businessman's Guide to Continuous Quality Improvement.* It was authored by John Ryan.

One story in it tells about a Japanese quality expert who stresses the need for patience and discipline. He likens the quality process to farming bamboo. Once the bamboo seed is planted, the farmer waters it every day. He does that for four years before the tree even breaks ground. But when it finally does, it grows 60 feet in the next 90 days.

It's that kind of commitment to the long view that marks the companies which have been most successful in achieving outstanding quality.

## 886. How Quality Was Born in Japan

A good place to start a history of Total Quality would be a sweltering July evening in 1950 at the Industry Club in downtown Tokyo. Gathered there was a group of 21 prominent Japanese business leaders who came together to listen to an outside expert, a man who had gained some visibility in Japan recently with a series of technical lectures on statistical process control.

His name was Dr. W. Edwards Deming (1990-1993). Over the past 30 years he had worked for Western Electric, at its legendary Hawthorne Plant in Chicago, as well as the Department of Agriculture and the Census Bureau, developing and applying statistical processes to help achieve quality control.

Deming had taught statistical techniques to thousands in American industry and government during the war, to considerable acclaim. But he had become increasingly appalled by what he came to see as American management's unwillingness to accept responsibility to permanently build statistical-based improvements into our technology and management. Instead, American managers were content to simply apply statistics to solve the problem of the moment, to fight today's fire.

Once the war was won, few in the U.S. were willing to listen to Deming. So at age 50, his philosophy (and career) were languishing. But when he came into that room in Tokyo in 1950, something magical began to happen. Because, while Deming talked, the 21 Japanese — representing a lot of wealth and power — actually listened.

What he told them was this: "You can produce quality. You have a method for doing it. You must carry out consumer research, look toward the future and produce goods that will have a market years from now. You have to do it to eat. You can send quality out and get food back.

The Japanese, he had already noted, were putting up with poor quality in incoming materials — off-gauge and off-color. "I urged them to work with the vendors and to work on instrumentation. A lot of what I urged them to do came very naturally to the Japanese, though they were not doing it. I said, "You don't need to receive the junk that comes in. You can never produce quality with that stuff. But with process controls that your engineers are learning about — consumer research, redesign of products — you can. Don't just make it and try to sell it. But redesign it and then again bring the process under control with ever-increasing quality.

On a blackboard he drew a flow chart that began with suppliers and ended with consumers, which is now a staple in his seminars. "The consumer is the most important part of the production line," he told them. This, he realized, "was a new thought to Japanese management." Until then they had sold their wares to a captive market.

He made two more trips to Japan in 1951. Two more in 1952. Now Japan was on its feet and beginning to walk.

## 887. Measures of Quality

The following statistics were compiled by the Communications Division of Insight, Syncrude Canada Ltd. If 99.9 PERCENT IS GOOD ENOUGH, then...

- Two million documents would be lost by the United States IRS this year.

- 811,000 faulty rolls of 35 millimeter film will be loaded this year.

- 22,000 checks will be deducted from the wrong bank accounts in the next 60 minutes.

- 1,314 phone calls will be misplaced by telecommunication services every minute.

- 12 newborns would be given to the wrong parents daily in the U.S.

- 268,500 defective tires will be shipped this year.

- 14,208 defective personal computers will be shipped this year.

- 103,260 income tax returns would be processed incorrectly this year.

- 2,488,200 books would be shipped in the next 12 months with the wrong covers.

- 5,517,200 cases of soft drinks produced in the next 12 months would be flatter than a bad tire.

- Two plane landings daily at O'Hare International Airport in Chicago would be unsafe.

- 3,056 copies of tomorrow's *Wall Street Journal* would be missing one of the three sections.

- 18,322 pieces of mail would be mishandled per hour.

- 291 pacemaker operations would be performed incorrectly this year.

- 880,000 credit cards in circulation would turn out to have incorrect cardholder information on their magnetic strips.

- $9,690 will be spent today, tomorrow, next Thursday, and every day in the future on defective, often unsafe sporting equipment.

- 55 malfunctioning automatic teller machines will be installed in the next 12 months.

- 20,000 incorrect drug prescriptions would be written in the next 12 months.

- 114,500 mismatched pairs of shoes would be shipped per year.

- $761,900 will be spent in the next 12 months on tapes and compact discs that won't play.

- 107 incorrect medical procedures will be performed by the end of the day today.

- 315 entries in *Webster's Third New International Dictionary of the English Language* would be misspelled.

## 888. Handiwork Quality

When weaving a blanket, a Native American woman leaves a flaw in the weaving of that blanket to let the soul out.

## 889. Scarcity of Quality

When Queen Victoria (1819-1901) once complained to William Gladstone (1809-1898), her prime minister, that there were not many good preachers, he is said to have replied, "Madam, there are not many good anythings."

## 890. Roman Quality Standards

In ancient Rome, when the scaffolding was removed from a completed Roman arch, the law read that the Roman engineer who built the arch had to stand beneath it.

The point was, if the arch came crashing down, he would experience the responsibility first hand. As a result, the Roman engineer knew that the quality of his work was crucial and would have a direct personal impact on his life.

# READING

## 891. Loneliness

When Benjamin Franklin was dining out in Paris during his diplomatic duties there, someone posed this question to the assembled dinner guests.

"What condition of man most deserves pity?"

After each guest had given their answer to the question, Franklin offered the following:

"A lonesome man on a rainy day who does not know how to read."

## 892. Love Letters

Mortimer J. Adler (1902 -2001), American philosopher and editor once said of reading, "There is only one situation I can think of in which men and women make an effort to read better than they usually do. When they are in love and reading a love letter, they read for all they are worth. They read every word three ways; they read between the lines and in the margins. They may even take the punctuation into account. Then, if never before or after, they read.

## 893. Purpose of Reading

Francis Bacon (1561-1626), English lawyer, philosopher and essayist, said of reading, "Read not to contradict and confute; nor to believe and take for granted; nor to find talk and discourse; but to weigh and consider.

"Some books are to be tasted, others to be swallowed, and some few to be chewed and digested; that is, some books are to be read only in parts, others to be read, but not curiously, and some few to be read wholly, and with diligence and attention.

"Some books also may be read by deputy, and extracts made of them by others; but that would be only in the less important arguments, and the meaner sort of books; else distilled books are like common distilled waters, flashy things.

"Reading makes a full man, conference a ready man, and writing an exact man."

## 894. The Koran

Rana Kabbani, Syrian cultural historian, said that reading the Koran "becomes prosaic in any tongue but its own...A Muslim reading the Koran in Arabic and a non-Muslim reading it in translation are simply not reading the same book."

## 895. Speed Reading

Woody Allen (Allen Stewart Konigsberg) (1935- ), American writer, film director and actor, said about reading, "I took a course in speed reading, learning to read straight down the middle of the page, and I was able to go through 'War and Peace,' in twenty minutes. It's about Russia."

# REFORM

## 896. Streamlining Government

When President Harry Truman (1884-1972) announced his intention to streamline the government by getting rid of what he felt were unnecessary government bureaus, a woman wrote to tell him she was building a new house and needed furniture. "Would you mind," she asked, "sending on a few of the discarded bureaus?"

Truman wrote back that he had disposed of the bureaus already but that, if she were interested, he had a "second-hand no-damned good cabinet I'd like to get rid of."

## 897. Reforms from Hoover

In the years after he left office, President Herbert Hoover (1874-1964) once proposed a set of reforms in American life that included these which are recorded in the Herbert Hoover Library and Museum.

• four strikes in baseball "so as to get more men on bases; the crowd only gets worked up when somebody is on second base;"

• an end to political ghostwriters;

• and the scheduling of all after-dinner speakers "before" dinner "so that the gnaw of hunger" would speed things up.

# RELIGION

## 898. Sermon Topic

President Calvin Coolidge (1872-1933) went to church alone one Sunday because his wife was unable to attend with him.

On his return, she asked him what the sermon was about.

"Sin," he replied.

"But what did he say about it?" asked Mrs. Coolidge.

"He was against it," replied Coolidge.

Note: the story is probably apocryphal. Mrs. Coolidge reportedly said this was just the sort of thing he would have said. Coolidge himself said it would be funnier if it were true.

## 899. A Mother's Advice

The comedian Carol Burnett (1933- ) was asked by Charles Osgood on his Sunday morning television program how she had been able to carry on so serenely after the many troubles she has endured during her life.

Carol credited her Arkansas grandmother with teaching her this priceless piece of wisdom, "Leave it lay where Jesus flung it."

## 900. Lincoln and the Heavens

An anecdote about Abraham Lincoln's sense of the universe, as told by Captain Gilbert J. Greene:

"As we walked on the country road out of Springfield, Lincoln turned his eyes to the heavens full of stars and told me their names and their distance from us and the swiftness of their motion.

"He said the ancients used to arrange them so as to make monsters, serpents, animals of one kind or another out of them."

"During the walk, Lincoln said, "I never behold them that I do not feel that I am looking in the face of God. I can see how it might be possible for a man to look down upon the earth and be an atheist, but I cannot conceive how he could look up into the heavens and say there is no God."

## 901. Biblical Expertise

Like most of the other pioneer movie moguls in Hollywood, studio head Harry Cohn (1891-1968) loved to gamble. Cards, horses, roulette. He would bet on anything!

Once he bet his brother Jack (1889-1956) $50 that Jack couldn't recite the Lord's Prayer.

Jack responded immediately saying, "Now I lay me down to sleep..."

"O.K., O.K.," interrupted Harry and gave him the money. "That's enough. I didn't realize you knew it."

## 902. Heaven and Hell

Mark Twain (Samuel Clemens) once attended a dinner party at which the subject of heaven and hell was raised. Throughout the heated discussion, Twain said nothing.

Finally, the hostess asked, "Why haven't you said something, Mr. Clemens? Surely you must have an opinion on this subject."

"Madam, you must excuse me," Mark Twain replied, "I am silent because of necessity. I have friends in both places."

## 903. The Importance of Love

There is an ancient story in the Talmud about a man who lived such a righteous life that the angels of the Lord gave him a choice no other man had ever been given.

On his death, the man was asked: "Would you like to go to Heaven or to Hell?"

The man paused and thought for a while, then asked, "Is there love in Hell?"

"Love in Hell? Of course not! It is Hell" was the answer.

"Then," said the man, "I shall go into Hell and take some love there."

## 904. Keeping Your Cool

Abraham Lincoln liked to tell this story about a traveling preacher who was visiting a frontier family. The preacher severely criticized the young couple for not being more religious, saying, "You don't even have a Bible in the house."

Angered, the frontier wife said they did so own a Bible and dispatched her children to find it in the other room. A few minutes later, the children returned holding up a few tattered pages.

The frontier mother, however, never lost her cool.

Looking the minister right in eye, she said calmly, "I had no idea that we were so near out."

## 905. Vigorous Old Age

The famous clergyman John Wesley (1703-1791) traveled 250,000 miles on horseback, averaging 20 miles a day for 40 years, preached 4,000 sermons, produced 400 books, and knew ten languages.

At 83, he was annoyed that he could not write more than 15 hours a day without hurting his eyes, and at 86, he was ashamed he could not preach more than twice a day.

He complained in his diary that there was an increasing tendency to lie in bed until 5:30 in the morning.

## 906. War and Religion

Abraham Lincoln, during the darkest hours of the Civil War, in response to the question whether he was sure God was "on our side", replied:

"I do not know: I have not thought about that. But I am very anxious to know whether we are on God's side."

## 907. Twain's Religion

The famous author Mark Twain (Samuel Clemens) was not the atheist he was sometimes accused of being. He believed there was a God, but not the God of orthodox religious tradition. In his private notebook in 1898, Twain wrote:

"The Being who to me is the real God is the One who created this majestic universe and rules it. He is the only originator, the only originator of thoughts; thoughts suggested from within, not from without...He is the only creator. He is the perfect artisan, the perfect artist."

Mark Twain's belief was that to know God was to know Nature. He believed the ways of God were the ways of Nature and that they can be observed in the natural world. In the introduction to "Letters From the Earth," he affirmed his doctrine that divine law is natural law:

"Natural Law is the LAW OF GOD — interchangeable names for one and the same thing."

## 908. A Village Rabbi

Once there was a small Jewish village in Europe whose rabbi vanished early every Friday for several hours. The village elders said that during these hours their beloved rabbi ascended to Heaven to talk with God. But a skeptical newcomer came to town and decided to find out just where the rabbi really went on those Friday mornings.

So before dawn one Friday morning, the newcomer hid near the rabbi's house. Undetected, he watched the rabbi rise, say his prayers, and put on clothes of a working man.

Following at a safe distance, the newcomer watched the rabbi take an ax and go into a nearby forest where he chopped a large bundle of firewood. He gathered the wood into a large bundle and carried it to a hovel in the poorest section of the village where an old woman lived. There, the rabbi left the wood and quietly returned to his own house, unseen by anyone else in the village.

The story goes that the skeptical newcomer stayed on in the village and became a disciple of the rabbi. And whenever he would hear one of his neighbors say that "On Friday mornings our rabbi ascends all the way to Heaven," the newcomer would quietly add, "If not higher."

## 909. The Collection Plate

Mark Twain (Samuel Clemens), the author and humorist, was attending a meeting at which a missionary had been invited to speak. Twain was deeply impressed. Later he gave this account:

"The preacher's voice was beautiful. He told us about the sufferings of the natives, and he pleaded for help with such moving simplicity that I mentally doubled the 50 cents I had intended to put in the collection plate.

"He described the pitiful misery of those savages so vividly that the dollar I had in mind gradually rose to five.

"Then that preacher continued, and I felt that all the cash I carried on me would be insufficient. I decided to write a large check.

"But he kept right on. He went on and on and on about the dreadful state of those natives, and I abandoned the idea of the check.

"Still he continued. And in my mind I got back to five dollars. When he didn't stop, I revised my contribution to four dollars, then two and then, one.

"Still he went on. When the collection plate finally came around, I took 10 cents out of it."

## 910. Shortest Sermon on Record

President Ronald Reagan (1911-2004) liked to tell this story about the best sermon he had ever heard.

As a boy in Dixon, Illinois, Reagan said he once attended church on the hottest day of the year. "You could have fried eggs on the steps of the town's Civil War Memorial," he said, "and the humidity was so high the air was like soup."

When it came time for his sermon, the preacher mounted the steps to the pulpit and, wiping his forehead with a big handkerchief, faced the congregation.

Pointing his finger downward, the minister said, "It's hotter down there." With that he descended from the pulpit.

"That was the end of his sermon," said Reagan.

## 911. Lincoln's Religion

A friend once asked Abraham Lincoln to describe his religion.

Lincoln said his religion was like that of an old man he had once heard speak at a church meeting in Indiana.

The old man said, "When I do good, I feel good; and when I do bad, I feel bad."

"That," said Lincoln, "is my religion."

## 912. The Bible Is Hopeful

There once was an old man who had many troubles. Life seemed to hand him one thing after another, but he faced each obstacle with a smile and a cheery disposition.

An acquaintance of the man's finally asked him how he managed to stay so happy despite his hardships.

The old man quickly answered: "Well, the Bible often says, 'And it came to pass,' but never once does it say, 'It came to stay.'"

## 913. Biblical Scholar

W.C. Fields (1880-1946), the famous comedian, juggler, and we might add, prodigious consumer of alcoholic spirits, was visited by a friend while Fields was in the hospital.

When the friend entered Fields' room, he was startled to see the comedian deeply engrossed in reading the Bible.

Knowing that Fields was a lifelong agnostic who did not believe in religion, the friend asked Fields what he was doing.

"Looking for loopholes," replied Fields.

## 914. Lincoln's Ghost-Writer

John Wycliffe (1320-1384), Professor of Divinity at Oxford University, was banished by Oxford because he had authored a masterful translation of the Old and New Testament from Latin into an English vernacular version of the Bible.

Wycliffe, who was a major force behind Protestant Reformation, was driven into virtual exile by a hypocritical alliance of church and state authorities who wanted to discredit his Biblical version.

In defiance, Wycliffe wrote in the flyleaf of his Bible, "This Bible is translated and shall make possible a government of the people, by the people, and for the people."

Five hundred years later, President Abraham Lincoln used the same words in his famous Gettysburg Address, in which he dedicated a blood-drenched battlefield of America's Civil War.

## 915. FDR's Favorite Joke

A young man brought the latest addition to their Episcopal church's staff in to meet his father, a staunch, slightly deaf, and dyed-in-the-wool Republican.

"Father," the boy said, "I want you to meet our new deacon."

"New Dealer?" snarled the old man.

"New deacon," repeated the young man, "he's the son of a bishop."

"Ha!" sneered the old man, "They all are!"

### 916. Prayer

Sydney Smith (1771-1845) was a well-known humorist in his day and his quotations still are sprinkled through thousands of quotation books.

Sydney always prayed aloud and a friend said he once overheard Smith say during his prayer, "Now Lord, I'll tell you an anecdote."

### 917. The Important Things

There is an old Jewish legend about the origin of praise.

After God created mankind, says the legend, He asked the angels what they thought of the world He had made.

"Only one thing is lacking," they said. "It is the sound of praise to the Creator."

So, the story continues, "God created music, the voice of birds, the whispering wind, the murmuring ocean, and planted melody in the hearts of men."

# RENEWAL

### 918. Legend of the Phoenix

Most of us have heard the myth of the Phoenix — an Egyptian bird of great beauty that was found in the Arabian Desert. There was only one and it lived for hundreds of years. When it sensed that it was about to die, it built its own funeral pyre, lighted it by fanning its wings, then flew into the fire and arose young again from the ashes.

The Phoenix came to be associated with the sun god who disappeared as an old man each night and appeared as a child the following morning. For centuries the Phoenix has become a symbol of rebirth and renewal.

### 919. Idea for Business

Dr. Dwayne Orton (1903-1971),
Editor, IBM's *Think Magazine*, one wrote:

Every business organization should have a vice-president in charge of constant renewal.

### 920. Business in a Rut

John W. Gardner (1912-2002) American educator and government official, said in his book about renewal, "Most human organizations that fall short of their goals do so, not because of stupidity or faulty doctrines, but because of internal decay and rigidification. They grow stiff in the joints. They get in a rut. They go to seed."

### 921. Searching for Excellence

Robert H. Waterman, Jr., American management consultant and author, in one of his many books on management wrote, "The highest expression of management art is the manager's ability to renew a department, a division, a company, himself. Without renewal there can be no excellence."

### 922. Your Ideas

Frank Gelett Burgess (1866-1951), American designer and author, once said, "If in the last few years you haven't discarded a major opinion or acquired a new one, check your pulse. You may be dead."

# RESPECT

### 923. Volunteers Are Nice People

Norman Augustine (1935- ), when he was chairman of Lockheed Martin, liked to tell this story about an incident that happened when he was Under Secretary of the Army.

While visiting the 82nd Airborne Division, Augustine was introduced to a grizzled old sergeant who had over 1,000 parachute jumps on his record.

I said, "You sure must like to jump."

To which he replied, "No, I hate to jump."

When I asked why he was in an all-volunteer Army in an all-volunteer parachute unit if he hated to jump, he answered, "Because I like to be around the kind of people who do."

## 924. What Makes a Lady

In George Bernard Shaw's famous play, *Pygmalion*, the serving girl, "Eliza Doolittle," spoke this way to a visitor to the house, a Mr. Pickering, about the British class system. "You see, really and truly, apart from the things anyone can pick up (the dressing and the proper way of speaking, and so on) the difference between a lady and a flower girl is not how she behaves but how she's treated. I shall always be a flower girl to Professor Higgins, and always will; but I know I can be a lady to you, because you always treat me as a lady, and always will."

## 925. Characteristics that Earn Respect

Robert Louis Stevenson (1850-1894), Scottish essayist, novelist and poet, described in this way the personal characteristics that bring respect from others, "That man is a success who has lived well, laughed often and loved much; who has gained the respect of intelligent men and the love of children; who has filled his niche and accomplished his task; who leaves the world better than he found it, whether by an improved poppy, a perfect poem or a rescued soul; who never lacked appreciation of earth's beauty or failed to express it; who looked for the best in others and gave the best he had."

## 926. Respect for American Arts

An inscription on the John F. Kennedy Center for the Performing Arts in Washington D.C., drawn from a speech made by President Kennedy (1917-1963), reads as follows: "I look forward to an America which will reward achievement in the arts as we reward achievement in business or statecraft. I look forward to an America which will steadily raise the standards of artistic accomplishment and which will steadily enlarge cultural opportunities for all of our citizens. And I look forward to an America which commands respect throughout the world not only for its strength but for its Civilization as well."

### 927. Respect in Business

The following is by an unknown Author:

- A customer is the most important person in any business.

- A customer is not dependent on us. We are dependent on him.

- A customer is not an interruption of our work. He is the purpose of it.

- A customer does us a favor when he comes in. We aren't doing him a favor by waiting on him.

- A customer is part of our business, not an outsider.

- A customer is not just money in the cash register. He is a human being with feelings and deserves to be treated with respect.

- A customer is a person who comes to us with his needs, and his wants. It is our job to fill them.

- A customer deserves the most courteous attention we can give him.

- He is the lifeblood of this and every business.

- He pays our salary.

- Without the customer, we would have to close up.

- Don't ever forget it

# RESPONSIBILITY

### 928. Truman's Daily Walk

Harry Truman's (1884-1972) biographer, David McCullough, tells this charming story about the ex-president.

After Truman's retirement to the family home in Independence, Missouri, he continued his lifelong habit of taking a vigorous, long walk before breakfast. Frequently, he was accompanied by a Presbyterian minister who lived next door.

The minister told McCullough that the two always walked by a giant ginko tree around the corner and that Truman used to talk to the tree as he passed by.

"What did he say to the tree?" asked McCullough.

"You're doing a good job." reported the minister.

## 929. When the Wind Blows

Once upon a time there was a farmer who was desperate to find a reliable hired man.

While interviewing an applicant for the job, the farmer asked what skill he was proudest of.

"I can sleep when the wind blows," the man answered.

The farmer thought this was a strange answer but he needed someone right away so the man got the job.

A few nights later a storm came up, filled with lightning, rain, wind and hailstones the size of big marbles. Alarmed, the farmer jumped out of bed and ran to the barn to see if everything was all right.

Sure enough, the barn was locked tightly, all the farm implements had been carefully put away, the animals inside were calm, and everything had been secured against the onslaught.

Then the farmer checked on the little bunkhouse near the barn. Inside he found the hired man fast asleep while the wind and lightning roared around him.

The farmer then realized what the man had meant when he said, "I can sleep when the wind blows." The hired man was able to sleep because he had done all his work properly and had prepared his area of responsibility for every eventuality.

## 930. Passing Blame Around

This is a old story about four characters named Everyone, Anyone, Someone, and No One.

There was a big job to do and Everyone was responsible for doing it. But Everyone concluded that, since Someone was bound to do it (he always did), he needn't bother to do it. Of course, Anyone could have done the job, but as it turned out, No One did.

This made Someone very angry because it had been made clear that it was Everyone's responsibility, not just Anyone's. However, No One had envisioned that Everyone would neglect to do the assignment.

When an explanation was asked for, Everyone pointed a finger at Someone only to be told that No One had managed to do what Anyone could have done.

# RETIREMENT

## 931. Being out of Power

After President Giscard d'Estaing (1926- ) of France left office, he was asked by a news reporter how it felt to be out of power. He responded:

"How does it feel? About the same way you feel when you write a story that doesn't get in the paper."

## 932. Advice to the Young

Stephen Leacock (1869-1944), Canadian economist and humorist had this to say about retirement, "But as to this retirement business, let me give a word of advice to all of you young fellows around fifty.

"Some of you have been talking of it and even looking forward to it. Have nothing to do with it. Listen, it's like this. Have you ever been out for a late autumn talk in the closing part of the afternoon, and suddenly looked up to realize that the leaves have practically all gone? You hadn't realized it. And you notice that the sun has set already, the day gone before you knew it – and with that a cold wind blows across the landscape? That's retirement."

## 933. Reagan on Retirement

Ronald W. Reagan (1911-2004), the fortieth President of the United States, once said, "Two weeks ago I went into retirement. Am I glad that's over! It took all the fun out of Saturdays."

## 934. Justice Holmes on Retirement

Oliver Wendell Holmes, Jr. (1841-1935), a distinguished Justice of the U.S. Supreme Court, said in a radio broadcast celebrating his 90th birthday (March 8, 1931):

"The riders in a race do not stop short when they reach the goal. There is a little finishing canter before coming to a standstill. There is time to hear the kind voice of friends and to say to one's self: 'The work is done.' But just as one says that, the answer comes: 'The race is over, but the work never is done while the power to work remains.' The canter that brings you to a standstill need not be only coming to rest. It cannot be, while you still live. For to live is to function. That is all there is to living."

## 935. Money in Retirement

Jackie Mason (1934- ), an irrepressible stand-up comedian most popular in New York, said of retirement, "I have enough money to last me the rest of my life, unless I buy something."

## 936. Idleness in Later Life

Blaise Pascal (1623-1662), French mathematician, physicist and man of letters, said of retirement, "Nothing is so intolerable to man as being full at rest, without a passion, without business, without entertainment, without care. It is then that he recognizes that he is empty, insufficient, dependent, ineffectual."

# SCAM

### 937. Beware of Big Promises

Damon Runyon (1884-1946) was a New York City newspaperman who also wrote charming short stories about Broadway gamblers and various types of con men. The musical "Guys and Dolls" was based on one of his stories. One of Runyon's characters in the musical had this advice on avoiding pitfalls among the sporting fraternity:

"One of these days in your travels, a guy is going to come up to you and show you a nice brand new deck of cards on which the seal is not yet broken. And this guy is going to offer to bet you that he can make the jack of spades jump out of the deck and squirt cider in your ear. But, son, do not bet this man, for as sure as you stand there, you are going to get an earful of cider."

### 938. Potemkin Villages

What were Potemkin Villages and why have they become synonyms for sham and pretense. The story is a fascinating one.

Grigory Aleksandrovich Potemkin (1739-1791) was a courtier in the court of Russian Empress Catherine the Great (1729-1796). An ambitious cavalry officer, Potemkin contrived to make Catherine's acquaintance during the coup that brought her to power. During the Russo-Turkish War of 1768-74, Potemkin distinguished himself by his valor, and he became Catherine's lover in 1774.

Catherine appointed him to a series of important posts, eventually making him governor-general of the southern Ukraine and Crimea. To show off his accomplishment to Catherine during a tour she was making of the Ukraine and Crimea, Potemkin did everything he could to make the villages look as prosperous as possible.

Before her arrival, orders went out to hide beggars, to paint facades, and perhaps even erect occasional false fronts to conceal hovels of the poor. Thus has come down to us the term "Potemkin Village" as a synonym of falseness, a phony "stage set" of prosperity to cover decrepit reality.

### 939. Phony Offers

In a song titled "Ocean Front Property," Hank Cochran, Royce Porter and Dean Dillon had this to say:

"I got some ocean front property in Arizona.
From my front porch you can see the sea.
I got some ocean front property in Arizona.
If you'll buy that, I'll throw the Golden Gate in free."

### 940. Scamming

One of America's greatest showmen, P.T. Barnum (1810-1891), who was a hokum artist extraordinaire, once observed, "You can fool most of the people most of the time."

### 941. Twain on Scamming

Mark Twain (Samuel Clemens) (1835-1910) once said about being taken in by false claims, "By and by you sober down, and then you perceive that you have been drunk on the smell of somebody else's cork."

# SCIENCE

### 942. Scientific Illiteracy

More than 30 years ago, C.P. Snow (1905-1972), the English scientist and novelist, was appalled at the lack of technological understanding on the part of much of the public. He would occasionally ask an individual if they could describe the Second Law of Thermodynamics.

He almost always got a negative response. "Yet," said Snow, "that is about the scientific equivalent of 'Have you read a work of Shakespeare's?'"

Not too many years ago, only five of 435 members of the U.S. House of Representatives held engineering degrees. There were none in the Senate and none in the Cabinet. Of the 50 governors, only three held engineering degrees. These figures don't change much from election to election.

The danger to all when those to whom we entrust our well being do not understand even the rudimentary technological aspects of critical issues was eloquently noted by the late Isaac Asimov, a famous science writer, who wrote:

"Increasingly, our leaders must deal with dangers that threaten the entire world, where an understanding of those dangers and the possible solutions depends on a good grasp of science. The ozone layer, the greenhouse effect, acid rain, questions of diet and heredity. All require scientific literacy. Can Americans choose the proper leaders and support the proper programs if they themselves are scientifically illiterate?

"In order to survive in the technologically driven twenty-first century it will not suffice merely for engineers to be exposed to the liberal arts — although that will be necessary. There will be an equally compelling need for our universities to offer physics for poets. It is one thing to be unable to program one's DVD player or Tivo; it is quite another to sit in the United States Senate and have not an inkling of what causes the greenhouse effect, what are the implications of genetic engineering, or what is the consequence of losing a leadership position in the manufacture of dynamic random access memory devices."

## 943. Einstein in Heaven

Albert Einstein (1879-1955), generally acknowledged as one of the greatest scientists who ever lived, was a modest man but he was also very certain about his scientific conclusions.

When Einstein died and went to Heaven, God gave him an immediate audience and said to him, "I presume there is much in the world of physics that puzzled you during your lifetime."

Einstein nodded in agreement.

"You will be glad to know," continued God, "that you now have the opportunity of understanding everything, including the unified theory that you never completed." With this, God handed Einstein a thick sheaf of papers filled with numbers.

Einstein gladly accepted the papers and looked through them rapidly. Then with a sigh he handed them back to God, saying, "No, still wrong."

## 944. Power of Mathematics

Often you hear or read that something is growing at an exponential rate.

To appreciate what that means, consider the story of a rancher who brought his horse to be shod and asked what it would cost.

The blacksmith said he would charge a penny for the first nail, 2 cents for the second, 4 cents for the third, and so on.

The rancher, innocent of mathematics, agreed. For eight nails in each shoe, or 32 nails altogether, his bill came to $42,949,642.95.

An exponential rate of growth is an awesome thing.

## 945. Value of a Ph.D.

One of America's most famous physicists was Robert A. Millikan (1868-1953). His wife was walking down the hall of their home when she heard their cleaning woman talking to someone on the telephone.

"Yes," said the cleaning woman, "this is where Dr. Millikan lives, but he's not the kind of doctor that does anybody any good."

## 946. A Scientific Credo

At a reception in Albert Einstein's (1879-1955) honor at Princeton, when asked to comment on some dubious experiments that conflicted with both relativistic and prerelativistic concepts, he responded with a famous remark — a scientific credo that was overheard by an American professor Oswald Veblen (1880-1980), who must have jotted it down.

Years later, in 1930, when Princeton University constructed a special building for mathematics, Veblen requested and received Einstein's permission to have the remark inscribed in marble above the fireplace of the faculty lounge. It was engraved there in the original German:

"Raffiniert ist der Herrgott, aber boshaft ist er nicht," which may be translated: "God is subtle, but he is not malicious."

In his reply to Veblen, Einstein explained that he meant that Nature conceals her secrets by her sublimity and not by trickery.

## 947. A Lesson from Scientific History

Take this lesson from history: In 1589 Galileo (1564-1642) summoned a collection of the world's most learned professors to the Leaning Tower of Pisa for a demonstration that would disprove a 2,000-year-old physics principle of Aristotle's — that the heavier an object is, the faster it will fall to earth.

From the top of the tower, Galileo simultaneously dropped a ten-pound and a one-pound weight, which both landed at the same time. The result? Conventional wisdom was so powerful and change so threatening that the professors all denied the truth as seen by their own eyes.

Moral: At times you may have to preach truth to people who refuse to believe it, even after seeing it with their own eyes.

## 948. Scientists in the Military

During the First World War a representative of the American Chemical Society called on the Secretary of War and offered the services of the nation's chemists.

The Secretary thanked him and asked him to return the next day for an answer. When he did, the Secretary of War expressed appreciation for the offer but said it was unnecessary.

"I have looked into the matter," said the Secretary, "and find that the War Department already has a scientist."

## 949. Research Facilities

Before they emigrated to the U.S., the famous scientist Albert Einstein (1879-1955) and his wife had endured severe economic hardships in Germany between the two world wars. Mrs. Einstein saved old letters and other scraps of paper for Albert to write on and to continue his work.

Years later, Mrs. Einstein was pressed into a public relations tour of an impressive scientific research center in the U.S. Dutifully, she plodded through lab after lab filled with gleaming new scientific equipment. Though they were trying to be polite, the American scientists who were her guides frequently explained things in that peculiarly condescending way we all treat non-native speakers of our own language.

Finally, Mrs. Einstein was ushered into a high-chambered observatory and came face to face with still another huge scientific contraption.

"What's this one for?" she asked.

"Mrs. Einstein," said her host with an important tone in his voice, "we use this equipment to probe the deepest secrets of the universe."

"Is THAT all!" she replied. "My husband did that on the back of old envelopes!"

## 950. Calculating Risk

Isidor Rabi (1898-1988), a professor at Columbia, was asked to visit the great Enrico Fermi (1901-1954) to ask his opinion of whether a chain reaction could result from the fission of uranium.

Fermi's reply was that it was a "remote" possibility.

"What do you mean by remote?" Rabi asked.

"Well," Fermi replied, "ten percent."

Then Rabi quietly uttered the reply that those in the room remembered for years after. He said, "Ten percent is not a remote possibility...if we may die of it."

# SELF-CONFIDENCE

## 951. Self-Worth

A well-known speaker started off his seminar by holding up a $20 bill. In a room of 200 people, he asked "Who would like this $20 bill?"

Hands immediately went up. He said, "I am going to give this $20 bill to one of you, but first let me do this." He proceeded to crumple the bill into a tight wad of paper.

He then asked, "Who still wants it?" Still the hands remained in the air.

"Well," he replied, "what if I do this?"

And he dropped it on the ground and ground it into the floor with his shoe, so now the bill was not only crumpled, but also dirty.

"Now who still wants it?" Still the hands remained in the air.

"My friends, you have all learned a very valuable lesson. No matter what I did to the money, you still wanted it because it did not decrease in value. It was still worth $20. Many times in our lives, we are dropped, crumpled, and ground into the dirt by the decisions we make and the circumstances that come our way.

"We feel as though we are worthless. But no matter what has happened or what will happen, you will never lose your value in the eyes of those who love you.

"You are each special and don't ever forget it."

## 952. Nelson Mandela on Self-Confidence

Nelson Mandela (1918- ), South African political activist, who helped free his country from apartheid after being imprisoned by the government for many years, said of confidence in self the following:

"We ask ourselves, who am I to be brilliant, gorgeous, talented, and fabulous? Actually, who are you not to be? You are a child of God. You playing small doesn't serve the world. There is nothing enlightened about shrinking so that other people won't feel insecure around you.

"We are born to make manifest the Glory of God that is within us. It's not just in some of us, it's in everyone, and as we let our own light shine, we consciously give other people permission to do the same. As we are liberated from our own fear, our presence automatically liberates others."

## 953. Michael Jordan's Confidence

Michael Jordan (1963 - ) is arguably the best basketball player who ever took part in the sport. He led the Chicago Bulls to several championships in the National Basketball Association. He once said, "Once I get the ball, you're at my mercy. There's nothing you can say or do about it. I own the ball. I own the game. I own the guy guarding me. I can actually play him like a puppet."

## 954. Emerson on Confidence

Ralph Waldo Emerson (1803-1882), American poet, essayist and philosopher, in his essay on "Self Reliance," said, "A man should learn to detect and watch that gleam of light which flashes across his mind from within, more than the luster of the firmament of bards and sages. Yet he dismisses without notice his thought, because it is his. In every work of genius we recognize our own rejected thoughts; they come back to us with a certain alienated majesty."

## 955. Walt Disney's Trust in Himself

Walt Disney (1901-1966), the famed creator of animated films and entertainment theme parks, said of his own talents, "I think it's important to have a good hard failure when you're young. I learned a lot out of that. Because it makes you kind of aware of what can happen to you. Because of it I've never had any fear in my whole life when we've been near collapse and all of that. I've never been afraid. I've never had the feeling I couldn't walk out and get a job doing something."

## 956. General MacArthur's View of Confidence

General Douglas MacArthur (1880-1964) was a prominent military leader during both World Wars I and II. About self-confidence, he said, "You are as young as your faith, as old as your doubts; as young as your self-confidence, as old as your fear; as young as your hope, as old as your despair."

## 957. Dangers to Self-Confidence

Eric Hoffer (1902-1983), a San Francisco longshoreman who earned national recognition for his philosophical writings, said, "Man staggers through life yapped at by his reason, pulled and shoved by his appetites, whispered to by fears, beckoned by hopes, small wonder that what he craves most is self-forgetting."

## 958. Great People Have It

Yousuf Karsh (1908-2002), a Canadian photographer who earned world-wide recognition for his portraits of famous people, said, "I have found that great people do have in common...an immense belief in themselves and in their mission. They also have great determination as well as an ability to work hard. At the crucial moment of decision, they draw on their accumulated wisdom. Above all, they have integrity."

# SELFISHNESS

## 959. A Selfish Collector

Luigi Tarisio, an Italian collector of violins, failed to learn that important lesson. One morning in 1855, he was found dead in his rundown farmhouse that contained almost no creature comforts. Yet a search of the house following his death discovered an attic crammed with 246 exquisite violins. The best of them were located in the bottom drawer of an old rundown chest.

Tarisio's blind devotion to the violin and his personal selfishness concerning his collection, had robbed the world of all the music these instruments might have given other music lovers. Other collectors before him apparently had done the same with some of the instruments in his collection. When the greatest of his collection, a priceless Stradivarius, was played, it was determined that it had not been used in 147 years.

## 960. Lincoln on Selfishness

On hearing children crying in the street, one of Abraham Lincoln's neighbors in Springfield, Illinois, rushed out of his house to investigate. There he found Lincoln with two of his sons, both of whom were sobbing uncontrollably.

"Whatever is the matter with the boys, Mr. Lincoln?" he asked.

"Just what's the matter with the whole world," replied Lincoln. "I've got three walnuts, and each wants two."

## 961. Dog in the Manger

This ancient Aesop fable demonstrates selfishness as well as anything else.

A dog was lying in a manger full of hay. An ox, being hungry, came near, and offered to eat of the hay.

But the envious, ill-natured dog, getting up and snarling at him, would not let the ox touch it.

At this, the ox said, in the bitterness of his heart, "A curse light on thee, for a malicious wretch, who will neither eat hay himself, nor suffer others to do it."

## 962. True Selfishness

George Bernard Shaw (1850-1950), Irish-born British playwright and critic, said this about selfishness, "The true artist will let his wife starve, his children go barefoot, his mother drudge for his living at seventy, sooner than work at anything but his art."

# SEX

### 963. Job Application

The American author Sinclair Lewis (1885-1951) once received a letter from a very young and very pretty woman who wished to become his secretary.

She said she could type, file, and anything else, and concluded, "When I say anything, I mean anything."

Lewis turned the letter over to his wife, Dorothy Thompson (1894-1961), who wrote to the young woman saying, "Mr. Lewis already has an excellent secretary who can type and file. I do everything else, and when I say everything, I mean everything."

### 964. Shaw on Sex

The famous Irish author George Bernard Shaw (1856-1950) was attending a dinner party when he was unexpectedly called upon to deliver an after-dinner toast on the subject of sex. This was at the turn of the century and sex was considered quite a scandalous word.

Shaw stood up, raised his glass, and addressed the guests by saying: "It gives me great pleasure..." and sat down.

### 965. Generation Gap

Harry Hershfield (1885-1974), the comic artist and humor writer, used to telephone birthday greetings every year to the eminent financier Bernard Baruch (1870-1965) no matter where he was in the world.

On Baruch's 95th birthday, Hershfield put through the call as usual, and, during their conversation, queried Baruch as follows: "Bernie, do you think there's as much love in the world today as there was years back?"

"Yes," was the old man's reply, "but there's another bunch doing it."

## 966. Be Careful What You Read

The comedian Phyllis Diller (1917- ) was traveling in Australia when she was injured in an auto accident. At the hospital, she was encased in a body cast covering the entire upper part of her body.

The following week, she had to play an engagement at Las Vegas and she searched for a story to explain her appearance. Finally, the solution came to her.

When she walked on stage, she announced to the shocked audience, "Ladies and Gentlemen, I would like to explain this body cast, and also make a public announcement. If there is anyone in the audience who has just bought the book *The Joy of Sex*, there is a misprint on page 182."

## 967. Vicarious Reading

Edward Bernays (1891-1995), often called the "Father of Public Relations", lived to be 104 years old.

Late in his life, a visitor asked him why he was still reading *Playboy Magazine*.

Bernays replied, "For the same reason I read *National Geographic*. I want to see places I know I am never going to visit."

## 968. Job Resume

One of Great Britain's most famous actresses was Mrs. Patrick Campbell (1865-1940), who created the role of Eliza Doolittle in George Bernard Shaw's (1856-1950) *Pygmalion*.

Mrs. Campbell went to Hollywood in the early 1930s to pursue a film career and a studio functionary handed her the customary publicity form to fill out.

As the form requested, she filled in her name, the color of her hair and eyes, her height, her interests, etc.

In the blank headed "Experience," she wrote in, *Edward VII*.

## 969. Washington Apology

This was some time ago, and things do change, but still...

Senator Margaret Chase Smith (1897-1995) of Maine was a guest speaker at a meeting of the Women's Press Club in Washington.

Among other things, she was asked what she would do if she woke up one morning and found herself in the White House. "The first thing I'd do is go straight to the President's wife and apologize," she replied.

Senator Smith did become the first woman ever nominated for President at a major political party convention — the Republican convention in 1964.

## 970. Sex Appeal

A highly desirable young lady was taken out to dinner, first by William Gladstone (1809-1898), the famous British Labour politician, and, the following evening, by the dashing Conservative politician Benjamin Disraeli (1804-1881).

Later, a friend asked her what impressions the two political rivals had made upon her.

"When I left the dining room after sitting next to Mr. Gladstone, I thought he was the cleverest man in England," she replied.

"But after sitting next to Mr. Disraeli, I thought I was the cleverest woman in England."

## 971. Women's View of Men

Mrs. Patrick Campbell (1865-1940) was a British actress famed both for her beauty and for her sharp tongue.

At dinner once evening, a pompous man asked her, "Why do you suppose it is that women so utterly lack a sense of humor?"

"God did it on purpose," Mrs. Campbell answered with fire in her eye, "so that we may love you men instead of laughing at you."

# SLEEP

## 972. Insomnia

President Calvin Coolidge (1872-1933) kept a copy of Milton's *Paradise Lost* by his bedside. Reading a few pages every night helped him to go to sleep.

Charles Dickens (1812-1870), like many Victorians, kept the head of his bed lined up precisely with the North Pole. By doing this, he believed that the earth's magnetic field would pass longitudinally through his body, and ensure him a good night's sleep. Some Islamic believers point their beds toward Mecca, using a similar logic.

One of America's richest men, Cornelius Vanderbilt (1794-1877), was an insomniac and also a believer in the occult. He could not fall asleep unless the four legs of his bed were planted in dishes filled with salt. He believed this kept malevolent spirits from attacking him.

## 973. About Sleep

Miguel de Cervantes (1547-1616), Spanish novelist, playwright and poet, described sleep in this way, "Blessings on him who invented sleep, the mantle that covers all human thoughts, the food that satisfies hunger, the drink that slakes thirst, the fire that warms cold, the cold that moderates heat, and, lastly the common currency that buys all things, the balance and weight that equalizes the shepherd and the king, the simpleton and the sage."

## 974. Sleep as Medicine

John W. Gardner (1912-2002), American educator and government official, once said, "The greatest psychotherapeutic medicine we know anything about is sleep. When your prevailing mood becomes one of anxiety or fear or hostility or misery, take the medicine! Sleep!"

### 975. Time in Bed

Philip Doddridge (1702-1751), an English pastor and religious thinker, once calculated how much of our lives we spend in bed. His calculations went like this, "The difference between rising at five and seven o'clock in the morning for forty years, supposing a man to go to bed at the same hour at night, is nearly equivalent to the addition of ten years to a man's life."

# SMALL TOWNS

### 976. You Live In a Small Town If...

- A small town is where, if you get the wrong phone number, you can talk for 15 minutes anyway.

- In the class play, there's a part for everybody.

- The City Council meets at the coffee shop.

- You decide to walk somewhere for exercise and five people pull over and ask if you need a ride.

- You were nine years old before you found out your town was not named "Resume Speed."

- The local telephone book has one yellow page.

- The big Saturday night activity is to go down to the filling station, stomp on the hose, and listen to the bell ring.

- Second Street is on the edge of town.

- You drive into the ditch five miles out of town and the word gets back before you do.

- You don't use your turn signal because everyone knows where you are going anyway.

- Directions are given by using the grain elevator as a reference.

- Anyone you want can be found at either the Dairy Queen or the store.

- You once used the "f" word and your parents knew within the hour.

- Everyone in small towns knows what everybody else is doing, but they read the weekly newspaper to see who got caught at it.

- The town jail is usually empty.

- The small town policeman has a first name and you call him by it.

- You miss a Sunday at church and receive get-well cards.

- The townspeople will sympathize with you in trouble and, if you don't have any, they will hunt some up for you.

- The town is so small the post office puts up wanted posters of all the people who have books overdue at the library.

- People walk around a dog enjoying a nap on the downtown sidewalk.

## 977. A Place to Start

"What is this place known for?" asked a traveler stopping in a small town.

Replied an old-time resident, "Why, mister, this is the starting point for any place in the world. You can start right here and go anywhere you want to go."

# SPEAKING

## 978. Brevity

Hubert Humphrey (1911-1978), who was Vice-President in President Lyndon Johnson's administration, was once asked to limit a commencement speech to twelve minutes.

Humphrey, who was famous for loving to talk, replied: "The last time I spoke for only twelve minutes was when I said hello to my mother."

## 979. Short and Long

Speaking of brevity, it is worth mentioning that the shortest inaugural address was George Washington's (1732-1799) — just 135 words.

The longest in U.S. history was William Henry Harrison's (1773-1841) in 1841. He delivered a two-hour, 8,578 word speech into the teeth of a freezing northwest wind. It would have been longer had not Daniel Webster (1782-1852) shortened it by eliminating several flowery, classical allusions.

Actually, the lengthy speech may have caused the death of the 68-year-old Harrison. Despite the cold, raw weather, he refused to wear either a hat or a coat. He then led the inaugural parade to the White House and attended three inaugural balls.

He came down with a cold the following day, and a month later he died of pneumonia.

## 980. The Great Demosthenes

The greatest orator of ancient Greece was a man named Demosthenes (c. 384 BC-322 BC). He achieved his incredible speaking skills despite having been born with a severe stammer.

To cure his stammer, Demosthenes stuffed his mouth with pebbles and practiced speaking with them ever so slowly.

He learned to overcome audience noise by going to the seashore and practicing speaking above the roar of the waves.

He practiced breath control by reciting poetry as he ran uphill. To resist the temptation of going out into society until he was ready, Demosthenes shaved one side of his head so that he would be too embarrassed to show himself in public.

He stood beneath a suspended sword to train himself not to favor a shoulder that kept hitching. He practiced facial expressions in front of a mirror.

With these devices, Demosthenes honed his speaking skills until he was able to hold his fellow Athenians spellbound, on any subject and under any conditions.

His fame as a speaker became so great that many centuries later his name is still synonymous with extraordinary speaking ability.

## 981. The Gettysburg Address

The Myth: Abraham Lincoln (1809-1865) hurriedly composed his most famous speech – The Gettysburg Address – on the back of an envelope while riding on a train from Washington, D.C. to the site of the speech in Gettysburg, Pennsylvania.

Background: The story apparently originated with Lincoln's son, Robert (1843-1926), who first created it in a letter he wrote after his father was assassinated.

The Truth: Lincoln actually started writing the speech two weeks before the event, and wrote at least five drafts before even leaving Washington for Gettysburg. He wasn't particularly keen on speaking spontaneously — in fact, he even refused to say anything to the crowd that met him at the Gettysburg train station because he was afraid he might say something foolish.

Consisting of approximately 272 words (the exact length is frequently in dispute), Lincoln's Gettysburg Address is now considered to be one of the greatest speeches ever made. But we are told that, just after delivering the famous oration, Lincoln was greatly disappointed in it.

Stepping down from the speaker's platform, Lincoln said to a friend, "That speech won't scour."

The word "scour" in Lincoln's day was a farming term describing a plow that could pass through the earth without soil clinging to the blade.

In other words, Lincoln didn't think his speech worked with the audience.

## 982. How to Be a Good Speaker

In an interview with *The New York Times*, James Humes, a former speechwriter for presidents and an authority on Winston Churchill. described five simple points he makes while tutoring executives as public speakers. Here they are:

1.  Begin strongly. The opening moments of a speech are 'prime time.' Everyone's listening and thinks you have something interesting to say. And so you should not dissipate that psychological advantage. Never waste it by saying the expected. Complimenting and thanking your audience at the beginning of a speech is not the best use of prime time.

2.  Use one theme. Keep it simple and single. And make sure there's a theme. Churchill once sent back a pudding because he said it had no theme.

3.  Use simple language. Don't make listeners plow through jargon. Those who comprehend it won't be impressed and those who don't will start reading a book.

4.  Talk in pictures. Give case examples that tell a story to illustrate cost benefit or delivery of service. When I teach, I have my students work on their 'I.R.A.'s' — incident recorded accounts. I make them come up with 15 incidents — being fired, going to camp — and show them how to use them to illustrate points.

5.  Use an emotional ending. The emotions that stir people in their private lives — pride, love, hope — are the same themes that motivate wallboard executives and vacuum cleaner salesmen. C.E.O.'s tell me, 'Listen, Jim, I'm not trying to save England, I'm just trying to get a message across to the company.' Well, you still want to ask the employees to join you in something. End on an emotional pitch. Work that audience up.

## 983. The Rule of Three

Many people follow this ancient mathematical law of proportion in ways they don't even think about. Abraham Lincoln learned it in his one-room school house. Even Aristotle (384 BC-322 BC), in his *Art of Rhetoric*, referred to "three types of speeches" and "three forms of proof," although he also divided ideas into two parts and four parts as well.

Lewis Carroll (1832-1898), who in addition to writing the "Alice in Wonderland" stories was a mathematician at Oxford, referred to the Rule of Three more than once in his writings. In his "Mad Gardener's Song," he writes:

> He thought he saw a Garden-door
> That opened with a key:
> He looked again, and found it was
> A double Rule of Three:
> "And all its mystery," he said,
> "is clear as day to me."

Later on in "The Hunting of the Snark," he writes:

> I have said it twice:
> That alone should encourage the crew.
> I have said it thrice:
> What I tell you three times is true.

Suffice to say, irrespective of the mathematical overtones, the number three is truly magical. Speech coaches insist that people can most easily remember something if it is said three different times. Shakespeare (1564-1616) used it. ("Friends, Romans, Countrymen"). Thomas Jefferson (1743-1826) used it. ("Life, Liberty and the Pursuit of Happiness"). U.S. Marine Corp instructors teach that a Marine should limit his or her attention to three tasks or goals. And the Jay Lenos of the comedy world frequently follow this formula. (The first comment names the topic, the second sets a pattern, and the third unexpectedly switches the pattern, which is funny.)

The Rule of Three is an excellent tool in the art of persuasion.

## 984. Using Quotations

President Lyndon Johnson (1908-1973) was a consumate politician who never forgot that you shouldn't get too fancy when trying to communicate with people.

One day while reviewing with a speechwriter the text of an upcoming address, he stumbled on a fancy quotation by the Greek philosopher Aristotle.

Johnson liked the quotation but said, "Half the people I'm talking to won't even know who Aristotle was."

"Hell," added Johnson, crossing out Aristotle's name, "let's just say, 'As my dear ole Daddy used to say.'"

## 985. Keep Your Speech Simple

There are frequent debates about just what qualities a candidate needs to get elected to political office. Sometimes they could surprise you.

The humorist Mark Twain (Samuel Clemens) (1835-1910) liked to tell about a man named Jim Watrous who ran five times for an office in the Missouri state legislature. And he lost every time. There was one problem. He used such big words in his speeches that no one in his farming district could understand him.

For example, he referred to himself as "your humble aspirant." He referred to his audience as "my enlightened constituency." He talked of "obtaining a mandate" for his "legislative mission."

"However," said Twain, "Watrous was milking a cow one morning and practicing one of his speeches at the same time. And the cow kicked him in the jaw, causing him to bite off the end of his tongue."

"That must have put an end to his career as a politician," said a friend to Twain.

"Not at all," Twain replied, "After that he could use only words of one syllable and that made him such a hit with the farmers that he was elected overwhelmingly and served in the legislature for many years."

## 986. Speech Preparation

Someone once asked Woodrow Wilson (1856-1924) how long it took him to write a speech.

He replied, "It depends. If I am to speak for ten minutes, I need a week for preparation. If fifteen minutes, three days. If for half an hour, two days. If an hour, I am ready now."

Note: Wilson (1856-1924), a Democrat, served as the twenty-eighth President of the United States from 1913 to 1921.

## 987. Testimonial Speeches

Orville (1871-1948) and Wilbur Wright (1867-1912), the flight pioneers, were both very shy men.

Once, during a testimonial dinner, the toastmaster called on Wilbur to make a speech. Wilbur rose to his feet and said in a stammering voice, "There must be a mistake. I think you want my brother." And Wilbur sat down.

The toastmaster then called on Orville, who replied, "Wilbur just made the speech."

## 988. Long Speeches Are Nothing New

Insufferably long speeches have been with us through the ages. A memorable illustration of that can be seen in a painting by George Catlin (1796-1872) which is part of the Paul Mellon Collection at the Virginia Museum of Fine Arts.

Catlin was a 19th century American artist who is best remembered for his realistic depictions of the everyday life of American Indians. One of the paintings, done more than 100 years ago, is titled "The Long Speech."

In the background are a few teepees with some women and children standing in front of them. It is snowing, and they are stolidly watching a lone Indian who is in the foreground and standing in the middle of a circle of individual mounds of snow. A bit of leather headdress can be seen emerging from the top of each of these mounds of snow. The painting is called "A Long Speech."

## 989. A Lifesaving Speech

Having a prepared speech text on you before making a speech can save your life. Consider this true story from the life of one of our great presidents — Theodore Roosevelt (1858-1919).

It was October 14, 1912 and Roosevelt was in Milwaukee campaigning for the Presidency as a third-party candidate, not unlike the Texas billionaire Ross Perot's candidacy some years ago.

On his way to making a speech, Roosevelt stood in an automobile bowing to a cheering crowd. Suddenly a shot rang out. A half-crazed fanatic had shot the former president.

They wanted to rush him to a hospital. But Roosevelt said, "You get me to that speech! It may be the last I shall deliver, but I am going to deliver it."

As he entered the hall where he was to speak, someone exclaimed, "Look, Colonel, there's a hole in your overcoat!"

Roosevelt looked down, saw the hole and, putting his hand inside his coat, withdrew it with blood on it.

"It looks as though I have been hit," he said calmly, "but I don't think it is anything serious."

Three physicians, summoned from the audience, examined the wound, which was in his right breast, and recommended that he be taken at once to a hospital. But Roosevelt would have none of it.

Beginning his speech, he told the audience, "I am going to ask you to be very quiet and please excuse me from making a long speech. You see there is a bullet in my body. But it is nothing. I'm not hurt badly."

When he took the folded manuscript of his speech from his coat's inside pocket, he saw that a bullet had passed completely through it, having first passed through a metal eyeglasses case.

Brandishing the bullet-pierced speech manuscript before the crowd, Roosevelt roared: "It takes more than that to kill a Bull Moose!"

Holding a bloody handkerchief to the wound, Roosevelt spoke for an hour and a half. Several times he seemed to weaken but, when persons on the platform rose to help him, he shook them off, saying, "Let me alone, I'm all right."

Roosevelt finished his speech and was taken by special train to Chicago, arriving there at half past three the next morning. Even then he insisted on walking to the ambulance and into the hospital itself.

"I'm no weakling to be crippled by a flesh wound," the former Rough Rider declared.

Roosevelt remained in the hospital until October 21, when he returned to his suburban home in Oyster Bay, Long Island. And 10 days later he addressed an audience of 15,000 persons in New York City's Madison Square Garden.

The shredded speech manuscript, the mangled spectacle case and the torn shirt he was wearing that fateful day are on display today in a reproduction of Theodore Roosevelt's home in New York City — a tribute to a stubbornly brave man whose life may have been saved by a thick speech manuscript in his coat pocket. Who needs a teleprompter anyway?

## 990. Fear of Speaking

An old friend of Mark Twain's (Samuel Clemens) (1835-1910) came to New York to attend a dinner where he was the guest of honor.

As the dinner progressed, Twain asked his friend, "Don't you feel well? You look whiter than a fish-belly."

"I'm scared to death," said the friend. "because I know they are going to ask me to speak. I'm afraid I won't even be able to get up from my chair. When I stand up, my mind sits down!"

"Don't worry," said Twain reassuringly, "just remember they don't expect much."

## 991. Speech Honorariums

In this day and age when famous speakers are paid fees of up to $100,000 and beyond, the following story has a particular poignancy.

Oliver Wendell Holmes Sr. (1809-1894) was an American physician who was also famous for his writing. He once returned the following message when asked to deliver a lecture:

"I have at hand your kind invitation. However, I am far from being in good physical health. I am satisfied that, if I were offered a $50 bill after my lecture, I would not have strength enough to refuse it."

## 992. Stage Fright

Even famous public figures who are constantly called upon to make speeches must deal with butterflies in their stomach.

Winston Churchill (1874-1965) found that a simple fantasy helped him to conquer his stage fright. Whenever he stood before a crowd, he tried to imagine that every man and woman he was addressing had a hole in his sock.

President Eisenhower (1890-1969) is said to have taken his fantasies one step further and formed a mental picture of his audience as sitting before him without wearing any clothes.

## 993. A Speaker's Afterthoughts

William Lyon Phelps (1865-1943), the famous Yale professor and lecturer, once said that he got credit for only one-fourth of his after-dinner speeches.

"Every time I accept an invitation to speak, I really make four addresses. First is the speech I prepare in advance. That is pretty good.

Second is the speech I really make.

Third is the speech I make on my way home, which is the best of all.

The fourth is the speech the newspapers the next morning say I made, which bears no relation to any of the others.

## 994. A Trick by Demosthenes

One of the most famous orators of ancient times was a Greek named Demosthenes (c.384 BC-322 BC). Normally, he held audiences spellbound but this time his audience in the city of Athens booed and hissed him so loudly that he could not get started with the speech he had come to deliver.

Thoroughly frustrated, Demosthenes said "Let me tell you one short story." And the crowd immediately became quiet.

Once, said Demosthenes, a young man hired a donkey and its owner to take him on a journey to a distant city.

It was very hot and, at high noon, the young men decided to rest in the shade of the donkey. But the donkey's owner insisted that he should rest in the small shadow cast by the donkey, and not the young man. And they began pushing each other to enjoy the meager shade.

"But I have hired the donkey for this journey," protested the young man, "and therefore I am entitled to rest in its shade."

"But I am the donkey's owner, said the other man, and I only rented the donkey to you, not its shadow."

The crowd remained silent, waiting for the story's outcome. At this point, Demosthenes thanked the crowd and began to leave. But the audience protested he had not told them the end of the story, and begged him to continue.

"How is it," said Demosthenes angrily, "that you insist upon hearing a story about the shadow of a donkey, and yet will not give your attention to matters of great importance to our city? The audience immediately quieted down and listened to what Demosthenes had to say.

The mystery of who had the right to rest in the donkey's shadow remains unresolved, even to this day.

## 995. An Audience Proposition

There have been many opinion surveys quoting people as saying they would rather die that have to make a speech. Abraham Lincoln (1809-1865) liked to tell this story about a man who felt the same way but found a way to surmount it. It goes like this:

"Out in my state of Illinois, a man was nominated for Sheriff of the county where I lived," said Lincoln. "He was a good man for the office, brave, determined, and honest. But he was not much of a speaker. In fact, he couldn't make a speech to save his life.

"His friends knew that he was a man who would preserve the peace of the county and perform its demanding duties well. But the people of the county didn't know it. His friends wanted him to come out boldly at political meetings and state his convictions and principles. People were downright suspicious of a man who was afraid to open his mouth.

"At last, the candidate gave in and consented to give a speech at the next political meeting. When he was called upon, he walked right up front and there was a glint of determination in his eye.

"Feller Citizens," he said in a quiet voice. "I'm not a speakin' man. I ain't no orator and I never stood up before a lot of people in my life before. So I am not going to make no speech 'cept to say that I can lick any man in the crowd."

Note: Lincoln told this story in defense of General Ulysses S. Grant (1822-1885).

## 996. The Wright Brothers

Early in the development of flight, the Wright brothers (Orville (1871-1948) and Wilbur (1867-1912)) had to go abroad to get proper recognition for their aeronautical achievements.

The French government welcomed them and gave the brothers an opportunity to demonstrate what they had done. But as a group, the French could not conceal their jealousy of the two modest Yanks.

To honor the accomplishments of the two Wright brothers, a banquet was arranged in Paris. The chief speaker at the dinner was a distinguished Frenchman who devoted most of his remarks to claiming that France had led the world in aviation exploration and would do so in the future. The speaker had very little to say in praise of the two American guests.

When Wilbur Wright was called upon to speak, he rose slowly to his feet, "I am no hand at public speaking," said Wilbur, "and so I must on this occasion content myself with a few words. As I sat here listening to the speaker who preceded me, I heard his comparisons made to the eagle, to the swallow, and to the hawk as typifying skill and speed in mastery of the air. But somehow or other, I could not keep from thinking of the parrot which, of all the ornithological kingdom is the poorest flier and the best talker."

## 997. Rewards of Brevity

A young clergyman who was to deliver his first sermon came to Disraeli (1804-1881) while he was British Prime Minister and asked for some pointers on public speaking.

"It's not so much what you say that counts," cautioned Disraeli. "It's how long it takes you to say it. If your sermon lasts an hour, you'll never be heard of again. If it lasts 30 minutes, your parishioners will snore. If it lasts 15 minutes, you may eventually become a success. But if you preach for five minutes only, you will be a bishop in three years."

## 998. The Talking Stick

This excerpt from *The Circle is Sacred: A Medicine Book for Women* by Dr. Scout Cloud Lee says a lot about the power of speaking and its role in leadership. Something called a "talking stick" was used by Native Americans as they sat in council on important subjects.

"The talking stick has been a way of life among the elders since people using words first sat in council...It seems that our elders would first pass the pipe and smoke in silence until all hearts beat as one.

"Then they would pass the talking stick. It is a very powerful microphone. When one holds the talking stick, everyone listens. The person with the stick speaks into the center of the circle with no thought of influencing others. They simply speak their truth.

"A powerful beginning for the one who holds the talking stick is this: 'I am Cloud, and I will speak.'

"Holding the stick seems to magically streamline what one will say. When the speaker has finished it is powerful to say, 'I am Cloud and I have spoken!'

Note: The tribes represented in Dr. Scout Cloud Lee's book include: Seminole, Cherokee, Choctaw, Seneca, Lakota, and Iroquois.

## 999. Proliferation of Words

Abraham Lincoln (1809-1865) delivered his Gettysburg Address well over a century ago. Based on research by *USA Today*, take a look at how his words compare to some examples of today's writing.
 Number of Words

Gettysburg Address 272
Bag of Frito Lay's Potato Chips 401
IRA Form 1040 EZ 418
Average *USA Today* cover story 1,200

## 1000. What Makes a Good Speech

During a cabinet meeting, Winston Churchill (1874-1965) once looked over at a speech that lay on the table in front of his Foreign secretary, Anthony Eden (1897-1977), who sat just across from him.

"It's a bad speech, Anthony," volunteered Churchill.

"How can you tell?" replied Eden. "Surely you can't read upside down!"

"I can too," replied Churchill, "because there are too many semicolons and never a dash."

Note: Churchill believed that the words of a speech should be typed out in bite-size phrases, just as a person talks, with lots of bold underlining, pauses, and punctuation marks such as dashes.

## 1001. A Churchill Technique

Winston Churchill was said to have used a simple trick to make people believe he did his public speaking without a text in front of him.

The fact is, he read virtually all his speeches, but he always used a few quotations in the body of his speech. When he got to a quote, he would put on his eyeglasses to make it appear that he needed them to read.

## 1002. Brevity Insurance

An isolated but civilized and cultured tribe in sub-Saharan Africa has a method for avoiding overly long speeches, which they consider injurious to both the speaker and the audience. The custom is that the speaker must stand on one leg while addressing his audience. As soon as his second foot touches the ground, he must stop.

## 1003. Unprepared Speaker

The British politician, Harold MacMillan (1894-1986), who would become his country's Prime Minister in the 1950s, made his "maiden speech" in the House of Commons in 1925. Afterward, he asked fellow legislator Winston Churchill what he thought of it

Churchill's critique went like this: "Harold, when you rose you didn't know what you were going to say, when you were speaking you didn't know what you were saying, and when you finished you didn't know what you had said."

Churchill's remarks underscore how important it is for a speaker to organize his/her thoughts prior to speaking in public.

## 1004. Time to Say Farewell

President Calvin Coolidge (1872-1933) was returning to Washington from an American Legion convention in Omaha, when his train stopped for coal and water at a small town.

The stop had been publicized and 2500 people were waiting when the train pulled into the station. An aide informed Coolidge about the crowd and the President walked back to the rear platform. When he appeared, the crowd applauded. Mrs. Coolidge was then introduced and got an even bigger ovation.

The local master of ceremonies then took center stage. "Now folks, keep quiet," he said. "I want absolute silence. The President is about to address us." A hush descended upon the crowd. "All right," the man said, "Mr. President, you may speak now."

At that point there was a hiss of air as the train brakes were released, and the train slowly began to move out of the station. The President smiled, waved to the crowd, and said, "Goodbye."

# SPORTS, BASEBALL

## 1005. The Baseball Bat

Babe Ruth is credited with the invention of the modern baseball bat. He was the first player to order a bat with a knob on the end of the handle, with which he hit 29 home runs in 1919.

The company that produced the bat was Louisville Slugger, which has been producing baseball bats ever since.

## 1006. The National Anthem and Baseball

"The Star Spangled Banner," now America's national anthem, was played at the beginning of a baseball game for the first time in Boston in 1918 before a game between the Boston Red Sox and the Chicago Cubs.

There is an interesting story behind this event. It was during World War I and many wounded veterans were in the stands, ready and excited about watching the approaching contest.

What the veterans did not know was that the Boston players had refused to take the field because they were disgruntled about not getting a bigger share of the World Series purse. Negotiations extending over an hour had failed to settle the matter and people in the stands became impatient.

Finally, the players reluctantly agreed to play ball for the sake of the soldiers. The Red Sox owner was so overjoyed that he quickly had the band strike up "The Star Spangled Banner." Although the tune had not yet been made the official national anthem, the audience stood and doffed their hats in respect, beginning what is now a national tradition.

"The New York Times" was so impressed that it gave the event a banner headline.

## 1007. Satchel Paige

Leroy Robert "Satchel" Paige (1906-1982) is generally conceded to be one of the greatest baseball pitchers to ever play the game. However, he was barred from playing major league baseball until very late in his career because he was black.

Richard Donovan, a writer for *Collier's Magazine*, was preparing a 1953 profile on the famous pitcher who seemed ageless. Donovan reportedly asked Paige for some typical quotes and they appeared in a box within the article's layout. Paige apparently happily accepted them as his own and they have become famous as his philosophy of life ever since. Here they are:

- Avoid fried meats which angry up the blood.

- If your stomach disputes you, lie down and pacify it with cool thoughts.

- Keep the juices flowing by jangling around gently as you move.

- Go very light on the vices, such as carrying on in society. The social ramble ain't restful.

- Avoid running at all times.

- Don't look back. Something might be gaining on you.

## 1008. Yankee Uniforms

Why do the New York Yankees wear pinstriped uniforms?

We do not know if the story is apocryphal or not, but the story goes that, because of Babe Ruth's (1895-1948) bulky figure, the owner of the Yankees, Jacob Ruppert (1867-1939), decided to dress the Yankees in the now-traditional pinstripe uniform and dark blue stockings. Ruppert felt the new uniform would make the Babe look slimmer.

The Yankees also introduced uniform numbers to the major leagues in 1929. Ruth's number was number 3 because he batted third, Lou Gehrig's (1903-1941) 4 because he batted fourth, and so on.

## 1009. Pep Talk

One of baseball's most colorful managers was Casey Stengel (1890-1975). Here is a portion of a pep talk he gave to the Toledo Mud Hens in 1929 when he was managing the team.

"Now, you boys haven't been playing very well, but I know there's been a lot on your minds. I see a lot of you reading about the stock market, and I know you're thinking about it.

"Now, I'm going to do you a favor, since you're so interested in Wall Street. I'm going to give you a tip on the market. (Pause.) Buy Pennsylvania Railroad. (Pause.) Because ( whack! ) if you don't start playing better ball there's gonna be so many of you riding trains out of here that railroad stocks are a cinch to go up."

## 1010. Rogers Hornsby

There is nothing like having a reputation for excellence, for good judgment and integrity.

An example of someone who had all three was a baseball player named Rogers Hornsby (1896-1963). Many people consider Hornsby to be the greatest right-handed hitter in baseball history. His lifetime batting average was .358. In 1924 he hit .424 with the St. Louis Cardinals.

The story goes that Hornsby came to bat one day against a flashy rookie pitcher with a blazing fast ball.

"Whoosh" went the first pitch past the plate.

"Ball one," said the umpire.

"Whoosh" came the second pitch to Hornsby, who kept his bat cocked.

"Ball two," said the umpire.

Then came the third pitch and the umpire called that a ball too.

Angry and frustrated, the young pitcher shouted at the umpire, "Those balls were strikes!"

"Young man," replied the umpire, "when you throw a strike, Mr. Hornsby will let you know."

## 1011. Jackie Robinson's Worst Day

Even if they aren't baseball fans, almost everyone knows the story of how Jackie Robinson (1919-1972) became the first African-American to play major league baseball. But few know what happened on what Robinson himself called the worst day of his career.

When Robinson was signed with the Brooklyn Dodgers, he became a target for racial hate mail and even death threats. Before one game, Robinson received a threatening phone call that left him so shaken that he was unable to concentrate on the game.

Robinson struck out in one inning with bases loaded. In another inning, he committed a fielding error. The crowd screamed obscenities at him.

A time-out was called and the Dodger shortstop, Pee Wee Reese (1918-1999), walked up to the shaken Robinson, put his arm around him, and said: "Jackie, you are the greatest ballplayer I have ever seen. You can do it. And I know something else. One of these days you are going into the Hall of Fame. So, hold your head up high, and play ball like only you can do it."

Robinson was so encouraged by these words that he went on to deliver a game-winning hit for his team. Many years later, Robinson recalled the incident when he was inducted into the Baseball Hall of Fame at Cooperstown. He said of Pee Wee Reese: "He saved my life and my career that day. I had lost my confidence, and Pee Wee picked me up with his words of encouragement. He gave me hope when all hope was gone."

## 1012. Babe Ruth Had No Equal

Before the age of weight programs, personal trainers, free agency, juiced-up baseballs — and bodies — George Herman Ruth (1895-1948) did it all. He routinely pitched nine innings, then took the field on other days, all the while smacking home runs, stealing bases and throwing out runners from every angle on the diamond.

No baseball player, despite what record books claim, has ever equaled Ruth's awesome performance. When his power erupted, in 1919, home runs were as rare as rubies. In 1915 the Boston Red Sox as a team slugged only 17. The famous "Home Run" Baker never hit more than 12 in a season; in fact, between 1904 and 1919, no one had hit more than 12. But in 1921, Ruth tagged a cool 59.

## 1013. A Baseball Anomaly

Can you imagine a major league baseball player leading the league in making the most errors...in being struck out the most times...in hitting into the most double plays — and still being voted Most Valuable Player for that year?

It happened. In 1942 Joe Gordon (1915-1978) did all those things, yet still won the MVP award that season in the American League.

What's the lesson in this? Joe Gordon's case shows that even though you have faults, you can overcome them and be recognized for your good points.

## 1014. Why Is It Called the "World Series?"

The "world" in World Series comes not from the synonym for the globe but rather from the name of the *New York World*, the newspaper that originally sponsored the games.

## 1015. Negotiation

After a poor year pitching for the New York Yankees in the 1930s, legendary pitcher Lefty Gomez (1908-1989) was asked to accept a salary cut from $20,000 to $7,500 a year.

Reeling, Gomez asked the Yankees, "How about you keep the salary and pay me the cut."

## 1016. Little Things Mean a Lot

Little things can be important in achieving success.

When the famous baseball player Ty Cobb (1886-1961) got on first base he had what seemed to be a nervous habit of kicking the bag. It wasn't until he retired from baseball that the secret came out.

By kicking the bag hard several times, Cobb was able to move it a full two inches closer to second base. A terror on the bases, Cobb figured this tiny advantage was enough to improve his chances of stealing second or making it safely on a hit. Anything to win the game! The mark of a real competitor.

## 1017. Character in Sports

The great Boston Red Sox star Ted Williams (1918-2002) was nearing the end of his career when he had a bad season because of a pinched nerve in his neck.

"The thing was so bad," he later explained, "that I could hardly turn my head to look at the pitcher."

For the first time in his career, Williams batted under .300, hitting just .254 with 10 home runs. He was the highest salaried player in sports, making $125,000. The next year, the Red Sox sent him a new contract at the same salary level.

When he got the contract, Williams sent it back with a note saying that he would not sign it until they gave him the full pay cut allowed.

"I was always treated fairly by the Red Sox when it came to contracts," Williams said. "Now they were offering me a contract I didn't deserve. And I only wanted what I deserved."

Williams cut his own salary by 25 percent, raised his batting average by 62 points, and closed out a brilliant career by hitting a home run in his final time at bat.

## 1018. Baseball Statistics

Mickey Mantle (1931-1995), the great New York Yankee outfielder, once said, "During my 18 years I came to bat almost 10,000 times. I struck out about 1,700 times and walked maybe 1,900 times.

"You figure a ballplayer will average about 500 at bats a season. That means I played seven years without ever hitting the ball."

Since Mantle was one of the great hitters of all time, the above should give us some perspective about the failures and mistakes that life hands us from time to time.

## 1019. Positive Thinking

A little boy was talking to himself as he entered his backyard, baseball cap in place, and carrying a baseball and bat.

"I'm the greatest baseball player in the world," he said proudly. Then he tossed the ball in the air, swung and missed.

Undismayed, he picked up the ball, threw it into the air and said to himself again, "I'm the greatest player ever!" As the ball descended, he swung at it again, and again he missed.

He paused a moment to examine the bat and ball carefully. Then once again he threw the ball into the air and said, "I'm the greatest baseball player who ever lived." As the ball came down, he gave another mighty swing and missed the ball again.

"Wow!" he exclaimed. "What a pitcher!"

## 1020. The Inventor of Baseball

Abner Doubleday (1819-1893) did not invent baseball. Publications about the game were issued as early as 1835, when Doubleday was only sixteen.

Further, though he is credited with inventing baseball in Cooperstown, New York, in 1839, it is known that Doubleday was enrolled at West Point from 1838 to 1842.

At that time a West Point cadet was not allowed to leave campus until his last years in school; thus it was impossible for Doubleday even to have visited Cooperstown before 1841.

Doubleday was, however, distinguished in other ways. He was a Union general during the Civil War and played a leading part in the Battle of Gettysburg.

Note: in 2005 a definitive history of baseball's origins was published by the University of Nebraska Press titled "A Search for the Roots of the Game," by David Block.

## 1021. Hot Weather

It was a miserably hot and humid day in New York City and Yankee baseball great Yogi Berra (1925- ) was on stage to receive the key to New York City from Mayor John Lindsay.

The mayor's wife, Mary, complimented Berra on how cool he looked.

Ever the king of malaprops, Berra replied, "You don't look so hot yourself."

## 1022. Professional Pride

Joe DiMaggio (1914-1999) of the New York Yankees had a fierce pride about always doing his best.

The Yankees were on the road for a doubleheader against the St. Louis Browns. The day was not only boiling hot, the Browns were last place in the league.

Despite this, DiMaggio made an off-hand comment that he was looking forward to playing that day.

"In this heat!" said an amazed sportswriter. "How can you enjoy playing a doubleheader in stifling weather like this?"

Glancing toward the grandstand, DiMaggio said, "Maybe somebody out there has never seen me play before."

## 1023. Not Playing It Safe

Ted Williams (1918-2002) of the Boston Red Sox was one of baseball's all-time great hitters — not to say gentlemen.

Going into the last day of the season in 1941, Williams was batting something like .39955, and if you rounded it off, you could honestly say he was a .400 hitter for the year. Ammunition for a big salary negotiation, right?

Faced with a doubleheader to end the season, Williams might have considered sitting out both games and icing his .400 percentage.

It is a measure of Williams's character that he didn't sit out the game. Instead he got enough hits to end the season at .406.

Williams had the confidence of a winner and wasn't afraid to take risks. This attitude marked his entire distinguished career and, of course, earned him an early place in baseball's Hall of Fame.

## 1024. Baseball Autographs

Mickey Mantle (1931-1995), the great New York Yankee baseball Hall of Famer, by his own admission, lived quite a wild life full of carousing.

At Mantle's funeral, his good friend, sportscaster Bob Costas, told a story that Mantle liked to tell on himself. It goes like this.

Mickey pictured himself at the pearly gates of Heaven where he was met by St. Peter.

"Mick," said St. Peter shaking his head, "we looked at your record and we know some of the things that went on. So we are sorry we can't let you in. But before you go, God wants to know if you'd sign these six dozen baseballs."

## 1025. Dizzy Dean

The great baseball pitcher Dizzy Dean (1910-1974) for the St. Louis Cardinals often puckishly told different reporters that he was born in different birthplaces.

Depending on his mood and the last person he talked to with a pad and pencil, Diz would look reporters straight in the eye and say he hailed from Lucas, Arkansas...or Holdenville, Oklahoma...or Bond, Mississippi, or somewhere else in the general vicinity — the vicinity being someplace in "America."

When he was pressed on the matter, Dean replied, "I was helpin' the writers out. Them ain't lies; them's scoops."

Dizzy Dean was anything but modest. Once he said, "If Satch (Satchel Paige was a famous black baseball pitcher who was barred for many years from playing in the major leagues because of his race) were pitching on the same team, we'd cinch the pennant by July 4 and go fishing until World Series time. Between us, we'd win 60 games."

After Dean retired from baseball as an active player, he became a popular baseball sportscaster who mangled the English language like you couldn't believe until you heard him.

Once, he was interviewed by a British reporter who asked him, "Mr. Dean, don't you know the king's English?"

Diz thought for a moment. "Sure I do," he said, "And so's the queen."

Note: Dean's proper name was Jay Hanna Dean

## 1026. Hitting Prowess

Casey Stengel (1890-1975), great baseball player and manager of many championship teams, was once asked if Babe Ruth (1895-1948) used a heavy bat.

"He could have used his sleeve," replied Stengel, "or a rolled up copy of the 'Police Gazette.' Wouldn't have made a bit of difference."

## 1027. Baseball Fame

Some newspaper reporters once asked famed Italian tenor Enrico Caruso (1873-1921) what he thought of Babe Ruth (1895-1948).

Caruso replied he didn't know because unfortunately he had never heard her sing.

## 1028. Pay for Performance

During the Depression of the 1930s, the New York Yankee baseball great Babe Ruth was (1895-1948) asked to take a cut in salary. Stubbornly, he held out for his $80,000 salary. In the negotiations, one of the Yankee officials protested, "But that's more money than Herbert Hoover got for being president last year."

Ruth replied, "I know, but I had a better year than he did."

Note: Yankee owner Jacob Ruppert (1867-1939) gave Ruth the $80,000 he demanded.

## 1029. Optimism

A man passing near a local playground stopped to watch a Little League baseball game. To get himself up to speed, he asked one of the youngsters what the score was.

"We're behind 16 to nothing," the boy answered.

"I must say you don't seem discouraged." the man said, "Why is that?"

"Discouraged?" said the boy. "Why should we be discouraged? We haven't been up to bat yet."

## 1030. Time to Retire

The famous Pittsburgh Pirate outfielder Paul Waner (1903-1965) was once asked how did he know when it was time to quit baseball.

"Well," said Waner, "as you get older, you slow down and the infielders back up because they've got more time to throw you out at first. At the same time you lose a little power, so the outfielders move in because you aren't hitting the ball so far."

Then he added, "When they can shake hands, it is time to retire."

## 1031. An Umpire Speaks

One afternoon when American League umpire Bill Guthrie was working behind the plate, the catcher of the visiting team repeatedly protested his calls.

Guthrie endured this for three innings. But in the fourth inning when the catcher started to complain, Guthrie stopped him.

"Son," he said gently, "you've been a big help to me calling balls and strikes and I appreciate it. But I think I've got the hang of it now. So I'm going to ask you to go to the clubhouse and show them how to take a shower."

# SPORTS, BASKETBALL

## 1032. Greatness Is in the Details

The great college and NBA basketball star Bill Walton (1952- ) still remembers how he got prepared for "greatness" by the famous Hall of Fame UCLA coach John Wooden (1910- ).

Walton, a big redhead from San Diego, arrived at UCLA in the fall of 1970 after the UCLA Bruins had already won an unprecedented six NCAA titles in seven years.

So the eager college freshman Walton couldn't wait to study at the feet of the Wizard of Westwood. He was almost dizzy imagining the strategic secrets this great basketball coach would soon impart to him.

Walton recalls the first day of practice when Wooden came in, sat down on a stool, and motioned for the rookies to gather around him. "This is it," thought Walton excitedly.

"Gentlemen," began Wooden, "today we are going to learn how to tie our shoes properly."

Then the famous coach showed his new recruits, step by painstaking step, how to knot their shoelaces so they would never, ever come undone during a game.

Then he took off his socks and showed them how to put on sweat socks so they would never, ever bunch up inside the sneakers and cause a blister.

Then it was on to the rest of the uniform: how to tuck in the jersey so the shirttail would never, ever fall out, and how to tie the drawstring in the shorts.

After that it was lessons on how to warm up, how to eat and sleep properly, how to organize one's time and how to dry one's hair after practice.

In this way Walton learned that greatness in anything depends not only on God-given talent, but on mastering the tiniest details of a game or profession.

## 1033. High Point Man

Stacey King, who was a rookie NBA basketball player with the Chicago Bulls during Michael Jordan's (1963- ) tenure there, will never forget one of his first games playing with the superstar.

Michael Jordan scored 69 points and King scored 1, defeating their opponent.

After the game, a reporter asked King for his reaction to the Bulls' victory and he replied:

"I'll always remember this as the night Michael and I combined for 70 points."

## 1034. Poetry as Inspiration

Phil Jackson (1945- ), the highly-successful coach of the Chicago Bulls and the Los Angeles Lakers professional basketball teams, frequently reads poetry to his players.

To inspire his players on the subject of teamwork, he once read the following lines from Kipling's 1895 poem "The Law of the Jungle":

Now this is the Law of the Jungle —
 As old and as true as the sky;
And the Wolf that shall keep it may prosper,
 But the Wolf that shall break it must die.
As the creeper that girdles the tree-trunk
 The Law runneth forward and back —
But the strength of the Pack is the Wolf,
 And the strength of the Wolf is the Pack.

## 1035. Basketball Is Born

On December 21, 1891, the game of basketball was invented by Dr. James Naismith (1861-1939), a physician and ordained minister. The place was the International YMCA Training School in Springfield, Massachusetts.

According to sports historian Dr. Tony Ladd of Wheaton College and Naismith's grandson (also named James Naismith) Dr. Naismith's motive was to invent a game to encourage healthy exercise by young men kept indoors by the winter weather.

The 30-year-old Dr. Naismith asked the janitor to fasten two peach baskets on the gymnasium railing at a height of 10 feet. Within an hour, Naismith had created thirteen rules for the game and play began using a soccer ball.

No other sport is known to owe its origin to one person. Dr. Naismith never patented his invention or made any money from it. Basketball is the only popular American game that does not have English origins.

The rules Naismith devised have been changed little in nearly 100 years.

## 1036. When Winning Was Everything

The Incas of ancient Peru played a primitive form of basketball, the object of which was to shoot a solid rubber ball through a stone ring placed high on a wall.

The winner was traditionally awarded the clothes of all spectators present. The loser was put to death.

## 1037. Later Doesn't Win Ball Games

When he was 14, Shaquille O'Neal (1972- ), now the superstar center for the Miami Heat NBA team, enrolled in a basketball camp expecting to amaze the coaches with his basketball prowess. He was in for an unpleasant shock.

Although Shaquille had been a star at his San Antonio high school, at the basketball camp he was just one of many outstanding athletes. Frequently ignored by the coaches, he began to worry that maybe he wasn't good enough to make the grade. His self-confidence hit rock bottom.

Totally discouraged, he asked his parents for advice and his mother said: "You must fulfill your dreams while there's still room for you to do so. Attack them with a full head of steam. There's no opportunity like now. This is the time you can show people."

His confidence almost gone, Shaquille tried to brush his mother off by saying, "I can't do that right now. Maybe later."

Then, says Shaquille, his mother gave him some motherly advice that he says totally changed his life.

"Later," said his mother, "doesn't always come to everybody."

## 1038. John Wooden's Pyramid of Success

John Wooden (1910- ), the famous UCLA basketball coach who led his Bruins to 10 national championships in 12 years, drilled his players over and over on what he called the Pyramid of Success.

Basketball great Kareem Abdul-Jabbar (1947- ), who played his college years under Wooden, once told a reporter he thought the Pyramid was kind of corny when he first saw it, but he later came to the conclusion that it had a great effect on his career and later life.

If you would like to construct a visual picture of Coach Wooden's Pyramid of Success, get a pencil and paper. Construct the pyramid out of rectangular blocks as did the Egyptians. Into each of the blocks write one of Wooden's "secrets" of success.

On the bottom layer, fill in five blocks and label them: industriousness, friendship, loyalty, cooperation, enthusiasm.

On the next layer above, fill in four blocks with these labels: self-control, alertness, initiative, intentness.

On the third layer toward the top of the pyramid, place three blocks and label them: condition, skill, team spirit.

On the fourth layer, place two building blocks and label them: poise, confidence.

The fifth and next to last layer has only one block. It bears the label: competitive greatness.

Finally, the triangular crown of the pyramid is divided into two halves with the labels: faith, patience.

Wooden always maintained that the order and placement of each block was essential to the pyramid's success. Considering his success with this teaching tool, who could contradict him.

## 1039. About Teamwork

"I don't believe in statistics. What determines a player's salary is his contribution to winning — not his statistical accomplishments. Players' livelihoods depend on their contribution to the Celtics, not to themselves," said Red Auerbach (1917-2006), the former coach of the Boston Celtics.

Auerbach told how he brought backup center Bill Walton (1952- ) out of a slump during the 1985-86 season. Walton simply wasn't scoring. Auerbach told Walton it didn't matter what Walton scored; all Auerbach cared about was his contribution to the team. After that conversation, Walton's performance greatly improved.

"He became loose," said Auerbach, "and he never looked to see what he scored. All he looked at was: 'Did we win?' And it was 'we,' not 'I.'"

# SPORTS, OARSMEN

### 1040. Synchronized Rowing

When you ask oarsmen to describe their perfect moments in a boat, they don't talk so much about winning a race as to the feel of the boat – all eight oars in the water together, the synchronization almost perfect. When that happens, they say, the boat seems to lift itself right out of the water. Oarsmen describe that as the moment of "swing."

Olympics contender John Bigelow relished that moment, but what he liked best about it was that it "allowed you to totally trust the other men in the boat."

A boat does not have "swing" unless everyone is putting out in exact measure. Because of that, and only because of that, there is the possibility of true trust among oarsmen.

# SPORTS, BOXING

### 1041. Time for Some Humility

Champion boxer Muhammad Ali (1942- ) was aboard an airliner awaiting takeoff when the female flight attendant reminded him to fasten his seat belt.

"Superman don't need to seat belt," said Ali.

The flight attendant replied, "Superman don't need no airplane, either."

Ali fastened his belt.

Note: Muhammad Ali was world heavyweight champion from 1964-1971 and 1974-1978). He changed his name from Cassius Marcellus Clay when he became a Muslim. For three years, he was deprived of his heavyweight title for refusing to serve in the U.S. Army during the Vietnam War.

# SPORTS, FOOTBALL

## 1042. Shula's 24-Hour Rule

"Success is not forever and failure isn't fatal."

When Don Shula (1930- ) was head coach of the Miami Dolphins football team, that was his favorite quotation. It governed a great deal of his behavior during his long and distinguished career as the "winningest" coach in the NFL.

Shula had a 24-hour rule. Following a game, he allowed himself, his coaches, and his players a maximum of 24 hours to celebrate a victory or bemoan a defeat. During that time, they were encouraged to experience thoroughly the thrill of victory or the agony of defeat as much as humanly possible.

However, once the 24-hour deadline had passed, they were taught to put these emotions behind them and to focus their energies on getting ready for the next opponent.

Shula's rule is well worth remembering. Don't get conceited when you win or too discouraged when you lose. Keep things in perspective. Success is not forever, and failure isn't either.

## 1043. How the Huddle Was Invented

When players of American football want to talk about the next play, they form a "huddle" in which they all face inward in a tight group.

But the huddle has not always been part of the game. Prior to the 1890s, football players just stood around discussing the play, far enough away from the other team that they could not be overheard.

The huddle was invented in 1894 by Paul Hubbard, quarterback for Gallaudet University's Bisons. Gallaudet was a university for deaf people, located in Washington, D.C., and the players used sign language to discuss strategy. The tight huddle was a way to hide the sign language from anyone on the opposing team who might be able to understand it.

Another early user of the huddle was Herb McCracken, coach of the Lafayette College football team. It was 1924 and McCracken discovered that his hand signals had been scouted and decoded by Penn, his upcoming opponent.

On game day, McCracken responded by ordering his players to "huddle" together, several yards behind the line of scrimmage, and talk over the next play in a whisper. This procedure immediately became a ritual at Lafayette and eventually became standard practice in the game of football.

## 1044. Winning Attitude

Joe Theismann (1949- ) quarterbacked the Washington Redskins to two consecutive Super Bowl appearances in the 1980s. His team won in 1983, but lost the following year.

Today, he wears both his winner's ring and his loser's ring as reminders concerning the necessity of effort.

During the first championship game, he was thrilled to be there and gave his very best effort. A year later things were different. He stated, "I was griping about the weather, my shoes, practice times, everything." His focus was more on convenience and comfort than unbridled effort.

Theisman says, "The difference in those two rings lies in applying oneself and not accepting anything but the best."

Further evidence that full-blown effort always carries a greater probability of success.

## 1045. Profanity in Sports

Bear Bryant (1913-1983), the great University of Alabama football coach, had a strict system of fines for profanity on the practice field.

The fines: a quarter for any player heard cursing, a dollar for assistant coaches, $5 for himself.

One practice session everything went wrong and Bryant finally blew his top. One swear word followed another.

Finally, scrambling down from the coaching tower, Bryant handed $200 to the team manager and said, "When that runs out, run me a tab!"

## 1046. Who's Got the Ball?

One could say this is one of the oddest, and funniest, football stories of all time.

Reporting on the first big West Coast football game, which had taken place on March 18, 1892, in San Francisco, the "San Francisco Chronicle" said there had been an unexpected delay when Stanford University and the University of California at Berkeley lined up to play.

Nobody had brought a football. They had to send someone out to get a ball.

Moral: what is everybody's responsibility is nobody's responsibility.

## 1047. A Mental Triumph

Tom Dempsey (1947- ) was born with only half a right foot and a deformed right hand. But his parents never made him uncomfortably aware of his handicap. As a result, the boy did everything all the other kids did. As he grew older, Tom wanted to play pro football. He found he could kick the football farther than anybody. And without ever giving a negative thought to his handicap he begged for a chance to try out for the New Orleans Saints.

The coach was doubtful, but was impressed by the boy's belief in himself, and so took him on.

Two weeks later the coach was even more impressed when Tom Dempsey kicked a 55-yard field goal in an exhibition game. That got him the job of regular kicker for the Saints, and in that season he scored 99 points for his team.

Then came the big moment. The stadium was packed with 66,000 fans. The ball was on the 45-yard line. There was time for only one play. The coach shouted for Dempsey to go in and try for a field goal.

As Tom ran onto the field he knew his team was 63 yards from the goal posts. The longest kick ever in a regular game had been 55 yards.

The snap of the ball was perfect. Dempsey put his foot into the ball squarely. The 66,000 spectators watched breathlessly. The ball had cleared the bar by inches. The team won, 19-17. The stands went wild, thrilled by the longest field goal ever kicked. And by a player with half a foot and deformed hand!

"Unbelievable!" someone shouted. But Dempsey smiled. He remembered his parents. They had always told him what he could do, not what he couldn't do. He accomplished this tremendous feat because, as he put it, "They never told me I couldn't."

## 1048. The Forward Pass

Very few people know that President Theodore Roosevelt (1858-1919) was the man most responsible for adding the forward pass to the game of football.

President Roosevelt convened an urgent meeting at the White House in October of 1905, whose purpose was to discuss the growing violence in football. The game had become so violent that more than 100 student players had been killed playing it. College presidents were discontinuing the sport. Several state legislatures were thinking seriously of making football illegal.

Responding to pressure from Roosevelt, a new rules committee was formed and charged with making major changes in the game. During the meeting, an idea long advocated by legendary coach John Heisman (1869-1936) – making the forward pass legal – was proposed.

The idea was called "radical" by *The New York Times* and the head of the rules committee was opposed to it. However, in 1906, a new rule permitting the forward pass was adopted. Other rules were passed outlawing holding and unnecessary roughness.

College football's first forward pass occurred on September 22, 1906, when the Saint Louis University quarterback threw the ball to Jack Schneider in a game against Carroll College. Now the forward pass is one of the game's most popular features.

## 1049. Under Oath

A Notre Dame football center named Frank Szymanski, who played in the 1940s, was called as a witness in a civil suit at South Bend, Indiana.

"Are you on the Notre Dame football team this year?" the judge asked.

"Yes, Your Honor," he replied.

"What position?"

"Center, Your Honor."

"How good a center?"

Szymanski hesitated for a moment, and blushed a little, but replied firmly, "Sir, I am the best center Notre Dame has ever had."

In the courtroom was the famous Notre Dame coach Frank Leahy (1908-1973) and he was surprised at Szymanski's seemingly boastful statement. When the court session was over, Leahy took Szymanski aside and asked why he had been so immodest about his abilities.

"I hated to do it, Coach," Szymanski said. "But, after all, I was under oath."

# SPORTS, GOLF

### 1050. Supreme Confidence

Annoyed by the constant boast of champion boxer Muhammad Ali (1942- ) that "I am the greatest," a colleague asked Ali what he was like in golf.

"I'm the best," replied Ali, "I just haven't played yet."

### 1051. How Golf Got Its Name

The name of the game may originate from the days of its origins in Scotland, when it was strictly a "Gentlemen Only, Ladies Forbidden" sport — hence GOLF.

### 1052. Integrity

At the 1925 U.S. Open, golfing great Bobby Jones (1902-1971) insisted on penalizing himself a stroke when his ball moved slightly in the rough as the blade of his iron touched the turf.

Nobody else could possibly have seen the ball move. The penalty dropped Jones into a tie with golfer Willie McFarlane, who went on to win the playoff.

Tom Kite did the same thing 53 years later in 1978. The self-imposed penalty caused him to lose the Hall of Fame Classic at Pinehurst by one stroke.

Reporters asked both men why they took the penalties. And both said essentially the same thing, "There's only one way to play the game."

### 1053. Thin Margins

During one year in the 1960s, near the peak of his skills, golfer Jack Nicklaus (1940- ) earned approximately $400,000 on the PGA tour.

Another golfer on the tour that year was Bob Charles. As a professional, he was not as successful as Jack Nicklaus. During the same year, Bob Charles earned approximately $40,000 on the PGA tour, one-tenth that of Jack Nicklaus (excluding income from endorsements and other revenue generating activities).

It might surprise you to learn that the difference in their respective per round stroke average was less than half a stroke. Imagine that!

The difference between the greatest golfer of all time and a very good golfer was less than half a stroke per round.

## 1054. General Grant and Golf

On a visit to Scotland, General Ulysses S. Grant (1822-1885) was treated to a demonstration of a game he'd never heard of before, something called golf. His host wanted to show Grant how the game was played, even though he wasn't much of a golfer himself.

While Grant watched, the man placed a ball on a tee, stood back, and took a swing. Although he missed the ball, he did tear up a patch of grass. He tried again, with the same result. Again and again he sent patches of dirt and grass into the air without once hitting the ball.

Grant looked from his perspiring host to the ball, then back to his host. "There seems to be a fair amount of exercise in the game," he said, "but I fail to see the purpose of the ball."

## 1055. The Little Red Book

Success came late in life for Harvey Pennick (1906-1995), author of *Harvey Pennick's Little Red Book*, which sold more than a million copies.

In the 1920's, Pennick bought a red spiral notebook and began jotting down observations about golf. He never showed the writings to anyone except his son, until 1991, when he shared it with a local writer and asked if he thought it was worth publishing. The writer showed it to Simon & Schuster and left word with Pennick's wife that the publisher had agreed to print the book for an advance of $90,000.

When the writer saw Pennick the next day, the golfer seemed troubled and finally explained that with all his medical bills, there was no way he could advance Simon & Schuster $90,000.

### 1056. Stay Focused

Golf great Ben Hogan (1912-1997) stood over a crucial putt. Suddenly a loud train whistle blared in the distance.

After he had sunk the putt, someone asked Hogan if the train whistle had bothered him.

"What whistle?" Hogan replied.

### 1057. Bad Golfer

President Richard Nixon (1913-1994) returned to Camp David and proudly announced, "I scored 126."

In a flattering voice, Henry Kissinger (1923- ), his national security advisor, said, "Your golf is improving, Mr. President."

Nixon snapped back, "I was bowling."

# SPORTS, HOCKEY

### 1058. Failure to Take Risks

Wayne Gretzky (1961- ), the hockey player, reported the comment of an early coach who was frustrated with his lack of scoring in an important game.

The coach made his point when he said, "You miss 100 percent of the shots you never take."

# SPORTS, THE OLYMPICS

## 1059. History of the Olympic Games

The first organized Olympic Games were held in Greece in 776 B.C. They were held every four years as a tribute to the god Zeus. It is thought that competitive athletic games had been held in Greece since about 800 B.C., but not as an organized festival.

The only event at the first Games was the stadium foot race, a 600 foot (183 meter) sprint. In later Games, many other competitions were added, including javelin throws, horse racing, and wrestling.

The early Games were men-only affairs. Women were not allowed to compete, nor even to observe. The games were considered so important that, when they were held, trade was suspended and wars were often postponed.

Even after the Romans conquered Greece, the Games continued. However, in 394 A.D., the Roman emperor Theodosius ended the Games. He had become a convert to Christianity and considered the Games to be a glorification of ancient Greek gods.

For the next 1500 years, the Olympic Games were nothing but a distant memory. But in 1892, a 27-year-old French baron named Pierre de Coubertin (1863-1937) went about reviving the Olympic ideal. His motive was to improve the physical fitness of the French, so that his countrymen could be better prepared should there be war with Germany.

At first, the response from athletic officials was to ignore Coubertin's proposal. But Coubertin's stubborn devotion to the idea eventually carried the day. So in 1896 the first modern Olympiad was held in Athens, Greece, with 311 athletes competing, far fewer than the 10,000 that compete in the Olympics today.

## 1060. The Chariot Race

The Roman Emperor Nero was a contestant in an Olympics chariot race held in Rome in 65 AD. He won but he had more than a little help.

Driving a team of 10 horses, he lost control during the race and was thrown from the chariot. Bystanders reportedly helped him climb back in the chariot.

Although he could not finish the race, Nero was nonetheless awarded the crown of victory.

Note: Nero's full name was: Lucius Domitius Ahenobarbus (37-68 AD).

## 1061. Women in the Olympics

As stated elsewhere in this section, women were barred for years from competing in the Olympics. As late as 1960, women could not run in any race longer than 200 meters.

Women did compete in the 800 meters in 1928 in Amsterdam but, when several of them collapsed at the finish, it was determined that distances longer than 200 meters were possibly injurious to their health.

Therefore, no women's race longer than 200 meters was allowed until the 800 was run again at the 1960 Games.

## 1062. Statues of Cheaters

The athletes entrance to the stadium at Olympia, where the original Olympic Games were held, is lined with statues. But these are not representations of those athletes who achieved great and courageous victories, but of those who cheated.

Twenty-seven centuries later, those stone statues still shout out their message of contempt.

## 1063. Olympics in the Nude

The modern Olympics date from 1896, when the ancient competition between nations was revived in Athens.

But today's Olympics differ from the original Greek Games in an important way. Many of the original Olympics contests were conducted in the nude. This curious phenomenon resulted from an accident.

During the fifteenth Olympics in 720 B.C., while running in a footrace, an entrant by the name of Orsippus of Megara suddenly lost his loincloth. However, in spite of losing his loincloth, he won the race.

Other runners quickly credited Orsippus' victory to his absence of clothing, and soon many of them chose to emulate his triumph by wearing no clothes at all.

Their reasoning was certainly not wrong. Wearing no clothing during a race reduced wind friction and enabled runners to reduce their running times. Soon other athletes, liking the freedom of movement, shed their loincloths too. Thus, the ancient Olympics contests became nude events, thanks to the accidental loss of a runner's loincloth.

## 1064. The Mind Is a Powerful Thing

Russian Olympian star Vasily Alexeev was trying to break a weight-lifting record of 500 pounds. He had lifted 499 but couldn't for the life of him, lift 500.

Finally, his trainers put 501.5 pounds on his bar and rigged it so it looked like 499 pounds. Guess what happened? He lifted it easily.

Once Alexeev broke the 500-pound barrier, other weight lifters went on to break his record. Why? Because now they knew it was possible.

## 1065. Commitment

At 6:50 p.m. as evening fell in Mexico City in 1968, John Stephen Akwari of Tanzania painfully hobbled into the Olympic stadium — the last man to finish the punishing marathon race.

The victory ceremony for the winning runner was long over and the stadium was almost empty as Akwari — his leg bloody and bandaged — struggled to circle the track to cross the finish line.

Watching from a distance was Bud Greenspan (1926- ), a documentary film maker famous for his Olympic movies. Intrigued, Greenspan walked over to the exhausted Akwari and asked why he had continued the grueling run to the finish line.

The young man from Tanzania did not have to search for an answer. "My country," he said, "did not send me 9,000 miles to start the race. They sent me 9,000 miles to finish the race."

## 1066. Why We Call It the Marathon

A marathon is a long-distance race — a race of over 26 miles. The reason it is called that is because of something that happened after the Battle of Marathon in the year 490 B.C.

The Greeks were pitted against an invading army of Persians in that battle, and the Greeks were expected to lose.

Not only did the Persians outnumber the Greeks more than two to one, but they had also gained a reputation for invincibility as a result of previous conquests. The Persians had conquered everything from what is now Iran through Iraq, Syria and Turkey. They had rolled over everything in their path. They did not expect to run into much resistance from the Greeks.

With a surprise dawn attack, the Greeks totally routed the Persians on the plains of Marathon. The Persians lost 6,400 men in the battle while the Greeks lost only 192. What was left of the Persian army fled to the coast and escaped by boat.

Notwithstanding his great victory, the commander of the Greek forces was seized with the fear that the Persians would proceed down the coast to Athens. If word of the victory did not reach the city soon enough, the Athenian people, already expecting the worst, would almost certainly capitulate.

Therefore the Greek commander dispatched his swiftest runner to take the good news to Athens. This runner (Pheidippides (530 BC-490 BC) by name) ran the whole way, more than twenty miles. He arrived, gasping, "Rejoice; we conquered." Then he died of exhaustion.

It was in honor of him that the Marathon was established as a modern Olympic event.

The Battle of Marathon marks one of the great turning points in history. Having withstood the challenge mounted by the Persians, the Greeks went on to achieve a surpassing greatness of their own. They laid the foundations of western culture and civilization.

# SPORTS, SOCCER

## 1067. Soccer Was Once Illegal

What is probably the world's most popular sport today – soccer – was banned by King Edward II (1284-1327) of England in 1314.

True enough, soccer then was totally different than the way the game is played today. Town against town were often pitted against each other, with hundreds of players on a side brawling across fields and down roads. The "sport" was very popular with the common people but the King's royal edict made it illegal and harsh prison terms were given those caught violating the law.

Through the years, King Edward had a lot of royal company who legislated against the sport. Also extending the ban were Edward III, Richard II, and Henry IV. King James IV of Scotland in 1457 banned not only soccer but the game of golf.

Why did these two sports so bother the royal rulers? It was because the kings believed they were distracting men from archery practice. And, without a nation of good archers, it was not possible to raise good armies during times of crisis.

It was the people's love of the two sports that kept them alive despite the royal persecution. People kept on engaging in them despite the heavy penalties until the laws banning them were finally forgotten.

# SPORTS, GENERAL

### 1068. History of Sports

Originally, sport had a religious basis and was preparation for life. Its roots were in man's desire to gain superiority over real and unseen foes, to influence natural forces, and to encourage fertility among his crops and cattle.

As a word, Sport is an abbreviation: the shortened form of "disport," a diversion and an amusement. Rooted in Latin, it literally means "carry away" (from desporto).

Millions of people today, whether as spectators or participants, amateurs or professionals, are carried away by the sport they love. It gives them release from the cares of their daily toil, their anxieties and frustrations. It allows them to enter a world of relaxation and emulation, excitement and thrills.

### 1069. Finding the Zone

"Finding the Zone" is that magical moment when performance seems inspired and effortless. Basketball players say that when they play "in the zone," the basket seems larger — the shots come easier.

Ted Williams (1918-2002), the Boston Red Sox legend, said that when he was "in the zone," everything was so clear to him that he could see the seams on a pitched ball.

Jazz musicians say they're "in the zone," when they're in their groove, and the instrument almost plays itself. There are times when opera singers suddenly experience a remarkable phenomenon — and hit high and low notes they could never reach before.

Being "in the zone" is that moment in which performance "transcends the normal or usual." "In the zone" can be a one time phenomenon — or it can be an incredible breakthrough that continues year after year.

## 1070. Hey Coach!

Why is the man or woman in charge of a sports team or athlete called coach? Carriages were originally named after the Hungarian town of Koes (pronounced "coach") where they were first made in the 16th century.

In the 19th century some university wit applied the term to a private tutor who prepared candidates for their examinations. A coach was a very luxurious and stately carriage and the idea, apparently, was that the student was being "carried" by the tutor.

About 40 years after the name "coach" was applied to a tutor, the term was extended to one who trained others for athletic contests.

## 1071. Steinbeck on Sports

The author John Steinbeck (1902-1968) put down some of his thoughts about sports in an article published in *Sports Illustrated*. Here is an excerpt:

"It seems to me that any sport is a kind of practice, perhaps unconscious, for the life-and-death struggle for survival. Our team sports simulate war, with its strategy, tactics, logistics, heroism and/or cowardice.

"Individual competition of all kinds has surely ingredients of single combat, which was for x millions of years the means of going on living. The Greeks, who invented realism and pretty much cornered the market, began the training of a soldier by teaching him dancing. The rhythm, precision and coordination of the dance made the hoplite (sic) one hell of a lot better trooper.

"In this connection, it is interesting that the hill men of Crete in their all-male dancing go through the motions of using shield and spear, of defense and dodge and parry, of attack, thrust and retreat. I don't imagine they know this, but it is what they do."

### 1072. Attitude in Sports

A winning attitude is critical to success in sports. A baseball manager with an interesting slant on winning said, "You only have to bat 1,000 in two things, flying and heart transplants. Everything else you can go four for five."

Unfortunately, some teams, like some businesses, have attitudes that inevitably guarantee failure. A Pittsburgh Pirates coach once said, "I managed a team that was so bad, we considered a 2-and-0 count a rally."

And a former Pirates manager knew he was in for a tough season when on opening day as the team lined up for the playing of the national anthem, he heard one of his players say, "Every time we hear that song, we have a bad game."

# STATISTICS

### 1073. Reliability of Statistics

The original source of statistics may easily be the weakest link. A good example is this story about how statistics are gathered in India.

A young man quoted some statistics to a Judge, an Englishman, and a very good fellow. The Judge said, "When you are a bit older, you will not quote Indian statistics with that assurance. The Government are very keen on amassing statistics. They collect them, add them, raise them to the nth power, take the cube root and prepare wonderful diagrams. But what you must never forget is that every one of those figures comes in the first instance from the 'chowty dar' [chowkidar] (village watchman), who just puts down what he damn pleases."

### 1074. Pickles and Cancer

The following is from the *Journal of Irreproducible Results*:

Statistics prove that pickles cause cancer, war, communism, airline tragedies and auto accidents. About 99.9% of cancer victims have eaten pickles at some time in their lives. So have 100% of all soldiers, 96.8% of all communists and 99.7% of those involved in car and air accidents. Moreover of those born in 1839 who ate pickles, none are alive today.

## 1075. Defense of Statistics

James Dunwoody Brownson De Bow (1820-1867), American statistician and editor, defended his profession this way, "Statistics are far from being the barren array of figures ingeniously and laboriously combined into columns and tables, which many persons are apt to suppose. They constitute rather the ledger of a nation, in which, like the merchant in his books, the citizen can read, at one view, all of the results of a year or of a period of years, as compared with other periods, and deduce the profit or loss which has been made, in morals, education, wealth or power."

## 1076. Analogy about Statistics

Ely Devons (1913-1967), a distinguished English economist composed this novel analogy about statistics, "The experience of falling in love could be adequately described in terms of statistics. A record of heart beats per minute, the stammering and hesitation in speech, the number of calories consumed per day, the heightening of poetic vision, measured by the number of lines of poetry written to the beloved. I won't go on; no doubt you can think of further measures."

## 1077. Defense of Statistics

Eric T. Bell (1883-1960), distinguished and sometimes controversial American mathematician, said, "The technical analysis of any large collection of data is a task for a highly trained and expensive man who knows the mathematical theory of statistics inside and out. Otherwise the outcome is likely to be a collection of drawings — quartered pies, cute little battleships, and tapering rows of sturdy soldiers in diversified uniforms — interesting enough in a colored Sunday supplement, but hardly the sort of thing from which to draw reliable inferences."

## 1078. Twain on Statistics

Mark Twain (Samuel Clemens) (1835-1910), American writer and humorist on every subject, had this to say, "Statistics are like ladies of the night. Once you get them down, you can do anything with them."

## 1079. A Measure of Civilization

Daniel J. Boorstin (1914-2004), American historian and former Librarian of Congress, said of statistics, "The science of statistics is the chief instrumentality through which the progress of civilization is now measured and by which its development hereafter will be largely controlled."

## 1080. Phony Statistics

Rex Stout (1886-1975), American author of mystery stories, once said, "There are two kinds of statistics, the kind you look up and the kind you make up."

## 1081. Persuading People

Tom Peters (1942- ), popular American business journalist and consultant, said, "People, including managers, do not live by pie charts alone — or by bar graphs or three inch statistical appendices to 300 page reports. People live, reason and are moved by symbols and stories."

# SUBSTANCE ABUSE

## 1082. Ignoring Danger

This story was told by a Native American actor named Iron Eyes Cody (1904-1999), who became famous for an anti-litter TV spot he did for the "Keep America Beautiful" campaign.

The story goes like this. Many years ago, Indian youths would go away in solitude to prepare for manhood. One such youth hiked into a beautiful valley, green with trees and bright with flowers.

There he fasted. But on the third day, as he looked up at the surrounding mountains, he noticed one tall rugged peak, capped with dazzling snow. "I will test myself against that mountain," he thought.

He put on his buffalo-hide shirt, threw his blanket over his shoulders and set off to climb the peak. When he reached the top he stood on the rim of the world. He could see forever, and his heart swelled with pride.

Then he heard a rustle at his feet and, looking down, he saw a snake. Before he could move, the snake spoke.

"I am about to die," said the snake. "It is too cold for me up here and I am freezing. There is no food and I am starving. Put me under your shirt and take me down to the valley."

"No," said the youth. "I am forewarned. I know your kind. You are a rattlesnake. If I pick you up, you will bite, and your bite will kill me."

"Not so," said the snake. "I will treat you differently. If you do this for me, you will be special. I will not harm you."

The youth resisted awhile, but this was a very persuasive snake with beautiful markings. At last, the youth tucked the snake under his shirt and carried it down to the valley where he laid it gently on the grass. Suddenly the snake coiled, rattled and struck, biting him on the leg.

"But you promised..." cried the youth.

"You knew what I was when you picked me up," said the snake as it slithered away.

Iron Eyes Cody told this story especially to young people who might be tempted by drugs.

"I want them to remember," he said, "the words of the snake."

"You knew what I was when you picked me up."

## 1083. Shakespeare on Abstinence

William Shakespeare (1564-1616) wrote frequently about what was necessary to break dangerous habits. Here is one example, "Refrain tonight, and that shall lend a hand of easiness to the next abstinence; the next more easy; for use can almost change the stamp of nature, and either curb the devil or throw him out with wondrous potency."

## 1084. Breaking Bad Habits

John Boyle O'Reilly (1844-1890) an Irish-born poet and novelist, wrote a poem titled "A Builder's Lesson" about the difficulty of breaking bad habits. It goes like this:

"How shall I a habit break?
 As you did that habit make,
 As you gathered, you must lose;
 As you yielded, now refuse,
 Thread by thread the strands we twist
 Till they bind us, neck and wrist,
 Thread by thread the patient hand
 Must untwine, ere free we stand.
 As we builded, stone by stone,
 We must toil, unhelped, alone,
 Till the wall is overthrown."

## 1085. An Addict's Testimony

Billie Holiday (1915-1959), American jazz singer of great popularity, was quoted in a movie of her life, *Lady Sings the Blues*, "Dope never helped anybody sing better or play music better or do anything better. All dope can do for you is kill you and kill you the long, slow, hard way. And it can kill the people you love right along with you."

## 1086. We Can Be Our Own Worst Enemy

A cartoon strip character conceived by Walt Kelly (1913-1973) was used for an Earth Day poster in 1971. It's message was, "We have met the enemy and he is us."

# SUPERSTITIONS

## 1087. Celebrity Superstitions

Luciano Pavarotti (1935-2007): "I won't sing a note or act a word until I find a bent nail onstage. It's like a good-luck charm for me. If I can't spot my nail onstage, I search the wings."

Larry Bird (1956- ) (basketball player): Always made sure to rub his hands on his sneakers before a game to give himself "a better feel" for the ball.

Lena Horne (1917- ) (singer): Thinks peanut shells in her dressing room brings bad luck.

Winston Churchill (1874-1965): Thought it was unlucky to travel on Fridays. He tried to arrange his schedule so he could "stay put" on that day.

Tony Curtis (1925- ) (actor): Wears only slip-on shoes. Thinks laces are unlucky.

Cornelius Vanderbilt (1794-1877) (America's richest man in the 1860s): Had the legs of his bed placed on dishes of salt, to ward off attacks from evil spirits.

Drew Barrymore (1975- ) (actor): Says "peas indicate good luck."

Jim Kelly (1960- ) (Buffalo Bills quarterback): Vomits for good luck before each game. He's been doing it since high school.

Queen Elizabeth II (1926- ): Insists on making a token payment for scissors used to cut ribbons at official openings. (It's bad luck to accept scissors as a gift and return nothing.)

Babe Ruth (1895-1948): Always stepped on first base when he came in from his right field position.

Zsa Zsa Gabor (1917 to 1919- ) (celebrity personality): Thought it was bad luck to have goldfish in the house.

Wayne Gretzky (1961- ) (NHL's all-time leading scorer): Puts baby powder on his stick before every game, and tucks only one side of his jersey into his pants.

Joan Rivers (1933- ): (comedian) "I knock on wood so often I have splinters in all ten knuckles."

Princess Diana (1961-1997): Had a lock of hair sewn into her wedding dress (for good luck).

## 1088. Edwin Land on Superstition

Edwin H. Land (1900-1993), American inventor of the Polaroid camera and businessman, had this to say, "We work by exorcising incessant superstition that there are mysterious tribal gods against you. Nature has neither rewards nor punishments, only consequences. You can use science to make it work for you. There's only nothingness and chaos out there until the human mind recognizes it."

## 1089. Causes of Superstition

Bertrand Russell (1872-1970), noted English philosopher and mathematician, at 78, said, "Fear is the main source of superstition, and one of the main sources of cruelty. To conquer fear is the beginning of wisdom."

## 1090. Analysis of Superstition

Francois Marie Arouet Voltaire (1694-1776), French satirist, philosopher and writer, made this observation about superstitions, "Superstition is to religion what astrology is to astronomy: the mad daughter or a wise mother."

# TACT

### 1091. Dealing with Enemies

Abraham Lincoln once was criticized for referring to the Confederates in kind terms.

The woman critic asked the President how he could speak generously of his enemies when he should rather destroy them.

"Why, Madam," replied Lincoln, "do I not destroy them when I make them my friends?"

### 1092. How to Make People Dislike You

Benjamin Franklin (1706-1790), probably with his tongue in cheek, wrote up some suggestions on how to make people dislike you. Here they are:

- If possible, engross the whole discourse...talk of much of yourself, your education, your knowledge, your successes.

- When you are out of breath, watch his words, and you will probably find something to contradict and raise a dispute about. If that fails, criticize his grammar.

- If another shall be saying an indisputably good thing, say it has already been said by Bacon, Locke, or another eminent writer, and thus you deprive him of the reputation he might have gained from it.

### 1093. Perfect Tact

Once President Abraham Lincoln was visited by two rival hatters, each of whom presented him with a hat he had made. After the presentation, both hatters stood back expectantly awaiting Lincoln's comments.

Lincoln looked over the two hats very carefully, and then remarked solemnly, "Gentlemen, they mutually excel each other."

## 1094. Personal Delicacy

Abraham Lincoln had accompanied a young lady to one of the hospitals in Washington where she expressed her sympathy to a wounded soldier. To all her questions as to the location of the wound, the soldier would only answer: "At Antietam."

"Yes, but where did the bullet strike you, exactly?" she asked.

"At Antietam," repeated the wounded soldier.

Discouraged, the young lady left the hospital ward but asked President Lincoln to find out for her.

When Lincoln rejoined her, she asked him just where the soldier had been wounded.

With a hint of a smile creasing his craggy face, Lincoln replied, "My dear girl, the ball that hit him would not have injured you."

## 1095. Modern Art

Abraham Lincoln was once shown a picture done by a mediocre painter and was asked to give his opinion of it.

"Why," said President Lincoln, "the painter is a very good painter, and he observes the Lord's commandments."

A well-known Senator standing nearby asked, "What do you mean by that, Mr. Lincoln?"

"I mean," said the tactful Lincoln, "that he hath not made to himself the likeness of anything that is in the heaven above, or that is in the earth beneath, or that is in the water under the earth."

# TAXES

## 1096. Tax Resistance

The subject of taxes — and peoples' resistance to paying them — is as old as time.

For years the Athenian statesman Themistocles (c.524 BC-459 BC) had alienated friendly allies of Athens by extorting money from them. Despite this, he accompanied a heavily armed naval fleet to the Andrian islands with a demand to pay him more money.

"I come with two gods," he told the islanders, "Persuasion and Compulsion."

The islanders replied that they already had two great gods on their side who hindered them from giving Themistocles any more money – "Penury and Despair."

## 1097. A Lady Called Godiva

A story first mentioned in 1236 by the chronicler Roger of Wendover relates how a young English noblewoman named Lady Godiva, in the year 1057, exasperated her husband by persistently pleading with him to reduce the taxes on the people of Coventry.

Her husband, Leofric, to shut her up, declared he would do so only if she agreed to ride horseback naked through the town's marketplace.

The 17-year-old Godiva called his bluff and set out for the town next day riding her horse completely naked. She concealed most of her body with her long and copious tresses of hair. This served both her own modesty and her husband's pride, enabling Leofric to reduce the taxes without loss of face.

Whether it is true or not, the legend is that the townspeople, in gratitude for Godiva's action, refused to look at her nakedness as she rode through the town.

Note: Lady Godiva's birth year is listed as around 1040. Could it be a coincidence that the U.S. standard income tax form bears the same number?

## 1098. Lincoln and the Income Tax

The four-page income tax form issued during the Civil War was far simpler than that of today's. But the Civil War tax form was sufficiently complicated that even a capable Illinois lawyer named Abraham Lincoln was unable to understand all its provisions.

The fact is, eight years after his assassination, it was discovered that in 1864 President Lincoln had overpaid his taxes by $1,250. The money was returned to his estate.

## 1099. English Domination of Ireland

Jonathan Swift (1667-1745), author of the famous *Gulliver's Travels*, also held the influential post of Dean of St. Patrick's Cathedral in Dublin.

In this capacity, Swift was renowned for his defense of the rights and liberties of the Irish people at a time when Ireland was being harshly ruled by England.

Once, when the wife of the English viceroy to Ireland casually remarked to Swift that she thought the air of Ireland was remarkably good, Swift fell to his knees in mock supplication exclaiming, "For God's sake, madam, don't say so in England. They will tax it!"

## 1100. Misunderstanding

Terry Sanford (1917-1998), the former governor of North Carolina, was recalling a speech he made during one of his gubernatorial campaigns.

"It was in a fairly remote county," he said, "and I made a strong speech about the need to improve public education in North Carolina."

"When I was finished, a woman stood up and demanded, 'Where are you going to get the money for all this stuff?'

"I decided to give her a blunt answer and said, 'Where do you think we will get the money? From taxes, of course.' And the audience broke out in loud applause."

"Later I turned to an aide and said, "Do you realize what we experienced tonight? Voters actually applauding when I said we would get new money from taxes. That's a real first!'

Replied the aide, "Governor, they thought you said Texas."

# TEAMWORK

## 1101. Lesson from the Redwoods

The huge redwood trees in California are considered the largest things on earth and the tallest trees in the world. Some of them are three hundred feet high and over 2,500 years old.

One would think that trees so large would have a tremendous root system reaching down hundreds of feet into the earth. The redwoods actually have a very shallow system of roots, but they all intertwine. They are locked to each other. When the storms come or the winds blow, the redwoods stand. They are locked to each other, and they don't stand alone, for all the trees support and protect each other.

## 1102. Stone Soup

Once upon a time, somewhere in Eastern Europe following a destructive war, there was a great famine in which people jealously hoarded whatever food they could find, hiding it even from their friends and neighbors. One day a wandering soldier came into a village and began asking questions as if he planned to stay for the night.

"There's not a bite to eat in the whole province," he was told. "Better keep moving on."

"Oh, I have everything I need," he said. "In fact, I was thinking of making some stone soup to share with all of you." He pulled an iron cauldron from his wagon, filled it with water, and built a fire under it. Then, with great ceremony, he drew an ordinary-looking stone from a velvet bag and dropped it into the water.

By now, hearing the rumor of food, most of the villagers had come to the square or watched from their windows. As the soldier sniffed the "broth" and licked his lips in anticipation, hunger began to overcome their skepticism.

"Ah," the soldier said to himself rather loudly, "I do like a tasty stone soup. Of course, stone soup with cabbage, that's hard to beat."

Soon a villager approached hesitantly, holding a cabbage he'd retrieved from its hiding place, and added it to the pot.

"Capital!" cried the soldier. "You know, I once had stone soup with cabbage and a bit of salt beef as well, and it was fit for a king."

The village butcher managed to find some salt beef. . . . and so it went, through potatoes, onions, carrots, mushrooms, and so on, until there was indeed a delicious meal for all. The villagers offered the soldier a great deal of money for the magic stone, but he refused to sell and traveled on the next day.

Moral: Working together, with everyone contributing what they can, a greater good is achieved for all.

## 1103. Climbing Mount Everest

Just how important is teamwork? Some of us may be old enough to remember a dramatic day in May of 1953, when for the first time in recorded history two men climbed to the top of Mount Everest, at 29,000 feet the highest point on earth.

The two men were Edmund Hillary (1919-2008), a New Zealand bee keeper and explorer, age 34, and a Nepal Sherpa mountaineer and guide named Ten-Zing Norgay (1914-1986), age 39. They reached the summit successfully, a little before noon, planted a banner, ate some mint cake, and radioed the news to the base camp below, where an army of reporters was awaiting them.

What many people do not remember is that, on the way down from the summit, Hillary lost his footing and started to slip. Norgay, an experienced and courageous mountaineer, instantly sensed what was happening: he immediately dug in his ice-ax, braced the rope connecting him to his climbing partner, and unquestionably saved Hillary's life.

The rest of their descent was uneventful. When they reached the bottom, Hillary was quick to tell the press of Norgay's heroic action. The press quickly surrounded Norgay, exploding hundreds of flashbulbs, and shouting dozens of questions at the sherpa guide.

Amid all this commotion, flashbulbs, shouted questions, Norgay remained calm and collected, and offered one simple but profoundly effective answer:

"Mountain climbers always help each other."

## 1104. The Body's "Teamwork"

This Aesop fable dramatically demonstrates the miracle of how well the human body's many complex parts work together to promote health and well-being.

In olden days, when all a man's limbs did not work together as peacefully as they do now, but when each had a will and way of its own, the Members began to criticize the Belly for enjoying a life of idleness and luxury, while they spent all their time working to feed it. So they entered into a conspiracy to cut off the Belly's supplies in the future.

The Hands were no longer to carry food to the Mouth, nor would the Mouth receive the food, nor the Teeth chew it.

They had not long followed this plan of starving the Belly, when they all began, one by one, to fail and flag, and the whole body began to waste away.

Then the Members realized that the Belly, too cumbersome and useless as it seemed, had an important function of its own; that they could no more do without it than it could do without them; and that if they wanted to keep the body in a healthy state, they must work together, each in his proper sphere, for the common good of all.

Moral: Only by working together can the greatest good for all be achieved.

## 1105. Sticking Together

Once upon a time there was a father whose sons were always fighting with each other. The father pleaded with them again and again to stop their constant quarreling but nothing seemed to do any good.

Finally, the father asked his sons to bring him a bundle of sticks. He took the sticks and, handing them to his eldest son, asked him to break the bundle in two. The eldest son tried with all his strength to do so, but finally gave up. The other sons, in turn, failed as well.

Then the father separated the sticks and placed one into each son's hand, asking them to break the sticks in two. And, of course, they did so easily.

Then the father said, "My sons, if you are of one mind, and help each other, you will be like the bundle of sticks. No one can break you apart. But if you are divided among yourselves, you will be broken as easily as a single stick."

After this demonstration, the fights among the brothers soon ceased and there was unity in the family from that day forward.

## 1106. Rocky Balboa

The movie *Rocky* contains a memorable line that perfectly sums up the power of teamwork and synergy.

In the movie, the boxer Rocky Balboa (played memorably by Sylvester Stallone (1946- )) describes the relationship that exists between himself and his girlfriend, whose personality is so different from his.

"I've got gaps, she's got gaps," says Rocky. "Together, we've got no gaps."

## 1107. The Power of Music

Robert Shaw (1916-1999), an American choral director, earned worldwide his fame for his ability to blend together hundreds of voices into unforgettable music.

Once Shaw was asked how he was able to do this, often with very short rehearsal times. His answer says a lot about what it takes to bring about winning combinations of people and organizations.

"Once we find each other," he said simply, "the miracle begins."

## 1108. Lincoln on Teamwork

Abraham Lincoln once told a story about a hunting party that went out to track a wild boar.

While engaged in the hunt, the wild boar jumped out from behind a tree unexpectedly and the hunters all scrambled toward the treetops — all except one, the bravest hunter of them all.

Seizing the fierce animal by the ears, he hung on for dear life, but none of his hunting mates came to help him.

After holding the ferocious boar for some time, and finding his strength giving way, the hero cried out to his companions hiding in the trees: "Boys, come down and help me let go!"

# TESTIMONY

## 1109. Nothing but the Truth

Since the Romans had no Bibles on which to swear, it was the custom to place one's right hand on one's testicles when swearing to tell the truth.

The English word "testimony" is derived from this practice.

## 1110. Will Rogers on Testimony

Will Rogers (1879-1935), American humorist and actor, said of testimony in Washington, "I think of all the bunch on the witness stand in Washington that lawyers are the worst. A lawyer has so many angles that he is trying to use a little of all of them and he winds up making everybody believe that he didn't tell half he knew, and didn't know half he told."

## 1111. Watergate Testimony

George S. Danielson (1915-1998), Democrat congressman from California, said of Attorney General John N. Mitchell's testimony during the Watergate hearings held by the House Judiciary Committee in Washington in July of 1974, "Trying to obtain information from Mr. Mitchell was like trying to nail a drop of water to the wall."

# THRIFT

## 1112. Prepare for the Future

This Aesop fable, written in the Sixth Century B.C., makes a powerful point about the need to set something aside for the future.

In a field one summer's day a Grasshopper was hopping about, chirping and singing to its heart's content. An Ant passed by, bearing along with great toil an ear of corn he was taking to his nest.

"Why not come and chat with me," said the Grasshopper, "instead of toiling in that way?"

"I am helping to lay up food for the winter," said the Ant, "and I recommend you do the same."

"Why bother about winter," said the Grasshopper; "we have got plenty of food at present."

But the Ant went on its way and continued its toil. When the winter came the Grasshopper had no food, and found itself dying of hunger, while it saw the ants distributing every day corn and grain from the stores they had collected in the summer.

Then the Grasshopper knew: It is best to prepare for the days of necessity.

## 1113. Ben Franklin and the Whistle

When Ben Franklin was seven years old, he was given a small gift of money. He went immediately to a toy shop and, being charmed by the sound of a whistle being blown by another boy, he paid all of his money for one just like it.

Franklin went home much pleased with his purchase and proceeded to drive everyone in the house crazy by constantly blowing his whistle. His pleasure was soon ended when his family told him he had paid four times more for the whistle than he should have.

"This discovery," said Franklin, "gave me more chagrin than the whistle gave me pleasure."

During Franklin's long career, he became a wealthy businessman, a respected scientist, and an admired American diplomat in the royal courts of France and England. But, despite his many successes, he never forgot the lesson of the whistle.

"When I saw a man sacrifice everything for royal favor," Franklin said, "I would say to myself, 'That man gives too much for his whistle.'

"When I see misers giving up every kind of comfortable living, all the pleasure of doing good to others, all the esteem of his fellow-citizens, and the joys of benevolent friendship for the sake of accumulating wealth, I say to myself, 'Poor man, you pay too much for your whistle.'

"When I see a beautiful, sweet-tempered girl married to an ill-natured brute of a husband, I say to myself, 'What a pity that she should pay so much for a whistle!'"

"In short," said Franklin, "I conceived that a great part of the miseries of mankind were brought upon them by the false estimates they have made of the value of things, and by their giving too much for their whistles."

## 1114. Actions Speak Loudest

An old farmer was once asked by a young man how it was he had become so wealthy.

"It's a long story," said the old man, "and while I'm telling it we may as well save the candle." And he put it out.

"You need not tell the story," said the youth. "I understand."

## 1115. You Get What You Pay For

This story by Ben Franklin illustrates the fact that sometimes you can drive too hard a bargain. Franklin said he once knew a shoemaker in Philadelphia who planned to travel by coach to New York to visit his brother. And to do that he needed to find a stable where he could leave his horse.

The first stable owner he went to told him, "We charge twenty dollars a month for the feeding and watering of your horse, but we give you back two dollars for our use of the manure."

The penurious shoemaker thought twenty dollars for stabling his horse was way too much so he went to see a second livery stable nearby. The liveryman there said they charged ten dollars a month, "but we give you back a dollar for the manure."

The shoemaker shook his head and asked the second liveryman if he knew someone who would stable his horse for less.

"Well," said the second liveryman, "there's an old Quaker off Arch Street who charges only five dollars a month. You might try him."

Encouraged, the shoemaker hurried over to the Quaker owner's address on Arch Street and asked him about his fees.

"Yes," said the Quaker, "we charge only five dollars a month for keeping your horse."

"And what about the manure?" asked the shoemaker.

"Manure!" said the Quaker. "At five dollars a month there won't be any manure!"

## 1116. Practice What You Preach

Benjamin Franklin is identified with thrift, having coined such maxims as "A penny saved is a penny earned," but he himself was a compulsive spender.

While serving as ambassador to France, he shipped home loads of extravagant purchases, including fine china, silverware, carpets and a harpsichord. He set up a wine cellar stocked with 1,203 bottles.

While in France he spent an average of $12,000 a year, an astonishing amount of money at the time. Franklin admitted that frugality was "a virtue I never could acquire in myself."

Researchers have found that his account at Philadelphia's Bank of North America was overdrawn at least three times a week.

## 1117. Saving

This is an old New England maxim about thrift:

"Use it up,
Wear it out,
Make it do,
Or do without."

## 1118. Benjamin Franklin on Thrift

Although late in life he admitted he was never good at it, Benjamin Franklin (1706-1790), American statesman, scientist and philosopher, wrote often about the virtues of thrift. Here is a sample:

"Remember, that time is money. Remember, that credit is money. Remember, that money is of the prolific, generating nature. Remember, that six pounds a year is but a groat a day. Remember this saying, The good payer is lord of another man's purse, He that is known to pay punctually and exactly to the time he promises, may at any time, and on any occasion, raise all the money his friends can spare. In short, the way to wealth, if you desire it, is as plain as the way to market. It depends chiefly on two words, industry and frugality; that is, waste neither time nor money, but make the best use of both."

## 1119. A Story of Saving

Helen Bevington (1906-2001), American poet, author, and educator, told this amusing story about a friend's mother: "My neighbor Howard says his mother saved everything. His mother made little cloth bags to hold pieces of string, each bag carefully labeled as to the length of the pieces. After her death, they found one small bag of string labeled "too short to save."

# TRAVEL, TRANSPORTATION

## 1120. Travel Times

In 1789, it took George Washington eight days to travel the 200-odd miles from his home, Mount Vernon, to the scene of his inauguration as President in New York City.

The fact that it required eight days is not significant. The important fact is that the time was the same as it would have taken 2,000 years before. No real progress had been made in transportation in twenty centuries.

Moses or Nebuchadnezzar could have traveled just as rapidly. Julius Caesar could have stepped from the first century into the nineteenth more easily than Benjamin Franklin could have stepped into 1976. Now for the first time in history, no man dies in the historical epoch in which he was born.

## 1121. Ocean Sickness

On one of his many trips to Europe, the writer and humorist Mark Twain (Samuel Clemens) became terribly seasick.

Recounting the experience later to a friend, Twain said, "At first you were afraid you would die and then you got so sick you were afraid you wouldn't die."

## 1122. Hitchhiking

A gentleman driving along the Springfield road in Illinois was hailed by a young Abraham Lincoln, who said: "Will you have the goodness to take my overcoat to town for me?"

"With pleasure," said the stranger, "but how will you get it again?"

"Oh, very readily," said Lincoln, "as I intend to remain in it."

## 1123. The Constant Traveler

Clifton Fadiman (1904-1999), the well-known American writer and editor, once teased the globe traveling novelist John Gunther (1901-1970) about where was he going to go next to write one of his famous "Inside" books.

"What are going to do when you run out of continents?" asked Fadiman.

"I thought I'd try incontinence," replied Gunther.

## 1124. Luggage

The writer and humorist Mark Twain (Samuel Clemens) asked a baggage handler at Union Station (Railroad) in Washington, D.C., "Is that satchel strong enough to go in the baggage car?"

Lifting the satchel above his head and hurling it to the pavement with all his might, the baggage handler said, "That is what it will get in Philadelphia."

Then the baggage man smashed the satchel against the side of the baggage car five or six times. "That," he said, "is what it will get in Chicago."

Next he threw the satchel up in the air as high as he could, and when it landed on the pavement, he jumped up and down on it repeatedly. "And that," he said, "is what it will get in Sioux City."

Looking directly at Twain, the baggage man added: "If you are going any farther than Sioux City, you'd better take it in the Pullman Car with you."

# TRUST

### 1125. The Acid Test

The famed aerialist Zumbrati once walked a shaky tightrope across Niagara Falls despite a gusty wind that almost caused him to lose his footing. He was very relieved to have made it safely across.

Waiting for him on the other side was a fan with a wheelbarrow.

"I believe you could walk back across pushing this wheelbarrow," the fan said.

Zumbrati shook his head and said he was lucky to have made it across without a wheelbarrow.

"But I know you can do it," the fan persisted. "Just give it a try."

Zumbrati shook his head again but the fan kept after him.

Finally, Zumbrati said, "You really believe in me, don't you?"

"Oh, I do," said the fan.

"Okay then," said Zumbrati, get into the wheelbarrow and we'll start."

### 1126. Good Advice

The story goes that a Bedouin entered the prophet's mosque, leaving his camel untied outside. When he was told to go and tie it up, he came up to the prophet saying that he only trusted in God, therefore he had left the camel untied.

"Go and tie it up first, then trust it to God, O son of the Arabs," replied the prophet.

## 1127. The Stock Market

Soon after President Kennedy (1917-1963) blocked a steel price hike in 1961, he was visited by a prominent businessman who was gloomy about the economy.

"Things look great," JFK reassured the businessman. "Why, if I weren't President, I'd be buying stock myself."

"If you weren't President," replied the businessman, "so would I."

## 1128. Decentralization

Chris Argyris (1923- ), business theorist and professor emeritus at the Harvard Business School, said about trust, "Built into decentralization is the age-old tug between autonomy and control: superiors want no surprises, subordinates want to be left alone. The subordinates push for autonomy; they assert that by leaving them alone, top management will show its trust from a distance. The superiors, on the other hand, try to keep control through information systems. The subordinates see the control devices as confirming their suspicions — their superiors don't trust them."

## 1129. Drucker on Trust

Peter F. Drucker (1909-2005), Austrian-born American management consultant and author, said of trust, "In the ethics of interdependence there are only obligations, and all obligations are mutual obligations. Harmony and trust — that is, interdependence — require that each side be obligated to provide what the other side needs to achieve its goals and to fulfill itself."

## 1130. Dr. Spock and Trust

Dr. Benjamin Spock (1903-1998), eminent American pediatrician whose books on child care were faithfully followed by thousands of parents around the world, said, "Trust yourself. You know more than you think you do....It may surprise you to hear that the more people have studied different methods of bringing up children, the more they have come to the conclusion that what good mothers and fathers instinctively feel like doing for their babies is usually best."

### 1131. Brand Loyalty

Michael Perry (1934- ) British business executive, said, "Brands are all about trust. You buy the brand because you consider it a friend."

# TRUTH

### 1132. Lincoln on Truth

Abraham Lincoln once said of a man who was attacking him, "He's the biggest liar in Washington."

Lincoln said the man reminded him of an old fisherman who had the reputation for stretching the truth. The fisherman bought a pair of scales and insisted on weighing every fish he caught in the presence of witnesses.

One day a doctor borrowed the fisherman's scales to weigh a new-born baby and the baby weighed 47 pounds.

### 1133. Truth and the Devil

There is a story that as God and Satan were walking down the street one day, the Lord bent down and picked something up. He gazed at it glowing radiantly in His hand.

Satan, curious, asked, "What's that?"

"This," answered the Lord, "is Truth."

"Here," replied Satan as he reached for it, "let me have that — I'll organize it."

### 1134. Truth Is Tough

Oliver Wendell Holmes, Sr. (1809-1894), father of the famous Supreme Court jurist, was a physician and a man of letters. He wrote, "Truth is tough. It will not break, like a bubble, at a touch; nay, you may kick it about all day, like a foot-ball (sic), and it will be round and full at evening."

## 1135. Isaac Newton and Truth

Isaac Newton (1642-1727) was an English scientist and mathematician whose discoveries live on to this day. He wrote, "I do not know what I may appear to the world, but to myself I seem to have been only like a boy playing on the seashore, and diverting myself in now and then finding a smoothe (sic) pebble or a prettier shell than ordinary whilst the great ocean of truth lay all undiscovered before me."

## 1136. Truth Is Ladylike

William F. Buckley, Jr. (1925-2008) was an American intellectual and editor who transformed American conservatism during his lifetime. He wrote, "Truth is a demure lady, much too ladylike to knock you on the head and drag you to her cave. She is there, but the people must want her and seek her out."

## 1137. Kennedy on Truth

John F. Kennedy (1917-1963), one of America's most popular presidents, said in a commencement address at Yale University in 1962, "The great enemy of the truth is very often not the lie — deliberate, contrived, and dishonest — but the myth — persistent, persuasive and unrealistic."

## 1138. Sherlock Holmes and Truth

Sherlock Holmes was a fictional detective created by Sir Arthur Conan Doyle (1859-1930). The Holmes stories are so popular that he seems like a real person. In one of his books, Doyle has Holmes saying, "How often have I said to you that when you have eliminated the impossible, whatever remains, however improbable, must be the truth."

## 1139. Churchill on Truth

Winston Churchill (1874-1965), Great Britain's famous wartime leader, said "Men stumble over the truth from time to time, but most pick themselves up and hurry off as if nothing happened."

### 1140. Truth Will Out

Ben Bradlee (1921- ), former executive editor of *The Washington Post* who played a key role in exposing the Watergate scandal which brought down the Richard Nixon (1913-1994) presidency, had a favorite saying. It was "truth emerges."

### 1141. Truth Always Wins

Dudley Field Malone (1882-1950), a prominent American attorney argued unsuccessfully that scientific testimony defending evolution should be admitted in the Scopes "monkey" trial in 1925, said, "There is never a duel with the truth. The truth always wins, and we are not afraid of it. The truth is no coward. The truth does not need the law. The truth does not need the forces of government. The truth is imperishable, eternal, and immortal and needs no human agency to support it."

# UNEXPECTED CONSEQUENCES

### 1142. Pandora's Box

In dealing with some of today's problems, it would be wise for us to remember the legend of Pandora's Box. The legend beautifully illustrates the law of "unexpected consequences."

According to Greek mythology, Pandora was the first woman on earth. She had been sent by the Greek god Zeus to be the lovely bride for [Epimetheus], the brother of Prometheus, who loved mankind and had been given the gift of fire.

Zeus was jealous of Prometheus so he arranged for Pandora to be given the box into which Prometheus had shut all the evils that might plague the world. This was to be part of Pandora's dowry and she was not told what was in the box. In addition, she was made to promise that she would never, ever open the box under any conditions.

But her situation was something like the one we face today. Pandora was not able to stand not knowing what was in the box and she opened it — thus releasing all the adversities and evil that have beset mankind ever since.

We must be very careful that in dealing with problems today that we don't open a Pandora's box of trouble that we will be totally unprepared to deal with.

## 1143. Unintended Consequences

Garrett Hardin (1915-2003) was a controversial American ecologist who wrote widely on the danger of overpopulation. He earned fame for the following observation, "You can never do merely one thing. The law applies to any action that changes something in a complex system. The point is that an action taken to alleviate a problem will trigger several effects, some of which may offset or even negate the one intended."

## 1144. One of Murphy's Laws

Arthur Bloch (1948- ) was a well-known American writer who authored the Murphy's Law books. This is his wording of one of the laws, "Inside every large problem is a small problem struggling to get out. Inside every small problem is a larger problem struggling to get out."

# VANITY

## 1145. Foolish Pride

This wonderful tale by Hans Christian Andersen (1805-1875), with its obvious moral for all of us, has become part of our culture and our language. Read on:

Many years ago there was an Emperor who was so excessively fond of new clothes that he spent all his money on them. He cared nothing about his soldiers, nor for the theater, nor for driving in the woods, except for the sake of showing off his new clothes. He had a costume for every hour in the day.

One day two swindlers came to town and passed themselves off as weavers. They said they could weave the most beautiful cloth imaginable. Not only that, they said that clothes made from these marvelous fabrics had the peculiar quality of becoming invisible to any person who was not fit for the office he held, or if he was impossibly dull.

"These must be splendid clothes," thought the Emperor. "By wearing them, I should be able to discover which men in my kingdom are unfit for their posts. I shall distinguish the wise men from the fools. Yes, I certainly must order some of that stuff to be woven for me." And he paid the two swindlers a lot of money in advance so that they might begin their work at once.

The two swindlers set up looms and were soon busy weaving imaginary cloth. Anxious to know of their progress, the Emperor sent one key government official after another to see the magic cloth. None of the ministers could see anything but empty looms but they were too embarrassed to say so because they did not want to admit that they were not fit for the powerful offices they held. Finally, the Emperor went to see for himself.

"What," thought the Emperor. "I see nothing at all! This is terrible! Am I a fool? Am I not fit to be Emperor?"

So the Emperor exclaimed that the invisible cloth was amazingly beautiful and his ministers all recommended that he have a suit made from it at once, and that he wear it in a great procession which was soon to take place. The Emperor was so pleased at the prospect that he gave each of the two rogues a knighthood and the title of "Gentlemen Weavers."

When the big day came, the two swindlers proceeded to "dress" the Emperor. "See," they said, "these are the trousers, this is the coat, here is the mantle," and so on. "It is as light as a spider's web. One might think one had nothing on, but that is the very beauty of it."

"Yes," agreed all the courtiers, but they could not see anything, for there was nothing to see.

Soon after the Emperor walked proudly in the public procession wearing his beautiful new clothes and everybody in the streets exclaimed, "How beautiful the Emperor's new clothes are!" No one would let it appear that he could see nothing, for then he would not be fit for his post, or else he was a fool.

"But he has got nothing on," exclaimed a little child watching the procession. "The Emperor is naked." "Hush," said the boy's father.

But the Emperor writhed, for he knew it was true, but he thought the procession must go on nevertheless. So he held himself stiffer than ever, and the chamberlains held up his invisible train, and they marched back to the castle.

## 1146. Indispensable Man

Many successful people have larger than ordinary personal vanity, as this anonymous poem demonstrates:

"Some day when you're feeling important -
Some day when your ego's in bloom,
Some day when you take it for granted
You're the best-qualified man in the room -
Take a bucket and fill it with water,
Put your hands in it, up to the wrist,
Pull them out and the hole that remains
Is a measure of how you'll be missed!
The moral of this is quite simple,
You must do the best that you can.
Be proud of yourself - but remember!
There is no indispensable man."

## 1147. Pride and Vanity

Arthur Schopenhauer (1788-1860), German philosopher, had this to say about vanity, "Pride is an established conviction of one's own paramount worth in some particular respect, while vanity is the desire of rousing such a conviction in others. Pride works from within; it is the direct appreciation of oneself. Vanity is the desire to arrive at this appreciation indirectly, from without."

## 1148. Vanity in Advertising

Many clients of advertising agencies are egotistical in the extreme, as this little poem shows:

"When the client moans and sighs
Make his logo twice the size.
If he still should prove refractory,
Show a picture of his factory.
Only in the gravest cases
Should you show the clients' faces."

# WAR

## 1149. American War Dead

In his award-winning PBS documentary on the Civil War, producer Ken Burns (1953- ) stated that 876,000 soldiers were killed during that terrible episode in America's history.

It is even more shocking to look at that figure this way. And that is that the number of soldiers killed in the Civil War was greater than all the lives lost in all other United States wars. This includes the Revolutionary War, the War of 1812, the Spanish-American War, World War I, World War II, the Korean War, the Vietnam War, Desert Storm, the Iraq War, and Afghanistan.

## 1150. Alexander the Great

At the age of 20, in 336 B.C., Alexander the Great (356 BC-323 BC) inherited his father's throne of Macedon in Greece. Two years later he was conquering the world. When he died at the age of 33, he had conquered almost all the known ancient world.

Evidence of Alexander's gift for inspiring his men and intimidating his enemies is shown by the following story.

One day Alexander and a small company of soldiers approached a strongly defended, walled city. Alexander stood outside the walls, demanding to see the king. The walled city's king, approaching the battlements above the invading army, agreed to hear Alexander's demands.

"Surrender to me immediately!" commanded Alexander.

The king laughed. "Why should I surrender to you?" he said, pointing out that his forces far outnumbered those of Alexander.

In answer to the king, Alexander ordered his men to line up in single file. He then ordered them to start marching straight toward a cliff that overlooked rocks hundreds of feet below.

The king and his soldiers watched in shock and disbelief when, one by one, Alexander's soldiers marched without hesitation right off the cliff to their deaths.

After ten of Alexander's soldiers had gone over the cliff, Alexander ordered the rest of his men to stop and return to his side.

Without further argument, the king and his soldiers quickly surrendered and opened the gates to the city.

## 1151. Using Military Resources Wisely

In March of 1864, President Abraham Lincoln promoted Ulysses S. Grant (1822-1885) to lieutenant general and placed him in command of all Union armies.

General Grant recalled later that, after receiving his new commission, Lincoln asked to speak to him privately. After a brief reference to all the unsuccessful Union generals who had preceded Grant, Lincoln said he could best express his hopes for the new commander by telling him this story.

"At one time," said Lincoln, "there was a great war among the animals, and one side had great difficulty in getting a commander who had sufficient confidence in himself to do the job.

"Finally they found a monkey by the name of Jocko, who said he thought he could command their army if his tail could be made a little longer.

"So they got more tail and spliced it onto the monkey's caudal appendage. He looked at it admiringly, and then thought he ought to have a little more still.

"The additional tail was added, and again Jocko called for more. The splicing process was repeated many times until they had coiled Jocko's tail around the room, filling all the space.

"Still Jocko called for more tail and, there being no other place to coil it, they began wrapping it around his shoulders. He continued his call for more, and they kept on winding the additional tail around him until its weight finally broke him down."

At this point, recalled Grant, he rose from his chair and said to Lincoln, "Mr. President, I will not call for more assistance unless I find it impossible to make do with what I already have."

Grant went on to win the war and became a national hero. He and Lincoln understood each other.

## 1152. Disarmament, a Fable

Once upon a time all the animals in the zoos decided that they would disarm, and they arranged to have a conference to arrange the matter.

So the Rhinoceros said when he opened the proceedings that the use of teeth was barbarous and horrible and ought to be strictly prohibited by general consent. Horns, which were mainly defensive weapons, would, of course, have to be allowed.

The Buffalo, the Stag, the Porcupine, and even the little Hedgehog all said they would vote with the Rhino, but the Lion and the Tiger took a different view. They defended teeth and even claws, which they described as honorable weapons of immortal antiquity.

The Panther, the Leonard, the Puma and the whole tribe of small cats all supported the Lion and the Tiger. Then the Bear spoke. He proposed that both teeth and horns should be banned and never used again for fighting by any animal. It would be quite enough if animals were allowed to give each other a good hug when they quarreled. No one could object to that. It was so fraternal, and that would be a great step towards peace.

However, all the other animals were very offended with the Bear, and the Turkey fell into a perfect panic. The discussion got so hot and angry, and all those animals began thinking so much about horns and teeth and hugging when they argued about the peaceful intentions that had brought them together that they began to look at one another in a very nasty way.

Luckily the keepers were able to calm them down and persuade them to go back quietly to their cages, and they began to feel quite friendly with one another again.

## 1153. Battle of the Bulge

When Creighton W. Abrams, Jr. (1914-1974) was named commander of American forces in Vietnam, his admirers recalled what he had said to rally his troops when they found themselves surrounded by the German Army at the Battle of the Bulge during World War II.

Abrams told his men, "They've got us surrounded again, the poor bastards."

## 1154. Coffee Break

What may have been history's first coffee break during battle occurred during the Civil War just outside Sharpsburg, Maryland.

The Union troops had just crossed Antietam Creek and were meeting heavy resistance from the Confederates. A 19-year-old sergeant in the Ohio regiment carried a bucket of hot coffee and some hot rations to the men in his regiment who were fighting on the front line.

The date was September 17, 1862, and a monument to that coffee break stands today on the site of that battlefield.

By the way, the sergeant who served the hot coffee was named William McKinley, who later became the 25th President of the United States.

## 1155. The Atom Bomb

Dr. Robert Oppenheimer (1904-1967) was an American physicist who was often called the "Father of the Atom Bomb." He played a crucial role in its development during World War II at a laboratory in Los Alamos, New Mexico.

In 1954, Dr. Oppenheimer was declared a security risk after charges that he had once belonged to some communist organizations. His name was cleared in 1963.

As a member of the Manhattan Project that developed the bomb, Dr. Oppenheimer was asked the question: "Doctor, is there any defense against such a nuclear weapon?"

"Certainly," he replied.

"What is that, Doctor?"

"Peace," Oppenheimer replied.

### 1156. No Exit Strategy

When one of Lincoln's generals presented a plan that entailed sending an army deep into the South, Lincoln expressed his concern with the following story:

"That reminds me of a barrel maker out my way," said Lincoln. "He was new to the trade and he became much annoyed because the top of the barrel kept falling in as he was attaching the hoops around the barrel.

"Then he had the bright idea of putting his young son inside the barrel to hold up the cover while the barrel maker fitted the staves into place. This technique worked wonders except that the question then was how to get the boy out.

Lincoln turned to the General and said, "Your plan is feasible, sir, but how are you going to get the boy out?"

### 1157. Defense Strategy

At the Constitutional Convention a member moved that "the standing army be restricted to no more than 5,000 men."

When George Washington heard this, he turned to a friend and remarked that the resolution was fine with him — so long as the convention agreed to an amendment prohibiting armies from invading the United States with more than 3,000 troops.

### 1158. Lincoln's Forgiving Nature

The famous Union General William T. Sherman (1820-1891) once asked Abraham Lincoln whether the Civil War President wanted Sherman to capture Jefferson Davis, president of the Confederacy.

In reply, Lincoln told a story about an old temperance lecturer who was very strict about total abstinence from liquor.

One day, after a long ride in the hot sun, the lecturer stopped at the house of a friend who offered to make him a cold lemonade. As he mixed the lemonade, his host asked the lecturer if he would like a drop of something stronger to brace his nerves after such a long, hot ride.

"Absolutely not," replied the temperance lecturer indignantly, "I couldn't think of it! I am opposed to liquor in principle."

Then, glancing at the inviting black bottle at his host's elbow, the lecturer quickly added, "However, if you could manage to put in a drop unbeknownst to me, I guess it wouldn't hurt me much."

"Now," said Lincoln to General Sherman, "I am bound to oppose the escape of Jeff Davis; but if you could manage to let him slip out unbeknownst-like, I guess it wouldn't hurt me much."

## 1159. Grandstand Act

During the Civil War, President Lincoln replaced the timid and slow-moving General McClellan (1826-1885) with another well-known general, Joseph Hooker (1814-1879), hoping to get a more aggressive approach to the war.

To demonstrate that he was a man of action, General Hooker on his first day in command sent to the President a dispatch datelined: HEADQUARTERS IN THE SADDLE.

Mr. Lincoln was not exactly impressed. "The trouble with Hooker," he remarked, "is that he's got his headquarters where his hindquarters ought to be."

Note: There is some disagreement as to whether this story should be attributed to General Hooker or General John Pope (1822-1892). The Hooker reference is taken from "Abe Lincoln Laughing" by P.M. Zall, a noted Lincoln authority. However, even he mentions there is disagreement about which General should be credited with the story.

## 1160. Communications

Trafalgar, 1805, the battle that was to lead to the eventual undoing of Napoleon (1769-1821) was won because Admiral Horatio Nelson (1758-1805) had a secret weapon: signal flags.

The technique of communicating over long distances by coded flags had only recently been invented by the Royal Navy. It revolutionized naval warfare.

The system enabled the British ships to cover vast expenses of ocean, looking for the enemy, while remaining in close contact with the fleet commander. It also allowed tactical flexibility once battle had been joined. Other navies were bound by rigid battle plans agreed upon in face-to-face councils long before the first broadside. They were confounded by the British and their talking flags.

The result of Trafalgar, and in large part this communications system, was that Britain enjoyed undisputed rule of the seas and over a century of relative peace; a Pax Britannica.

History is peppered with anecdotes of communications breakdowns leading to fiascos. It has been called the fog of war.

## 1161. Timid Command

During the Civil War, Abraham Lincoln had more trouble with General George McClellan than any other military leader. McClellan, who was the Union's highest ranking commander, continually pestered Lincoln for more men, more guns, and more horses, and he made each demand seem more urgent than the previous one.

In response, Lincoln pressured McClellan to provide more detailed reports on why he needed more resources. This angered McClellan, who began to send Lincoln all kinds of trivial messages. One dispatch read:

President Abraham Lincoln
Washington, D.C.

We have just captured six cows. What shall we do with them?

George B. McClellan

Lincoln immediately dispatched this reply:

George B. McClellan
Army of the Potomac

As to the six cows captured — milk them.

A. Lincoln

## 1162. Spartan Courage

Leonidas, who was king of Sparta from 487 to 480 B.C., was faced with an invasion by a powerful Persian army.

The Persians sent an envoy to Leonidas to tell him the futility of resisting the advance of their large army. "Our archers are so numerous," said the envoy, "that the flight of their arrows will darken the sun."

"So much the better," replied Leonidas, with his hand on his sword, "for we shall then fight in the shade."

## 1163. Bad Advice

This concerns a very wealthy man named Croesus — a man so wealthy that we still use the term "wealthy as Croesus."

Croesus lived in the Sixth Century B.C. and he was not only wealthy, he was very powerful. So powerful that he wanted to take over the country next to him — the ancient empire of Persia.

King Croesus was a man who didn't take any chances. So he went looking for answers in the best place he knew — the famed Oracle of Delphi. The Oracle at Delphi was sacred to Apollo, the god of prophecy, and they were quick to come up with answers to any question put to them.

So Croesus asked the Oracle, "If I go to war with the Persians, will I win?"

The Oracle replied in very direct terms. "Go to war with the Persians," it said, "and you will destroy a great empire."

Emboldened by that answer, Croesus invaded the Persian territory, only to be decisively beaten. Not only that, the Persians then invaded his territory, captured its capital, and threw Croesus himself into chains.

Angrily, King Croesus sent an ambassador to Delphi with the demand, "Why did you deceive me?"

The priestess of the Oracle replied that she had not deceived him – that Croesus had indeed destroyed a great empire — his own.

## 1164. Lincoln on Preemptive Strikes

The United States today has an official policy of engaging in preemptive strikes against any nation it believes is threatening its security. Below is the text of a letter from Abraham Lincoln in 1848 to William Herndon explaining his opposition to war against Mexico:

"Allow the President to invade a neighboring nation whenever he shall deem it necessary to repel an invasion...and you allow him to make war at pleasure...If today he should choose to say he thinks it necessary to invade Canada to prevent the British from invading us, how could you stop him?

"You may say to him, 'I see no probability of the British invading us,' but he would say to you, 'Be silent: I see it if you don't.'"

Abraham Lincoln

Note: The letter was cited by Senator Robert Byrd (1917- ) (Democrat from West Virginia) in opposing Congressional approval for President George W. Bush to order an invasion of Iraq, and the administration's new foreign policy of preemptive action, replacing the 50-year-old policy of containment to handle threats to world peace. "Harper Magazine's" editor Lewis H. Lapham reported that, within three days of his speech to Congress in October, 2002, Senator Byrd had received nearly 70,000 supporting letters, e-mails and telephone calls.

## 1165. Disobeying Orders

At the battle of Copenhagen, Lord Horatio Nelson (1758-1805). the British naval commander, reportedly put his telescope to his blind eye to ignore the signal for his squadron to retreat.

The British naval hero later explained his refusal to follow orders by saying, "I have only one eye. I have a right to be blind sometimes."

## 1166. History of the Stirrup

In 1066 one of the most decisive battles in the history of the world was fought. William, Duke of Normandy, launched an invasion of England in the face of a formidable opponent. But what gave him confidence to try such a risky undertaking was that he had a recently invented technological edge that the English did not. That edge was the stirrup.

While the English rode by horseback to the battlefield, they fought on foot. The conventional wisdom was that the horse was too unstable a platform from which to fight.

But the Norman cavalry, standing secure in their stirrups were able to ride down the English, letting the weight of their charging horses punch their lances home.

This technological edge led to the conquest of Britain. Without it, William might never have attempted such a perilous war. Advanced technology has been helping win battles ever since, both on the battlefield and in business as well.

## 1167. Personal Responsibility

Before the Allied invasion of Normandy during World War II, General Dwight D. Eisenhower wrote out a note that he put in his billfold. Its wording was to be used in a press release if the invasion was repelled by German forces.

Eisenhower's note, which now resides in the Eisenhower Presidential Library in Abilene, Kansas, reads as follows:

"Our landings in the Cherbourg-Havre area have failed to gain a satisfactory foothold and I have withdrawn the troops. My decision to attack at this time and place was based on the best information available. The troops, the Air and the navy did all that bravery and devotion to duty could do. If any blame or fault attaches to the attempt it is mine alone."

Eisenhower told his naval aide, Captain Harry Butcher, that he had written similar notes for every amphibious operation in the war but that he had later torn them all up.

Note: The punctuation and capitalization of General Eisenhower's note is reproduced exactly as he wrote it.

## 1168. Lincoln's Jokes

It was his robust sense of humor that kept Abraham Lincoln sane in the face of personal tragedy and a raging Civil War.

Asked how he could tell jokes at a time when the nation was bleeding, Lincoln replied, "I laugh because I must not cry."

## 1169. Origin of "Gung-Ho"

U.S. Marine Lt. Col. Evans F. Carlson (1896-1947) was an observer with the Chinese Army in the late 1930s when he heard the Chinese slogan, "Gung-Ho."

Carlson's Raiders adopted the slogan and used it to mean "ready to go." Soon other Marines began using the expression and, in time, it came to mean, "very enthusiastic."

## 1170. Pride in Fitness

During World War II one of Britain's most famous generals was Field Marshal Bernard Law Montgomery (1887-1976), a soldier famed for his flinty and often arrogant personality.

In Montgomery's memoirs he recalls having dinner with Winston Churchill and Churchill asked him what he wanted to drink with the meal.

"Water," Montgomery said, adding that "I neither drink or smoke and I am 100 percent fit."

In a flash, Churchill replied, "I drink and I smoke and I am 200 percent fit."

## 1171. Poise Under Pressure

For two weeks Colonel Lewis (Chesty) Puller (1898-1971) had commanded the rear of the First Marine Division which had been cut off in the Chosin reservoir region during the Korean War by hundreds of thousands of Chinese Communist troops.

The Colonel was visiting a hospital tent where a priest was administering last rites to a Marine wounded when a messenger came with an urgent message.

"Sir," said the messenger, "Do you know they have cut us off? We're entirely surrounded."

Replied Puller, "Those poor bastards. They've got us right where we want them. We can shoot in every direction now."

## 1172. Constant Optimism

During World War II, British Prime Minister Winston Churchill had a sign posted on his cabinet room desk facing the commanders of the armed forces.

The wording was a statement originally said by Queen Victoria (1819-1901) to some generals who were having a difficult time during the Boer War. The wording was as follows:

"Please understand there is no depression in this house and we are not interested in the possibilities of defeat, they do not exist."

## 1173. Statues in the Park

- If a statue in the park of a person on a horse has both front legs in the air, the person died in battle;

- If the horse has one front leg in the air, the person died as a result of wounds received in battle;

- If the horse has all four legs on the ground, the person died of natural causes.

## 1174. A Trophy with a Message

In a German monastery hangs a very unusual trophy of mounted deer antlers.

What is unusual about the display is that it is not just one set of antlers — but two. And they remain hopelessly entangled just as they were when two young bucks got themselves fatally tied to each other during some kind of winner-take-all turf fight using their antlers as weapons.

In the fury of each buck trying desperately to free himself from the other, both deer died. They had each obviously entered the battle with the intent of proving superiority over the other — only to die in humiliating disgrace.

There are many lessons humans can draw from this tragic happening in the animal kingdom and that is why these strange tangled antlers are on permanent display for the monks to gaze upon.

## 1175. Too Many Chiefs

Abraham Lincoln once told this story to illustrate why he wanted to cut down on commissioning more generals in the Union Army:

"Suppose you had a large cattle yard full of all sorts of cattle, cows, oxen, and bulls. And suppose you kept selling your cows and oxen, taking good care of your bulls.

"By and by, you would have a yard full of nothing but old bulls, good for nothing under heaven. And so it will be with our Army if we don't stop making brigadier generals."

## 1176. War and Peace

"There have been very few times in the history of civilization when there hasn't been a war going on somewhere," said Victor Davis Hanson (1953- ), a military historian and classicist at California State University in Fresno, California.

Hanson was so quoted in "The New York Times"

Hanson cited a brief period between A.D. 100 and A.D. 200 as perhaps the only time of world peace, the result of the Roman Empire's having everyone, fleetingly, in its thrall.

## 1177. West Point

These words are carved in stone on the main athletic building at West Point, the United States military academy:

"On the fields of friendly strife are sown the seeds, that on other fields, on other days, will bear the fruits of victory."

## 1178. The Unnecessary War

During one of Winston Churchill's stays at the White House during World War II, President Roosevelt told Churchill he was asking publicly for suggestions about what the war should be called.

Churchill immediately replied, "The Unnecessary War."

Source: In the Preface to Volume 1, "The Gathering Storm," published in 1948, of Churchill's "The Second World War," Churchill explained why he felt this way. Here is the relevant text:

"There never was a war more easy to stop than that which has just wrecked what was left of the world from the previous struggle. The human tragedy reaches its climax in the fact that after all the exertions and sacrifices of hundreds of millions of people and of the victories of the Righteous Cause, we have still not found Peace or Security, and that we lie in the grip of even worse perils than those we have surmounted. It is my earnest hope that pondering upon the past may give guidance in days to come, enable a new generation to repair some of the errors of former years and thus govern, in accordance with the needs and glory of man, the awful unfolding scene of the future."

## 1179. A Little-Known World War II Story

At the beginning of World War II, George Catlett Marshall (1880-1959) was head of the U.S. Joint Chiefs of Staff and widely respected by all branches of the military. That immense respect was shared by President Franklin Roosevelt (1882-1945). Although he never said so publicly, many believed that Marshall's fondest ambition was to leave his staff job and be named Supreme Commander of Operation Overlord, the planned invasion of northern Europe by the thousands of allied troops and materiel being assembled in England for a strike against the heavily fortified Normandy coast across the English Channel.

In December of 1943, General Marshall was with President Roosevelt in Cairo for a meeting with all the Allied leaders. At one point, FDR sent for General Marshall and dictated to him a brief message that he wanted sent to Marshal Joseph Stalin (1879-1953) of Russia without delay. It read:

"From the President to Marshal Stalin:

"The immediate appointment of General Eisenhower to command of Overlord operation has been decided upon." The message was signed "Roosevelt" in the President's own hand.

After sending the message to Stalin, Marshall took the piece of foolscap on which he had written the President's message and to it affixed a personal note of his own to General Dwight D. Eisenhower (1890-1969) which read:

Cairo, December 7, 1943

"Dear Eisenhower. I thought you might like to have this as a memento. It was written very hurriedly by me as the final meeting broke up yesterday, The President signing it immediately. (signed) G.C.M."

We do not know what, if any, explanation about the decision was given to Marshall by President Roosevelt. But there is no question that it must have been a bitter disappointment to General Marshall. We do know that President Roosevelt had such a high regard for Marshall that he once said, "I trust George so much that I can't sleep when he is out of the country."

Although General Marshall did not get the field command of his dreams, he did go on after the war to become the U.S. Secretary of State and had the Marshall Plan, which rebuilt wartorn Europe, named after him. In 1958 he was awarded the Nobel Peace Prize.

For his part, General Eisenhower had framed the piece of foolscap sent him by Marshall and on which Marshall had written his own personal note of congratulations. Eisenhower kept the framed announcement of his promotion and Marshall's note hanging over his desk for the rest of his life wherever he was located.

# WATER

## 1180. Use of Water

An increasing number of experts predict that water will become the world's scarcest and most valuable resource during the 21st Century. With that in mind, the following statistics have important relevance.

Each time your toilet is flushed, it uses 5 to 7 gallons of water — in fact, 40% of the pure water you use in your house is flushed down the toilet.

A running faucet puts 3-5 gallons of water down the drain every minute. In fact, you use 10 to 15 gallons of water if you leave the tap running while you brush your teeth. If you just wet and rinse your brush when you brush your teeth, you use 1/2 gallon of water.

Showers account for a whopping 32% of home water use. A standard shower head has a flow rate of 5 to 10 gallons of water per minute. So a 5-minute shower uses around 25 gallons.

## 1181. Clean Water

Isaac Asimov (1920-1992), arguably the greatest and most prolific science writer America has ever produced, said of water, "In many nations it is impossible to get clean water except under very unusual circumstances. That was one reason why people started drinking beer and wine — the alcohol killed the germs, and if you didn't drink that, you died of cholera. But there are places where you can supply clean water for nearly everyone. The United States probably supplies clean water for a larger percentage of its population than almost any other nation can."

## 1182. Ralph Nader on Water

Ralph Nader (1934- ) the American consumer watchdog and political spoiler, said, "Water is the most precious, limited natural resource we have in this country... But because water belongs to no one — except the people — special interests, including government polluters, use it as their private sewers."

## 1183. Invaluable Resource

Donald Culross Peattie (1898-1964), American botanist, naturalist and gifted writer, and Noel Peattie, said of water in "A Cup of Sky" in 1950, "The earth holds a silver treasure, cupped between ocean bed and tenting sky. Forever the heavens spend it, in the showers that refresh our temperate lands, the torrents that sluice the tropics. Every suckling root absorbs it, the very soil drains it down; the rivers run unceasing to the sea, the mountains yield it endlessly... Yet none is lost; in vast convection our water is returned, from soil to sky, and sky to soil, and back gain, to fall as pure as blessing. There was never less; there could never be more. A mighty mercy on which life depends, for all its glittering shifts, water is constant."

## 1184. Chemical Makeup of Water

Benjamin Harrow, a British scientist, wrote in a book of chemistry in 1935, "If the constituent atoms in a tumbler of water could all be labeled for later identification, and the water were then mixed with all the water in the world, and if, after thorough mixing, the tumbler were again filled, it would contain two thousand of the original atoms."

# WINNING

## 1185. Competitiveness

There is an old saying in Africa that goes like this:

Every morning a gazelle gets up and knows that it must out-run the fastest lion or it will get eaten.

And every morning, a lion gets up and knows that it must out-run the slowest gazelle or it will starve to death.

So, whether you are a gazelle or a lion, every morning when you get up, you'd better be running.

## 1186. Self-Control and Winning

The Chinese character for money is composed of three symbols. One symbol means "gold." The other two represent "spears."

The first "spear" represents the outward struggle for survival. The second "spear" represents the battle within.

Before one can fight and win the outward battle, one must win the battle within.

## 1187. Danger of Coasting

The famous naturalist Jane Goodall (1934- ) told this story during a speech to the Commonwealth Club of California in San Francisco.

"It makes me think of a fable my mother used to read to me and my sister when we were little, about the birds coming together to have a competition: who could fly the highest?

"The mighty eagle is sure he will win, and majestically with those great, strong wings he flies higher and higher, and gradually the other birds get tired and start drifting back to the ground. Finally, even the eagle can go no higher, but that's all right, because he looks down and sees all the other birds below him.

"That's what he thinks, but hiding in the feathers on his back is a little wren, and she takes off and flies highest of all."

## 1188. A Winning Strategy

One of my favorite Greek myths celebrates Atalanta — the fleet-footed huntress who refused to entertain a marriage proposal from any man who couldn't beat her in a race.

And no man could. Even Hippomenes, her eventual husband, had to cheat a bit. At crucial times in their footrace, Hippomenes rolled three golden apples off the course. Each time Atalanta veered off to scoop up the gilded enticement — a detour which allowed Hippomenes to stay just one step ahead of the gold-laden maiden at the finish line.

# WOMEN'S RIGHTS

## 1189. Changing Gender Roles

Several years before the Gulf War, TV journalist Barbara Walters (1929- ) did a story in Kuwait on the different gender roles of men and women there. Among other things, she reported that women customarily walked about 10 feet behind their husbands.

After the Gulf War, she returned to Kuwait and noticed that the men now walked several yards behind their wives.

Walters approached a woman there and said, "This is marvelous. Can you tell me what enabled women here to achieve this unusual reversal of roles in such a short time?"

The answer was, "Land mines."

## 1190. Queen Victoria's Views

In a letter to Sir Theodore Martin in 1870, Queen Victoria of England (1819-1901) said, "The Queen is most anxious to enlist everyone who can speak or write to join in checking this mad, wicked folly of "Woman's Rights" with all its attendant horrors on which her poor, feeble sex is bent, forgetting every sense of womanly feeling and propriety...It is a subject which makes the Queen so furious that she cannot contain herself."

## 1191. Hillary Clinton's Views

Hillary Rodham Clinton (1947 - ), wife of U.S. President Bill Clinton, said in her remarks to a United Nations forum on women's rights held in Beijing, China, on September 5, 1995, "As long as discrimination and inequities remain so commonplace around the world — as long as girls and women are valued less, fed less, fed last, overworked, underpaid, not schooled and subjected to violence in and out of their homes — the potential of the human family to create a peaceful, prosperous world will not be realized."

## 1192. A Women's Rights Pioneer

On her 80th birthday, pioneer American women's suffragist Susan B. Anthony (1820-1906), said, "I am not accustomed to demonstrations of gratitude or of praise. I have ever been a hewer of wood and a drawer of water to the movement. I have known nothing of oratory or rhetoric. Whatever I have done has been done because I wanted to see better conditions, better surroundings, better circumstances for women."

## 1193. Early American Women's Rights

Abigail Adams (1744-1818), wife of John Adams, the second President of the United States and a leading pioneer in the founding of America, wrote to him on March 31, 1776, expressing her hopes that a new government would redress the legal subjection of married women. She wrote, "In the new code of laws which I suppose it will be necessary for you to make, I desire you would remember the ladies and be more generous and favorable to them than your ancestors. Do not put such unlimited power into the hands of husbands. Remember, all men would be tyrants if they could. If particular care and attention is not paid to the ladies, we are determined to foment a rebellion, and will not hold ourselves bound by any laws in which we have no voice or representation."

## 1194. African-American Feminist

Sojourner Truth (c.1797-1883), African-American abolitionist and feminist, in speaking to the Ohio Women's Rights Convention in 1850, said, "That man over there says that women need to be helped into carriages, and lifted over ditches, and to have the best place everywhere.

"Nobody ever helps me into carriages, or over mud puddles, or gives me any best place! And ain't I a woman?

"Look at me! Look at my arm. I have ploughed and planted and gathered into barns, and no man could head me! And ain't I a woman?

"I could work as much and eat as much as a man when I could get it and bear the lash as well! And ain't I a woman?

"I have borne thirteen children and seen most all sold off to slavery, and when I cried out with my mother's grief, none but Jesus heard me! And ain't I a woman?"

# WORK

## 1195. Picked for the Job

When a recalcitrant Northern governor threatened to not carry out one of President Abraham Lincoln's decrees, Lincoln said it reminded him of a ship launching he had once seen.

"When everything was ready," said Lincoln, "the ship builders sent a boy under the ship to knock away the supports holding the ship in place. After knocking the supports loose, all the boy had to do was to lie flat while the ship slid over him into the water."

The boy did everything right except he yelled out as if he were being murdered.

"I thought the boy had his skin scraped right off his back," said Lincoln, "but he wasn't hurt at all."

The yard master told Lincoln they always chose this boy for the job even though he always yelled like he was being hurt. Said the yard master, "He only wants to make you understand how hard his task is, and how good he is in performing it."

As usual, Lincoln drew a parallel between the shipyard boy and the Northern Governor's loud complaints.

## 1196. Importance of Work

Fyodor Dostoevsky (1822-1881), the Russian novelist, once described the psychological value of work in this manner: "To crush, to annihilate a man utterly, to inflict on him the most terrible punishment so that the most ferocious murderer would shudder at it beforehand, one need only give him work of an absolutely, completely useless and irrational character."

## 1197. Work Defined

In her biography, the English aviator and author Beryl Markham (1902-1986) defined what is and is not work in this way: "No human pursuit achieves dignity until it can be called work, and when you can experience a physical loneliness for the tools of your trade, you see that the other things — the experiments, the irrelevant vocations, the vanities you used to hold — were false to you."

## 1198. Work and Happiness

Lin Yutang (1895-1976), Chinese philologist, essayist and writer, wrote of the happiness that can come from satisfying work: "Of all the unhappy people in the world, the unhappiest are those who have not found something they want to do. True happiness comes to him who does his work well, followed by a relaxing and refreshing period of rest. True happiness comes from the right amount of work every day."

# WRITING

### 1199. More Editing

Thomas Jefferson (1743-1826) is correctly honored as the author of America's Declaration of Independence, but he had a lot of help. He would have said, "too much help."

Before approving the Declaration, Congress cut out about 500 of Jefferson's words and made many other changes that Jefferson referred to as "mutilations."

Jefferson had originally written: "We hold these truths to be sacred and undeniable." The Congress changed that along with Jefferson's contention that "all men are created equal and independent, that from that equal creation they derive rights inherent and inalienable, among which are the preservation of life and liberty and the pursuit of happiness."

The edited version says that "all men are created equal, that they are endowed by their Creator with certain unalienable Rights, that among these are Life, Liberty and the pursuit of Happiness."

### 1200. Growth of Information

When writing was first invented, information was limited to a person's memory. As it evolved to writing with pencil and paper, knowledge was stimulated. Printing quickened the pace. Now we have a quantum leap into electronic writing. Speeds of calculation and projections — trillions of calculations a second — are beyond the dreams of the wildest science fiction writers.

It took from the time of Christ to the mid-eighteenth century for knowledge to double. It doubled again 150 years later, and then again in only 50 years. Today it doubles every four or five years. More new information has been produced in the last 30 years than in the previous 500.

## 1201. Invention of the Envelope

In 1820, the average person in England wrote only three letters a year. One reason for this was that letters in those days were mailed without a cover and could be read by anyone.

But William Mulready had an idea to ensure privacy — the envelope. On a visit to France, Mulready had noticed that written messages from an important person were often completely enclosed in "a little paper case, impervious to the peering eyes of the curious."

The idea of sending letters kept private from curious eyes was an instant success. The number of letters handled by the British postal service soared beyond anyone's expectations.

Thanks to the little paper envelopes invented by Mulready, thousands of letters travel daily around the world, shielded from prying eyes.

## 1202. Speechwriting

According to Liz Carpenter (1920- ), a journalist and White House staff member who worked closely with both President Lyndon Johnson and Mrs. Johnson, the President believed that every man or woman was a potential speechwriter. He asked Dick Goodwin, who had worked for the Kennedys, to write a speech declaring his war on poverty. And it got a great response.

President Johnson quickly started sending all his speech assignments to Goodwin. For three months, LBJ peppered him with every assignment. Finally Goodwin ran out of words and escaped to the Virgin Islands to replenish his brain cells. Even LBJ's long arm and telephone couldn't reach him to say, as he often did, "This is yoah (sic) President speaking."

LBJ was hurt. He brooded over the desertion for a few days. But later, riding around his Texas ranch looking at his cattle with Liz Carpenter, he was philosophical about it:

"Well," he told Carpenter, "I guess a, speechwriter is just like a breed bull. There are just so many shots in him."

## 1203. Dietary Advice

A young man who wanted to be a famous author once wrote Mark Twain (Samuel Clemens) asking what was the ideal diet for a writer. He particularly wanted to know if, as Professor Agassiz of Harvard had said, fish was good brain food. Unimpressed with the young writer's work and the tone of his letter, Twain replied in this fashion:

"Yes, Agassiz does recommend authors eat fish, because the phosphorus in it makes brain. So far you are correct.

"But I cannot help you to a decision about the amount you need to eat — at least, not with certainty. If the specimen composition you sent is about your fair usual average, I should judge that perhaps a couple of whales would be all you would want for the present."

## 1204. Research

Nicholas Murray Butler (1862-1947), the legendary president of Columbia University, and Professor Brander Matthews, were discussing an article Matthews had written on plagiarism.

"In the case of the first man to use an anecdote," said Professor Matthews, "there is originality; in the case of the second, there is plagiarism; with the third, it is lack of originality, and with the fourth it is drawing from a common stock."

"Yes," broke in President Butler, "and in the case of the fifth, it is research."

## 1205. Writing Classes

The novelist Sinclair Lewis (1885-1951) was an acerbic man who didn't mince words. Once, he was giving a lecture at Columbia University on the subject of writing.

"How many here are really serious about being writers?" he asked the audience. Almost everyone in the audience raised their hand.

"Then why in hell aren't you all home writing?" grumped Lewis, and ended the lecture.

## 1206. Titling a Story

Successful writers are often besieged by young writers seeking advice. This story concerns a young writer who approached the highly-successful English writer W. Somerset Maugham and said:

"Mr. Maugham (1874-1965), I've just written a novel but I haven't been able to come up with a suitable title. You seem to have such a knack for titles, sir, *Cakes and Ale*, *The Razor's Edge*, etc. I wonder if you would read my novel and give me some suggestions."

"I don't need to read your novel," said Maugham. "Are there drums in it?"

"No, it's not that sort of a story," said the young writer. "You see, it deals with the alienation of..."

"Are there any bugles in it?" asked Maugham, interrupting.

"No, sir."

"Then call it *No Drums, No Bugles*." said Maugham

## 1207. Poets

A young man approached the famous poet Robert Frost (1874-1963) and Frost asked him what he did.

The young man replied, "I am a poet."

"You shouldn't use the word 'poet,'" said Frost, "that is a gift word."

"What do you mean?" asked the young man.

Said Frost, "Someone else has to call you a poet, you can't call yourself one."

## 1208. Bureaucratic Brevity

Winston Churchill was so anxious to get his cabinet colleagues to communicate simply and clearly that he took time out from his pressing wartime duties as Prime Ministers to write the following memorandum. Note how Churchill follows his own advice, and numbers his points to improve clarity.

SECRET – War Cabinet
9th August, 1940

BREVITY

Memorandum by the Prime Minister

To do our work, we all have to read a mass of papers. Nearly all of them are far too long. This wastes time, while energy has to be spent in looking for the essential points.

I ask my colleagues and their staffs to see to it that their Reports are shorter.

(1) The aim should be Reports which set out the main points in a series of short, crisp paragraphs.

(2) If a Report relies on detailed analysis of some complicated factors, or on statistics, these should be set out in an Appendix.

(3) Often the occasion is best met by submitting not a full-dress Report, but an outline consisting of headings only, which can be expanded orally if needed.

(4) Let us have an end to such phrases as these: "It is also of importance to bear in mind the following considerations..." or, "Consideration should be given to the possibility of carrying into effect..." Most of these wooly phrases are mere padding, which can be left out altogether, or replaced by a single word. Let us not shrink from using the short, expressive phrase, even if it is conversational.

Reports drawn up on the lines I propose may at first seem rough as compared with the flat surface of officialese jargon. But the saving in time will be great, while the discipline of setting out the real points concisely will prove an aid to clearer thinking.

W.S.C. (Churchill's initials)

## 1209. Ghost Writers

The demanding pioneer movie producer Samuel Goldwyn (1882-1974) hired a ghostwriter to write a series of articles to be published under Goldwyn's byline.

Goldwyn was pleased with the work but unfortunately the writer fell ill during the assignment and had to be replaced.

When the explosive producer read the substitute's work, he was very upset.

"It's not up to my usual standard!" he complained.

## 1210. To Insure Brevity

The legendary Supreme Court Justice Oliver Wendell Holmes, Jr. (1841-1935), wrote his opinions standing beside a special high desk.

A new assistant asked him one day, "Mr. Justice, why do you write your opinions standing up?"

"It's very simple," said Holmes. "If I sit down, I write a long opinion and don't come to the point as quickly as I should. If I stand up, I write as long as my knees hold out. When my knees give out, I know it's time to stop."

## 1211. Words

Gwendolyn Brooks (1917- ), American writer and poet, said of words, "Words do wonderful things. They sound, purr. They can urge, they can wheedle, whip, whine. They can sing, sass, singe. They can churn, check, channelize. They can be a hup, 2, 3, 4. They can forge a fiery army out of a hundred languid men."

# YOUTH

### 1212. Arrogance of Youth

In ancient Greece, Alcibiades (450 BC-404 BC) was telling Pericles (495 BC-429 BC) how Athens should be governed.

Annoyed by the young man's tone and manner, Pericles said, "Alcibiades, when I was your age I talked just the way you are talking."

Alcibiades looked Pericles in the face and replied, "How I should like to have known you when you were at your best."

### 1213. What Is a Boy?

The following delightful essay about youth and boyhood was written by Dale Evans Rogers:

"Between the innocence of babyhood and the dignity of manhood we find a delightful creature called a boy. Boys come in assorted sizes, weights, and colors, but all boys have the same creed: To enjoy every second of every minute of every hour of every day and to protest with noise (their only weapon) when their last minute is finished and the adult males pack them off to bed at night.

"Boys are found everywhere — on top of, underneath, inside of, climbing swinging from, running around, or jumping to. Mothers love them, little girls hate them, older sisters and brothers tolerate them, and Heaven protects them.

"A boy is Truth with dirt on its face. Beauty with a cut on its finger. Wisdom with bubble gum in its hair, and the hope of the future with a frog in its pocket.

"When you are busy, a boy is an inconsiderate, bothersome, intruding jungle of noise. When you want him to make a good impression, his brain turns to jelly or else he becomes a savage, sadistic jungle creature bent on destroying the world, and himself with it.

"A boy is a composite — he has the appetite of a horse, the digestion of a sword swallower, the energy of a pocket-size atomic bomb, the curiosity of a cat, the lungs of a dictator, the imagination of a Paul Bunyan, the shyness of a violet, the audacity of a steel trap, the enthusiasm of a fire-cracker, and when he makes something he has five thumbs on each hand.

"He likes ice cream, knives, saws, Christmas, comic books, the boy across the street, woods, water (in its native habitat), large animals, trains, Saturday mornings, and fire engines.

"He is not much for Sunday school, company, schools, books without pictures, music lessons, neckties, barbers, girls, overcoats, adults, or bedtime.

"Nobody else gets so much fun out of trees, dogs, and breezes. Nobody else can cram into one pocket a rusty knife, a half-eaten apple, three feet of string, two gumdrops, six cents, a slingshot, a chunk of unknown substance, and a genuine supersonic code ring with a secret compartment.

"A boy is a magical creature — you can lock him out of your workshop, but you can't lock him out of your heart. You can get him out of your study, but you can't get him out of your mind.

"You might as well give up. He is your captor, your jailer, your boss, and your master — a freckled-faced, pint-sized, cat-chasing bundle of noise. But when your dreams tumble down and the world is a mess, he can put together the broken pieces in just a twinkling, with a few magic words..."I love you.""

## 1214. What Is a Girl?

The following essay about young girls was written by Dale Evans Rogers:

"Little girls are the nicest things that happen to people. They are born with a little bit of angel-shine about them and though it wears thin sometimes there is always enough left to lasso your heart — even when they are sitting in the mud, or crying temperamental tears, or parading up the street in Mother's best clothes.

"A little girl can be sweeter (and badder) oftener than anyone else in the world. She can jitter around, and stomp, and make funny noises that frazzle your nerves, yet just when you open your mouth, she stands there, demure, and with that special look in her eyes.

"A girl is innocence playing in the mud. Beauty standing on its head, and Motherhood dragging a doll by the foot.

"Girls are available in five colors — black, white, red, yellow or brown, yet Mother Nature always manages to select your favorite color when you place an order. They disprove the law of supply and demand — there are millions of little girls, but each is as precious as rubies.

"God borrows from many creatures to make a girl. He uses the song of a bird, the squeal of a pig, the stubbornness of a mule, the antics of a monkey, the spryness of a grasshopper, the curiosity of a cat, the speed of gazelle, the slyness of a fox, the softness of a kitten, and to top it all off He adds the mysterious mind of a woman.

"A little girl likes new shoes, party dresses, small animals, first grade, noise-makers, the girl next door, dolls, make-believe, dancing lessons, ice cream, coloring books, makeup, cans of water, going visiting, tea parties, and one boy.

"She doesn't care much for visitors, boys in general, large dogs, hand-me-downs, straight chairs, vegetables, snowsuits, or staying in the front yard. She is the loudest when you are thinking, the prettiest when she has provoked you, the busiest at bedtime, the quietest when you want to show her off, and the most flirtatious when she absolutely must not get the best of you again.

"Who else can cause you more grief, joy, irritation, satisfaction, embarrassment, and genuine delight than this combination of Eve, Salome, and Florence Nightingale?

"She can muss up your home, your hair, and your dignity — then, just when your patience is ready to crack, her sunshine peeks through and you're lost again.

"Yes, she is a nerve-racking nuisance, just a noisy bundle of mischief. But when your dreams tumble down and the world is a mess — when it seems you are pretty much of a fool after all — she can make you a king when she climbs on your knee and whispers, "I love you best of all!"

# TIME

## 1215. New Definition of Deadline

The Latin American popular singer Julio Iglesias was being interviewed by a British television host when he used the word "manana." (a Spanish word pronounced (mun-yahna).

The TV host asked him to explain what the word meant. He said the term in Spanish means "maybe the job will be done tomorrow, maybe the next day, maybe the day after that. Perhaps next week, next month, next year. Who cares?"

The host turned to an Irish guest who was also on the show and asked him if there was an equivalent term in Ireland.

"No," he said, "In Ireland we don't have a word to describe that degree of urgency."

## 1216. Punctuality

Winston Churchill was once asked why he always seemed to miss trains and airplanes.

"I am a sporting man," he said. "I always give them a fair chance of getting away."

## 1217. Danger of Being Too Busy

The Chinese word for "busy" is composed of two characters: "heart" and "killing."

When we make ourselves so busy that we are always rushing around trying to get this or that "done," or "over with," we kill something vital in ourselves, and we smother the quiet wisdom in our heart.

## 1218. Thoughts about Time

The following excerpt is from a book titled *Zadig*," or *The Book of Fate* by Voltaire (1694-1778).

"Of all the things in the world, which is the longest and shortest, the quickest and the slowest, the most divisible and the most extensive, the most disregarded and the most regretted, without which nothing can happen, which devours everything that is little, and gives life everything that is great?

"The answer is time. Nothing is longer, since it is the measure of eternity. Nothing is shorter, since it is lacking in all our plans. Nothing is slower for him who waits. Nothing is quicker for him who enjoys. It extends to the infinitely little. All men disregard it. All men regret the loss of it. Nothing happens without it. It makes forgotten everything unworthy of posterity, and it immortalizes the great things."

## 1219. Time Zones

One little-known but hugely important by-product of the invention of trains was the standardization of time. In the years before the coming of the railroads — and for all human history up to then — time was strictly a local affair. A town or village generally set time based on the position of the sun relative to the area's tallest structure (often a church steeple). Not only was this imprecise, but towns 50 or 60 miles apart on an east/west axis would naturally record the sun's apogee, high noon, at a slightly different time (owing to the rotation of the earth). However, such differences were inconsequential when it took more than two days to travel 60 miles.

With the advent of the railroad, travelers were suddenly faced with the need to reset their timepieces at nearly every stop; train schedules in such a system were all but meaningless. In 1883 American and Canadian railroads simply decreed there would be five standard time zones running across the continent from east to west. In each time zone, on Sunday, November 18, people were required to stop and reset their clocks by anywhere from two to thirty minutes when the railroad said it was officially noon.

The practicality of the system was hard to refute. The following year the International Meridian Council met and instituted the system used worldwide today, with Greenwich, England serving as the prime meridian and 24 more-or-less equally spaced time zones circling the globe from there. In the United States, local time technically remained a local prerogative until the federal adoption of daylight savings in 1918.

Internationally, the time zone system was not fully adopted in all major countries until 1929.

## 1220. Where Your Time Goes

Have you ever wondered where all your time goes?

The average person spends seven years in the bathroom, six years eating, four years cleaning house, five years waiting in line, two years trying to return phone calls to people who aren't there, three years preparing meals, one year searching for misplaced items, six months sitting at red lights, and eight months opening junk mail.

That's nearly thirty years and doesn't include a lot of what you might need or want to do. Prioritizing our time should be a top priority.

## 1221. Love and Time

Once upon a time there was an island where all the feelings lived; Happiness, Sadness, Knowledge, and all the others, including Love.

One day it was announced to all of the feelings that the island was going to sink to the bottom of the ocean. So all the feelings prepared their boats to leave.

Love was the only one that stayed. She wanted to preserve the island paradise until the last possible moment. When the island was almost totally under, she decided it was time to leave.

She began looking for someone to ask for help. Just then, Richness was passing by in a grand boat. Love asked, "Richness, can I come with you on your boat?"

"I'm sorry," replied Richness, "but there's a lot of silver and gold on my boat and there would be no room for you anywhere."

Then Love decided to ask Vanity for help who was passing in a beautiful vessel.

Love cried out, "Vanity, help me please."

"I can't help you," Vanity said. "You are all wet and will damage my beautiful boat."

Next Love saw Sadness passing by.

Love said, "Sadness, please let me go with you."

Sadness answered, "Love, I'm sorry, but I just need to be alone now."

Then Love saw Happiness. Love cried out, "Happiness, please take me with you."

But Happiness was so overjoyed that he didn't hear Love calling to him.

Love began to cry. Then she heard a voice say, "Come, Love, I will take you with me."

It was an elder. Love felt so blessed and overjoyed that she forgot to ask the elder his name. When they arrived on land, the elder went on his way.

Love realized how much she owed the elder. Love then found Knowledge and asked, "Who was it that helped me?"

"It was Time," Knowledge answered.

"But why did Time help me when no one else would?" Love asked.

Knowledge smiled and with deep wisdom and sincerity answered, "Because only Time is capable of understanding how great Love is."

# Index

## A

AARP  345
Abbott, Bud  271
Abdul-Jabbar, Kareem  499
Abolitionist  172, 566
Abrams, Creighton W., Jr.  549
Accountant  2, 149
Accounting  **1**, 2
Action  **3**-4, 27, 36, 99, 119, 310, 389, 525, 529, 534, 543, 551, 554
Actors  **5**-6
Actors' Home  272-73
Adair, Red  159
Adam  24
Adams, Abigail  341, 565
Adams, John  31, 146, 215, 341, 565
Adaptability  **7**-8
Adaptation  8
Adler, Mortimer J.  438
Administerium  50
Adversity  **8**-10, 174, 412, 542
Advertising  **10**-16, 170, 545
Aerialist  538
Aeschines  389
Aesop fable  7, 120, 162, 191, 378, 398, 463, 529, 532
Africa  41, 184, 186, 244, 563
Agriculture  **16**, 18-19, 434
Ahenobarbus, Lucius Domitius  510
Akwari, John Stephen  511
Alabama  17

Alaska  30
Alcibiades  574
Alcohol  **19**-22, 275, 445, 561
Alcoholic  21
Alcott, Louisa May  155
Alexander the Great (King of Macedonia)  94, 179, 274, 422, 546-47
Alexandria  93, 184, 354
Alexeev, Vasily  511
Algebra  130
Ali, Muhammad  328-29, 500-501, 506
Alighieri, Dante  8
Allen, Woody  375, 438
Alps  245, 318-19
Ambition  **23**-24, 92, 109, 211, 560
Amen  93, 354
Americana  **24**
American Booksellers Association  49
American Chemical Society  458
American Express  324
American Medical Association  309
Anaximander  186
Andersen, Hans Christian  543
Andover  91
Andrews, Julie  345
Angelou, Maya  382
Anger  **32**-33, 196, 311, 336
Animals  **34**
Annapolis  362
Anthropologist  136, 144-45, 199
Antony, Marc  303
Apache  271

Page numbers listed in **bold** represent the first page of a section on the subject.

Apollo   425, 553
Appert, Nicholas   166
April Fool's Day   208
Architect   138, 306, 350, 360-61
Argyris, Chris   539
Aristippus   77
Aristotle   173, 324, 458, 472-73
Arizona   455
Arkansas   440, 493
Arlington   369
Arlington National Cemetery   107, 109,
    210-11, 361
Asia   186, 298, 422
Asimov, Isaac   456, 561
Assyrians   144, 301
Astaire, Fred   148, 155
Atalanta   564
Athens   131, 149, 172, 478, 509-10, 512,
    525, 574
Atlantic Journal   125, 177
Atlantic Monthly   130, 154, 157
Atlantic Ocean   30, 178, 186, 342
Attila the Hun   298
Attitude   **46**-47, 317, 492, 502, 516
Auden, Wystan Hugh   382
Auerbach, Red   499-500
Augustine, Norman   448
Austerlitz, Frederich   155
Austin   27
Australia   465
Automobiles   246-47, 252, 261
Autumn   216, 245, 318, 385, 452

## B

Babylonia   144, 289
Bacon, Francis   35, 438
Baghdad   16, 193
Balboa   151
Baldwin, Stanley   400
Ball, Lucille   155, 375
Baltimore   87, 215, 238, 364, 370, 405
Bananas   44
Bank of New York   61
Bannister, Roger   7
Barksdale, James   60
Barnum, P.T.   10, 423, 455
Barrymore, Drew   521
Barrymore, John   21
Bartholdi, Frederic Auguste   149
Barton, Clara   313
Baruch, Bernard   408, 464
Barzun, Jacques   87
Baseball   167, 439, **484**, 486, 489-93
Basketball   461, **495**-99, 514, 521
Bathing   313
Bathroom   313, 579
Bauby, Jean-Dominique   79
BBC   53
Beatles, The   155, 324-25
Bedell, Grace   396
Beer   222
Beethoven, Ludwig Van   8, 109, 155, 179,
    181, 326, 328, 334
Bell, Alexander Graham   156, 254, 257,
    374
Bell, Eric T.   517

Page numbers listed in **bold** represent the first page of a section on the subject.

Bell, Joseph   315

Bellamy, Francis   212

Benchley, Robert   72

Beran, C. Raymond   175

Berlin   246, 334

Berlin, Irving   365

Berlin, Isaiah   37

Bornays, Edward   465

Bernstein, Leonard   329-31

Berra, Yogi   491

Berton, Nicholas   269

Bessie, Simon   233

Bevington, Helen   536

Bible   8, 58, 80, 93, 132, 293-94, 367,
    394-95, 442, 445-46, 531

Bikini   2

Billroth, Theodor   315

Bird, Larry   521

Bismarck, Otto von   123-24, 345, 351

Black Hills   25

Blacksmith   199-200, 457

Blackwell, Alexander   145

Blarney Castle   263

Blarney Stone   263-64

Bloch, Arthur   543

Boabdil (King of Granada)   94

Boat   397, 433, 500, 512, 579

Bombeck, Erma   85

Books   **47-48**

Boorstin, Daniel J.   518

Borglum, Gutzon   25

Boston   86-87, 184, 259, 396, 484

Boston Red Sox   484, 488-89, 492, 514

Boswell, James   294

Boxing   **500**

Boxing Day   225, 231

Boyle, Hal   206

Braddock, Bessie   399

Bradford, William   219

Bradlee, Ben   542

Brady, Diamond Jim   167

Brahma   78-79

Brass   65, 180

Braxton, Carter   371

Brenner, Sydney   67

Brevity   469, 481, 483, 572-73

Bridge   65, 139-40, 196-97, 278, 400

Bronfman, Gerald   323

Bronfman, Sam   323

Bronowski, Jacob   40

Bronxville   267

Brooklyn   30, 139, 487

Brooklyn Bridge   30, 139-40

Brooklyn Dodgers   487

Brooks, Gwendolyn   573

Brooks, Mel   110, 408

Brown University   321

Bryan, William Jennings   393

Bryant, Bear   503

Buckley, William F., Jr.   541

Buffett, Warren   65, 68

Buick   419

Bulbs   58-59, 140, 225, 249

Bulls   337, 558, 569

Bumblebees   35

Bunyan, John   8

Burbank, Luther   115

Bureaucracy   3, 45, **49**-51, 53, 239, 242,
    269, 572

Bureau of Standards   53

Page numbers listed in **bold** represent the first page of a section on the subject.

Buren, Martin Van  76

Burgess, Frank Gelett  448

Burnett, Carol  440

Burns, George  352

Burns, Ken  546

Bush, George H.W.  402

Bush, George W.  89, 554

Business  5, 13-14, 35, 43-44, **55**, 57, 63,
    65-66, 70, 154-55, 205, 213, 222-23,
    239, 253-54, 278, 317-18, 329-30, 348,
    402, 448-50

Butler, Nicholas Murray  570

Butler, Samuel  390

Butterfield, Daniel  336

Buttons  88, 90, 361

Byrd, Robert  554

## C

Caesar, Julius  9, 185, 536

California  24, 246, 527, 532, 558

California State University  558

Callas, Maria  330

Cambridge  63

Camel  194, 224, 268, 415, 538

Campbell, Mrs. Patrick  52, 465-66

Canada  39, 49, 53, 209, 213

Canada Day  213-14

Candy  209, 224

Capitol of the United States  242, 360-61,
    403

Career  6, 14, 17, 23, 48, 52, **72**, 137, 168,
    179, 236, 260, 270, 281-82, 332, 388,
    414, 434, 465, 487, 489

Carlson, Chester  156, 374

Carlson, Evans F.  556

Carlyle, Thomas  377-78

Carnegie, Andrew  24, 392

Carnegie, Dale  264

Carol (King of Rumania)  73

Carpenter, Liz  569

Carrier, Willis  242

Carroll, June A.  246

Carroll, Lewis  75, 426, 472

Carroll College  505

Carson, Johnny  95

Carson, Rachel  84

Caruso, Enrico  156, 327, 494

Casals, Pablo  352

Caterpillars  75, 105, 357

Catherine the Great  54, 454

Catholic  172, 182, 292-93

Catlin, George  475

Celtic  216-17

Celtics  499

Centennial Exposition  362

CEO  51, 61

Cervantes, Miguel de  467

Chagall, Marc  353

Change  38, 48, **74**-75, 93, 173, 192, 219,
    256, 268, 270, 306, 310, 458, 466, 519

Character  8, 18-19, 23, **77**, 79, 82-83, 148,
    489, 492

Charities  66, 304, 391-93

Charles, Bob  506

Charles, Ray  332

Charles II (King of Great Britain)  90, 293

Chemistry  130, 344-45, 562

Chessboard  304-5

Chesterton, G.K.  80

Page numbers listed in **bold** represent the first page of a section on the subject.

Chicago   12, 85-87, 393, 434, 436, 476, 537

Chicago Bulls   461, 496

Chicago Cubs   484

Chickens   36, 46, 169-70, 207

Child, Julia   156, 168

Children   18, 31, **83**-85, 104, 135-36, 194, 200, 202, 212-13, 216, 220, 224, 227-29, 232, 265, 305, 341, 357, 372, 376, 442

China   56, 183, 241, 243-44, 295, 535, 565

Christian   129, 182-83, 204, 207, 209, 216-17, 219, 224, 228, 304

Christmas   30, 49, 136, 221, 223-31, 234, 272, 383, 575

Christmas Day   230-31

Christmas Eve   228, 230

Chrysler Corporation   71

Churchill, Winston   22, 43, 96, 106, 108, 111-12, 141-42, 145, 154, 177, 269-70, 295, 389, 399, 402, 471-72, 482-83, 541, 556-57, 559, 572-73

Cigars   74, 280, 292, 348-49

Citadel Military College   82

Cities   **85**

Civil War   8, 32, 207, 210, 213, 223, 240, 335, 343, 397, 403-4, 422, 442, 446, 491, 526, 546, 549, 551-52, 556

Cleese, John M.   389

Cleopatra   94, 185, 303

Clergymen   22, 124, 165, 195, 210, 266, 295, 362, 442, 445, 451, 481, 544

Cleveland   316

Cleveland Clinic, The   316

Clinton, Bill   565

Clinton, Hillary Rodham   565

Clothing   15, **88**-89, 158, 189, 199, 219, 222, 511

Clowns   234-35

Coach   496, 498-99, 501-5, 508, 515

Cobb, Ty   489

Coca Cola Company   375

Cod   67, 222

Code of Hamurabi   57

Cody, Iron Eyes   518-19

Coffin, William Sloan   91

Cognac   74

Cohen, Paul   375

Cohn, Harry   441

Cohn, Jack   441

Cole, Henry   224

Collier's Magazine   485

Colorado   280

Columbia University   570

Columbus, Christopher   8, 27, 152-54, 168, 212, 221, 244, 335

Commitment   31, 67, **91**-92, 110, 188, 378, 434, 511

Communication   53, 61, **92**, 95-98, 140, 226, 255, 286, 309, 389, 435, 552

Community Service   **99**

Competitiveness   43, 563

Compromise   **102**, 361

Comstock, Henry   374

Confidence   137, 174, 238, 254, 286, 311, 378, 417, 460-62, 487, 492, 498-99, 547, 555

Conformity   45, **104**-6

Confucius   92, 418

Connecticut   66, 262, 291, 317

Page numbers listed in **bold** represent the first page of a section on the subject.

Connelly, Marc   21
Consequences   95, 128, 522
Constitutional Convention   361, 550
Constitution of the United States   368
Continental Congress   212, 214-15, 219, 221, 363-65
Conwell, Russell H.   193
Cook, James   39
Coolidge, Calvin   23, 158, 213, 307, 394, 404, 439-40, 467, 483
Cooperstown   487, 491
Coppersmith, Joshua   259
Cornelia   83-84
Cornwallis, Charles   371
Cortes, Hernando   151
Coryate, Thomas   165
Costello, Lou   271
Courage   31, **106**-10, 196, 215, 266, 320, 364
Cousins, Norman   48, 315, 317
Coventry   525
Cows   22, 63, 91, 245, 267, 322, 474, 552-53, 558
Cox, Channing   404
Crampton, C. Ward   310
Creativity   **109**, 232
Credit   4, 78, 134, 168, 170, 222, 225, 237, 248, 258, 330-31, 478, 535
Cremona   12
Crimea   454
Criticism   5, **111**-12, 276, 400, 402
Croesus (King of Lydia)   553-54
Cromwell, Oliver   66, 223, 225, 395
Crowds   30, 104, 124, 209, 211, 250, 278, 328, 346, 370, 394, 439, 471, 476, 478-80, 483-84, 487

Crystal, Billy   5-6
Cultural Decline   **114**
Curiosity   11, 71, **115**, 117, 243, 575-76
Curley, James Michael   396

**D**

D'Antonio, Agostino   110
Dahlgren   246
Dallas   63, 87
Danielson, George S.   532
Darrow, Charles   378
Darrow, Clarence   280
Darwin, Charles   7, 179
David (King of Israel)   94, 185
Da Vinci, Leonardo   306
Davis, Bette   233
Davis, David   395
Davis, Jefferson   271, 550
Day, Clarence   47
Daylight Saving Time   178
Dean, Dizzy   493
Death   8, 84, 94, **117**-18, 129, 142, 162-64, 180, 183, 195-96, 230, 316, 371, 498
De Bow, James Dunwoody Brownson   517
Debussy, Claude   333
Decca Records   155, 375
Decision Making   **118**
Declaration of Independence   28-29, 31, 98, 122, 211, 214-15, 257, 323, 361-68, 371-72, 568
De Coubertin, Pierre   509
De Gaulle, Charles   138
De Hegerman-Lindencrone, Lillie   329

Page numbers listed in **bold** represent the first page of a section on the subject.

Delphi  553-54

Deming, W. Edwards  434

Democrats  394-95, 397, 399, 404, 474,
532, 554

Demosthenes  389, 470, 478-79

Dempsey, Tom  503-4

Denial  **120**

Denny, John W.  157

Department of Agriculture  17, 434

Department of State  362

Devons, Ely  517

Diamonds  83, 193-94, 488

Diana (Princess of Wales)  195, 266, 522

DiBacco, Thomas  222

Dickens, Charles  467

Dickinson, Emily  161

Diller, Phyllis  465

DiMaggio, Joe  491-92

Diocletian (Emperor of Rome)  129

Diogenes  77

Dionysius  223

Diplomacy  71, **121**-22

Discouragement  **125**

Disney, Walt  156, 461

Disraeli, Benjamin  267, 466, 481

Diversity  **126**-27

Dizzy Dean  493

Doctors  7, 79, 164, 253, 259, 281, 309-17,
348, 457, 540, 549

Dodd, Mrs. John B.  213

Doddridge, Philip  468

Dogg, Snoop Doggy  364

Dolphin, The  340-41

Donkey  104, 163, 398, 479

Donovan, Richard  485

Doolittle, Eliza  52, 449, 465

Dostoevsky, Fyodor  567

Doubleday, Abner  490-91

Douglas, Stephen  19, 406

Douglass, Frederick  24, 172

Dover  9, 51

Doyle, Arthur Conan  315, 541

Dragons  151, 354

Drucker, Peter F.  61, 173, 255, 429, 539

Druid  216

Dublin  526

Ducks  36, 45, 169

Dukas, Helen  88

Duke, Vernon  325

Du Maurier, Daphne  196

Durant, Ariel  429

Durant, Will  429

Dylan, Bob  156

Dyson, Freeman J.  245

## E

Eagles  43, 46, 480, 563

Earth Day  520

Easter  207, 327

Easter Sunday  207

Eastwood, Clint  156

Eaton, John  275

Ecology  **127**-28

Economics  **128**-29, 232

Eddington, Arthur  40

Eden, Anthony  482

Education  18, 24, 125, **130**-32, 134,
136-37, 178, 183, 238, 315, 341, 347,
372, 517, 523, 526

Page numbers listed in **bold** represent the first page of a section on the subject.

Educator  87, 120, 195, 245, 448, 467, 536
Edward II (King of Great Britain)  513
Edward III (King of Great Britain)  513
Eggs  46, 152, 165, 167, 207, 299, 381
Ego  5-6, 38, **138**-39, 158, 237, 545
Egypt  128
Einstein, Albert  30, 88, 117, 131, 154, 157, 160, 179-81, 247, 306, 323, 328, 387, 456-59
Eisenhower, Dwight D.  72, 91, 106, 137, 212, 275, 478, 555-56, 560
Elephants  24-25, 36, 43, 108, 126, 384-85
Elizabeth I (Queen of Great Britain)  263
Elizabeth II (Queen of Great Britain)  521
Elle (Magazine)  79
Elman, Mischa  334
Emancipation Proclamation  118, 366
Emerson, Ralph Waldo  77, 84, 340, 461
Encyclopedia Britannica  185
Engineering  **139**-40, 256, 429, 455-56
Engineers  39, 62, 90, 139-40, 247, 256-57, 262, 295, 306, 320, 360, 379, 416, 419-20, 435, 437, 456
English Channel  9, 560
ENIAC  248
Eratosthenes  184
Eriksson, Leif  27
Erik the Red  27
E.R. Squibb and Sons  16
Ethics  **142**, 539
Etiquette  **143**
Euphrates River  193
Europe  29, 135, 141, 164, 184, 209, 256, 303, 344, 443, 536
European Economic Community (EEC)  98

Eve  24
Excellence  80, **147**, 448, 486
Exploration  **150**, 243, 262

F

Fabre, John Henry  105
Fadiman, Clifton  537
Fahrenbach, T. R.  31
Failure  34, 44-45, 73, 108, 127, **154**-55, 241, 276-77, 321, 490, 501, 508
Fame  109, 152, **158**-59, 211, 227, 246, 328, 331, 334, 350, 470, 494, 530, 543
Faraday, Michael  179, 261
Farmer  17-18, 58, 73, 91, 101-2, 148, 169-70, 177, 190, 283, 371, 380, 412, 418, 422-23, 434, 451, 474, 534
Farmington  248
Fate  42, **160**-61, 227, 372, 412
Fathers 33, 55-57, 73, 79, 99, 104, 106, 133, 158, 161, 178, 212-13, 283, 301, 343, 349, 359, 385-86, 412-13, 530, 539-40
Father's Day  212-13
FBI  49
Fear  9, 19, 34, 45, 80, 104, 113, 123, 144, 151, **161**-62, 172, 195, 218, 259, 290, 308, 316, 346, 461-62, 522
Federalist Party  394
Feistritzer, C. Emily  240
Fellowes, Jane  195
Fences  33, 236, 323
Fermi, Enrico  459
Feynman, Richard P.  148
Fields, W.C.  21, 230, 324, 445
Fildes, Samuel Luke  316

Page numbers listed in **bold** represent the first page of a section on the subject.

Financial World  69

Fitzherbert, John  57

Flag Day  211-12

Flags  107, 211-12, 363, 368, 370-71, 529, 552

Fleas  37

Florida  270, 429

Food And Utensils  **164**

Football  **501**-4

Ford, Henry  56, 99-100, 157, 238, 375, 420, 428-29

Ford, Henry, II  238

Ford Motor Company  99, 289, 420

Forks  46, 165, 359

Fort Knox  362

Fortune Magazine  63

Foster, Stephen  30

Fountain of Youth  387

Fox  37, 120, 332-33, 378, 576

Foxx, Jamie  332

France  4, 90, 106, 122, 124, 138, 141-42, 149, 170, 206, 208, 224, 243, 395, 452, 480, 533, 535, 569

Francis of Assisi, Saint  10, 118, 226, 265

Freedom  28-31, 49, 122, **171**-73, 204, 315, 352, 511

French Revolution  377

Fresno  558

Freud, Sigmund  94

Fridays  89, 207, 443-44, 521

Friedman, Milton  129

Friendship  32, 71, **173**-76, 205, 303, 499, 533

Frogs  38, 279, 574

Frontinus, Julius Sextus  247

Frost, Robert  154, 157, 352, 571

Fry, Arthur  250

Fuller, R. Buckminster  320

Fulton, Robert  250, 259

Funk, Wilfred J.  98

Future  160, 162, **176**, 177, 202, 206, 232, 248, 304, 341, 408, 532

**G**

Gabor, Zsa Zsa  521

Galilei, Galileo  258, 306, 458

Gallaudet University  502

Gandhi
  Indira  78
  Mahatma  78, 89, 203-4, 352

Gardens  35, 46-47, 118, 169, 191, 193-94, 262, 276, 414

Gardner, John W.  120, 448, 467

Garland, Judy  108

Gaul  9

Geese  38-39, 41, 169, 191, 230

Gehrig, Lou  485

Geisel, Theodore  376

General Electric  178-79, 225, 416

General Motors  3, 251, 419

Genies  192-93

Genius  11, 131, 137, **178**-81, 257, 306, 321, 416, 461

Genoa  335, 391

Geometry  130, 184-85

George II (King of Great Britain)  275, 368

George III (King of Great Britain)  121, 214

George V (King of Great Britain)  89

George Washington University  3

Page numbers listed in **bold** represent the first page of a section on the subject.

Gerhardt, Charles   311

Germany   166, 187, 226, 230, 259, 270, 288, 458, 509

Gerry, Melville G.   281

Gettysburg   471, 491

Gettysburg Address   28, 109, 446, 471, 482

Giamatti, Bartlett   97

Gibbon, Edward   114, 172

Gimbel's   223

Giraffe   126

Giscard d'Estaing, Valéry   452

Gladstone, William Ewart   123, 261, 267, 437, 466

Glenn, John   352

Global   62, **182**-83, 185, 226

Gloves   89, 303

God   17, 19, 21, 24, 31, 101, 123, 136, 198-200, 207, 219, 235-36, 303-4, 321, 358, 440, 442-43, 447, 456, 461, 538

Goddard, Mary Katherine   215, 364, 405

Godiva, Lady   525

Goethe, Johann Wolfgang von   258, 352

Goldwyn, Samuel   233-35, 262, 573

Golf   **506**-8, 513

Goliath   57

Gomez, Lefty   488

Goodall, Jane   563

Goodwin, Dick   569

Gorbachev, Mikhail   358

Gordian Knot   422

Gordium   422

Gordon, Adam Lindsay   266

Gordon, Joe   488

Government   42, 53, 73, 76, 92, 112, 134, 138, 173, 219, 256, 263, 270, 278, 304, 342-43, 369, 381, 405, 434, 439

Graham, Ben   68

Graham, Billy   30

Grains   42, 44, 201-2, 304-5, 532

Grand Ole Opry   157

Grange, John   269

Grant, Cary   353

Grant, Ulysses S.   73, 275, 335, 480, 507, 547

Grapes   120

Grasshoppers   532, 576

Gratitude   145, 525, 565

Great Britain   9, 28, 32, 52, 59, 66, 73-74, 76, 86, 89-90, 103, 106, 108, 111, 116, 130, 141, 182, 209, 216-17, 231, 254, 266, 269, 274-75, 297-99, 395, 400, 465-66, 526, 555-56

Greece   77, 130-31, 149, 203, 330, 470, 509, 546, 574

Greed   44, **188**-89, 191

Greeley, Horace   28, 30

Green Bay Packers   159

Greene, Gilbert J.   440

Greenland   27

Greenspan, Bud   511

Greenwood, Chester   248

Gregorian, Vartan   321

Gretzky, Wayne   508, 522

Grey, Zane   196

Grief   **195**-96, 576

Groundhog   204

Gujarat   202

Gulf of Mexico   151

Page numbers listed in **bold** represent the first page of a section on the subject.

Gulf Stream   178
Gulf War   564
Gunther, John   15, 537
Gustav III (King of Sweden)   164
Guthrie, Bill   495
Gwenn, Edmund   272-73

H

Haley, Alex   236
Halloween   216-18
Haloid Company   156, 374
Hamburg   166, 287
Hamilton, Alexander   61, 367
Hammerstein, Oscar   150
Hancock, John   214, 365-66
Hankin, Joseph   267
Hanks, Tom   32
Hannibal   83
Hannibal (Missouri)   324
Hanson, Victor Davis   558
Hanukkah   226
Happiness   10, 18, 100, 160-61, 173, 194,
     202, 300, 314, 381, 473, 567-68, 579-80
Hardin, Garrett   128, 543
Harding, Gilbert   53
Hare   378, 434
Harper and Row   233
Harrison, William Henry   470
Harrow, Benjamin   562
Harrow School   108
Hart, John   372
Hartford   291
Harvard Business School   341, 539
Harvard University   71, 130, 246, 570

Hawaii   30, 380
Hayes, Helen   330
Hayes, Rutherford B.   156, 374, 395
Hay Theory of History   245
Heart   9, 32, 47, 104, 174-75, 198, 235, 286,
     288, 294-95, 302-3, 310, 364, 389, 413,
     433, 447, 463, 518, 575, 577
Heaven   86, 98, 102, 186, 198, 200, 202,
     218, 220, 258, 282, 288, 302, 326, 406,
     408, 440-41, 443-44, 456, 492, 524
Hedgehogs   37, 548
Heine, Heinrich   91
Heinlein, Robert A.   390
Heisman, John   504
Helping Others   192, **196**
Henry Ford   289
Henry IV (King of Great Britain)   24, 513
Henry VIII (King of Great Britain)   24, 296
Hepburn, Audrey   266
Hercules   336, 425
Herndon, William   23, 554
Hershfield, Harry   464
Highfield, Roger   228
Hillary, Edmund   528-29
Himalayas   78, 186
Hindu   78, 182, 202, 228, 292-93, 304
Hippomenes   564
Hiroshima   97
Hitchcock, Alfred   6
Hitchhiking   537
Hitler, Adolph   49, 395
Hobson, Thomas   63
Hockey   **508**
Hoffer, Eric   29
Hoffman, Felix   311

Page numbers listed in **bold** represent the first page of a section on the subject.

Hogan, Ben  508

Holidays  76, **201**, 204-5, 207, 209, 212, 220, 223, 226, 229-32, 387

Hollerith  244-45

Holly, Buddy  375

Hollywood  21, 52, 66, 180, **233**-34, 307, 353, 441, 465

Holmes, Oliver Wendell, Jr.  135, 453, 573

Holmes, Oliver Wendell, Sr.  240, 477, 540

Homer  277

Honeymoon  289, 295

Hooker, Joseph  551

Hoover, Herbert C.  2, 146, 255, 295, 439, 494

Hoover, J. Edgar  49

Hopkinson, Francis  211-12, 363

Hopper, Grace Murray  246

Horne, Lena  521

Hornsby, Rogers  486-87

Horses  171

Horsley, John Calcott  224

Hospitality  146

Hospitals  79, 100, 106, 135, 311, 445, 465, 476-77, 524

Hotchner, A.E.  66

Hot Dogs  55-56, 167-68

Houghton & Mifflin  142

House of Commons  53, 111, 114, 257, 483

Houston  87

Howard, Carole  391

Howe, Elias  251

Hubbard, Paul  502

Huddle  501-2

Hugo, Victor  176

Humanity  48, 320

Humes, James  471

Humility  **236**, 304, 500

Humphrey, Hubert  469

Hunter, Holly  143

Hurt, William  143

Hutchins, Robert  284

Hydrochloric acid  53-54

I

IBM  45, 106, 237, 244, 320, 448
  founder of  320-21

Ice cream  419-20, 575-76

Iceland  27

Iglesias, Julio  577

Illinois  32, 85, 102, 160, 319, 393, 395, 444, 463, 479, 526, 537

Illustrators  223, 227, 369

Impala  34

Impeachment  395

Incas  184

Incompetence  **238**-39

Independence  28, 450

India  186, 202-4, 352, 422, 516

Indiana  505

Indianola  16

Industrial Revolution  226, 243-44, 428

Inferiority Complex  **240**, 320

Ingalls, John J.  395

Insomnia  467

Institute for the Future  61

Internet  253, 262

Inventions  137, 157, **242**, 247, 260-61, 334, 416
  New  259-61

Page numbers listed in **bold** represent the first page of a section on the subject.

Iowa 16
Ireland 99, 206, 216-17, 263, 299, 526, 577
Irish **263**
Irving, Washington 227
Isabella (Queen of Spain) 153
Ismael, Abdul Kassem 267
Israel 277, 352
Italy 12, 101, 110, 165, 179, 224, 227, 330, 391

J

Jackson, Andrew 370
Jackson, Phil 496
Jacksonville 429
Jacquard, Joseph-Marie 248
James IV (King of Scotland) 513
Japan 71, 93, 148, 202-3, 270, 434-35
Jar 41, 381
Jarvis, Anna May 210
Jefferson, Thomas 30-31, 35, 122, 124, 146, 196-97, 215, 271, 308, 363, 394, 405, 473, 568
Jenner, Edward 260
Jesus Christ 101, 185, 207, 209, 224, 226, 301, 304, 440, 566, 568
Jewelry 302, 324
Jigsaw Puzzles 182
Jim Crow 26
Jischke, Martin C. 261
John F. Kennedy Center for the Performing Arts 449
John Murray Anderson Drama School 155, 375
Johnson, Andrew 219, 395

Johnson, Edward 225
Johnson, Lyndon Baines 139, 210, 213, 376, 405, 469, 473, 569
Johnson, Samuel 11, 294
Joint Chiefs of Staff 4, 560
Jones, Bobby 506
Jones, James Earl 157
Jones, John Paul 30, 221
Jordan, Michael 461, 496
Journalism 143, 308
Jowett, Benjamin 237
Juliet 205
Julius I (Pope) 223
Julius III (Pope) 239

K

Kangaroo 39
Kansas 30, 72, 91, 135, 395, 555
Kansas City 87
Keaton, Buster 234
Keller, Helen 8
Kelly, Jim 521
Kelly, Walt 520
Kennedy, John E. 15
Kennedy, John F. 109, 117, 205, 319, 342, 352, 369, 399, 429-30, 449, 539, 541
Kennedy, Robert Francis 107
Kentucky 362
Kettering, Charles F. 251, 425
Keynes, John Maynard 75
Khrushchev, Nikita 319
Kierkegaard, Søren 45
Kindness 174-75, 196, 198, 203, **264**-66, 357

Page numbers listed in **bold** represent the first page of a section on the subject.

King, Benjamin Franklin 339
King, Martin Luther, Jr. 30, 172, 203
King, Stacey 496
Kingsport 276
Kipling, Rudyard 116
Kissinger, Henry 508
Kiswahili 232
Kite, Tom 506
Kites 85, 409
Kitty Hawk 375
Knebel, Fletcher 87
Knowledge 11, 17, 25, 41, 48-49, 75, 120,
    130-31, 157, 236, 266, 306, 316, 353,
    364, 424, 429, 523, 568, 579-80
Koran 438
Krakow 344
Kremlin 209, 307, 358
Ku, Pan 285-86
Kuhn, Margaret 41
Kuwait 564
Kwanzaa 226, 231-32

L

Laboratory 16, 130, 181, 258, 549
Labor Day 167, 209
Lafayette College 502
La Guardia, Fiorello 282, 289
Lakota 81, 481
Lancaster 362
Land, Edwin H. 522
Language 123, 175, 206, **267**, 286, 472
Lansdowne House 342
Lapham, Lewis H. 554
Laplace, Pierre 258

Lasker, Albert 15
Las Vegas 253, 465
Latin 23, 93, 130, 322, 356, 446, 514
Laughter 235, **271**, 282, 304, 314, 317
Laurel, Stan 234
Law Enforcement **273**
Lawyer 35, 211, 235, 280-84, 363, 371,
    405-6, 438, 526, 531
Leacock, Stephen 452
Leadership 106, 154, 243, **274**-79, 395,
    423, 456, 481
Leahy, Frank 505
Le Conte, Joseph 247
Lee, Robert E. 356
Legal **280**, 302, 425
L'Enfant, Pierre Charles 360-61
Lennon, John 324-25
Leofric (Earl of Mercia) 525
Leonidas 553
Lewis, Francis 372
Lewis, Sinclair 464, 570
Liberty Bell 28, 367-68
Lighthouses 48
Lincoln, Abraham 19, 23-24, 32, 34, 60,
    102, 111-12, 118-19, 219-20, 240,
    271-72, 279-84, 343, 366-68, 384,
    394-407, 471-72, 523-24, 547-48,
    550-54, 566-67
Lincoln, Robert 471
Lindsay, John 491
Lion 43, 107, 343, 548, 563
Lippard, George 28
Listening 55, 232, **285**-86, 338, 471, 480
Little, Brown and Company 228
Liverpool 59

Page numbers listed in **bold** represent the first page of a section on the subject.

Livy   430
Lobster   40, 45
Lombardi, Vince   157, 159
London   59, 63, 74, 80, 82, 106, 121, 170,
      184, 195, 246, 271, 342, 351, 367, 407
Loneliness   437
Longevity   48
Long Island   477
Loop, Floyd D.   316
Lorillard, Pierre   90
Los Alamos   549
Los Angeles   5, 71, 87, 167, 496
Louisville Slugger   484
Louis XVI (King of France)   121
Love   198, 204, 229, **287**, 290, 292, 301,
      303-4, 317, 343, 365, 396, 413, 438,
      441, 449, 460, 464, 466, 472, 579-80
Love Letters   35, 438
Luck   14, 187-88
   Bad   188, 295, 521
   Good   14-15, **187**-88, 203, 292, 297,
      521-22
Lundstrom, J.E.   249
Luther, Martin   8
Luther Burbank   115
Lyautey, Marshal Hubert   3

**M**

MacArthur, Douglas   375, 462
MacCarthy, Cormac MacDermot   263
MacDonald, Bill   273
Mackay, Harvey   64, 69
MacMillan, Harold   483
Macy, R. H.   157

Madison, James   220
Madison Square Garden   477
Mailer, Norman   87
Maimonides, Moses   392
Maine   30, 248, 466
Making Decisions   119
Malarkey   269
Malone, Dudley Field   542
Malone, Joseph D.   256
Manchester Guardian   358
Mandela, Nelson   460
Manhattan   87, 139, 322
Manhattan Project   549
Mantle, Mickey   490, 492
Marathon, Battle of   512-13
Marathon Race   512
Marcus, Stanley   57, 65
Markham, Beryl   567
Markham, Edwin   411
Mark II   246
Marquis de Lafayette   122
Marriage   155, 227, 287-89, 292-94,
      300-303, 564
Marshall, George Catlett   560-61
Marshall, John   368
Marshall, Peter   318
Martin, Mary   330
Martin, Theodore   565
Maryland   222, 322, 362, 549
Masai   145
Maslow, Abraham   80
Mason, Jackie   453
Massachusetts   26, 28, 113, 214-15, 219,
      222-23, 230, 256, 365, 369, 404, 497
Mathematics   243, **304**-6, 457

Page numbers listed in **bold** represent the first page of a section on the subject.

Matthews, Brander  570
Maugham, Somerset  74, 351, 571
May Day  209
Mayflower  25-26
Mayo, Charles  236
Mayo, William  236
McCartney, Paul  325
McClellan, George B.  240, 551, 553
McClure, Alexander K.  405
McCormack, John Francis  326
McCracken, Herb  502
McCullough, David  450-51
McFarlane, Willie  506
McKean, Thomas  371
McKinley, Willliam  247, 549
McMann, Ed  82
Mead, Carver A.  428
Mead, Margaret  199
Media  **307**, 309
Medicine  **309**, 315-16, 345, 349, 467
Mediterranean  128, 245
Meir, Golda  352
Memorial Day  167, 210
Mencken, H.L.  430
Mendelssohn, Moses  287-88
Menninger, Karl  99
Mestral, George de  90
Mexico  49, 151, 209, 224, 554
Mexico City  511
Michelangelo  109-10, 147, 350
Michener, James  137-38, 380
Middle Kingdom  418
Miletus  186
Mill, John Stuart  377
Millikan, Robert A.  457

Milwaukee  475
Misawa, Chiyoshi  93
Misawa Homes  93
Mississippi  272, 493
Mississippi River  342, 397
Missouri  14, 85, 119, 169, 264, 324,
    450, 474
Mistakes  145, **318**-21, 398, 402, 409, 411,
    475, 490
Mistletoe  229, 292
Mitchell, John N.  532
Molnar, Ferenc  111
Mondale, Walter  403
Money  18, 57, 59, 70, 74, 87, 159, 188,
    193-94, 218, 225-26, 231, 280-81, 308,
    **321**-24, 331, 453, 525-28, 533, 535-36,
    543-44
Monk, Thelonious  333
Monkeys  40-41, 44, 354, 542, 547, 576
Monopoly  378-79
Monroe, Marilyn (Norma Jean Mortenson)
    157, 233
Montagu, John  170
Montgomery, Bernard Law  556
Moock, Harry G.  71
Morgan, J.P.  343
Morison, Elting E.  52
Morison, Samuel Eliot  221
Morris, Ralph  225
Morris, Robert  367
Morrow, Walter  129
Moscow  246
Moses  536
Moses, Grandma  352
Moslems  182

Page numbers listed in **bold** represent the first page of a section on the subject.

Mothers   32, 76, 83-84, 113, 117, 121, 131, 134-35, 137, 157, 178, 187, 202, 209-10, 323, 341, 356-58, 360, 498, 536, 574-75
Mother's Day   209-10
Motivation   80, 157, 325, 356, 429
Mountbatten, Louis (1st Earl Mountbatten of Burma)   141
Mount Vernon   364, 536
Mozart, Wolfgang Amadeus   179, 331
Mt. Rushmore   25
Mulberry Leaves   105
Mulcahy, Anne   63
Mulready, William   569
Murphy, Edward A.   140
Murphy's Law   140, 543
Music   **325**
Mustard   168, 198, 332

## N

Nader, Ralph   562
Nagasaki   97
Nails   26, 33, 74, 340, 380, 457, 532
Naismith, James   497
Napoleon   51, 166, 179, 185, 552
Nast, Thomas   227, 370
Natchez   272
National Aeronautics and Space Administration (NASA)   253, 407
National Center for Education Research   240
Naturalists   7, 105, 118, 174, 384, 562-63
Naval Museum   246
Nazi Party   395
NCAA   495

Nebraska   65, 393
Nebuchadnezzar (King of Babylon)   93, 536
Negative Thinking   250, **336**, 338, 409
Negotiation   235, 291, **342**-43, 484, 488, 492, 494
Neiman Marcus   57
Nelson, Harmon O., Jr.   233
Nelson, Horatio   552, 555
Nelson, Thomas, Jr.   371
Nero (Emperor of Rome)   509-10
Netherlands   58
Netscape   60
New England   86, 216, 369
Newhart, Bob   2
New Jersey   88, 211, 222, 259, 362-63
Newman, Paul   66
New Mexico   549
New Orleans   87, 397
News
    Bad   93-94
    Good   326, 409, 512
Newton, Isaac   541
New Year's Day   146, 201, 203, 366
New Year's Eve   203
New York   20, 53, 76, 86-87, 90, 117, 149, 156-57, 167-68, 207, 239, 244, 246, 251, 255, 267, 283, 313, 327-28, 369, 374-75
New York City   68, 167, 255, 282, 289, 345, 360, 430, 454, 477, 491, 536
New York Philharmonic   329
New York Public Library   321
New York Times, The   205, 364, 414, 471, 484, 505, 558
New York University   375

Page numbers listed in **bold** represent the first page of a section on the subject.

New York Yankees   327, 485, 488-92, 494
New Zealand   20, 528
Niagara Falls   121, 538
Nicholas, St.   227
Nicklaus, Jack   506
Nightingale, Florence   576
Nilsson, Birgit Marta   331
Ninth Wave   355
Nixon, Richard M.   4, 429, 508
Noah   21
Nobel, Alfred Bernhard   344-45
Nobel Peace Prize   172, 203, 561
Nobel Prize   134, **344**-45
Norgay, Ten-Zing   528-29
Normal and Industrial Institute   17
North America   27, 53, 213, 535
North Carolina   375, 526
North Pole   467
Norton, Oliver Willcox   336
Notre Dame   505
Nurses   312-13
Nuts   41, 43, 217, 226, 299
Nuttail, Thomas   153

## O

O'Hare International Airport   436
O'Reilly, John Boyle   520
Oarsmen   **500**
Odysseus   277-78
Ogilvy, David   13
Ohio   140, 259, 316, 403, 549, 566
Oklahoma   493
Old age   **345**, 347-48, 350, 353
Olympia   510

Olympic Games   376, **509**-11
Omaha   65, 483
Omaha Beach   141
O'Neal, Shaquille   498
O'Neill, Tip   404
Operas   330, 332-33
Oppenheimer, Robert   549
Opportunity   73-74, 137, 151, 286, **354**, 356, 409, 456, 480, 498
Optimist   62, 409
Oracle   553-54
Orchids   59
Orton, Dwayne   448
Oscar   233, 352
Osgood, Charles   440
Oxford English Dictionary   25, 40, 254
Oxford University   7, 133, 237, 446, 472
Oyster Bay   477

## P

Paar, Jack   307
Pacific Ocean   97, 151
Packer, Alfred G.   280-81
Paderewski, Ignace Jan   157, 331
Paganini, Niccolo   332, 335
Paige, Leroy Robert "Satchel"   485, 493
Paine, Thomas   31
Pakistan   290
Panama   151
Pandora's Box   542
Pangea   186
Parentenal Love   360
Parenting   **356**
Paris   4, 35, 50, 122, 169, 246, 278, 325, 330, 342, 437, 480

Page numbers listed in **bold** represent the first page of a section on the subject.

Parker, Dorothy   283, 311
Parker Brothers   378-79
Pascal, Blaise   453
Passy   243
Patara   227
Patent Office   247, 362
Patents   180, 248-49, 258, 260
Patrick, Saint   205-6
Patriotism   **360**, 364-65
Patronage   53
Pavarotti, Luciano   327, 521
Peanut   16-17, 236
Pearl Harbor   21, 30, 362, 395
Peattie, Donald Culross   562
Pennick, Harvey   507
Pennsylvania   30, 84, 222, 322, 362,
     367-68, 379-80, 471
Pepper, Claude   270
Pericles   574
Perkins, Maxwell   286
Perot, Ross   3, 475
Perrault, Charles   268
Perry, Michael   540
Perseverance   372, 374
Persia   93, 162, 193, 207, 267, 512-13,
     553-54
Persistence   **372**, 374, 380
Personal Growth   39, **380**, 383
Personal Health   **384**
Perspective   332-33, 382, **385**-87, 490, 501
Persuasion   15, **387**-90, 473, 525
Pessimist   62, 140, 339, 409
Peter, Lawrence J.   239
Peter, Saint   74, 85-86, 94, 123, 326-27,
     350, 492

Peter Principle, The   239
Peters, Tom   518
Peter the Great (Czar of Russia)   94
Petty, William (Lord Shelburne)   342
PGA   506
Pheidippides   512
Phelps, William Lyon   136, 478
Phidias   149
Philadelphia   28, 30, 61, 86-87, 89, 124,
     184, 193, 211, 214, 223, 362-63, 365,
     368, 534-35, 537
Philanthropy   **391**-93
Philologist   567
Phoenix   447
Physicians   20, 240, 309, 314-17, 352, 476,
     497, 540
Physics   130, 148, 154, 185, 228, 345, 456,
     458
Picasso, Pablo   352-53
Pickens, T. Boone   3
Pickersgill, Mary Young   370
Pickles   229, 516
Pierpont, James   226
Pilgrims   25-26, 185, 204, 220-22
Pineapple   146
Pinehurst   506
Pitney Bowes   61
Pittsburgh Pirates   516
Plato   173
Pledge of Allegiance   212
Plymouth   26, 222
Plymouth Rock   25-26
Pneumonia   376, 470
Poinsettia   224
Poland   344

Page numbers listed in **bold** represent the first page of a section on the subject••

Politics   177, **393**, 397-98, 404
Polk, James K.   327
Polo, Marco   183
Pope, John   551
Popular Mechanics   248
Population Reference Bureau   186
Portugal   244
Positive Thinking   313, 317, 330, **407**, 490
Post, Emily   144
Potatoes   17, 167, 169-70, 528
Potemkin, Grigory Aleksandrovich   454
Potemkin Villages   454
Powell, Colin   274
Prairie chickens   46, 169
Preece, William   257
President's Day   364
Presley, Elvis   157
Princeton University   135, 457
Problem Solving   **416**
Productivity   **427**, 429
Profanity   119, **429**-30, 503
Prometheus   542
Protestant   103, 172, 182, 231, 446
Proust, Marcel   387
Providence   321
Prudence   **431**
Ptolemy (King of Egypt)   93
Puerto Rico   337
Puller, Lewis (Chesty)   557
Pumpkin   218, 222
Purdue University   261
Puritans   209, 223, 225, 230
Pythagoras   304

Q

Quaker   271, 534
Quality   64, 68, 166, 170, **433**-35, 437, 543
Quality Control   51, 433, 434

R

Rabi, Isidor   134, 459
Radford, Arthur William   4
Raleigh, Walter   8
Reader's Digest   391
Reading   23, 55, 58, 95, 135, 256, 268, 368, **437**-38, 465, 467
Reagan, Ronald   37, 76, 82, 237, 250, 402-3, 409-10, 444-45, 453
Red Sox   484, 489
Reese, Pee Wee   487
Reeve, Christopher   407
Reform   129, 172, **439**
Reformation   308
Reformer   277
Reforms   277, 439
Reindeer   228
Rejection   154, 156, 218, 374, 376, 378
Relaxation   139, 514
Religion   **439**, 442, 445
Renewal   **447**-48
Republican   284, 393-94, 429, 446, 466
Respect   103, 137, 285, 335, **448**-50, 484, 560
Responsibility   54, 115, 121, 172, 232, 269, 373, **450**
Retirement   274, 351, **452**-53, 494-95

Page numbers listed in **bold** represent the first page of a section on the subject••

Revolutionary War   26, 31, 219, 221, 342, 367, 371, 546
Reynolds, Burt   156
Rhode Island   321
Rice, Daddy   26
Richard II (King of Great Britain)   513
Richard Nixon   542
Rickover, Hyman George   352
Rivers, Joan   522
Roach, Robert   397
Roberts, Flora   331
Robert the Bruce   380
Robinson, Jackie   487
Rockefeller, David   392
Rockefeller, John D., Sr.   343
Rockefeller, Laurance   391-92
Rockefeller Foundation   323
Rodin, Auguste   158
Roebling, John   139
Roebling, Washington   139
Roger of Wendover   525
Rogers, Dale Evans   574-75
Rogers, Fred   265
Rogers, Will   30, 386, 531
Rollins, Jack   5-6
Roman Empire   114, 172, 245, 559
Roosevelt, Eleanor   117
Roosevelt, Franklin Delano   6, 49, 117, 135, 158, 171, 188, 219, 221, 270, 375, 446, 559-60
Roosevelt, Theodore   4, 475-77, 504
Rosh Hashanah   202
Ross, Betsy   30, 211, 363, 370
Royal Navy   552
Rubinstein, Arthur   325-26, 353

Rudolph, Wilma   376
Runyon, Damon   454
Ruppert, Jacob   485, 494
Rushmore, Charles E.   25
Russell, Bertrand   306, 387, 522
Russia   123, 194, 237, 298, 320, 353, 438, 560
Ruth, Babe   30, 327, 484-85, 488, 493-94, 521

S

Saint Louis University   505
Salk, Jonas   30, 375
Sandwich   167, 170
Sanford, Terry   526
San Francisco   29, 87, 368, 462, 503, 563
San Francisco Examiner   397
San Francisco News   129
San Juan Mountains   280
Santa Claus   227-28
Sargent, Malcolm   332
Satan   207, 540
Sayers, Dorothy L.   338
Scam   **454**
Scamming   455
Schieldorup-Ebbe, Thorlief   36
Schopenhauer, Arthur   160, 545
Schweitzer, Albert   352
Science   17, 48, 126, 176, 178, 306, 316, 321, **455**-56, 518
Scotland   203, 208, 301, 380, 506-7, 513
Seaton, George   272-73
Second Bank of the United States   61
Seidenberg, Ivan   253

Page numbers listed in **bold** represent the first page of a section on the subject ❖❖

Self-Confidence   10, 332, **460**, 462, 498
Self-Control   499, 563
Selfishness   **462**-63
Semantics   96
Semmelweiss, Joseph   316
Sex   402, **464**-66, 565
Shackleton, Ernest   150
Shakespeare, William   24, 40, 94, 205, 455, 473, 519
Sharks   78
Sharpsburg   549
Shaw, George Bernard   8, 52, 145, 180, 341, 353, 386, 449, 463-65
Shaw, Robert   530
Sherlock Holmes   315, 541
Sherman, William T.   550
Shofar   202
Sholes, C. L.   249
Shula, Don   501
Silver Pine Cones   187
Simon & Schuster   507
Simon, Paul   393
Simpson College   16
Sioux City   537
Sioux Indian   46
Sisyphus   419
Skelton, Red   414
Sleep   **467**
Small, William   94
Smallpox   260
Small towns   317, **468**-69, 483
Smathers, George A.   270
Smith, Margaret Chase   466
Smith, Sydney   447
Smithson, James   391

Smithsonian Institution   371, 391
Snakes   3, 20-21, 60, 206, 354, 519
Snow, C.P.   455
Soccer   **513**
Socrates   101-2, 142
Soldiers   9, 52, 73, 151, 274, 278, 369, 371, 484, 515-16, 524, 528, 543, 546-47, 556
Solid Rocket Boosters (SRBs)   257
Sondheim, Stephen   330-31
Sophocles   94
Sorbonne   4
Soule, John L.   28
South Bend   505
South Dakota   25
Spain   151-52, 224, 244
Speaking   **469**
Speech Honorariums   477
Speech Preparation   474
Speechwriting   569
Spiders   14-15, 380
Spock, Benjamin   539
Spokane   213
Sports   7, 114, 162, 215, 461, **484**, 489, 495, 497, 500-501, 503-4, 506, 508-9, 513-16
Sports Illustrated   515
Spring   18, 80, 177, 207, 209, 281, 318, 348, 385
Springer, Charles W.   244-45
Springfield   160, 440, 463, 497
Springfield Republican   259
Stalin, Joseph   307, 319, 560
Stallions   189, 432
Stallone, Sylvester   530
Standard Oil   349

Page numbers listed in **bold** represent the first page of a section on the subject••

Stanford University  503
Stanton, Edwin  34, 111
Starfish  197
Statistics  434-35, 455, 490, 499, **516**-18, 561, 572
Steinbeck, John  515
Steinmetz, Charles  178-79, 416
Stengel, Casey  486, 493
Stevenson, Adlai  121, 124, 173, 399
Stevenson, Robert Louis  449
Stirrups  254, 555
St. Louis  85, 87
St. Louis Browns  491
St. Louis Cardinals  486, 493
Stockholm  344
Stock Market  58, 65, 69-70, 486, 539
Stout, Rex  518
Stowe, Harriet Beecher  31
St. Patrick's Cathedral  526
St. Patrick's Day  205
St. Petersburg  94, 123
St. Peter's Church  74
Stradivarius, Anton  12, 463
Strauss, Richard  333
Substance Abuse  **518**
Summer  40, 43, 72, 90, 120, 124, 169, 213, 216, 340, 385, 532
Super Bowl  502
Superman  8, 500
Superstition  355, **521**-22
Sweden  164, 249, 344
Swift, Jonathan  526
Szymanski, Frank  505

**T**

Tact  **523**-24
Taft, William Howard  284, 401
Talmud  441
Tanzania  511-12
Tatars  166
Taxes  114, 261, 417, **525**-27
Taylor, Frederick Winslow  341, 429
Teachers  48, 132, 134-36, 138, 156-57, 240, 321
Teamwork  38-39, 286, 497, 499, **527**-31
Technologies  52, 198, 226, **242**-45, 255, 316, 428, 434
Telephone  156, 254-55, 257, 259, 374, 457, 569
Teller, Edward  321
Temple University  193
Tennessee  276, 376
Testimonial Speeches  475
Testimony  280-81, 284, 520, **531**-32, 542
Tet Nguyen Dan  202
Teutonic  225
Texas  27, 139, 159, 273, 377, 380, 395, 527, 569
Thanksgiving  219-23, 226
Theismann, Joe  502
Thompson, Adam  259
Thomson, Charles  214, 366
Thoreau, Henry David  48, 77, 174, 384
Thrift  **532**, 535
Tigers  43, 64, 354, 548
Tigris River  193
Time  2, 13, **577**

Page numbers listed in **bold** represent the first page of a section on the subject··

Times (of London)   150
Titanic   238
Titian   352
Titus   276
Tokyo   70, 183, 434-35
Tolstoy, Leo   3, 101, 189
Toronto   53
Tortoise   378
Toscanini, Arturo   333-34
Trafalgar   552
Transportation   36, 76, 89, 257, **536**
Trapeze   9
Travel   25, 38, 46-47, 71, 76, 87, 107, 179, 187, 193, 198, 202, 223, 227-29, 309, 324, 368, 411-12, 442, **536**-37, 578
Traveler   46-47, 247, 259, 309, 324, 411-12, 469, 537, 578
Travelers Home Equity Service   71
Trees   3, 7, 10, 27, 71, 104, 110, 116, 133, 225, 228-29, 258, 285, 292, 300, 318, 338, 380, 385, 451, 531
Trenton   362
Trigonometry   130
Troy   369
Truman, Harry S.   142-43, 158, 439, 450-51
Trust   **538**
Truth   **540**
Truth, Sojourner   566
Ts'ao, King   285
Tuchman, Barbara W.   48
Tudor   209
Turkey   44, 222-23, 227, 512, 548
Tuscany   165
Tuskegee   17
Tuxedo Park   90

Twain, Mark   14-15, 20, 49, 86, 133, 160, 169, 272, 291-92, 294, 308, 313-14, 324, 347, 397-98, 430, 441, 443-44, 455, 477, 536-37

U

UCLA   315, 317, 495, 498
UCLA School of Medicine   315, 317
Umpires   378, 486-87, 495
Uncle Sam   369-70
Unexpected Consequences   **542**
Union Station   537
United Nations   121, 124, 266, 565
United States Army   210, 240, 370, 448-49, 501, 558
United States Bill of Rights   363
United States Congress   29, 97, 155, 171, 210-11, 215, 221, 361, 364, 369-71, 429, 518, 554, 568
United States Constitution   61, 103, 341, 352, 363
United States House of Representatives   221, 270, 393, 455
United States Library of Congress   48, 362-63
United States Marine Corp   473
United States of America   2-3, 53, 71-73, 76, 86-87, 158, 182-83, 196-97, 203, 209-12, 220-21, 254-56, 259, 327, 363, 365, 394-96, 400-401, 434-36, 458-59, 549-50
United States Senate   155, 221, 270, 318, 376, 399, 455-56
University of Alabama   503

University of Bern  154, 157
University of California  247, 250
University of California at Berkeley  250,
    503
University of Chicago  284
University of Colorado at Boulder  281

V

Valentine's Day  205
Vanderbilt, Cornelius  259, 467, 521
    Jr.  307
Van Dyke, Dick  234
Van Dyke, Henry  195
Vanity  320, **543**, 545
Veblen, Oswald  457-58
Velcro  90
Verdi  352
Vermont  30, 158, 211, 370
Versailles  121, 124
Victoria (Queen of Great Britain)  296,
    437, 557, 565
Vienna  319, 328
Vikings  27
Vincent, Strong  336
Violins  12, 155, 323, 329, 332, 335, 462
Virginia  135-36, 215, 246, 322, 362, 364,
    371
Virginia Museum of Fine Arts  475
Voltaire, Francois Marie Arouet  522, 578

W

Wade, Benjamin  403
Wagner, Honus  72

Wakan Tanka  81
Waldorf Astoria Hotel  430
Wallenda, Karl  336-37
Wall Street Journal  61, 436
Walmart  70
Walnuts  82, 463
Walpole, Horace  187
Walruses  384
Walters, Barbara  407, 564
Walton, Bill  495, 500
Walton, Sam  70
Waner, Paul  494
War  **546**
Ward, William Arthur  409
Warner, Harry  6, 180
Warner Brothers Pictures  6, 180
Washakie County Museum and Cultural
    Center  132
Washington, Booker T.  17, 373
Washington, Bushrod  174
Washington, D.C.  53, 107, 109, 142, 210,
    242, 260, 266, 322, 360-62, 371, 391,
    449, 471, 502, 537, 552
Washington, George  18, 89, 122, 146,
    174, 211, 219-21, 275, 322, 360-61, 363-
    64, 366-67, 372, 384, 402, 469, 536, 550
Washington, Martha  322
Washington Post  117, 240, 542
Washington Redskins  502
Water  **561**
Watergate  532, 542
Waterloo  274
Waterman, Robert H.  448
Watson, Thomas J.
    Jr.  45, 106, 237, 244, 320, 385
    Sr.  244, 320-21, 385

Page numbers listed in **bold** represent the first page of a section on the subject••

Wayne, John  159
Weaver, Richard L., II  372
Webster, Daniel  97, 470
Wedding  287, 289, 292, 294-98, 300
Welk, Lawrence  268
Welles, Orson  6
Wellington, Arthur Wellesley  274
Wesley, John  442
Westchester Community College  267
Westminster Abbey  195
West Point  375, 491, 559
West Side Story  329
West Virginia  554
Whistler, James  113
White House  4, 24, 137, 143, 146, 255,
    271, 295, 307, 366, 401, 403, 405, 409,
    466, 470, 559, 569
Whitman, Walt  31
Whitney, Eli  30, 179
Whittaker, Otto  29
Wilde, Oscar  176, 328
Wilding, Michael  6
William (Duke of Normandy)  254, 555
Williams, Ted  489, 492, 514
Wilson, Samuel  369
Wilson, Woodrow  135, 210-11, 363, 474
Winfrey, Oprah  376, 382
Winning  105, 305, 378, 498-500, 516, **563**
Winter  43, 204, 216, 225, 245, 276, 385,
    417, 422, 532
Wirthlin, Richard  409-10
Wisconsin  159
Witches  216-18
Wolfe, James  275
Women's Rights  **564**-65

Wooden, John  495, 498
Woodford, William  275
**Work  566**
Worland  132
World Development Forum  182
World Series  30, 484, 488, 493
World War I  211, 226, 365, 370, 458, 462,
    484, 546
World War II  22, 52, 72, 101, 106, 138,
    141, 211, 269-70, 307, 365, 462, 546,
    549, 555-57, 559-60
Wren, Christopher  407
Wright, Leonard  269
Wright, Orville  375, 475, 480
Wright, Wilbur  375, 475, 480
Wrigley, Philip K.  12
Writing  264, 477, 482, **568**, 570
Wycliffe, John  446
Wyoming  132

## X

Xerox  63, 156

## Y

Yale Law School  284
Yale University  97, 136, 478, 541
Yale University Press  47
Yavlinsky, Gregory  129
Yeager, Chuck  375
York  362
Youth  116, 131, **574**

Page numbers listed in **bold** represent the first page of a section on the subject••

Printed in the United States
214121BV00004B/2/P